Understanding

Morality

Understanding Morality

Albert B. Hakim

Professor emeritus of Philosophy
Seton Hall University

Prentice Hall

Boston   Columbus   Indianapolis   New York   San Francisco   Upper Saddle River
Amsterdam   Cape Town   Dubai   London   Madrid   Milan   Munich   Paris   Montreal   Toronto
Delhi   Mexico City   Sao Paulo   Sydney   Hong Kong   Seoul   Singapore   Taipei   Tokyo

Editorial Director: Craig Campanella
Editor in Chief: Dickson Musslewhite
Publisher: Nancy Roberts
Editorial Project Manager: Kate Fernandes
Editorial Assistant: Nart Varoqua
Director of Marketing: Brandy Dawson
Senior Marketing Manager: Laura Lee Manley
Managing Editor: Maureen Richardson
Senior Project Manager: Harriet Tellem
Operations Specialist: Christina Amato
Cover Design Director: Jayne Conte
Cover Designer: Suzanne Duda
Cover Credit: Sand © Ben Stoate/Fotolia
Full-Service Project Management: Integra Software Services Pvt. Ltd.
Composition: Integra Software Services Pvt. Ltd.
Printer/Binder: Courier
Cover Printer: Courier
Text Font: New Baskerville 10/12

Credits and acknowledgments borrowed from other sources and reproduced, with permission, in this textbook appear on appropriate page within text or on pages 267.

Library of Congress Cataloging-in-Publication Data
Hakim, Albert.
Understanding moral/Albert B. Hakim.—1st ed.
    p. cm.
  ISBN-13: 978-0-205-83582-9 (alk. paper)
  ISBN-10: 0-205-83582-1 (alk. paper)
  1. Ethics.   2. Values.   I. Title.
BJ71.H285 2011
170–dc22
                                        2010033694

10 9 8 7 6 5 4 3 2 1

Prentice Hall
is an imprint of

www.pearsonhighered.com

ISBN 10:   0-205-83582-1
ISBN 13: 978-0-205-83582-9

for Irene

Contents

CHAPTER SIX Integrity of Life Questions   139

CHAPTER SEVEN The Environment   161

Readings

CHAPTER EIGHT War and Peace   195

Readings

Acknowledgments

Understanding Morality grew out of lecture notes over many years of teaching an introductory course in ethics and was made pertinent by continuous dialogue with students whose concerns contributed to its final shape. But it could not have reached publication without the input of my colleagues, particularly in the Department of Philosophy, whose cooperation I gratefully acknowledge. I would like to thank David O'Connor, who not only encouraged me all along the way, but critically perused the first four chapters, after which further requests for his insightful comments would have been a thoughtless imposition in light of his being deluged by his own writing commitments. Vicente Medina, always on top of political philosophy, supplied me with several valuable pages of comment which enabled me to fine-tune Chapter 5. Judith Stark, whose interest in ecology knows no bounds, read the first draft of Chapter 7 and, although we didn't see eye to eye on the focus of the chapter, her comments helped me to re-present it. From the Department of Biology, I should like to thank Carolyn Bentivegna, who assisted me on the terminology for the biologist's understanding of the humanity of the unborn, and Eliot Krause, who carefully read the pages on the process of human reproduction. Toni Malone, now emerita, had developed courses in human sexuality in the Department of Religious Studies and was able to give me welcome suggestions for improving Chapter 9. Jerome Bracken, Professor of Moral Theology in the School of Theology, was always ready to discuss moral issues with me and did me the courtesy of reading Chapter 10. I turned to Fred Booth, Department of Classical Languages, for much needed help in translating a tricky passage from Virgil's *Georgics* for Chapter 7.

Thank you to the reviewers of this book: Frank Schalow, University of New Orleans and Maureen Sander-Staudt, Arizona State University.

Introduction

Each of several different approaches to a text on morality has something to recommend it. One approach begins with a presentation of general moral principles and proceeds to draw out applications for particular cases; this offers the prospect of being logically air-tight and compelling. Another approach is to lay out a selection of chief moral systems that have proven influential over time to see how each might solve specific moral problems; this has the advantage of disclosing how complex morality really is. A third approach is a flat-out case study method wherein a number of cases are analyzed for their moral implications; the value of this is, while letting each case speak for itself, analysis develops a moral sensitivity helpful in solving others. Yet, as successful as these approaches may be, there are substantial considerations remaining to be made in each one. In the first approach, we still have to ask where the principles themselves come from. Does the mind, to begin with, first grasp the principles and then work from the top down? Or is it the other way around? The second approach gives us a sense of the historical importance of a major segment of philosophy, but does so without evaluating the systems presented or committing to any one of them. The third approach tends to make the study of morality a tool for problem solving without acknowledging that it is foremost a *philosophy* whose goal is to uncover the ultimate reasons for calling certain human actions "moral" in the first place. These considerations are required for a fuller understanding of morality and lie behind the composition of this text as an introduction for first-time students.

Understanding Morality is an invitation to students to join a philosophic journey of discovery, to learn afresh why morality is an extraordinary feature of our lives and a defining characteristic of being human. The journey begins from where all knowledge begins, from *experience*. Reflecting on our experiences will show the emergence of one aspect of human activity that is totally different from all other aspects and is distinctive enough to warrant a distinctive name, a name in fact that has been used by humans from time immemorial, *moral*, or its equivalent. We'll come to appreciate how terms like *right–wrong, good–bad, moral–immoral, ethical–unethical* describe our personal actions insofar as they square with humanity or demean it. What they tell us is not only that our actions have moral meaning, but also that in the last analysis moral meaning is personal and radically constitutive of the intrinsic character of the individual.

If it is true that moral meaning is personal, it is also true that nothing is more personal than *love*, without which human affairs would be far less than human. Yet the primacy of love is seldom, if ever, found in the general text on morality. Terms like *concern, care,* and *regard* are used often enough, though reticence prevails on the role of love as the grounding principle of morality. In recognizing, let's say, the primacy of oxygen in sustaining life, it doesn't follow that we always have to be talking about it, or even keeping it at the top of our minds, but it does follow that we have to keep it on the top of our practical consciousness so that nothing is allowed to interfere with our breathing. So too in recognizing the primacy of love in moral matters, it doesn't follow that we always have to be engaged in talking or thinking about it, but it does follow that we are always ready to act out of love as the virtue of deepest meaning for our personal life. The spirit of this book lies in the recognition of love as the foundation of morality and the answer to what it means to be human.

A glance at the Contents will give you a good idea of the range of the book. Viewed overall, the first half deals with the basic concepts of morality, while the second half generally deals with moral questions we face as individuals, or as members of society engaged in public controversy over any number of agonizing moral problems. Chapter 1 yields to the strong probability that this course will be the first and only course in philosophy many, if not most, of the students will take in their college career, although the author has the fond hope it will entice them into taking others. That being so, the opening pages of the chapter are devoted to an introduction to what philosophy tries to do and how we access the branch referred to as the *philosophy of morality.* The chapter then goes on to explore what is meant by the moral sense, the difference between acts called good and those called bad, whether this sense is natural to us or acquired, the meaning of moral freedom as against determinism, and whether human beings are summoned to be good. Chapter 2 takes up the all-important questions as to how we decide which acts are to be done and which avoided, whether morality is a private matter or the same for all, and how this ties in with the faculty of conscience presents an overview of several moral systems addressing these questions. Chapter 3 continues discussing the moral dimension but under the aspect of the moral law, with special attention given to natural law which has suffered much from popular misunderstanding. Chapter 4, devoted to the meaning of life, is the "heart" of the book. Here the problem of evil as the chief enemy of life is squarely faced while good is found to be its center; good is what is to be pursued and loved as the answer to what human life is all about.

If we are going to examine moral questions facing society today, what is first called for is an understanding of society itself, which is the subject of Chapter 5's inquiry into the common good, particularly the economy and its effect upon the poor. Physical life is an existential value we are directly aware of, along with the innate need to cherish its integrity. Assaults against the integrity of life are therefore considered in Chapter 6, which includes a discussion of abortion, euthanasia, physician-assisted suicide, capital punishment, and gun control. Life in general, and human life in particular, looks to an environment to thrive in, so Chapter 7, working from the universally accepted need for ecology, stresses the notion of nature-as-life, under the rubric that an appreciation of nature is an appreciation of life. War and peace, Chapter 8, is a disjunction man has had to live with since the dawn of time and demands that we stand back to see ourselves caught up in a cycle of self-destruction. The chapter, while it is a plea for destroying the engines of war, is primarily a plea for the very peace the human heart yearns for. Chapter 9 treats of the human self under the aspect of sexuality. If it is true that person-to-person relationships are the stuff of being human, then a unique instance is found in the relationship of male and female. It is profound in every sense and takes its place among the most telling experiences of love as the bedrock of what it means to be human. The final chapter, Chapter 10, rounds out the imperatives of the moral life described thus far with a discussion of virtue and vice, and leads to the conclusion that an interior readiness to do good is the signature of our humanity.

It should be clear that *Understanding Morality* is written in the tradition of its readers, the Western tradition, and is therefore consonant with Hebraic, Hellenistic, and Christian cultures, without any judgment implied as to the relative worth of other cultures like Hindu, Buddhist, or Confucian which have their own claim to special study.

A word about chapter structure: The first, and main, part of each chapter is the presentation and discussion of the material. This is followed by a selection of readings which are not intended to be "research" readings, but extensions, literary as well as academic, of points made in the first part and are integral to the chapter as a whole. The readings are keyed to the text by a reference, for example (R #1). A short bibliography is found at the end of the text that provides students who wish to expand their study with titles easily available. The index will prove helpful for any number of obvious reasons.

Chapter One

The Moral Sense

PHILOSOPHY AND THE ROLE OF EXPERIENCE

More often than not, in moving into a new area of study, our immediate impulse is to look for a clear definition of terms and then get underway. Some terms, however, are indefinable: There is no definition of the color yellow, or love, or existence, and yet we *know* them; we know the color yellow, we know when we're in love, and we know we exist. Other terms state what we know in another sense, such as Aristotle's definition of man as "rational animal," for which he uses his genus-species approach: Man belongs to the genus "animal" but is distinguished from other animals in that he is "rational." Aristotle could have distinguished man from other animals in a totally different way if he wanted to, even a humorous way, such as "man is a two-legged animal that cooks its own food," but that distinction would hardly have defined the *nature* of man. In a theistic tradition, St. Augustine would offer yet another definition of man as the "image of God," not to depart from the Aristotelian "rational animal" but to state the nature of man in its fundamental orientation. The most satisfactory way of getting to know the meaning of philosophy is to be engaged in it, by doing it, which any course in philosophy intends to do. But it would be helpful to set out by describing the pathways philosophy takes toward understanding the real world about us, especially for those students for whom this may be the only course they will enroll in during their college careers.

The etymological derivation of a word, in this case *philosophy*, often sheds some light on its meaning. *Philosophy* is compounded from the Greek words *philia* (love) and s*ophia* (wisdom), whence philosophy is the *love of wisdom*. Love can be understood in many ways, but all of them signify something thought worthy of being desired, sought, or pursued, in which sense "philosophy" becomes the *pursuit* or *search* for "wisdom." For its part, the word *wisdom* pertains to knowledge, of course, but a deeper level of knowledge than a mere catalogue of facts. We would never call a person "wise" merely because he has extensive command of facts or because his mind is like a warehouse of memorized data. This is the kind of knowledge we gain by direct observation or through everyday acquaintance, like the cost of items in the shop, or the gasoline consumption of a car, or the train schedule, or the chronology of events. Such factual knowledge is necessary for daily living and can even become the source of pleasantness in one's life. It would be folly to demean it or deny its importance. But it would not be demeaning to say that, as surface or horizontal knowledge, it has to be distinguished from knowledge on a deeper level, vertical if you will. Take the simple example of an apple. We can ask questions such as the following: What is its shape, color, and taste? How much does it cost? Where does it grow? But we can also ask questions of another kind: Why does the apple exist rather than not? Is it caused, or is it just there? What's in its make-up to distinguish it from a stone, a dog, or a man? Is there a reason why it exists? The questions of the first kind are questions of fact; they're on the surface; they're horizontal. The questions of the second kind go beyond the surface and reach to a level not given at immediate contact. Take a totally different example; two authors, let's say, write about the French Revolution; one gives just a sequential account of the facts, while the other tries to get beyond the facts to explore the meaning of this singular event in the history of the French as a people, the kind of knowledge for which the name "wisdom" is reserved, the kind that presses for the *understanding* of things, for their very *meaning* (R #1).

How we get to the meaning of things can be clarified by considering the *relationship* they have to each other. The meaning of "chair," for example, is grasped by seeing how this physical object is *related* to the shape of the human body and how it can be accommodated in a sitting position. The tile in front of you in the classroom is a blackboard because of how it's related to you in a teaching context, but put overhead it becomes a ceiling tile, or underfoot it becomes a floor tile; its meaning has changed because its relationship has changed.

Take a personal example. A friend of yours manifests a certain confusion, unsure of who he is, upset as to how he stands to the world, and he must "get his head together." You recommend that he see someone who can help, say a psychologist. The psychologist does help, mainly in bringing him to see that there *is* a relationship among the ideas floating around in his head at random and thus to see a unity between himself and the world he inhabits. The integration of disparate ideas in the young man's mind was the work of a skilled psychologist who, in his wisdom, was able to elicit a sense of unity from a tangle of disconnected ideas. Time and again, we see instances of how *many* things are brought together in a *unity*, as when all those free-standing figures are reduced to a unified statement by the accountant, or isolated notes are shaped into a melody by the composer, or the countless parts of a living body are seen working together as an organic whole. The chemist analyzes a compound to reveal what constituents are brought together into a unified whole, in order to be able to synthesize them again. Physicists today are expending huge amounts of intellectual energy to discern the reason why the myriad parts of the universe hold and function as one. The *underlying relationship of togetherness* is precisely what the philosopher is trying to determine. Where there is no sense of unity, there is no philosophy either.

Besides the etymological definition of philosophy as the love of wisdom, there is another extremely fruitful definition rising from the fact of *experience*. Experience is had only when an event involves you personally. If a friend tells you a wonderful story about himself, he is trying to share *his* experience with you, but the experience is his, not yours. Whence, a good definition of experience is *personal involvement in a happening*. Experience simply happens. It's an awareness, a realization, an opening-up to something hitherto unknown to you, or unfelt. Given such an experience, you could stop right there, without dwelling on it; but then again you may be impelled to think further about it, to reflect on it, and to ask questions about it, in short, to analyze it. When you go to an art gallery and look at a painting, it may be that there's no chemistry at all between you and the painting. And then again, there may be. It may be that the painting moves you, takes hold of you, quietly, serenely, and you say "It's beautiful!" And in trying to figure out why the experience occurred in the first place, a whole chain of questions is begun: What is it that makes it beautiful? What is there about the colors, the shapes, the harmony, or even its message that makes you so drawn to it? These are questions on the objective side. On the subjective side, you may be wondering what there is about you that makes you appreciate it so much; you did not will it to happen, you did not reason to it; it just happened. The experience has profound objective and subjective components to it. And thus, with the first question "why?" you are moving toward the philosophy of art.

Similarly, reflection on the experience of "before" and "after" leads to the philosophy of time, and thence to the philosophy of history. Reflection on yourself as a knowing being leads to the philosophy of knowledge, epistemology. Reflection on existence leads to the philosophy of being (metaphysics), and so on, with every area of philosophy. There is no experience so insignificant as not to merit some kind of reflection and to warrant the beginning of a new line of philosophical inquiry. Without experience, no reflection; without reflection, no philosophy (R #2).

A question may arise as to how philosophical reflection differs from any other kind of reflection. The accountant may indeed reflect on the best way to make an entry, but that's not philosophical. A dentist or a physician may reflect on which procedure to be used without calling their reflection philosophical. At times it's difficult or impossible to make a clear distinction as to where, in a continuum of reflection, one type ends and philosophical reflection begins, for example, as to where, in the art gallery episode, to draw the line between art criticism and the philosophy of art, or between physics and cosmology, or neurobiology and the philosophy of mind. The answer lies in what philosophy is trying to do. If, as presented above, philosophy begins in experience, it does not end there; it goes *beyond* experience, it goes to a place where experience does not and cannot go, to a *conclusion*, a conclusion that in itself is not experienced but is *required* to explain why the experience takes place at all. So the philosopher reaches the conclusion that the animal, which he experiences as a living material entity, is living for a reason that goes beyond the material, namely an immaterial entity, called soul.

The classical model holding for the role of experience was Aristotle, whose style in philosophy was given artistic rendering in Raphael's famous painting *The School of Athens*, in which one of the two central figures, Plato, is pointing upward, to the speculative, depicting our journey to knowledge as beginning from above, while the other figure, Aristotle, is pointing downward, depicting it as beginning from below, the distinction between rationalism and empiricism. True to this distinction, Aristotle begins his mighty work *Metaphysics* with a chapter on the workings of the intellect and, together with assertions from his other writings, lays out some tightly knit observations on the role of experience. Among the functions, or activities, of the intellect, there are three that pertain to the *pursuit of wisdom*, the higher meaning of things. One function is *speculative*—wisdom of the highest and theoretical order, called simply "wisdom" (*sophia*); a second function is *productive*—a wisdom called "art" (*techné*); and a third is *practical*—a wisdom he calls "practical wisdom" (*phronesis*). But none of these activities is possible without being initiated in experience. Once initiated, that is, once the intellect is activated by the senses, then its own proper functioning begins and, on the strength of particular knowledge delivered by the senses, rises to the level of universal knowledge and the ordering of things called wisdom. But speculative knowledge, untapped, has no direct consequence in the practical world and therefore has to re-engage itself in some way. (The Irish mother said it right, that her smart son had "brains" but no "head"!) That's where "art" and "practical wisdom" come in, knowing *how to produce results*: art as *general* know-how and practical wisdom as *particular* know-how. The doctor's "art" tells him that a type of tropical disease must be treated with quinine, and his "practical wisdom" tells him that this particular patient, Joe Smith, is sick with that disease and should be given quinine. That's why Aristotle sagely remarks, "With a view to action, experience seems in no respect inferior to art, and men of experience succeed even better than those who have theory without experience."

THE PHILOSOPHY OF MORALITY

There are innumerable ways we use the word *good*—good guess, good movies, good car, good teacher, good for you, and so on—but the philosophy of morality deals with identifying what "good" stands for when we say "this act is good," as opposed to "this act is bad." As pointed out earlier, people generally feel that they know what something means when they have a definition of it, even though there are things we know without being able to define them. That's why, early in the last century, George Edward Moore, the English moralist, in the beginning of his book *Principia Ethica*, stated, "how 'good' is to be defined is the most fundamental question of all Ethics." Generally we get to the definition of a term by resolving it into the simpler terms it's composed of, as "man" is a "rational animal," or "square" is a "right-angled plane figure of four equal sides," or "knife" is a "cutting instrument." But other terms or concepts have nothing simpler to explain them with, as the color 'yellow', or the sound B#, or the idea of circle, or the fact of existence, and so on, yet we *know* them. As Moore puts it, "My point is that 'good' is a simple notion, just as "yellow" is a simple notion; that, just as you cannot, by any manner of means, explain to any one . . . what yellow is, so you cannot explain what good is" (*Principia Ethica*, Chap. 1, pp. 5–7). We do not, and we cannot, define simple notions, even though we know them—that's the role of experience. Just as our knowledge of yellow, or B#, or circle, or existence originates in experience, so does our knowledge of good originate in experience: and *reflection on experience* gives us our primary insight as to what the philosophy of morality is all about; it is the principal focus of this book.

What, then, is the experience we have that leads to the philosophy of morality? Where does it begin? What is it that initiates the sense of morality that all of us have? These questions touch on the very foundation of morality. How we answer them will disclose whether or not there is a factor in our actions we can refer to in a time-honored tradition as the *moral* factor, or the *moral* dimension. This is the dimension we are alerted to when we use terms like *good* or *bad, ought* or *ought not, moral* or *immoral, ethical* or *unethical, human* or *inhuman,* and others similarly. If there is a difference between these terms, we should be able to discover it.

Take two sets of examples. The first set includes actions like choosing a green tie to go with your outfit, writing with a pen, investing in stocks, or reading a Charles Dickens novel. What difference would it make if, instead, you chose a red tie, wrote with a pencil, invested in real estate, or read a Toni Morison novel? The second set includes actions like helping an old lady cross the street, speaking gently to your neighbor, keeping your side of an agreement, giving sincere advice, or using a knife to cut bread with. Now again, ask what difference would it make if, instead, you gave the old lady's cane a swift kick, spoke disparagingly to your neighbor, rejected your side of an agreement, gave deceitful advice, or used a knife to hurt someone? It's clear that the two sets of examples show the difference to be a *personal* one. That is, in the first set, you are no more or less a human being, nor more or less a person, in choosing a red tie over the green one, for it's only a matter of fashion; in writing with a pencil instead of a pen, for it's only a matter of legibility; in investing in real estate instead of stocks, for it's only a matter of business choice; or in reading a Toni Morison novel instead of a Charles Dickens novel, for it's only a matter of literary taste. All of these choices have a relative importance, of course, but *none* of the differences touch on what it fundamentally means to be a *human being*.

The actions of the second set, however, tell a profoundly different story, for they indeed *are* personal; they *do* touch on what it means to be human. The examples show a sensitivity for things human, a feeling for humanity, a respect or regard for the other and for oneself, and a care for the goods and purposes of life; they are a matter of "soul," and are seen as befitting, in an important sense, what it means to be human. Contrariwise, in kicking the cane, in speaking disparagingly, in rejecting an agreement, in giving deceitful advice, or in using a knife injuriously, you are acting out of insensitivity for things human, disrespect for the other, and unconcern for the goods and purposes of life: Though we recognize that human beings are quite capable of such actions, and to that extent disclose the downside of human nature, we basically *understand* them to be contrary to what "truly human" means. All these aspects are unique to the human being and together pertain to the character of our acts signified above as their *moral dimension*.

What we are trying to appreciate here is that there are acts that proceed from us as *human* beings, acts that befit our humanity and allow us to say "this act is human and therefore *good*," or "this act is not human and therefore *bad*." We value them because they are manifestations of the human and give us a deeper grasp of what it means to be a human being; they nourish our humanity. Acts contrary to humanness subvert its very meaning, destroy the possibility of interpersonal relationships, and turn the agent into a tragedy of human isolation.

We have at our disposal several ways of expressing our experience, the chief one among them being the *language* we use to do so. Language is a kind of extension of our experience and helps us to understand what "moral" means, especially as it emerges from the various ways we use the word *ought*. We say, for example, that the stone ought to fall and, when we release it, it does. We say that zinc ought to react with hydrochloric acid and, when we insert a piece, it does. We say the rising sun ought to brighten the sky and, sure enough, it does. What does "ought" mean in these examples? Nothing other than that the activities mentioned take place according to physical laws. They take place in a determinate way by a *physical* necessity. Other examples of "ought" do not involve physical necessity, such as those pertaining to a distinct area of discourse and whose "ought" has meaning only within that area. This bridge, says one engineer, ought to be built of concrete, while another says it ought to be built of steel. The "ought" used here is plainly proper to engineering discourse, and nothing else. Likewise with the patient who needs medication, one doctor says medicine A ought to be given while another says medicine B; again, the "ought" involved is proper to medical discourse, and nothing else.

But there's another use of "ought" radically different from the "ought" in the examples just mentioned. If I say I ought to speak kindly to my neighbor, or a grocery clerk says he ought to give the proper weight, or a mother says she ought to attend to her sick child, or the young man says he ought to assist the old woman cross the street, the "ought" in these instances is far different from the "ought" of physical laws, or the "ought" in engineering or medical discourse; it is different because it is directly connected with what it means to be a human being. And insofar as the act in question fits the human context, it is good; if it does not fit, it is not good. Once again, by reflecting on our experience—this time on the meaning of "ought"—the *moral* aspect of our acts is disclosed.

If we inquire into the relationship between the "ought" and the "good," we face the dilemma Plato writes about in the dialogue *Euthyphro* between Socrates and his friend regarding the question, why is a thing called "holy"? Is it holy because it is loved by the gods, or do the gods love it because it is holy? Though no definitive answer is given, Socrates implies the latter, that is, because a thing is holy the gods love it (R #3). In the practical order, whether we say that what ought to be done is good, or that the good is what ought to be done, they carry the same weight. But there is a deeper level to look at. Compare the following questions: "Is it good to do what you ought?" with "Is what you ought to do, good?" Which, as it were, comes first, the good or the ought? Is it because an act *ought* to be done that it is good? Or is it because an act is *good* and therefore ought to be done? Does the ought found the good, or does the good found the ought? Does the ought come first, then good; or does the good come first, then ought? It sounds like the chicken and the egg dilemma. But if we place these questions in light of our previous discussion, we see a twofold response. In the *order in which we know things* (epistemologically), the ought comes first because it is what we first grasp, or perceive; but in the *order of nature* (metaphysically), the good comes first and is what is revealed by the ought. It is not the ought that makes the good, but the good that makes the ought, so that the good is what the ought is all about, and so is the moral act. This consideration helps us to formulate the basic moral axiom, *good is to be done and evil avoided* (R #4).

THE MORAL SENSE: NATURAL OR ACQUIRED?

The previous section dealt with the overall question of how, in our experience, we identify the sense of morality, which leads to another fundamental question: Is the *moral sense* natural, or is it acquired? It has to be either. I can "acquire" a car, a job, or a suntan because I do not have them in virtue of being a human being; I am a human being without them. Perhaps I acquire the moral sense as a capacity or a habit. But a moment's reflection will show how this involves a contradiction, for then I'd be obliged to say that I have a capacity to acquire a capacity, and so on *ad infinitum*. In casual conversation, if I say one must "acquire a moral sense," I mean something essentially different from "acquiring a car, a job, or a suntan." A human capacity of any kind—one that I cannot be human without—has to be natural, so the moral sense has to be a capacity that is *natural* too, an innate basic ability to tell right from wrong, with the correlative imperative to do one and avoid the other.

To ask, then, where this moral capacity comes from is, in a sense, a *false question*. A question is false when it has no relation to reality, such as, if it's raining and you ask, "why don't you take the covered walk?" when there is no such thing; or the favorite, popular trick question, "when did you stop beating your wife?" when you have never beaten her at all. The question, then, as to where the moral capacity comes from cannot be asked apart from the total human being. We don't ask where our capacity to see comes from, it being understood that as human beings we naturally possess a pair of eyes to see with. Likewise with the moral *capacity*, as human beings we naturally possess the capacity to tell right from wrong; it is natural.

Agreeing that the moral capacity is natural, different responses to the question as to how this is so were developed in the early eighteenth century by a number of British philosophers, notably David Hume. Much in keeping with his commitment to the empirical, Hume holds that we make a judgment on the rightness or wrongness of an action not as a decision made by reason but as the result of a feeling or sentiment that immediately moves us of itself. He would have no part in the rationalistic style of Descartes in deducing a particular truth from a general premise. Reason cannot be looked to as the *source* of moral discernment, which, he maintains, can be shown by introspection: Take any virtue or vice you want, explore it in whichever way, and you will never find a sentiment of approbation or disapprobation "till you turn your reflexions into your own breast" (R #5). Moral distinctions are not derived from reason; quite the contrary, "reason is the slave of passions and must obey them" (*A Treatise of Human Nature*, Book II, Sect III).

A softer Hume on the role of reason shows up, however, in his later treatise on morality where he lays out in some detail the plausibility of the arguments for both sides of the question as to the input of reason and sentiment into making moral distinctions. The arguments on each side "are so plausible, that I am apt to suspect, they may, the one as well as the other, be solid and satisfactory, and that *reason* and *sentiment* concur in almost all moral determinations and conclusions" (*An Enquiry Concerning the Principles of Morals*, Sect I). Yet, having sifted the matter of morality carefully and trying to come to an ultimate statement that would hold with his empiricism, he writes, "it is probable, I say, that the final sentence depends on some internal sense or feeling, which nature has made universal in the whole species" (*ibid*).

But having the moral capacity naturally does not mean that we have the *specific contents* of morality the same way. The basic capacity is there, but not the particularities of this individual action. The moral sense has to be refined, led by experience, cultivated by education, and learned from others; in short, *a human being develops the innate moral sense by living and resonating to the rhythms of human life.* Take the intellect as an analogous example. The intellect is the basic, raw ability to know but it doesn't know anything until it comes into contact with things knowable. Likewise the moral sense is the raw ability to know good and to do it, to know evil and avoid it, but it does not become active until it comes into contact with things choosable. We do not perform acts in a general sort of way; we perform them specifically. That is, any action we perform is a particular thing, performed in a particular set of circumstances, with a particular good in mind, and is unique as any individual thing is unique. A judgment, therefore, has to be made as to the morality of this particular act. How we make such a judgment is the subject of Chapter 2.

FREEDOM AND DETERMINISM

In a preceding section we were careful to distinguish the moral ought from other kinds of ought inasmuch as it is essentially composed by uniquely personal ingredients, one of which has to be considered more at length, the ingredient of *freedom*. How sure am I that the acts I place, and call human, are not of the same nature as those displayed in the physical world? A stone falls because it has to; it *must* do so according to the physical laws of gravity that determine its behavior. Why do I think my actions are any different? If the bee builds its honeycomb in a certain way, even though there appears to be less determination than in the case of the stone, it is still necessitated. Are my actions necessitated in the same way, though perhaps less determined? Here we are in the midst of a long-standing problem, the problem of *freedom vs. determinism*. With the evidence of determinism all about us—not only in the stone and the honeybee, but in the planets and the astrosphere beyond; in the atom and the sub-atomic world, where even the so-called Heisenberg principle of indeterminacy must be reconsidered in light of new thinking on chaos theory; in plant and animal life, wherein the huge and mysterious powers of nature conspire to produce hundreds of thousands of wonderful life types which respond to some kind of necessity—are we then to say that the human being is not determined as well? The human body is a physical thing, a vegetative thing, and an animal thing and, to the extent involved, is governed by laws of necessity. But there is yet to be considered the question of human freedom as the overarching difference between the human and the nonhuman, reminding ourselves, in the words of the French philosopher Henri Bergson, that freedom does not have to be everywhere to be somewhere.

It's perhaps true that most of our conversation about freedom is of a general kind and pertains to life in various social and political milieux, as when we speak of a free people, or the freedom of political activity, mobility, speech, or marital choice, and so on. Or we might frame our ideas along the lines of *positive* and *negative* freedom, a critical distinction made widely influential by the English philosopher Isaiah Berlin, in which *positive* refers to the freedom a person has to develop his or her own personal capacities from within and *negative* refers to the freedom a person has in the absence or reduction of external forces that would prevent action or coerce it. Every one of these aspects of freedom has a moral content that must be considered by the moralist, but our concern in this section is to address the forever problem of internal freedom, the *freedom of the will*, which characterizes the human domain over all others.

To think of human activity exclusively in terms of necessity and determinism has a powerful attraction about it. If we were to follow it, it would put us in line with traditional materialists and with those of a more modern mind-set who feel that the more science advances, the more human freedom recedes, which is why David Hume*um* pointedly described his work on human nature not as the philosophy of man but the "science" of man. In a way, perhaps, your own life might become easier to bear if you believed you had no control over it. But the price you have to pay is steep, for then you have to accept a reality in which, as William James bleakly noted, if freedom is denied, then necessity and impossibility between them rule the destinies of the world. The "dilemma of determinism," as James called it, invalidates determinism as a viable philosophy for understanding the world, thus leaving freedom (or "chance," a word James prefers in this context) as the only option: "Determinism, in denying that anything else can be in its stead, virtually defines the universe as a place in which what ought to be is impossible—in other words, as an organism whose constitution is afflicted with a taint, an irremediable flaw" (R #6).

An action is *determined* if only one course of action is open to an agent. A stone falls if it is released; to rise is a course not open to it. Heliotropic plants have no option but to grow toward the sun. Beavers build dams only in this way. But *freedom* means that more than one course of action is open to the agent so that it is not constrained by a built-in, constitutive necessity to take this one and only course. Is it possible to find such an action? Only experience can be our guide. Since you alone are aware of your own experiences, ask yourself if you are not aware that you are free to sit, or stand, or walk? That you can choose ice cream in one of fifty different flavors? That you can say yes or no to smoking? That you can speak respectfully to your friends or tear them into strips? That you can honor your promises or turn back on them? That you can be true to your parents, spouse, and family or not? That you can love or hate? When you are beset by a difficult situation calling for a hard decision on your part, can you not choose to ignore it or see it through? If the situation is one of life or death, do you not still choose one? Even if no external action is involved, you can internally respect or despise another, wish good fortune or bad, be at peace with yourself or angry over a presumed insult.

Going beyond this "free choice" aspect of freedom, there is the "humanizing" aspect of freedom that enhances the very meaning of "human." It is freedom that disposes us to another in love and affection and friendship, that brings music and the arts into the fabric of life, that endows us with the power to extend ourselves in creative works, that nurtures acts of charity and forgiveness. Freedom is found in the joy of spontaneity, in the mystery of acceptance, in the appreciation of the beauty and freshness of the natural world. Freedom binds all together to launch projects for the common good. Freedom is there in the willingness to adapt to changing circumstances, to the discernment of goals and the means to achieve them, and to respond to the invitations of rest and movement. Without freedom, human existence would be lifeless. To reject testimony we give ourselves regarding the meaning of freedom is tantamount to rejecting the value of experience itself, emptying self-awareness of all content.

As indicated earlier, there is a huge difference between a free act and a determined one. A free act runs contrary to the kind of activity universally present in the physical world, the *determined* cause and effect activity found therein. Freedom and determinism occupy opposite poles on a wide spectrum between them. If, at one end of the spectrum, an action is free, then determinism has no part in it; if, at the other end, an action is determined, then freedom has no part in it; they are mutually exclusive. Let's take a further look at this opposition from another angle. It is true that there cannot be a cause without an effect nor an effect without a cause, in which sense they are mutually self-defining; the same event necessarily includes cause and effect. There can be no such thing as a "causeless effect" or an "effectless cause." This holds not only for the physical world but for the moral world as well. How it holds for the physical world is clear, as we recall from earlier remarks, because it is the world in which freedom, necessity's opposite, in no way appears. But how it holds for the moral world has been the subject of much controversy over the years because it represents such a departure from the rest of the universe, though the terms used in the controversy, *compatible* and *incompatible*, are of recent vintage. The view of the *incompatibilist* is straightforward and uncomplicated: Freedom of the will and determinism cannot co-exist side-by-side; they are not compatible; an act cannot be free and necessitated at the same time. But the *compatibilist*, for whom free will and determinism *are* compatible, must find a way to defend the will's freedom without surrendering the necessity involved in the cause-and-effect event. The compatibilist feels he has found such a way by asking whether the agent could have done otherwise than he did; if the answer is "yes," then the agent (or the will) is free; if the answer is "no," then the agent is being coerced and therefore not free. But this solution is incomplete because it does not answer how the will gets to act even when there is no coercion; it must still be explained *how the will gets to act in the first place*. It can only get to act not from any cause outside itself (a "transient" cause) but from *within* itself (an "immanent" cause); it is in the nature of the will to act freely, not because it is coerced.

Putting it another way, it would be contradictory, as indicated in the previous paragraph, to say that a free act is caused to be free by a cause outside itself, for then it would be determined. So the cause has to be *from within*. A free act has, in some way, to be the *origin of its own freedom*. At first this may sound contradictory, but not when you consider that all life is from within. The *within-ness* of life characterizes every living thing; life is from within; life is immanent. It's true that the living body must receive nourishment from without, but the act of living is within. Or the intellect, as a living faculty, needs something real to know, but the act of knowing takes place *within* the intellect. In a similar way, the will needs an object to enact it, but the act of willing takes place in the will. How acts of life, various as they are, emerge from within themselves belongs to the mystery of life.

An interesting query: Could it be that nonhuman animals feel free, with a freedom analogous to ours? I remember many years ago a student expressed a similar quandary as to animal knowledge: "Professor, maybe there's more intelligence in one antenna of an ant than there is in all human beings collectively, and we just don't know it!" I cannot recall the exact wording of my answer, but I'm sure it was along the lines of, "well, if there were, we'd certainly know about it; intelligence is impossible to conceal." Some animals have knowledge, and they show it. Some are able to communicate, and they do. Some feel pain or sense impending danger, and exclaim it. So, perhaps, we ought not shut the door too quickly on the possibility that some animals *feel* free, but are incapable of knowing it. However, there's another consideration to keep in mind. As the ladder of life ascends, some animal activities on the borderline of the lower stage give the appearance of kinship with those of the higher, but we cannot therefore conclude from mere likeness that they are the same. What counts most of all against such a conclusion is the *totality of life* exhibited in each type. In our present concern, there is precious little evidence of self-awareness in animal life, as there is in human, without which an awareness of freedom is extremely unlikely, if not impossible.

Without the notion of human freedom (voluntariness, liberty), it would be impossible to have the notion of personal *responsibility*, which holds that the agent, or doer of the act, has to answer for it, has to respond for it, inasmuch as he is the fundamental cause of the act. Praise or blame, credit or discredit, can then be properly attributed to the one responsible. Morality is a human affair; non-human beings do not act responsibly. We cannot praise or blame a stone for falling, or a flower for facing the sun, or a beaver for building a dam. Still less can you blame your dog Fido for telling you a lie!

Often a roadblock is set up against the notion of human freedom by saying something like, well, hold it if you want to, but you can't *prove* it. The implication here is that one cannot know a thing is true if it cannot be proven. Laying aside the self-contradiction involved in such a proposition, truth (as we touched on earlier in this chapter) can be had in one of two ways, *directly* or *indirectly*: directly by self-evidence and indirectly by proof. Directly, by the fact that the thing is evident of itself: I know that I am, that I am not you, that the whole is greater than any of its parts, that it is the color I call yellow I now see, that my hat cannot be on my head and off at the same time. These kinds of things are self-evident to me: I know them immediately; I know them without any intermediary; I intuit them, or have an intuition of them. If I am to know what is not self-evident, then I have to know it indirectly, by arguing to it: for the dart to hit the bulls-eye, it must be targeted, because a dart doesn't target itself; if A is B, and B is C, then A is C; if all freshmen are smart, and if Helen is a freshman, then Helen is smart; if this key is a key because it is metallic, then everything metallic would be a key, but not everything metallic is a key, therefore a key is a key for some other reason than that it is nonmetallic. It's clear then that our knowledge of our own freedom is not of the second type, indirect; it is of the first type, direct, self-evident, not dependent on proof but on experience, and it has all the certainty that's attached to direct knowledge. As a corollary, if we did not have self-evident knowledge to begin with, we could never have any knowledge whatsoever. But with self-evident knowledge, we can move on to knowledge beyond the self-evident, beyond experience, to those things we *conclude* to. This is the domain of metaphysics and epistemology.

NO FREEDOM WITHOUT KNOWLEDGE

The expectation we have of an act's being placed freely (voluntarily) is that it is being placed *entirely* freely and that the ensuing responsibility is entire also. True, but some distinctions are in order. Common sense tells you that if a woman *unknowingly* walks off with a bag of groceries, not hers, from the supermarket, she cannot be accused of stealing. How can she choose what she doesn't know? The rule is obvious: *You cannot will what you do not know.* One of the functions of the intellect is to make a judgment, such as, "this act is good and ought to be done," which can be followed by, "and I *ought* to do it"; therefore, I *will* do it. But if I do not have full knowledge of what I am doing, I cannot *fully* will it. In other words, to the degree that knowledge is lacking, so is freedom. There is a direct ratio at work: more knowledge, more freedom; less knowledge, less freedom; and where knowledge is totally lacking (total ignorance), as in the supermarket example just given, freedom too is totally lacking. To the extent that our judgment-making ability is impaired, to that extent so is the will's freedom. Voluntariness and responsibility, then, can be lessened by things that infringe the mind, like fear, violence, concussion, or illness, and even destroyed in cases of extreme fear, violence, concussion, illness, or even, in modern times, by mind-altering treatment.

There is some slippery terrain here, for a lack of knowledge does not always mean a lack of voluntariness: Sometimes ignorance itself is voluntary! How often have you said, or heard, "Don't tell me, I don't want to know!"? That suggests there is something you *choose not to know*. If it pertains to knowledge you should have to make a morally good choice, or think you should have, then that kind of ignorance is blameworthy and referred to as *culpable ignorance*. Examples abound: You refuse to be told whether a low cost item you want to buy is "hot"; a corporation's CEO has spread it about that he does not want to hear about shady accounting practices; a president refuses to hear any evidence contrary to a policy decision he wants to make.

As mentioned earlier, the opposite of freedom is determinism and it would be helpful to describe several different *kinds of determinism* that have made an historical bid for attention. Among the early pre-Socratics, who touched upon an imposing list of perennial philosophical questions, we find the first espousal of *materialism* in its early, classical dress. The basis of this view is that all the things of this world are composed of small, indivisible particles called *atoms* and the differentiation among things is explained by the different ways the atoms are constellated together. One constellation is a mineral, another is a plant, another an animal, another a man, and all the activities of these physical things, of sense, of growth, of knowledge, are themselves explained by the movement of atoms in special ways according to the laws of nature. Even the soul, according to Democritus, is made up of exceedingly fine atoms at work in the larger body. In the seventeenth century, after Descartes had maintained that man is pure spirit and that the "living" body was nothing more than a robot operating on purely mechanical laws, the way was paved for several kinds of philosophy that saw no need whatsoever for the realm of the immaterial to explain life and sought to explain all human activities in terms of the physical as, for example, with the eighteenth-century physician/philosopher *La Mettrie*, for whom man is a machine that walks with walk-muscles and thinks with thought-muscles.

In the same century, as we saw earlier, David Hume was deeply committed to the role of experience and as a result made some acute observations on our discernment of virtue and vice by way of experienced feelings. His firm commitment to experience, however, made it difficult for him to admit the possibility of knowing anything beyond it. Accordingly, since we cannot *observe* the actual influencing of the thing called cause over the thing called effect, we must deny, or at least be skeptical of, the *necessary* relationship between them. This view on cause and effect so loosens the relationship between free will and the consequent act that it makes the assignment of responsibility impossible.

A century after Hume, the well-known English utilitarian John Stuart Mill, though his view on cause and effect is pure Hume, seems to have insisted more on his belief that the relation of effect to cause is absolutely invariable, which he stated as the "law of causation": "Every consequent has an invariable antecedent." This notion of causality prevails throughout all of nature and includes man as well. There is a large problem here. Mill held that man *is* responsible for his moral character, but how can that be true if man is as determined as the rest of physical nature? This is a restatement of the classical problem of freedom and determinism. Mill believed he found a way out by suggesting a midway point between them, in that man, by his desires, can alter the circumstances in which his character is formed. Not really a genuine response, because man would then have to be free in his desires: If man can alter them, he must be *free* to do so. Mill does give a hint that he was not really satisfied with his resolution of the dilemma, but it was "sufficiently established for the purposes of this treatise."

There are some psychologists in our day who quite agree with Mill that human activity can, or will, be explained in terms of a determinism proper to the human being. Such a view is subsumed under a broad category of tenets generally referred to as *behaviorism*, with the American psychologist B.F. Skinner as one of its main exponents. He was a widely respected psychologist who, in his admiration for the marvelous advances science makes, fully expected that scientists would ultimately uncover those "conditions or variables which can be used to predict and control behavior in a new, and increasingly rigorous, technology." Control, if properly used, can lead to "a world in which people are wise and good without trying, without 'having to be,' without 'choosing to be' " and such a world "could conceivably be a far better world for everyone" (R #7).

The temptation to foreclose the freedom of the will in the name of science, as seen in Hume, Mill, and Skinner, comes nearer to completion in the high-tech world of our day. The reach of the computer, for some, knows no bounds. As computers come to "solve" intricate problems far better than humans do, or to obtain results beyond human capacity, they increasingly encourage belief in artificial intelligence, and the time will come when these very computers are no longer artificially intelligent but actually so. Put another way, the human being will be totally understood as a computer. That being the case, to show how outrageous this can become, a computer/person will be able to download itself/himself, not into a mere clone, but into a second self! Handy to have around just in case the original one ceases to function! These are the sentiments of Ray Kurzweil, one of today's most imaginatively aggressive technologists, whose book *The Age of Spiritual Machines, When Computers Exceed Human Intelligence* we'll discuss in a later chapter. Suffice it to say here that Kurzweil foresees that by the year 2099, there will no longer be "any clear distinction between humans and computers."

It's not difficult to figure out how all this applies to the subject of freedom and determinism under discussion, for just as intelligence is to be transformed into a machine, so the will is destined to be transformed into a machine in the same way, and the notion of *free will* becomes a contradiction, that is, a non-entity, just like a square circle.

MORAL FREEDOM

With so much said about the freedom of the will, are we not obliged to take it all back when we talk about the *necessity* of the will to do what is right? Do we have the right to do what is wrong? Don't we *have to do* what is moral? Did we not agree above that there is an *imperative* to do good? What is, after all, the meaning of "ought" if we are not obliged to act or refrain from acting? To solve these questions, a distinction has to be made, a distinction between *natural freedom* (*constitutive, functional, "physical"*) and *moral freedom.* In the first sense, the will, by its nature, is free to do whatever it wills, that is, it can make a choice of one out of many, or it can choose to do or not to do, it can choose right or wrong, good or evil; it is *able* to do so. In the second sense, the will is not free; it *must* choose good and avoid evil. The will is indeed free, naturally but not morally: That is, the will is free, morally speaking, only when it chooses the good. Does this sound contradictory? Isn't the will really under constraint in its being obliged to do good? We won't have a satisfactory answer until we answer the further question as to whether freedom is an end in itself. But as we think about it we begin to realize that freedom cannot be an end in itself. Freedom is *for* something; freedom has achieved its goal when it has achieved what it is *for*, and in moral matters it's *for* the *good* (R #8). Our conclusion, then, is that the will *is* free *naturally* in whatever choice it makes, good or bad, and *morally* only in the choice of the good.

St. Augustine faced this question over 1,500 years ago, and according to him, "freedom consists in submission to the truth," that is, in the acceptance of the truth. The freedom he is speaking of lies in the making of choices befitting our humanity, in acts of charity, honesty, justice, respect, trust, and acceptance; so understood, freedom is the engine for enlarging our humanity. But if freedom is used to make choices contrary to humanity, such as acts of injustice, hatred, distrust, meanness, and unconcern, then it is not real freedom at all but its perversion; it is not human; it is wrong, it is sin. In a word, human nature is destined for the good (R #9 and #10).

DO WE HAVE TO BE GOOD?

Implied in what has been said so far is the answer to the nagging question, "Do we have to be good?" The answer, once again, is found in our experience, the experience of doing what I know has to be done. I realize that the imperative for acting is one with the very goodness of the act. In knowing the good, I simultaneously know that it's to be done, a truth we saw earlier in our treatment of the meaning of ought. It is not as though there are two separate acts taking place in sequence, first I recognize the good and then I recognize the imperative. Rather it is one act with two moments together, that of the good and that of the necessity of doing it. This is the heart of what Socrates has to say about wisdom, that the very *idea* of wisdom *includes* the *dynamic* aspect of doing it; a person is wise only if he knows the good and does it; whence, *ethical wisdom.* A person who knows the good and does not do it is not only unwise but is also in denial of his own humanity.

Ethical wisdom is the message tragically delivered in the *Apology*, Plato's literary presentation of Socrates' defense of himself before the court of Athens. It is Plato's legacy of honor to Western culture's great teacher and proves to be a clear window on the character and teaching of the man. The charges brought against Socrates can be summed up under one heading—that he misled the young people of Athens by instructing them in false doctrine and encouraging them to disrespect authority. The charge is a caricature of what Socrates was really trying to do, which was to impart to his young students a love for wisdom whose ultimate meaning was the kind of knowledge that leads to an ethical life. That's why he could say that "virtue is wisdom." Wisdom is a far cry from the mere accumulation of knowledge, as important as that is, for it is a deepening insight into what knowledge is that makes a person good. A man may be a good boat-builder but a terrible person, or a terrible boat-builder but a good person. True wisdom lies in the actual *doing* of good, whence wisdom is virtue, and virtue wisdom. Loving-and-doing the good is thus an essential component of wisdom, its dynamic aspect. In the end it is what happiness is all about.

To what extent Socrates himself was committed to wisdom/virtue can be seen at the moment of the deepest personal poignancy for him, the moment of his death. He viewed death as a life event, pregnant with philosophical importance, for in death, as in a prism, life can be seen as the unity of happiness, goodness, truth, and all the other characteristics identified with humanity. Though this is true for everyone, it was especially so for Socrates, who, under the sentence of death, was able to convert his last days into a privileged stillpoint for contemplating the end of life as he knew it. To be sure, in facing death, the first and only existential question— the meaning of life and its values—is the only question to be asked; he made an effort to answer it. Indeed, Socrates offered no more arresting description of philosophy than that it is "practicing death." Practicing death refers to what, with death in view, one does with his life, the way one lives, the ideals he holds, the convictions he has, and the practice in which he externalizes what is internal: *Death is a life-directing reality.* That is why, for those who have led a good life, a life of "holiness," the future holds no fears and death can be thought of only as a blessing. For Socrates, such a person "has fitted himself to await his journey to the next world."

READINGS

READING 1
Man's Place in the Universe
Bertrand Russell
(from *An Outline of Philosophy*)

I will take up another matter in regard to which what I have said may have been disappointing to some readers. It is sometimes thought that philosophy ought to aim at encouraging a good life. Now, of course, I admit that it should have this effect, but I do not admit that it should have this as a conscious purpose. To begin with, when we embark upon the study of philosophy we ought not to assume that we already know for certain what the good life is; philosophy may conceivably modify our views as to what is good, in which

case it will seem to the non-philosophical to have had a bad moral effect. That, however, is a secondary point. The essential thing is that philosophy is part of the pursuit of knowledge, and that we cannot limit this pursuit by insisting that the knowledge obtained shall be such as we should have thought edifying before we obtained it. I think it could be maintained with truth that *all* knowledge is edifying, provided we have a right conception of edification. When this appears to be not the case, it is because we have moral standards based upon ignorance. It may happen by good fortune that a moral standard based upon ignorance is right, but if so knowledge will not destroy it; if knowledge can destroy it, it must be wrong. The conscious purpose of philosophy, therefore, ought to be solely to *understand* the world as well as possible, not to establish this or that proposition which is thought morally desirable. Those who embark upon philosophy must be prepared to question all their preconceptions, ethical as well as scientific; if they have a determination never to surrender certain philosophic beliefs, they are not in the frame of mind in which philosophy can be profitably pursued.

But although philosophy ought not to have a moral purpose, it ought to have certain good moral effects. Any disinterested pursuit of knowledge teaches us the limits of our power, which is salutary; at the same time, in proportion as we succeed in achieving knowledge, it teaches the limits of our impotence, which is equally desirable. And philosophical knowledge, or rather philosophical thought, has certain special merits not belonging in an equal degree to other intellectual pursuits. By its generality it enables us to see human passions in their just propositions, and to realise the absurdity of many quarrels between individuals, classes, and nations. Philosophy comes as near as possible for human beings to that large, impartial contemplation of the universe as a whole which raises us for the moment above our purely personal destiny. There is a certain asceticism of the intellect

which is good as a part of life, though it cannot be the whole so long as we have to remain animals engaged in the struggle for existence. The asceticism of the intellect requires that, while we are engaged in the pursuit of knowledge, we shall repress all other desires for the sake of the desire to know. While we are philosophising, the wish to prove that the world is good, or that the dogmas of this or that sect are true, must count as weaknesses of the flesh— they are temptations to be thrust on one side. But we obtain in return something of the joy which the mystic experiences in harmony with the will of God. This joy philosophy can give, but only to those who are willing to follow it to the end, through all its arduous uncertainties . . .

Philosophy should make us know the ends of life, and the elements in life that have value on their own account. However, our freedom may be limited to the causal sphere, we need admit no limitations to our freedom in the sphere of values: what we judge good on its own account we may continue to judge good, without regard to anything but our own feeling. Philosophy cannot itself determine the ends of life, but it can free us from the tyranny of prejudice and from distortions due to a narrow view. Love, beauty, knowledge, and joy of life: these things retain their lustre however wide our purview. And if philosophy can help us to feel the value of these things, it will have played its part in man's collective work of bringing light into the world of darkness.

READING 2
The Role of Experience in Acquiring Knowledge
Aristotle
(from *Metaphysics*)

All men, by their very nature, desire to know. We indicate this by the way we acknowledge the senses for, even though they are useful to us, we acknowledge them for what they are in themselves . . . Animals too are born with

sense faculties; some of them possess the faculty of memory as well and so show more intelligence and learning capacity than the others . . . though they have little experience. But the human race, living as it does by art* and reason, employs memory to confirm experience in that many memories all together finally produce a full experience. Experience itself is very much like science and art; indeed it is through experience that men acquire both science and art for, as Polus says, "experience ends in art, but inexperience, chance." . . . To judge that Socrates, or any other individual, is suffering from a particular disease and is benefited by a particular treatment, is a matter of experience, but to judge that the same treatment will benefit all afflicted the same way is a matter of art.

From the viewpoint of practical action, it surely seems that experience is not at all

* "Art," in the Aristotelian sense, is the *general knowledge* (or *theory,* or *know-how*) of how things are to be done, e.g. the architect's knowledge of structure, or the doctor's know-how regarding a disease and its treatment. (abh)

inferior to art; as a matter of fact, men of experience succeed better than those who have theory but no experience . . . The reason for this is that experience is knowledge of the particular, whereas art is knowledge of the universal: it is Socrates, the individual, who is benefited by the physician, not man in general . . . It is not surprising that we think men who possess theoretical knowledge are wiser than those who possess only experience, because the former know the cause and the latter do not—thus master-craftsmen are superior to manual-workers because they know the why and wherefore things are done . . . Further, we do not think that *wisdom* is attached to any of the senses seven though they are the prime source of our knowledge of particulars; they do not tell us why fire is hot, only that it is.

READING 3
Why Is a Thing Called "Holy"?
Plato
(from *Euthyphro*)

EUTHYPHRO: Piety, then, is that which is dear to the gods, and impiety is that which is not dear to them.

SOCRATES: Very good, Euthyphro; you have now given me the sort of answer which I wanted. But whether what you say is true or not I cannot as yet tell, although I make no doubt that you will prove the truth of your words.

EUTH: Of course.

SOC: Come, then, and let us examine what we are saying. That thing or person which is dear to the gods is pious, and that thing or person which is hateful to the gods is impious, these two being the extreme opposites of one another. Was not that said?

EUTH: It was.

SOC: But I will amend the definition so far as to say that what all the gods hate is impious, and what they love pious or holy; and what some

of them love and others hate is both or neither. Shall this be our definition of piety and impiety?

EUTH: Why not, Socrates?

SOC: Why not! certainly, as far as I am concerned, Euthyphro, there is no reason why not. But whether this admission will greatly assist you in the task of instructing me as you promised, is a matter for you to consider.

EUTH: Yes, I should say that what all the gods love is pious and holy, and the opposite which they all hate, impious.

SOC: Ought we to enquire into the truth of this, Euthyphro, or simply to accept the mere statement on our own authority and that of others? What do you say?

EUTH: *We* should enquire; and I believe that the statement will stand the test of enquiry.

SOC: We shall know better, my good friend, in a little while. The point which I should first wish to understand is whether the pious or holy is beloved by the gods because it is holy, or holy because it is beloved of the gods. . . .

And what do you say of piety, Euthyphro is not piety, according to your definition, loved by all the gods?

EUTH: Yes.

SOC: Because it is pious or holy, or for some other reason?

EUTH: No, that is the reason.

SOC: It is loved because it is holy, not holy because it is loved? *Euth.* Yes.

SOC: And that which is dear to the gods is loved by them, and is in a state to be loved of them because it is loved of them?

EUTH: Certainly.

SOC: Then that which is dear to the gods, Euthyphro, is not holy, nor is that which is holy loved of God, as you affirm; but they are two different things.

EUTH: How do you mean, Socrates?

SOC: I mean to say that the holy has been acknowledged by us to be loved of God because it is holy, not to be holy because it is loved. *Euth.* Yes.

SOC: But that which is dear to the gods is dear to them because it is loved by them, not loved by them because it is dear to them.

EUTH: True.

SOC: But, friend Euthyphro; if that which is holy is the same with that which is dear to God, and is loved because it is holy, then that which is dear to God would have been loved as being dear to God; but if that which is dear to God is dear to him because loved by him, then that which is holy would have been holy because loved by him. But now you see that the reverse is the case, and that they are quite different from one another . . .

EUTH: One of the two must be true.

SOC: Then we must begin again and ask, What is piety? That is an enquiry which I shall never be weary of pursuing as far as in me lies; and I entreat you not to scorn me, but to apply your mind to the utmost, and tell me the truth. For, if any man knows you are he . . .

Another time, Socrates; for I am in a hurry, and must go now.

SOC: Alas! my companion, and will you leave me in despair? I was hoping that you would instruct me in the nature of piety and impiety.

READING 4
Good Is to Be Done, Evil Avoided
Plato
(from *Apology*)

Some one will say: And are you not ashamed, Socrates, of a course of life which is likely to bring you to an untimely end? To him I may fairly answer: There you are mistaken: a man who is good for anything ought not to calculate the charge of living or dying; he ought only to consider whether in doing anything he is doing right or wrong—acting the part of a good man or of a bad. Whereas, upon your view, the heroes who fell at Troy were not good for much, and the son of Thetis above all, who altogether despised danger in comparison with disgrace; and when he was so eager to slay Hector, his goddess mother said

to him, that if he avenged his companion Patroclus, and slew Hector, he would die himself—"Fate," she said, in these or the like words, "waits for you next after Hector"; he, receiving this warning, utterly despised danger and death, and instead of fearing them, feared rather to live in dishonour, and not to avenge his friend. "Let me die forthwith," he replies, "and be avenged of my enemy, rather than abide here by the beaked ships, a laughing-stock and a burden of the earth." Had Achilles any thought of death and danger? For wherever a man's place is, whether the place which he has chosen or that in which he has been placed by a commander, there he ought to remain in the hour of danger; he should not think of death or of anything but of disgrace. And this, O men of Athens, is a true saying.

Strange, indeed, would be my conduct, O men of Athens, if I who, when I was ordered by the generals whom you chose to command me at Potidaea and Amphipolis and Delium, remained where they placed me, like any other man, facing death—if now, when, as I conceive and imagine, God orders me to fulfil the philosopher's mission of searching into myself and other men, I were to desert my post through fear of death, or any other fear; that would indeed be strange, and I might justly be arraigned in court for denying the existence of the gods, if I disobeyed the oracle because I was afraid of death, fancying that I was wise when I was not wise. For the fear of death is indeed the pretence of wisdom, and not real wisdom, being a pretence of knowing the unknown; and no one knows whether death, which men in their fear apprehend to be the greatest evil, may not be the greatest good. Is not this ignorance of a disgraceful sort, the ignorance which is the conceit that man knows what he does not know? And in this respect only I believe myself to differ from men in general, and may perhaps claim to be wiser than they are:—that whereas I know but little of the world below, I do not suppose that I know: but I do know that injustice and disobedience to a better, whether God or man, is evil and dishonourable, and I will never fear or avoid a possible good rather than a certain evil. And therefore if you let me go now, and are not convinced by Anytus, who said that since I had been prosecuted I must be put to death (or if not that I ought never to have been prosecuted at all); and that if I escape now, your sons will all be utterly ruined by listening to my words—if you say to me, Socrates, this time we will not mind Anytus, and you shall be let off, but upon one condition, that you are not to enquire and speculate in this way any more, and that if you are caught doing so again you shall die;—if this was the condition on which you let me go, I should reply:

Men of Athens, I honour and love you; but I shall obey God rather than you, and while I have life and strength I shall never cease from the practice and teaching of philosophy, exhorting any one whom I meet and saying to him after my manner: You, my friend,—a citizen of the great and mighty and wise city of Athens,—are you not ashamed of heaping up the greatest amount of money and honour and reputation, and caring so little about wisdom and truth and the greatest improvement of the soul, which you never regard or heed at all? And if the person with whom I am arguing, says: Yes, but I do care; then I do not leave him or let him go at once; but I proceed to interrogate and examine and cross-examine him, and if I think that he has no virtue in him, but only says that he has, I reproach him with undervaluing the greater, and overvaluing the less. And I shall repeat the same words to every one whom I meet, young and old, citizen and alien, but especially to the citizens, in as much as they are my brethren. For know that this is the command of God; and I believe that no greater good has ever happened in the state than my service to the God. For I do nothing but go about persuading you all, old and young alike, not to take thought for your persons or your properties, but first and chiefly to care about the greatest improvement of the soul. I tell you that virtue is not given by money, but that from virtue comes money and every other good of man, public as well as private. This is my teaching, and if this is the doctrine which corrupts the youth, I am a mischievous person. But if any one says that this is not my teaching, he is speaking an untruth. Wherefore. O men of Athens. I say to you, do as Anytus bids or not as Anytus bids, and either acquit me or not; but whichever you do, understand that I shall never alter my ways, not even if I have to die many times.

· · ·

Some one will say: Yes, Socrates, but cannot you hold your tongue, and then you may go into a foreign city, and no one will interfere with you? Now I have great difficulty in making you understand my answer to this. For if I tell you that to do as you say would be a disobedience to the

God, and therefore that I cannot hold my tongue, you will not believe that I am serious; and if I say again that daily to discourse about virtue, and of those other things about which you hear me examining myself and others, is the greatest good of man, and that the unexamined life is not worth living, you are still less likely to believe me. Yet I say what is true, although a thing of which it is hard for me to persuade you.

READING 5
Sentiment as the Source of Moral Distinction
David Hume
(from *Treatise of Human Nature*)

But can there be any difficulty in proving, that vice and virtue are not matters of fact, whose existence we can infer by reason? Take any action allow'd to be vicious: Wilful murder; for instance. Examine it in all lights, and see if you can find that matter of fact, or real existence, which you call *vice*. In which-ever way you take it, you find only certain passions, motives, volitions and thoughts. There is no other matter of fact in the case. The vice entirely escapes you, as long as you consider the object. You never can find it, till you turn your reflexion into your own breast, and find a sentiment of disapprobation, which arises in you, towards this action. Here is a matter of fact; but 'tis the object of feeling, not of reason. It lies in your self, not in the object. So that when you pronounce any action or character to be vicious, you mean nothing, but that from the constitution of your nature you have, a feeling or sentiment of blame from the contemplation of it. Vice and virtue, therefore, may be compar'd to sounds, colours, heat and cold, which, according to modern philosophy, are not qualities in objects, but perceptions in the mind: And this discovery in morals, like that other in physics, is to be regarded as a considerable advancement of the speculative sciences; tho', like that too, it has little or no influence on practice. Nothing can be more real, or concern us more, than our own sentiments of pleasure and uneasiness; and if these be favourable to virtue, and unfavourable to vice, no more can be requisite to the regulation of our conduct and behaviour.

READING 6
The Dilemma of Determinism
William James
(from *The Will to Believe*)

To begin, then, I must suppose you acquainted with all the usual arguments on the subject. I cannot stop to take up the old proofs from causation, from statistics, from the certainty with which we can foretell one another's conduct, from the fixity of character, and all the rest. But there are two *words* which usually encumber these classical arguments, and which we must immediately dispose of if we are to make any progress. One is the eulogistic word *freedom*, and the other is the opprobrious word *chance*. The word "chance" I wish to keep, but I wish to get rid of the word "freedom." Its eulogistic associations have so far overshadowed all the rest of its meaning that both parties claim the sole right to use it, and determinists to-day insist that they alone are freedom's champions. Old-fashioned determinism was what we may call *hard* determinism. It did not shrink from such words as fatality, bondage of the will, necessitation, and the like. Nowadays, we have a *soft* determinism which abhors harsh words, and, repudiating fatality, necessity, and even predetermination, says that its real name is freedom; for freedom is only necessity understood, and bondage to the highest is identical with true freedom.

. . . What does determinism profess?

It professes that those parts of the universe already laid down absolutely appoint and decree what the other parts shall be. The future has no ambiguous possibilities hidden in its womb: the part we call the present is compatible with only one totality. Any other future complement than the one fixed from eternity is impossible. The whole is in each and every part, and welds it with the rest into an absolute unity, an iron block, in which there can be no equivocation or shadow of turning.

> "With earth's first clay they did the last man knead,
> And there of the last harvest sowed the seed.
> And the first morning of creation wrote
> What the last dawn of reckoning shall read."

Indeterminism, on the contrary, says that the parts have a certain amount of loose play on one another, so that the laying down of one of them does not necessarily determine what the others shall be. It admits that possibilities may be in excess of actualities, and that things not yet revealed to our knowledge may really in themselves be ambiguous. Of two alternative futures which we conceive, both may now be really possible; and the one become impossible only at the very moment when the other excludes it by becoming real itself. Indeterminism thus denies the world to be one unbending unit of fact. It says there is a certain ultimate pluralism in it; and, so saying, it corroborates our ordinary

unsophisticated view of things. To that view, actualities seem to float in a wider sea of possibilities from out of which they are chosen; and, *somewhere*, indeterminism says, such possibilities exist, and form a part of truth.

Determinism, on the contrary, says they exist *nowhere*, and that necessity on the one hand and impossibility on the other are the sole categories of the real. Possibilities that fail to get realized are, for determinism, pure illusions: they never were possibilities at all. There is nothing inchoate, it says, about this universe of ours, all that was or is or shall be actual in it having been from eternity virtually there. The cloud of alternatives our minds escort this mass of actuality withal is a cloud of sheer deceptions, to which "impossibilities" is the only name that rightfully belongs.

. . .

The stronghold of the deterministic sentiment is the antipathy to the idea of chance. As soon as we begin to talk indeterminism to our friends, we find a number of them shaking their heads. This notion of alternative possibility, they say, this admission that any one of several things may come to pass, is, after all, only a roundabout name for chance; and chance is something the notion of which no sane mind can for an instant tolerate in the world. What is it, they ask, but barefaced crazy unreason, the negation of intelligibility and law? And if the slightest particle of it exist anywhere, what is to prevent the whole fabric from falling together, the stars from going out, and chaos from recommencing her topsy-turvy reign?

Remarks of this sort about chance will put an end to discussion as quickly as anything one can find. I have already told you that "chance" was a word I wished to keep and use. Let us then examine exactly what it means, and see whether it ought to be such a terrible bugbear to us. I fancy that squeezing the thistle boldly will rob it of its sting.

The sting of the word "chance" seems to lie in the assumption that it means something positive, and that if anything happens by chance, it must needs be something of an intrinsically irrational and preposterous sort. Now, chance means nothing of the kind. It is a purely negative and relative term, giving us no information about that of which it is predicated, except that it happens to be disconnected with something else,— not controlled, secured, or necessitated by other things in advance of its own actual presence. As this point is the most subtile one of the whole lecture, and at the same time the point on which all the rest hinges, I beg you to pay particular attention to it. What I say is that it tells us nothing about what a thing may be in itself to call it "chance." It may be a bad thing, it may be a good thing. It may be lucidity, transparency, fitness incarnate, matching the whole system of other things, when it has once befallen, in an unimaginably perfect way. All you mean by calling it "chance" is that this is not guaranteed, that it may also fall out otherwise. For the system of other things has no positive hold on the chance-thing. Its origin is in a certain fashion negative: it escapes, and says, Hands off! coming, when it comes, as a free gift, or not at all.

· · ·

But for the deterministic philosophy the murder; the sentence, and the prisoner's optimism were all necessary from eternity; and nothing else for a moment had a ghost of a chance of being put into their place. To admit such a chance, the determinists tell us, would be to make a suicide of reason; so we must steel our hearts against the thought. And here our plot thickens, for we see the first of those difficult implications of determinism and monism which it is my purpose to make you feel. If this Brockton murder was called for by the rest of the universe, if it had to come at its preappointed hour, and if nothing else would have been consistent with the sense of the whole, what are we to think of the universe? Are we stubbornly to stick to our judgment of regret, and say, though it *could n't* be, yet it *would* have been a better universe with something different from this Brockton murder in it? That, of course, seems the natural and spontaneous thing for us to do; and yet it is nothing short of deliberately espousing a kind of pessimism. The judgment of regret calls the murder bad. Calling a thing bad means, if it mean anything at all, that the thing ought not to be, that something else ought to be in its stead. Determinism, in denying that anything else can be in its stead, virtually defines the universe as a place in which

what ought to be is impossible,—in other words, as an organism whose constitution is afflicted with an incurable taint, an irremediable flaw.

· · ·

We have thus clearly revealed to our view what may be called the dilemma of determinism, so far as determinism pretends to think things out at all. A merely mechanical determinism, it is true, rather rejoices in not thinking them out. It is very sure that the universe must satisfy its postulate of a physical continuity and coherence, but it smiles at any one who comes forward with a postulate of moral coherence as well. I may suppose, however, that the number of purely mechanical or hard determinists among you this evening is small. The determinism to whose seductions you are most exposed is what I have called soft determinism—the determinism which allows considerations of good and bad to mingle with those of cause and effect in deciding what sort of a universe this may rationally be held to be. The dilemma of this determinism is one whose left horn is pessimism and whose right horn is subjectivism. In other words, if determinism is to escape pessimism, it must leave off looking at the goods and ills of life in a simple objective way, and regard them as materials, indifferent in themselves, for the production of consciousness, scientific and ethical, in us.

· · ·

But this brings us right back, after such a long détour, to the question of indeterminism and to the conclusion of all I came here to say to-night. For the only consistent way of representing a pluralism and a world whose parts may affect one another through their conduct being either good or bad is the indeterministic way. What interest, zest, or excitement can there be in achieving the right way, unless we are enabled to feel that the wrong way is also a possible and a natural way,—nay, more, a menacing and an imminent way? And what sense can there be in condemning ourselves for taking the wrong way, unless we need have done nothing of the sort, unless the right way was open to us as well? I cannot understand the willingness to act, no matter how we feel, without the belief that acts are really good and bad. I cannot understand the belief that an act is bad, without regret at its happening. I cannot understand regret without the admission of real, genuine possibilities in the world. Only *then* is it other than a mockery to feel, after we have failed to do our best, that an irreparable opportunity is gone from the universe, the loss of which it must forever after mourn.

· · ·

But now you will bring up your final doubt. Does not the admission of such an unguaranteed chance or freedom preclude utterly the notion of a Providence governing the world? Does it not leave the fate of the universe at the mercy of the chance-possibilities, and so far insecure? Does it not, in short, deny the craving of our nature for an ultimate peace behind all tempests, for a blue zenith above all clouds?

To this my answer must be very brief. The belief in free-will is not in the least incompatible with the belief in Providence, provided you do not restrict the Providence to fulminating nothing but *fatal* decrees. If you allow him to provide possibilities as well as actualities to the universe, and to carry on his own thinking in those two categories just as we do ours, chances may be there, uncontrolled even by him, and the course of the universe be really ambiguous; and yet the end of all things may be just what he intended it to be from all eternity.

An analogy will make the meaning of this clear. Suppose two men before a chessboard—the one a novice, the other an expert player of the game. The expert intends to beat. But he cannot foresee exactly what any one actual move of his adversary may be. He knows, however, all the *possible* moves of the latter; and he knows in advance how to meet each of them by a move of

his own which leads in the direction of victory. And the victory infallibly arrives, after no matter how devious a course, in the one predestined form of check-mate to the novice's king.

Let now the novice stand for us finite free agents, and the expert for the infinite mind in which the universe lies. Suppose the latter to be thinking out his universe before he actually creates it. Suppose him to say, I will lead things to a certain end, but I will not *now* decide on all the steps thereto. At various points, ambiguous possibilities shall be left open, *either* of which, at a given instant, may become actual. But whichever branch of these bifurcations become real, I know what I shall do at the *next* bifurcation to keep things from drifting away from the final result I intend.

The creator's plan of the universe would thus be left blank as to many of its actual details, but all possibilities would be marked down. The realization of some of these would be left absolutely to chance; that is, would only be determined when the moment of realization came. Other possibilities would be *contingently* determined; that is, their decision would have to wait till it was seen how the matters of absolute chance fell out. But the rest of the plan, including its final upshot, would be rigorously determined once for all. So the creator himself would not need to know *all* the details of actuality until they came; and at any time his own view of the world would be a view partly of facts and partly of possibilities, exactly as ours is now. Of one thing, however, he might be certain; and that is that his world was safe, and that no matter how much it might zigzag he could surely bring it home at last.

READING 7
Control of Human Behavior
B. F. Skinner
(from *Science,* vol. 124)

Science is steadily increasing our power to influence, change, mold—in a word, control—human behavior. It has extended our

"understanding" (whatever that may be) so that we deal more successfully with people in nonscientific ways, but it has also identified conditions or variables which can be used to predict and control behavior in a new, and increasingly rigorous, technology.

. . . Until only recently it was customary to deny the possibility of a rigorous science of human behavior by arguing, either that a lawful science was impossible because man was a free agent, or that merely statistical predictions would always leave room for personal freedom. But those who used to take this line have become most vociferous in expressing their, alarm at the way these obstacles are being surmounted. . . .

A world in which people are wise and good without trying, without "having to be," without "choosing to be," could conceivably be a far better world for everyone. In such a world we should not have to "give anyone credit"—we should not need to admire anyone—for being wise and good. From our present point of view we cannot believe that such a world would be admirable. We do not even permit ourselves to imagine what it would be like. . . .

If the advent of a powerful science of behavior causes trouble, it will not be because science itself is inimical to human welfare but because older conceptions have not yielded easily or gracefully. We expect resistance to new techniques of control from those who have heavy investments in the old, but we have no reason to help them preserve a series of principles that are not ends in themselves but rather outmoded means to an end. What is needed is a new conception of human behavior which is compatible with the implications of a scientific analysis. All men control and are controlled. The question of government in the broadest possible sense is not how freedom is to be preserved but what kinds of control are to be used and to what ends. Control must be analyzed and considered in its proper proportions. No one, I am sure, wishes to develop new master–slave relationships to bend the will of the people to despotic rulers in new ways. These are patterns of control appropriate to a world without science. They may well be the first to go when the experimental analysis of behavior comes into its own in the design of cultural practices.

READING 8
Freedom, Consciousness, and Creative Life
Henri Bergson
(from *Creative Evolution*)

Radical therefore, also, is the difference between animal consciousness, even the most intelligent, and human consciousness. For consciousness corresponds exactly to the living being's power of choice; it is co-extensive with the fringe of possible action that surrounds the real action: consciousness is synonymous with invention and with freedom. Now, in the animal, invention is never anything but a variation on the theme of routine. Shut up in the habits of the species, it succeeds, no doubt, in enlarging them by its individual initiative; but it escapes automatism only for an instant, for just the time to create a new automatism. The gates of its prison close as soon as they are opened; by pulling at its chain it succeeds only in stretching it. With man, consciousness breaks the chain. In man, and man alone, it sets itself free. The whole history of life until man has been that of the effort of consciousness to raise matter, and of the more or less complete overwhelming of consciousness by the matter which has fallen back on it. The enterprise was paradoxical, if, indeed, we may speak here otherwise than by metaphor of enterprise and of effort. It was to create with matter, which is necessity itself, an instrument of freedom, to make a machine which should triumph over mechanism, and to use the determinism of nature to pass through the meshes of the net which this very determinism had spread. But, everywhere except in man, consciousness has let itself be caught in the net whose meshes it tried to pass through: it has remained the captive of the mechanisms it has set up. . . . But our brain, our society, and our language are only the external and various signs of one and the same internal superiority. They tell, each after its manner, the unique, exceptional success which life has won at a given moment of its evolution. They express the difference of kind, and not only of degree, which separates man from the rest of the animal world. They let us guess that, while at the end of the vast spring-board from which life has taken its leap, all the others have stepped down, finding the cord stretched too high, man alone has cleared the obstacle.

READING 9
Truth as Freedom
St. Augustine
(from *On Free Will*)

But remember that I promised to show you that there is something beyond the reach of our mind and our reason. It's right before you, Truth itself. Embrace it while you can. Rejoice in it. "Take delight in the Lord, and he will give you the desires of your heart." (Ps. 37,4) What more can you ask for, than to be happy? And what greater happiness is there than to enjoy the Truth, unshakable, unchanging and far above all else?

If men proclaim that they are happy in embracing the beautiful bodies they've been longing for, whether of their wives or even courtesans, should we at all doubt that we are happy in embracing the truth?

If men proclaim that they are happy when, with their throats parched from heat, come upon a stream, flowing and refreshing, or, when hungry, they find a welcoming supper or dinner prepared for them, should we deny that we ourselves are refreshed and nourished by the truth?

We often hear the happy voices of those who are brushing about in a field of roses or other flowers, and breathing in their delicate fragrance; yet what is more fragrant or more joyful than a breath of truth?

There are those who feel that their happiness is found in listening to song or the sound of stringed instruments or flutes; when they are not at hand they feel miserable when they are at hand they are transported with joy. Why are we wont to seek any other kind of happiness than that which suffuses our minds with the silence of truth, without noise, but with a gentle, quiet eloquence?

Others are dazzled by the brightness of gold, silver, gems, colors, whose light bathes our very eyes, or by the fire-light on earth, or the stars, or the moon, or the sun, and are held in thrall unless beset by some kind of trouble or need. They appear to themselves as happy and would choose this kind of life forever. And again, are you and I fearful of seeing our happiness in the light of truth?

And what is more, in as much as the highest good is known and grasped as truth and truth being wisdom, let us, in the wisdom we possess, see, grasp and enjoy the highest good. Happy is the one who enjoys the highest good.

It is this same truth that, in effect, reveals the truth that is found in all good things which, either singly or as a whole, the wise person rejoices in according to his degree of wisdom. . . . If truth in lesser things is a source of joy, all the more is the Truth itself.

Be sure of this, our liberty is precisely in yielding to this very Truth. It is our God Himself who frees us from death, that is, from our sinful condition. It is Truth, speaking as a human being among human beings, who says to those who believe in him, "If you remain faithful to my word, you are my disciples in earnest; you will come to know the truth and the truth will set you free." (Jn 8, 31–2)

READING 10

Freedom and Necessity: United in God

Benedict Spinoza

(from *Ethics*)

PART I

Definition vi

By *God* I mean a being absolutely infinite—that is, a substance consisting of infinite attributes, of which each expresses eternal and infinite essentiality.

Definition vii

That thing is called free, which exists solely by the necessity of its own nature, and of which the action is determined by itself alone. On the other hand, that thing is necessary, or rather constrained, which is determined by something external to itself to a fixed and definite method or existence or action.

PROPOSITION XVI

From the necessity of the divine nature must follow an infinite number of things in infinite ways—that is, all things which can fall within the sphere of infinite intellect.

PROOF: This proposition will be clear to everyone, who remembers that from the given definition of any thing the intellect infers several properties, which really necessarily follow therefrom (that is, from the actual essence of the thing defined); and it infers more properties in proportion as the definition of the thing expresses more reality, that is, in proportion as the essence of the thing defined involves more reality. Now, as the divine nature has absolutely infinite attributes (by Def. vi), of which each expresses infinite essence after its kind, it follows that from the necessity of its nature an infinite number of things (that is, everything which can fall within the sphere of an infinite intellect) must necessarily follow. *Q.E.D.*

COROLLARY I: Hence it follows, that God is the efficient cause of all that can fall within the sphere of an infinite intellect.

COROLLARY II: It also follows that God is a cause in himself, and not through an accident of his nature.

COROLLARY III:—It follows, thirdly, that God is the absolutely first cause.

PROPOSITION XVII

God acts solely by the laws of his own nature, and is not constrained by anyone.

PROOF: We have just shown (in Prop. xvi.), that solely from the necessity of the divine nature, or, what is the same thing, solely from the laws of his nature, an infinite number of things absolutely follow in an infinite number of ways; and we proved (in Prop. xv.), that without God nothing can be nor be conceived; but that all things are in God. Wherefore nothing can exist outside himself, whereby he can be conditioned or constrained to act. Wherefore God acts solely by the laws of his own nature, and is not constrained by anyone. *Q.E.D.*

COROLLARY I: It follows: 1. That there can be no cause which, either extrinsically or intrinsically, besides the perfection of his own nature, moves God to act.

COROLLARY II: It follows: 2. That God is the sole free cause. For God alone exists by the sole necessity of his nature (by Prop. xi. and Prop. xiv., (Coroll. i.), and acts by the sole necessity of his nature, wherefore God is (by Def. vii.) the sole free cause. *Q.E.D.*

NOTE: Others think that God is a free cause, because he can, as they think, bring it about, that those things which we have said follow from his nature—that is, which are in his power, should not come to pass, or should not be produced by him. But this is the same as if they said, that God could bring it about, that it should not follow from the nature of a triangle, that its three interior angles should not be equal to two right angles; or that from a given cause no effect should follow, which is absurd.

Chapter Two

On Making Moral Judgments

In the first chapter we saw that the basic sense of morality is natural to us; that is, we have the natural capacity to grasp the unique character of human acts referred to by the term *moral*. The moral sense is a fundamental capacity, but without any specific or particular content; the morality of a *specific* or *kind* act is not known innately, nor is the morality of a *particular* act; it is not a given. If, then, the moral *specifics* of an action are not given along with the capacity, the question emerges, "How do we get to know the morality of a specific or particular act?" The goal of this chapter is to answer that question. The knowledge we are looking for has to be in the form of a *judgment*, a mental act that is verbally expressed in a proposition in which something is said of something else: This apple is red; Socrates is a Greek philosopher; a triangle is a three-sided plane figure. What we want to arrive at is a *moral judgment* in which the morality of an action is assessed: to respect another's property is right; to withhold someone else's mail is wrong; for a mother to feed her child is good; to revel in another person's misery is bad. The more particular the act, the more complicated it becomes, and so does the difficulty of making a sound moral judgment.

MEANING OF NORM

Every judgment requires a measurement of sorts, a *standard* to give us assurance of its truth; a guide, a rule, or a principle: This pen is six inches long, as measured by a ruler; the time is 11:00 A.M., as measured by the clock; this budget entry is correct, as measured by accepted accounting procedures. The same holds true for morality because each act of ours requires a standard against which its moral quality can be measured and a judgment made. If the word *standard* has too much of an abstract, impersonal tinge to it, then *norm* would seem to be less abstract and more personal because it signifies the direction our action should take; a norm is *directive of behavior*. So the goal of this chapter can also be stated as *searching for the norm of morality*.

By now we should have come to expect that every time we turn a corner, we have to get ready to turn another. The next corner here is the question: Whose norm of morality are we talking about? Do Chinese think of moral matters the same way as Icelanders do? The French as Nigerians? Arctic Eskimos as American Indians? Does Socrates think the same moral thoughts as Don Juan? Does John Doe have the same moral norms as Jane Roe? The inquiry into the norm of morality seems doomed to failure from the very beginning (R #1). A dilemma arises: If the norm pertains to all in exactly the same way, then there's no room for the individual; if the norm varies from one individual to the next, then there's no room for a common norm; one negates the other. The question, Whose morality?, is a tough one and moralists have exercised themselves over it, yet that does not free us from exploring it.

MORALITY: OBJECTIVE OR SUBJECTIVE?

One way to begin is to look again at the very terms of the dilemma: humanity vs. the individual, the common vs. the particular, the same for all vs. proper to each, or, to put it in the usual terms for discussion, *objective* vs. *subjective*. As a question, then, is morality objective or subjective? Is it objective only and not at all subjective? Is it subjective only and not at all objective? Is it each partially, that is, can it be objective and subjective at the same time?

Let's clarify the meaning of the words involved. The meaning of the word *objective* is seen in the word itself, for the word *object* suggests something that is *there*, standing before you on its own. Just as the chemist has a piece of zinc in front of him as an object to be seen of itself, the moral questioner has an action in front of him as an object to be seen of itself: *The moral act is an object*. Morality is found in the act itself, irrespective of any other consideration: *Morality is absolute*. The moral act is there for all to assess: *Morality is public*. It is there for all to assess in the same way: *Morality is universal*. The moral act presents itself, as it is, to the inquirer; it is not for me to invent it, but to discover it; it is detached from personal implications: *Morality is impersonal*.

The meaning of the word *subjective* is quite the opposite. Morality is not found in the act as seen in itself, but as I, the individual, see it; it is not located in the object, but in the subject: *Morality is subjective*. The morality of an act cannot be considered in any other way but contextual, and as the context changes, so does morality: *Morality is relative*. There is nothing more personal to me than my own acts: *Morality is personal*.

But there are problems in saying that morality is objective only or subjective only. If it is *objective only*, then what place can we assign to cultural and particular differences? We possess individuality as well as commonality, so how does individuality, or subjectivity, fit in? Similar problems arise if we say that morality is *subjective only*, for then what happens to the universality implied in our common nature? If humanity is one, why not morality? True, we are individuals, but it is no less true that we share human nature with all human beings. If only subjective, how could we blame or fault others, even in law courts?

Putting a positive spin on the problem, there are solid reasons for saying that morality is objective, for everyone is a human being, and all possess the same nature. Would we not be upset with the proposition that some people are less human than others? Surely, if we are all equally human, then what is moral for one is equally moral for all. What chaos would ensue if each individual had a private, personal morality? Yet there are also solid reasons for saying that morality is subjective. After all, who's placing the act but the individual person, so much so, that there is nothing more personal than one's own acts. Each person is unique, induplicable, and so is each act. If no situation can be duplicated, neither can the act placed in *this* situation be duplicated.

The only resolution, then, to the dilemma between objective and subjective is to hold that morality is, in some way, *both objective and subjective*. But how? That's the next problem. It seems that the best route to take is the one that would get at the problem more naturally to begin with and would save us from worrying overmuch about Robert Frost's dilemma *The Road Not Taken!* Simply stated, it is the route that plain common sense recognizes as basic to the orderliness of human activity: *Morality is objective.* Our acceptance of objectivity as a starting point assures us of universality in countless areas other than morality, so why not morality itself? If, for example, two and two are four is true for me, it must be so for all rational beings. If fighting off invasive germs is good for the health of one person, it must be good for all. If the interior angles of a triangle equal 180 degrees is an intelligible equation, even though it may not be known to all, it is objectively true for all. In a similar way, the acceptance of objectivity allows us an assurance of universality in moral matters. So *the plan we'll follow here* is, once the claim of objectivity in morality has been explored, we will come back to the second claim, that of subjectivity, and explore it on the basis of what is unique to an individual, namely, *conscience.*

MORALITY AS OBJECTIVE: SOME PHILOSOPHICAL POSITIONS

There are a surprising number of paths philosophers may take to keep morality within the parameters of objectivity; we'll consider three of the more prominent ones, those of two individual philosophers, Immanuel Kant and John Stuart Mill, and the third of a traditional path to which the names of many philosophers belong.

1. Kantian: The Categorical Imperative

The reputation of Immanuel Kant (1724–1804) is firmly established in modern philosophy, based mainly on his profound epistemological inquiry into the conditions and boundaries of knowledge, often referred to by the term *criticism.* This is borne out in the titles of his trilogy *The Critique of Pure Reason, The Critique of Practical Reason,* and *The Critique of the Faculty of Judgment.* Though moral questions are referred to *passim* throughout his works, they are magisterially treated in *The Critique of Practical Reason* and *Foundations of the Metaphysics of Morals.* He was a life-long academic, spending the later years of his life as Professor of Philosophy at the University of Königsberg, a small unpretentious town in East Prussia. The concept of duty looms large in his writings but it was also the operative drive in his life. In his famous daily routine, Kant was a living example of German orderliness, rising each day at the same time and performing the day's activities, whether drinking coffee, preparing class, or taking lunch, all at a fixed hour. It was the poet Heine who wrote of this legendary metronome that "Neighbors knew it was exactly half past three when Immanuel Kant in his grey coat, with his bamboo cane in his hand, left his house door and went to Lime Tree Avenue, which is still called, in memory of him, the 'Philosopher's Walk.' "

A lengthy analysis of his philosophy of knowledge is not necessary at this juncture; it suffices to say that for Kant all knowledge begins in sense experience but is shaped for us by determinants, by "forms," internal to the knowing faculty "before" experience takes place, whence they are called *a priori forms*, without which reason could not do its work. But in the wider range of experience, we are also aware of an experience of another kind, totally different from sense experience, and eventually to be referred to as *moral.* It is an awareness of *duty* to begin with, an experience of obligation or oughtness we recognize in ourselves when we are called upon to act. Kant considers this aspect of oughtness, which we analyzed in Chapter 1, as a *given*;

we do not demonstrate its existence; we neither deduce it nor induce it; we have no need to prove it—it is a *datum*. Because it is a datum, it must be understood in terms of nothing but itself, which means that we are under compulsion to put that duty into practice: We must either positively place the action or negatively refrain from it. Whence, as Kant clearly sees, duty entails *freedom*; that is, we must be free to do what we ought; otherwise, we risk a stark contradiction in saying that we ought to do what we cannot do. As we saw in Chapter 1, if the rest of nature is governed by necessity, the will is not.

It could be said that Kant has not yet spoken of the of morality as objective because the acknowledgment of duty comes from within me *as an individual*; that's why he wants to make it unmistakably clear that what is *imposed on me is imposed on all*; thus the duty that binds *me* binds *all*, assuring us of its universality, thus taking on the character of *law*. Notice that the binding nature of the *moral law* comes from within itself, and not from any other consideration, even consequences; it is an imperative that brooks no option, whence the term *categorical imperative*. Kant gives several formulations of the categorical imperative but the one that most clearly fits the notion of objectivity is had in the first one: "Act only on a maxim through which you can at the same time will that it should become a universal law." That is, a moral principle is valid only if it can be *universalized*, if it can be seen as binding on all *without involving a contradiction*. For example, in the case of a man beset by a series of misfortunes, Kant asks, "whether it would not be contrary to his duty to himself to take his own life." He answers this by pointing out the contradiction involved in a system of nature whose special feature is the improvement of life to allow it to be destroyed. Suicide cannot be universalized; therefore it is morally wrong. Notice that Kant does not say suicide is wrong because, as a consequence, it would bring about chaos in society; no, it's wrong because it's wrong *in itself*, and therefore it would bring about chaos in society (R #2).

From the viewpoint of terminology, the moral system of Kant, and of others that stress the primacy of duty, the term *deontology* (from the Greek word *deon*, meaning duty) is often used. *Deontological* and *consequential* thus enter the discussion on objective/subjective with *deontological* enlisted as objective and *consequential* as subjective, but, as unambiguous definitions in morality are in short supply, a clarification has to be made. Deontology favors judging the morality of an act as seen in itself and is usually referred to as objective and therefore universal; consequentialism favors judging the morality of an act as seen in its results, so there is a tendency to refer to it as subjective. But, in an argumentative mood, one can insist, contrary to the deontologist, that duty is a private matter, and therefore subjective. So parents can say that their duty to their children is their business, and nobody else's. And nothing prevents one from insisting, contrary to the consequentialist, that consequences are a public matter, and therefore objective. A student then can say, in slipping the answer to an exam question to a friend, it's okay because I'm helping a worthy candidate to get into med school, which everybody would say is a good thing.

There are a number of ways in which the system of Kant can be challenged, or modified, as on the part of those moralists who insist that consequences should not peremptorily be dismissed as part of the act, or that in some cases they should be included in the very meaning of the act itself, as, for example, a doctor's action in prescribing a medicine is good *because* it has good results. Or a challenge may arise on the score of its being too absolute, with no clear regard for morality as relative. In any event, the objective value of the moral world was not to be surrendered by Kant, and modern philosophy has recognized this in the hard rock consistency expressed in the often-quoted Kantian phrase, "the starry heavens above and the moral law within."

2. Utilitarian: The Greatest Happiness Principle

The main reason for enlisting the *utilitarianism* of John Stuart Mill (1806–1873) as a contribution to the objectivity of morality is not to make an "objectivist" out of him but to recognize that, for all its difficulties, his "greatest happiness principle" is an attempt to establish a norm that could be accepted universally as reasonable. As to his overall philosophical bent, he can clearly be seen as working in the empirical tradition of his English predecessors, Locke, Berkeley, and Hume, but also as looking forward to contemporary philosophical issues in his championing personal values, his search for some way to ground humanity in view of a declining Christianity, and his efforts to improve the conditions of the working class of England.

There is a popular use of the word *utilitarian* which associates it with the achievement of a goal one has in mind; it's useful, or helpful, or practical such as acquiring a college degree, or procuring a lawnmower. Often it bespeaks a narrow self-interest: It's good for me; it's what I want; my personal satisfaction is my chief concern; values are what I make them to be. This is a far cry from what the author of *Utilitarianism* meant by the word. Toward the beginning of this work, Mill writes, "The creed which accepts as the foundation of morals, Utility, or the Greatest Happiness Principle, holds that actions are right in proportion as they tend to promote happiness, wrong as they tend to promote the reverse of happiness. By happiness is intended pleasure, and the absence of pain, by unhappiness, pain, and the privation of pleasure" (R #3).

Simple as this statement of principle sounds, Mill knew it was complex, particularly as regards the making of a moral judgment. If the making of a moral judgment is not fundamental to our nature, as Mill holds, then on what is it founded? If it is true, and it surely is, that we do not have direct knowledge of the moral value of each and every act, does that rule out direct knowledge of the *fundamental* distinction between good and bad, with further refinement to come later on through experience and education? If the "moral faculty" is not "part of nature," but is "a natural outgrowth from it," then it certainly means that the power of moral discernment is part of our nature, though Mill does not say so. Empirically we are aware of our moral feelings and Mill had no sympathy for those who would dare deny them, but they are not innate; they are acquired, brought about by education and experience and subject to rational control; the moral faculty is the depository of these moral feelings, yet "the moral faculty, if not part of our nature, is a natural outgrowth from it; capable . . . in a small degree, of springing up spontaneously; and susceptible of being brought by cultivation to a high degree of development."

Values, for Mill, are an integral part of the meaning of happiness and are not to be taken in any casual, reckless, selfish, or hedonistic sense. On the spectrum of values, some are of a higher order, some lower, therefore a *judgment* has to be made regarding the quality of an act: "Some *kinds* of pleasure are desirable and more valuable than others." Once we understand the level of dignity that attaches to the human being over other kinds of being and understand that there are different levels of value in human life, including moral values, we understand, as Mill puts it in a well-known quotation, that "It is better to be a human being dissatisfied than a pig satisfied; better to be Socrates dissatisfied than a fool satisfied."

To its credit, utilitarianism underscores the need of establishing a norm whereby our actions can be directed, some rule or guide that accounts for the decisions we make, some principle from which moral acts can emerge. It is also *contextual*, for it acknowledges the fact that no act can be evaluated in isolation, apart from every other consideration. But there are features that tell significantly against it. How is it possible to make a *quantitative* judgment regarding happiness? How can I decide that giving to a panhandler is better than giving to the Salvation Army? If one's answer is, "Well, I'm doing my best," one must understand that such an answer can be given to any question in any moral system and doesn't necessarily respond to what is objectively so. What justification does Peter Singer, for example, the most influential moralist today writing under the banner of utilitarianism, have in defending the abortion of a tragically defective fetus on the basis that it could result in the parents' giving birth to another baby, this one healthy, and therefore contributing to the increase of happiness in the world? One more example: Would the leader of a captured American platoon under orders from the Nazi commandant to kill one soldier of the platoon to save the rest from being killed, be right in doing so, and therefore decreasing the amount of pain in the world? Though there are attractive features to utilitarianism, problems like these give us pause in accepting it as a total foundation for moral rightness.

3. Traditional: Human Nature

The third path to moral objectivity is the traditional one: *human nature.* When we think of "norm" or "standard," we naturally tend to think of clear and precise blueprints for the action we intend to place. But do we have to think like that? Is it true, let's ask, of creative activity, like art, music, dance, and architecture? Take the last mentioned, the architect's design must fit into the context of landscape, environment, materials and the actual use of the building, and if it does not, it is neither artistic nor serviceable. Should not the same be said of *human acts*, particularly those we are calling *moral*? If they fit the context of "being human," they are moral; if they do not, they are immoral.

Draw this out a bit more. All of us understand phrases like, "it's the human thing to do," or such and such is "a terribly inhuman thing to do." We must therefore have some notion of what "to be human" means, to which an act must conform to be called "human." Because this is so, the use of the term *human nature* would be quite in order, for by it is signified *what it means to be human*, which is exactly how the term has traditionally been employed. It's a line that stretches from the golden age of Greek philosophy with Socrates, Plato, and Aristotle, through the later Stoics to Christian times, through some of the great names of medieval philosophy, like Thomas Aquinas, Duns Scotus, and, several centuries later, Francisco Suarez, to contemporary names like G.E.M. Anscombe and Philippa Foot so that, despite its being unwelcome by a number of modern philosophers, it deserves to be called the *traditional view.*

It's reasonably argued that Socrates (469–399 B.C.) set the moral tone for traditional moral philosophy because the main feature of his thought, and the one on which all other aspects of his philosophy depend, is that of *ethical wisdom,* seen in Chapter 1 as the recognition of the fundamental importance of the ethical in the life of man and of doing good as the basic principle of human activity. Socrates gave the concepts of virtue and goodness insistent attention, first by acknowledging virtues like courage, piety, and justice as good, and then by trying to discern their inward essence or nature, and then to define them. Aristotle praised him as the first philosopher who, in "seeking the universal in these ethical matters, fixed thought for the first time on definitions." What Socrates was clearly trying to do was to present virtue not as a mere ornament of the human being but as pertinent to its very essence. The virtuous person is the crowning achievement of ethical wisdom.

The Socratic spirit of ethical wisdom was continued in Plato (427–347 B.C.) but with insights properly his own. In the painting by Raphael mentioned earlier, the *School of Athens*, of the two central figures, Plato and Aristotle, it is Plato who is pointing heavenward, a pictorial representation of his belief that we must look above to understand what is below; he is sometimes referred to as a "top-down" thinker. His position holds for the existence of a higher reality, a realm above, variously called a world of *forms*, *ideas*, *essences*, and *natures*, in which things are found in all their perfection, where they are changeless, permanent, and outside of time. The things of the world we live in, however, are changing, transitory, and bound by time, but, though imperfect, they *participate* in the perfection of the higher world and as such are to be thought of as images or reflections of that world. We, in the world below, realize that we should bend our efforts more and more to make our actions in this quotidian life accord with *human nature* in its fullest sense. Plato's admonition is to strive for perfection by keeping our mind's eye in the direction of the flawless world above. In the course of speaking of light in a physical sense, he continues speaking of it in an analogous sense as the illumination supplied by our own natural reason: "Thus much let me say however. God invented and gave us sight to the end that we might behold the courses of intelligence in the heavens, and apply them to the courses of our own intelligence which are akin to them, the unperturbed to the perturbed, and we, learning them and partaking of the natural truth of reason, might imitate the absolutely unerring courses of God and regulate ours which have gone astray" (Timaeus, 47c).

The other central figure in Raphael's painting, Aristotle (384–322 B.C.), is pointing earthward, symbolizing his approach as just the reverse of Plato's: Begin with what you experience, and then move upward. His style of thinking is more practical, more action oriented, and more empirical than Plato's. A truly human act is not *any* activity a human being is capable of, but one that authentically resonates to what being human means, namely *moral* activity. It is the acting out of one's inner disposition, called a virtue, a ready sensitivity for placing morally good acts. Aristotle captures this tone of readiness in the way in which a morally sensitive person makes moral judgments: "to feel them at the right times, with reference to the right objects, towards the right people, with the right motive, and in the right way." A good action possesses due proportion, neither excessive nor defective, neither too much nor too little. Every action is to be measured, but measured in its rightness by *prudence* or, in a larger sense, by "practical wisdom." Practical wisdom is the application of principles directing our free and voluntary choices to ends befitting us as human beings; it is, again in Aristotle's words, "a true and reasoned state of capacity to act with regard to the things that are good or bad for men."

The acknowledgment of a real world, in which human nature is bound to find its way through countless felt relationships, continues through the late Greek period into the Christian period under the influence of *Stoic* philosophy. Though Stoic philosophy, over the course of many centuries, espoused a vast array of doctrines, it was its unfailing concern with matters of ethics that would designate it as a family of thought. Stoic philosophers had much to say on the kind of human behavior that would make living in the midst of Nature an enterprise worthy of rational being. There is no "outside" the universe, no "outside" God, no "outside" Nature; everything is "within," immanent, natural. In turn, this means that everything is one-with-God and thus there is a necessity by which all movement in the universe takes place according to the law of Nature. As the rational part of nature, we human beings must live in accordance with the order of nature as we understand it and if, at times, things look to us as crooked or chaotic, we are to remind ourselves that to the Eternal, things look otherwise, as the early Stoic, Cleanthes, wrote " . . . thou knowest to make crooked straight: chaos to thee is order."

Though much of what Cicero and Seneca wrote was inspired by Stoic thought, the two names most typical of the period are Epictetus (50–138 A.D.), teacher and former slave, and Marcus Aurelius (121–180 A.D.), Roman emperor. From Epictetus, one expects to find peace of mind as man's chief goal, admonitions of self-control, evenness of judgment, the wisdom of following Nature's (God's) will, how to judge good and evil, and how to use reason to temper the power of the senses. The doing of what we know to be right is within everyone's capacity, for everyone enjoys the power of reason and the power to discern right from wrong and good from evil: "Where then is man's good and man's evil, in the true sense, to be found? In that faculty which makes men different from all else." From Marcus Aurelius, in his private diary called *Meditations*, one expects to find similar reflections on the problems of life: Divine providence, Nature, virtue, the good life, happiness, ingratitude, treatment of others, pain, death, self-reliance, and tranquility. For him too, it is through the mediatorship of reason that man makes his way through life in understanding the unity of all things: "For there is one universe made up of all things and one God who pervades all things, and one substance, and one law, one common reason in all intelligent animals . . . " It's no wonder that many early Christians held that Stoic principles must have been leavened by Christian belief! (R #4).

Perhaps we should pause for a moment and ask, are not all moral philosophers fundamentally concerned with human nature and the human acts consonant with it? Though the idea of "human nature" is a staple among the philosophers we have been speaking of, it is not a term of choice among modern philosophers outside that tradition. However, even among them, very few would hold that the "meaning of man" is an empty phrase, except perhaps for some adherents of the movement called "existentialism," which gained popularity for a time right after World War II. A partial explanation for the reluctance to use human nature as a moral norm seems to lie in taking the term in too narrow a sense, that is, as an exact, fixed, static template against which acts can be measured, like a blueprint precisely directing what's to be done. This literalist style of making a copy is a perennial temptation but it must yield to the richer notion that man is a developing being, always unfinished, bound to grow, expanding horizons, and expressing new states of life and unexpected relationships, with problems insoluble, with joys unforgettable; human nature is a *nature on-the-move.*

With this vision in mind, a number of philosophers of the thirteenth and fourteenth centuries tried to employ a term more suitable to the myriad situations in which human beings find themselves, so they expanded the term *human nature* to something like *human nature fully considered.* That is, the *entire context* in which decision-making is demanded as it varies from person to person, from doctor, lawyer, and Indian chief to student, spouse, and grocery clerk, looking for human solutions to particular life situations. Practical decisions are not always easy to come by, for all too often you have to work your way through a web of intersecting and competing involvements to make a decision true to yourself as human. As Thomas Aquinas (1225–1274) succinctly puts it, "the nature of man is variable, and what is normally natural is not to be expected on every occasion." Aquinas wrote extensively on moral questions and can be turned to for a substantial contribution to the norm of morality. He was born of an aristocratic family in Aquino, near Naples, became a Dominican priest, and devoted his entire life to the study of theology and philosophy. His writings, though vast, were neat and spare, particularly his *Summa Theologiae*, and were, after some initial queasiness because of his reliance on the "pagan" Aristotle, profoundly influential across the centuries down to the present.

While accepting human nature as the norm of morality, Aquinas proceeds to focus on its primary aspect, namely the *rational* as the defining constituent of what it means to be human. In doing so, he locates the norm of morality precisely in man's understanding or *reason*, which is, in the matter of moral decision-making, the faculty whereby *moral judgments* are made. Often he uses the term *right reason*, which, though redundant, underscores the use of *reason* in its proper role, not unlike the prefix *ethical* in the Socratic term *ethical wisdom*. In his commentary on the *Ethics* of Aristotle, he writes that, since it belongs to man to be a rational animal, " . . . it must be that man's action is good if it is in accord with right reason. For the abuse of reason contradicts the very nature of reason." Or again, "Good and evil should be set in the context of what is proper to man as man. This is his rational life. Therefore a good or bad human act is tested by its agreement or disagreement with reason . . . " In simple, direct words, if an act is reasonable, it is good; if unreasonable, it is bad. There are, of course, some actions that, of themselves, do not touch on morality at all and are neither morally good nor bad, but "indifferent," for instance, to go for a walk, eating an orange, or scratching your head (R #5).

At this point someone may feel that "reason" is, in a way, too cold or too distant from the emotions and therefore cannot take into account the full range of human fulfillment. We'll recall from earlier comments how David Hume paid tribute to the emotions and, although "reason and sentiment concur in almost all moral determinations and conclusions," it would be unthinkable for us to call an action praiseworthy or blamable, or productive of happiness or misery, without appealing to "some internal sense or feeling, which nature has made universal in the whole species." He goes on to say that reason "is not alone sufficient to produce any moral blame or approbation" (R #6). There is much here Aquinas, along with Aristotle, would subscribe to, but they would hold that the function of reason is to *comprehend* how an individual action fits into the whole, to begin with experience and in that very experience to *understand* how it relates to human life. Love, for instance, is not at first an activity of intellect, but once experienced we begin to understand the meaninglessness of human life without it. And as our experience and reflection enlarge, our rational self reads them as a record of reality—of discerning relationships, values, orderliness, and all those other truths on the basis of which a human life plan can be built and principles of action discerned.

But principles are precisely that, principles. This means, in a broad sense, that they supply the *general direction* an action should take but they do not lay down with exactness the *particular* judgment that must be made in every set of concrete circumstances. As an analogy, take the sport of running. There are principles, or rules, for running well and, though the rules always apply, they must be applied to fit the particular circumstances: whether the surface is grass, gravel, or composition; whether the day is rainy or clear; whether the distance is short or long; and so on. So it is with moral action. You borrow twenty dollars, so it is to be repaid. When and how will depend on a range of variables—your ability, the lender's forbearance, or a special arrangement. If the lender gave you the loan in a spirit of friendliness, it's to be returned the same way; it would be sheer meanness to return it by crumpling up a twenty-dollar bill and tossing it at his feet. How to articulate from the abstract level to the particular is a matter of making a judgment as to how the action fits in with the entire context. To do so requires an appropriate reading of the setting, a delicacy of discretion, and a nuanced sensitivity for all concerned; it is the sign of a person's wisdom in making the right judgment, termed by Aristotle and Aquinas as *practical wisdom*. Recall the insightful words of Aristotle quoted earlier that such a judgment responds to the right time, the right object, the right people, the right motive, and the right way.

There's an increasing number of contemporary voices that speak a similar language regarding the role of the rational in the moral enterprise. Take, for example, the English moral philosopher Philippa Foot, who, in her small treasure of a book *Natural Goodness*, describes how she had to work her way beyond the language analysts who maintained that a mere analysis of statements about the good was an explanation of the good itself. For her, the evaluation of a moral act is to be had only by measuring it against what it means to be human. A moral good is to be seen as a form of natural wholeness; an evil as a defect. There's a lot of punch in her forthright question, "Why, then, does it seem so monstrous a suggestion that the evaluation of the human will should be determined by facts about the nature of human beings and the life of our own species?" (p. 24) (R #7).

MORALITY AS SUBJECTIVE: THE ROLE OF CONSCIENCE

Thus far in our discussion of the objective/subjective status of morality, we've seen that each position had a valid claim, but that objectivity had a prior, primordial claim in the commonness of human nature. We saw the reasonableness of considering objectivity first and then returning to subjectivity in terms of what is known as *conscience*, which is where we are now. In its everyday usage, in conversation or in writing, the word *conscience* has the meaning of a feeling or inward sentiment that an act of ours is either right or wrong. If we are comfortable with an act, if it generates satisfaction, if it represents sincerity in placing it, if it is a matter of "good faith," then we are warranted in saying that the act is right. If we are not comfortable with the act, if it generates a reaction of "guilt," if it offers a resistance to doing what we know we ought to do and is therefore a matter of "bad faith," then we are warranted in saying that the act is wrong. We often talk of conscience as an "inner voice," a clear prompting from within that a contemplated course of action is the right one and to be taken, or the wrong one and to be avoided. The clarity of the inner voice tends to make me think of conscience as addressed uniquely to me; it is private, it is my own, it is inalienable, it is personal, it is subjective. "I followed my conscience" is a testimony a person pays himself or herself for standing upright in face of other choices that could have been made; it's an assertion of moral integrity.

But there is much more that can be said about conscience than what we find in popular usage. The word *conscience* is derived from the Latin words *cum* and *scientia*, meaning "with knowledge," and therefore reflects what we here and now *know* of the morality of the act. This is expressed in a *judgment* by which we ensure the morality of an act for ourselves; it is the knowledge we bring to bear on this particular act, or, as Aquinas puts it, it is "knowledge applied to an individual case." We saw above that knowledge is critical in evaluating responsibility and that there is a direct proportion between them: the more a person knows about the act, the greater the responsibility; the less a person knows, less is the responsibility, because you cannot will what you do not know. What a person does or does not know, that is, the epistemological parameters within which a person's understanding takes place, can vary in a thousand different ways: native intelligence, physical formation, cultural upbringing, educational breadth, religious persuasion, and so on. So, the general principles of morality are mediated through the individual person who, with prudence and practical wisdom, applies them to this particular act. He or she, as the subject placing the act, is the sole arbiter of the morality of that act. It is precisely here that the claim of morality as subjective is met and cannot better be stated than in the words of St. Thomas:

> Disquisitions on general morality are not entirely trustworthy, and the ground becomes more uncertain when one wishes to descend to individual cases in detail. The factors are infinitely variable, and cannot be settled either by art or precedent. Judgement should be left to the people concerned. Each must set himself to act according to the immediate situation and the circumstances involved. The decision may be unerring in the concrete, despite the uneasy debate in the abstract. Nevertheless, the moralist can provide some help and direction in such cases.
>
> (*Com. on II 'Ethics,' lect.2*, tr. Gilby)

For their part, both Plato and Aristotle would agree with St. Thomas's position on the variability of human nature. Plato, without relinquishing his commitment to an unchanging Idea of man, could say that "the endless irregular movements of human things do not admit of any universal and simple rule . . . A perfectly simple principle can never be applied to a state of things which is the reverse of simple" (*Statesman*, 294 B.C.). And Aristotle, for whom, as we have seen, a good action is an action according to the rule of reason, could say, " . . . matters concerned with conduct and questions of what is good for us have no fixity, any more than matters of health" (*Eth.* II, 1, 1104a3–5).

The importance of the subjective aspect of morality, then, attaches to the individual making a particular judgment in a particular situation. Philosophically no one has written more poignantly about the individual facing a decision than the Danish philosopher Søren Kierkegaard (1813–1855) in his work *Fear and Trembling*. Of all the relationships an individual has, the most profound is the one he has with God; it is the relationship that makes actual the potentiality toward full personhood the individual possesses. Normally any individual is bound by the principles touching everyone in a given state of life, which principles Kierkegaard calls "universals." But something else becomes startlingly clear for him as he considers the case of the Old Testament patriarch Abraham, who is singled out in the Bible as the "father of all those who believe." Heeding God's command, addressed to him as an individual, Abraham, with all the sadness a human being can experience in surrendering what he dearly loves, was willing to sacrifice his son Isaac and proceeded to do so until his hand was stayed by the admonition of an angel. For Kierkegaard, one of the salient points of instruction in this event is the stance of Abraham before God as an *individual*, answering to no one but God, and inasmuch as Abraham was not following the universal standard of protective love of one's child, he is *breaking through the universal*. "The paradox of faith," writes Kierkegaard, "is this, that the individual is higher than the universal" (R #8).

The primacy of conscience can be seen in two ways: First, if the moral judgment is a true grasp of the actual state of affairs, it is *morally right* objectively; second, if the moral judgment is mistaken, it is still *morally right*, but subjectively. In either case, the person is making a judgment on what he or she holds to be true. A person who is uncertain, or unsure, depending on the gravity of the matter, will be correspondingly obliged to learn the truth. As observed in Chapter 1, once in a while, we've "protected" ourselves by the ruse, "Don't tell me! I don't want to know!" Moralists sometimes call this desire not to know "affected ignorance."

One may even be tempted to elide subjectivity and objectivity together, as in the following: No situation, in absolute terms, can be duplicated; but if, impossibly, someone else were precisely in the same situation as I am, he or she would make the very same decision as I did, so in that sense, what *I* did *everybody* would do. Or if you were to tell a friend about a decision someone else made who was in a terrible dilemma, and then you ask your friend, "What would you have done?" he might well answer, "I don't know, I haven't been there yet!"

Most of us are not public figures who have been called upon to take a stand "in conscience" against an established mode of life, like Jesus, Socrates, Gandhi, or Martin Luther King. Or like the many young conscientious objectors to the Vietnam War, or the whistle-blowers in the military or in the corporate scene of the last decade. There is a telling story about Henry David Thoreau, who was in jail overnight for his refusal to pay the war tax in the American–Mexican War and was visited by his friend Ralph Waldo Emerson. Emerson, talking with him through the jailhouse window, said, "Henry, what are you doing in there?" Thoreau answered, "Ralph, the real question is, what are you doing out there?"

The plain person is not normally visited with larger-than-life conscience calls but with countless, everyday calls, each one bearing its own moral weight and each to be made with knowledge sufficient for a moral decision. From time to time, there will be agonizing judgments to be made, like divorce, abortion, and detaching of life support systems, which require the utmost seriousness. Moral dilemmas may arise in professional or business situations; a nurse, for instance, who has a misgiving that the medicine she's taking to her patient is the right one, or a realtor who is bound by his agency not to sell to a minority couple. The human heart never takes a vacation from moral decision-making and is in constant search for the peace that comes from "A still and quiet conscience," as Shakespeare wrote.

In summary, in the very beginning of this chapter, we saw that the question of how we are to make moral judgments led to the question of a norm which, in turn, led to the question of whether morality is objective or subjective. We saw that verifiable claims can be made for both sides: Morality is objective, in the sense of universal, because human nature is common to all; and morality is subjective because human nature is found only in the individual, and it is the individual's existential context that dictates a particular practical judgment called conscience.

Making a judgment in response to two special questions:

1. *Does the end justify the means?*
2. *May an act be placed if it has two results, one good and the other bad?*

1. Does the end justify the means?

We seem to have a built-in tendency to think that if a person intends to do good, then the entire act leading to it also good. Contrariwise, we have no problem in seeing immediately that when one intends to do evil, then the entire act is evil, as when a person prays for another to suffer misfortune; praying in itself is good, but praying for something evil spoils it. In terms of "means" and "end," we can detach prayer from misfortune only in an abstract way, but in reality there is only *one act*, so that the *entire act* of praying-for-misfortune is immoral. But there can be a problem the other way around; that is, if the end is good, we can be inclined to feel that the means of achieving it are automatically good, that they are subsumed into the good of my intention. What the phrase "the end justifies the means" announces is that the good of my intention extends itself over the means and renders them good, or that the morality of the means is not to be considered apart from the good end. Consider the following example: A platoon is about to be captured and you are afraid that the sergeant, who has strategic information that would lead to the slaughter of an entire brigade, will reveal it, so you kill him. Clearly, what you're thinking about is that the saving of the lives of many cancels the malice of killing one innocent person. But it is never right to take an innocent life. The principle emerges that evil can never be done for the sake of the good; the means and the end both have to be good. In that sense, the end can never be used to justify the means. As always, prudence, or practical wisdom, applies this to particular cases.

Here are some additional examples to think about.

- A doctor is asked by his patient to tell her the absolute truth; but the doctor knows that the "absolute truth" will devastate her; so, without lying, he evades.
- A woman goes into prostitution to provide for her needy children.
- The specs call for a particular kind of cable, but the electrician uses another that's cheaper so that he can pocket the difference.
- To save the country from future terrorist attacks, prisoners, assumed to have firsthand knowledge of terrorist plots, are subjected to torture.
- Nancy, an honors student, helps Helen study for an exam so that she can score higher than Nancy's rival, Angela.
- A governor appoints the son of a rich contractor to a state post in return for a large campaign donation.

2. May an act be placed if it has two results, one good and the other bad?

One of the time-honored methods in ethics, as well as other studies, is the *case study method*, in which a situation is presented for analysis and for determining principles that may emerge for suitable application to other similar cases. Often a case is generated that is entirely hypothetical, or extremely unlikely to happen in real life, in order to make the factors involved stand out clearly, and once the moral picture is clear, you can move on to real-life cases where the moral picture is there but not as clear. So, let's take the case of two lumberjacks who, in a freak accident, wind up pinned under a huge log, one at either end. Lumberjack A is able to move and can free himself by pushing up his end of the log. But in doing so he knows he will kill Lumberjack B. May Lumberjack A free himself knowing that he will kill Lumberjack B? Nothing should be added to the case as presented that would change its nature, for example, A should wait for help to come, or should use his cell phone to call for help, and so on, because they are not presented with the case nor would they contribute to solving it as given.

There are indeed two effects, or two results: The freeing of A and the killing of B. So, what would A do if B were not there? He would of course push the log up, which shows us that the act itself is *morally good* or, at least, morally neutral. Is A's freedom brought about by B's death? That is, is B's death the cause of A's becoming free? Well, we just saw that A would push up on the log even if B were not there, so that we know that A's freedom is not caused by B's death; in other words, the good effect of A's freedom is *not caused* by the bad effect of B's death. B's death is foreseen by A but *not intended*; if it were intended, it would be immoral on that account. However, there is still a huge problem; B *is* a human being whose right to life is just as strong as A's right to life. There would be no problem if, let's say, it were a rabbit instead of a human being. What we are touching here is precisely the question of *proportion*. There is no proportion between human life and rabbit life; the comparison stands in favor of the human. But there is a proportion between a human life and another human life, which stands in favor of neither, so that B's life does not prevail over A's, who may thus free himself. Notice that what is being argued here is that A *may* free himself, not that he *must*.

Putting the discussion above into a statement of principle, what we have arrived at can be stated as follows: Whenever one action has two effects one good and one bad proceeding from it simultaneously, the act may be morally placed under the following conditions:

a. the act is good to begin with.

b. the good effect is not caused by the bad.

c. the evil is not intended.

d. there is a proportion between the two effects.

Together, these conditions are often referred as the *case of the double (two-fold) effect.* Analyze the following:

- Operating on a woman, three months pregnant, who has a cancerous uterus.
- Taking a powerful medicine for a migraine risking unforeseen consequences.
- A woman, about to be raped by an assailant, strikes him on the head with a poker from the fireplace.
- Jumping out of the window of a skyscraper's fiftieth floor to escape the blazing inferno within.
- A soldier throwing himself on a device about to explode to protect the others of his platoon.

READINGS

READING 1

Without God, Is Everything Lawful?

Fyodor Dostoyevsky

(from *The Brothers Karamazov*)

(*Here Alyosha [Alexei], a seminarian, is talking with his older brother, Ivan.*)

Alyoshka, why don't I call for champagne, let's drink to my freedom. No, if only you knew how glad I am!"

"No, brother, we'd better not drink," Alyosha said suddenly, "besides, I feel somehow sad."

"Yes, you've been sad for a long time, I noticed it long ago."

"So you're definitely leaving tomorrow morning?"

"Morning? I didn't say morning . . . But, after all, maybe in the morning. Would you believe that I dined here today only to avoid dining with the old man, he's become so loathsome to me. If it were just him alone, I would have left long ago. And why do you worry so much about my leaving? You and I still have God knows how long before I go. A whole eternity of time, immortality!"

"What eternity, if you're leaving tomorrow?"

"But what does that matter to you and me?" Ivan laughed. "We still have time for our talk, for what brought us together here. Why do you look surprised? Tell me, what did we meet here for? To talk about loving Katerina Ivanovna, or about the old man and Dmitri? About going abroad? About the fatal situation in Russia? About the emperor Napoleon? Was it really for that?"

"No, not that."

"So you know yourself what for. Some people need one thing, but we green youths need another, we need first of all to resolve the everlasting questions, that is what concerns us. All of young Russia is talking now only about the eternal questions. Precisely now, just when all the old men have suddenly gotten into practical questions. Why have you been looking at me so expectantly for these three months? In order to ask me: 'And how believest thou, if thou believest anything at all?' That is what your three months of looking come down to, is it not, Alexei Fyodorovich?"

"Maybe so," Alyosha smiled. "You're not laughing at me now, brother?"

"Me, laughing? I wouldn't want to upset my little brother who has been looking at me for three months with so much expectation. Look me in the eye, Alyosha: I'm exactly the same little boy as you are, except that I'm not a novice. How have Russian boys handled things up to now? Some of them, that is. Take, for instance, some stinking local tavern. They meet there and settle down in a corner. They've never seen each other before in their whole lives, and when they walk out of the tavern, they won't see each other again for forty years. Well, then, what are they going to argue about, seizing this moment in the tavern? About none other than the universal questions: is there a God, is there immortality? And those who do not believe in God, well, they will talk about socialism and anarchism, about transforming the whole of mankind according to a new order, but it's the same damned thing, the questions are all the same, only from the other end. And many, many of the most original Russian boys do nothing but talk about the eternal questions, now, in our time. Isn't it so?"

"Yes, for real Russians the questions of the existence of God and immortality, or, as you just said, the same questions from the other end, are of course first and foremost, and they should be," Alyosha spoke, looking intently at his brother with the same quiet and searching smile.

"You see, Alyosha, sometimes it's not at all smart to be a Russian, but still it's even impossible to imagine anything more foolish than what Russian boys are doing now. Though I'm terribly fond of one Russian boy named Alyoshka."

"Nicely rounded off," Alyosha laughed suddenly.

"Now, tell me where to begin, give the order yourself—with God? The existence of God? Or what?"

"Begin with whatever you like, even 'from the other end.' You did proclaim yesterday at father's that there is no God," Alyosha looked searchingly at his brother.

"I said that on purpose yesterday, at dinner with the old man, just to tease you, and I saw how your eyes glowed. But now I don't mind at all discussing things with you, and I say it very seriously. I want to get close to you, Alyosha, because I have no friends. I want to try. Well,

imagine that perhaps I, too, accept God," Ivan laughed, "that comes as a surprise to you, eh?"

"Yes, of course, unless you're joking again."

" 'Joking.' They said yesterday at the elder's that I was joking. You see, my dear, there was in the eighteenth century an old sinner who stated that if God did not exist, he would have to be invented: *S'il n'existait pas Dieu, il faudrait l'inventer*. And man has, indeed, invented God. And the strange thing, the wonder would not be that God really exists, the wonder is that such a notion—the notion of the necessity of God—could creep into the head of such a wild and wicked animal as man—so holy, so moving, so wise a notion, which does man such great honor. As for me, I long ago decided not to think about whether man created God or God created man.

. . .

"There is a force that will endure everything," said Ivan, this time with a cold smirk.

"What force?"

"The Karamazov force . . . the force of the Karamazov baseness."

"To drown in depravity, to stifle your soul with corruption, is that it?"

"That, too, perhaps . . . only until my thirtieth year maybe I'll escape it, and then . . . "

"How will you escape it? By means of what? With your thoughts, it's impossible."

"Again, in Karamazov fashion."

"You mean 'everything is permitted'? Everything is permitted, is that right, is it?"

Ivan frowned, and suddenly turned somehow strangely pale.

"Ah, you caught that little remark yesterday, which offended Miusov so much . . . and that brother Dmitri so naively popped up and rephrased?" he grinned crookedly. "Yes, perhaps 'everything is permitted,' since the word has already been spoken. I do not renounce it. And Mitenka's version is not so bad."

Alyosha was looking at him silently.

"I thought, brother, that when I left here I'd have you, at least, in all the world," Ivan suddenly spoke with unexpected feeling, "but now I see that in your heart, too, there is no room for me, my dear hermit. The formula, 'everything is permitted,' I will not renounce, and what then? Will you renounce me for that? Will you?"

Alyosha stood up, went over to him in silence, and gently kissed him on the lips.

"Literary theft!" Ivan cried, suddenly going into some kind of rapture. "You stole that from my poem! Thank you, however. Get up, Alyosha, let's go, it's time we both did."

They went out, but stopped on the porch of the tavern.

"So, Alyosha," Ivan spoke in a firm voice, "if, indeed, I hold out for the sticky little leaves, I shall love them only remembering you. It's enough for me that you are here somewhere, and I shall not stop wanting to live. Is that enough for you? If you wish, you can take it as a declaration of love. And now you go right, I'll go left—and enough, you hear, enough. I mean, even if I don't go away tomorrow (but it seems I certainly shall), and we somehow meet again, not another word to me on any of these subjects.

An urgent request. And with regard to brother Dmitri, too, I ask you particularly, do not ever even mention him to me again," he suddenly added irritably. "It's all exhausted, it's all talked out, isn't it? And in return for that, I will also make you a promise: when I'm thirty and want 'to smash the cup on the floor,' then, wherever you may be, I will still come to talk things over with you once more ... even from America, I assure you. I will make a point of it. It will also be very interesting to have a look at you by then, to see what's become of you. Rather a solemn promise, you see. And indeed, perhaps we're saying good-bye for some seven or ten years. Well, go now to your Pater Seraphicus; he's dying, and if he dies without you, you may be angry with me for having kept you. Good-bye, kiss me once more—so—and now go ... "

READING 2
The Categorical Imperative
Immanuel Kant

(from *Fundamental Principles of the Metaphysics of Morals*)

When I conceive a hypothetical imperative, in general I do not know beforehand what it will contain until I am given the condition. But when I conceive a categorical imperative, I know at once what it contains. For as the imperative contains besides the law only the necessity that the maxims shall conform to this law, while the law contains no conditions restricting it, there remains nothing but the general statement that the maxim of the action should conform to a universal law: and it is this conformity alone that the imperative properly represents as necessary.

There is therefore but one categorical imperative, namely, this: *Act only on that maxim whereby you can at the same time will that it should become a universal law.*

Now if all imperatives of duty can be deduced from this one imperative as from their principle, then, although it should remain undecided whether what is called duty is not merely a vain notion, yet at least we shall be able to show what we understand by it and what this notion means.

Since the universality of the law according to which effects are produced constitutes what is properly called *nature* in the most general sense (as to form), that is the existence of things so far as it is determined by general laws, the imperative of duty may be expressed thus: *Act as if the maxim of your action were to become by your will a universal law of action.*

We will now enumerate a few duties, adopting the usual division of them into duties to ourselves and to others, and into perfect and imperfect duties.

1. A man reduced to despair by a series of misfortunes feels wearied of life, but is still so far in possession of his reason that he can ask himself whether it would not be contrary to his duty to himself to take his own life. Now he inquires whether the maxim of his action could become a universal law of nature. His

maxim is: From self-love I adopt it as a principle to shorten my life when its longer duration is likely to bring more evil than satisfaction. It is asked then simply whether this principle founded on self-love can become a universal law of nature. Now we see at once that a system of nature of which it should be a law to destroy life by means of the very feeling whose special nature it is to impel to the improvement of life would contradict itself, and therefore could not exist as a system of nature; hence that maxim cannot possibly exist as a universal law of nature, and consequently would be wholly inconsistent with the supreme principle of all duty.

2. Another finds himself forced by necessity to borrow money. He knows that he will not be able to repay it, but sees also that nothing will be lent to him, unless he promises stoutly to repay it in a definite time. He desires to make this promise, but he has still so much conscience as to ask himself: Is it not unlawful and inconsistent with duty to get out of a difficulty in this way? Suppose, however, that he resolves to do so, then the maxim of his action would be expressed thus: When I think myself in want of money, I will borrow money and promise to repay it, although I know that I never can do so. Now this principle of self-love or of one's own advantage may perhaps be consistent with my whole future welfare; but the question now is, Is it right? I change then the suggestion of self-love into a universal law, and state the question thus: How would it be if my maxim were a universal law? Then I see at once that it could never hold as a universal law of nature, but would necessarily contradict itself. For supposing it to be a universal law that everyone when he thinks himself in a difficulty should be able to promise whatever he pleases, with the purpose of not keeping his promise, the promise itself would become impossible, as well as the end that one might have in view in it, since no one would consider that anything was promised to him, but would ridicule all such statements as vain pretences.

3. A third finds in himself a talent which with the help of some culture might make him a useful man in many respects. But he finds himself in comfortable circumstances, and prefers to indulge in pleasure rather than to take pains in enlarging and improving his happy natural capacities. He asks, however, whether his maxim of neglect of his natural gifts, besides agreeing with his inclination to indulgence, agrees also with what is called duty. He sees then that a system of nature could indeed subsist with such a universal law although men (like the South Sea islanders) should let their talents rest, and resolve to devote their lives merely to idleness, amusement, and propagation of their species—in a word, to enjoyment; but he cannot possibly *will* that this should be a universal law of nature, or be implanted in us as such by a natural instinct. For, as a rational being, he necessarily wills that his faculties be developed, since they serve him, and have been given him, for all sorts of possible purposes.

4. A fourth, who is in prosperity, while he sees that others have to contend with great wretchedness and that he could help them, thinks: What concern is it of mine? Let everyone be as happy as Heaven pleases, or as he can make himself; I will take nothing from him nor even envy him, only I do not wish to contribute anything to his welfare or to his assistance in distress! Now no doubt if such a mode of thinking were a universal law, the human race might very well subsist, and doubtless even better than in a state in which everyone talks of sympathy and good-will, or even takes care occasionally to put it into practice, but, on the other side, also cheats when he can, betrays the rights of men, or otherwise violates them. But although it is possible that a universal law of nature might exist in accordance with that maxim, it is impossible to *will* that such a principle should have the universal validity of a law of nature. For a will which resolved this would contradict itself, inasmuch as many cases might occur in which one would have need of the love and sympathy of others, and in which, by such a law of nature, sprung from his own will, he would deprive himself of all hope of the aid he desires.

READING 3
What Utilitarianism Is
John Stuart Mill

(from *Utilitarianism*)

The creed which accepts as the foundation of morals *utility,* or the *greatest happiness principle,* holds that actions are right in proportion as they tend to promote happiness, wrong as they tend to produce the reverse of happiness. By "happiness" is intended pleasure, and the absence of pain; by "unhappiness," pain, and the privation of pleasure. To give a clear view of the moral standard set up by the theory, much more requires to be said; in particular, what things it includes in the ideas of pain and pleasure; and to what extent this is left an open question. But these supplementary explanations do not affect the theory of life on which this theory of morality is grounded—namely, that pleasure, and freedom from pain, are the only things desirable as ends; and that all desirable things (which are as numerous in the utilitarian as in any other scheme) are desirable either for the pleasure inherent in themselves, or as means to the promotion of pleasure and the prevention of pain.

Now such a theory of life excites in many minds, and among them in some of the most estimable in feeling and purpose, inveterate dislike. To suppose that life has (as they express it) no higher end than pleasure—no better and nobler object of desire and pursuit—they designate as utterly mean and groveling; as a doctrine worthy only of swine, to whom the followers of Epicurus were, at a very early period, contemptuously likened; and modern holders of the doctrine are occasionally made the subject of equally polite comparisons by its German, French, and English assailants.

When thus attacked, the Epicureans have always answered that it is not they but their accusers who represent human nature in a degrading light; since the accusation supposes human beings to be capable of no pleasures except those of which swine are capable. If this supposition were true, the charge could not be gainsaid, but would then be no longer an imputation; for if the sources of pleasure were precisely the same to human beings and to swine, the rule of life which is good enough for the one would be good enough for the other. The comparison of the Epicurean life to that of beasts is felt as degrading, precisely because a beast's pleasures do not satisfy a human being's conceptions of happiness. Human beings have faculties more elevated than the animal appetites, and when once made conscious of them, do not regard anything as happiness which does not include their gratification. I do not, indeed, consider the Epicureans to have been by any means faultless in drawing out their scheme of consequences from the utilitarian principle. To do this in any sufficient manner, many Stoic, as well as Christian elements require to be included. But there is no known Epicurean theory of life which does not assign to the pleasures of the intellect, of the feelings and imagination, and of the moral sentiments, a much higher value as pleasures than to those of mere sensation. It must be admitted, however, that utilitarian writers in general have placed the superiority of mental over bodily pleasures chiefly in the greater permanency, safety, uncostliness, etc., of the former—that is, in their circumstantial advantages rather than in their intrinsic nature. And on all these points utilitarians have fully proved their case; but they might have taken the other, and, as it may be called, higher ground, with entire consistency. It is quite compatible with the principle of utility to recognize the fact, that some *kinds* of pleasure are more desirable and more valuable than others. It would be absurd that while, in estimating all other things, quality is considered as well as quantity, the estimation of pleasures should be supposed to depend on quantity alone.

If I am asked what I mean by difference of quality in pleasures, or what makes one pleasure more valuable than another merely as a pleasure, except its being greater in amount, there is but one possible answer. Of two pleasures, if there be one to which all or almost all who have experience of both give a decided preference, irrespective of any feeling of moral obligation to prefer it, that is the more desirable pleasure. If one of the two is, by those who are competently acquainted with both, placed so far above the other that they prefer it, even though knowing it to be attended with a greater amount of discontent, and would not resign it for any quantity of the other pleasure which their nature is capable of, we are justified in ascribing to the preferred enjoyment a superiority in quality, so far outweighing quantity as to render it, in comparison, of small account.

Now it is an unquestionable fact that those who are equally acquainted with, and equally capable of appreciating and enjoying, both, do give a most marked preference to the manner of existence which employs their higher faculties. Few human creatures would consent to be changed into any of the lower animals, for a promise of the fullest allowance of a beast's pleasures; no intelligent human being would consent to be a fool, no instructed person would be an ignoramus, no person of feeling and conscience would be selfish and base, even though they should be persuaded that the fool,

the dunce, or the rascal is better satisfied with his lot than they are with theirs. They would not resign what they possess more than he for the most complete satisfaction of all the desires which they have in common with him. If they ever fancy they would, it is only in cases of unhappiness so extreme, that to escape from it they would exchange their lot for almost any other, however undesirable in their own eyes. A being of higher faculties requires more to make him happy, is capable probably of more acute suffering, and certainly accessible to it at more points, than one of an inferior type; but in spite of these liabilities, he can never really wish to sink into what he feels to be a lower grade of existence . . . . It is indisputable that the being whose capacities of enjoyment are low, has the greatest chance of having them fully satisfied; and a highly endowed being will always feel that any happiness which he can look for, as the world is constituted, is imperfect. But he can learn to bear its imperfections, if they are at all bearable; and they will not make him envy the being who is indeed unconscious of the imperfections, but only because he feels not at all the good which those imperfections qualify. It is better to be a human being dissatisfied than a pig satisfied; better to be Socrates dissatisfied than a fool satisfied. And if the fool, or the pig, are of a different opinion, it is because they only know their own side of the question. The other party to the comparison knows both sides.

READING 4
Control of Oneself
Marcus Aurelius
(from *Meditations*)

3. Men seek retreats for themselves, houses in the country, sea-shores, and mountains: and thou too art wont to desire such things very much. But this is altogether a mark of the most common sort of men, for it is in thy power whenever thou shalt choose to retire into thyself. For nowhere either with more quiet or more freedom from trouble does a

man retire than into his own soul, particularly when he has within him such thoughts that by looking into them he is immediately in perfect tranquillity; and I affirm that tranquillity is nothing else than the good ordering of the mind. Constantly then give to thyself this retreat, and renew thyself; and let thy principles be brief and fundamental, which, as soon as thou shalt recur to them, will be sufficient to cleanse the soul completely, and to send thee back free from all discontent with the things to which thou returnest. For with what art thou discontented? With the badness of men? Recall to thy mind this conclusion, that rational animals exist for one another, and that to endure is a part of justice, and that men do wrong involuntarily; and consider how many already, after mutual enmity, suspicion, hatred, and fighting, have been stretched dead, reduced to ashes; and be quiet at last.— But perhaps thou art dissatisfied with that which is assigned to thee out of the universe.—Recall to thy recollection this alternative: either there is providence or atoms, fortuitous concurrence of things; or remember the arguments by which it has been proved that the world is a kind of political community, and be quiet at last.—But perhaps corporeal things will still fasten upon thee.—Consider then further that the mind mingles not with the breath, whether moving gently or violently, when it has once drawn itself apart and discovered its own power, and think also of all that thou hast heard and assented to about pain and pleasure, and be quiet at last.—But perhaps the desire of the thing called fame will torment thee.—See how soon everything is forgotten, and look at the chaos of infinite time on each side of the present, and the emptiness of applause, and the changeableness and want of judgment in those who pretend to give praise, and the narrowness of the space within which it is circumscribed, and be quiet at last. For the whole earth is a point, and how small a nook in it is this thy dwelling, and how few are there in it, and what kind of people are they who will praise thee.

This then remains: Remember to retire into this little territory of thy own, and above all do not distract or strain thyself, but be free, and look at things as a man, as a human being, as a citizen, as a mortal. But among the things readiest to thy hand to which thou shalt turn, let there be these, which are two. One is that things do not touch the soul, for they are external and remain immovable; but our perturbations come only from the opinion which is within. The other is that all these things, which thou seest, change immediately and will no longer be; and constantly bear in mind how many of these changes thou hast already witnessed. The universe is transformation: life is opinion.

12. A man should always have these two rules in readiness; the one, to do only whatever the reason of the ruling and legislating faculty may suggest for the use of men: the other, to change thy opinion, if there is any one at hand who sets thee right and moves thee from any opinion. But this change of opinion must proceed only from a certain persuasion, as of what is just or of common advantage, and the like, not because it appears pleasant or brings reputation.

49. Be like the promontory against which the waves continually break, but it stands firm and tames the fury of the water around it.

Unhappy am I, because this has happened to me.—Not so, but happy am I, though this has happened to me, because I continue free from pain, neither crushed by the present nor fearing the future. For such a thing as this might have happened to every man; but every man would not have continued free from pain on such an occasion. Why then is that rather a misfortune than this a good fortune? And dost thou in all cases call that a man's misfortune, which is not a deviation from man's nature? And does a thing seem to thee to be a deviation from man's nature, when it is not contrary to the will of man's nature? Well, thou knowest the will of nature. Will then this which has happened prevent thee from being just, magnanimous, temperate, prudent, secure against inconsiderate opinions and falsehood; will it prevent thee from having modesty, freedom, and everything else, by the presence of which man's nature obtains all that is its own? Remember too on every occasion which leads thee to vexation to apply this principle: not that this is a misfortune, but that to bear it nobly is good fortune.

READING 5
Reason as the Standard of Morality
Thomas Aquinas
(from *Summa theologiae*, I-II, 18; 21)

The morality of a human act is taken from its object according to the principles of moral activity, that is, according to a course of life as guided by reason. If the object is in accordance with a reasonable order of conduct, it will be a good kind of act; for instance, to help someone in need. But if the object of the act is contrary to reason, it will be a bad kind of act; for instance, to take to oneself what belongs to another. If, however, the object does not affect a reasonable course of life one way or the other, then the action is morally indifferent; for instance, to go for a walk or to pick up a straw.

Evil has a wider meaning than sin, just as good has a wider meaning than right. A privation of good in a thing is the essence of evil and, as far as sin is concerned, it lies precisely in an act's being out of harmony with its proper end. Now, that harmony, or ordered relationship, is measured by a standard which, given that things act according to their nature, is the very end to which their nature inclines them. There is a rightness, then, in an act that proceeds towards an end befitting its nature . . . when an act spoils that lightness, it is sinful . . . Thus the immediate standard for an act of the will is human reason, but the ultimate standard is the eternal law. When a human act is placed in harmony with the ordering of reason, then the act is right; but if it turns way from that rightness, it is called sin. From this it is clear that an act of the will is bad insofar as it departs from the order of reason, and from the eternal law too; good if it holds with reason, and with it the eternal law.

READING 6
The Moral Primacy of Sentiment
David Hume
(from *An Enquiry Concerning the Principles of Morals*)

These arguments on each side (and many more might be produced) are so plausible, that I am apt to suspect, they may, the one as well as the other, be solid and satisfactory, and that *reason* and *sentiment* concur in almost all moral determinations and conclusions. The final sentence, it is probable, which pronounces characters and actions amiable or odious, praise-worthy or blameable; that which stamps on them the mark of honour or infamy, approbation or censure; that which renders morality an active principle and constitutes virtue our happiness, and vice our misery: it is probable, I say, that this final sentence depends on some internal sense or feeling, which nature has made universal in the whole species. For what else can have an influence of this nature? But in order to pave the way for such a sentiment, and give a proper discernment of its object, it is often necessary, we find, that much reasoning should precede, that nice distinctions be made, just conclusions drawn, distant comparisons formed, complicated relations examined, and general facts fixed and ascertained. Some species of beauty, especially the natural kinds, on their first appearance, command our affection and approbation; and where they fail of this effect, it is impossible for any reasoning to redress their influence, or adapt them better to our taste and sentiment. But in many orders of beauty, particularly those of the finer arts, it is requisite to employ much reasoning, in order to feel the proper sentiment; and a false relish may frequently be corrected by argument and reflection. There are just grounds to conclude, that moral beauty partakes much of this latter species, and demands the assistance of our intellectual faculties, in order to give it a suitable influence on the human mind.

. . .

But though reason, when fully assisted and improved, be sufficient to instruct us in the pernicious or useful tendency of qualities and actions; it is not alone sufficient to produce any moral blame or approbation. Utility is only a tendency to a certain end; and were the end totally indifferent to us we should feel the same indifference towards the means. It is requisite a *sentiment* should here display itself, in order to give a preference to the useful above the pernicious tendencies. This sentiment can be no other than a feeling for the happiness of mankind, and a resentment of their misery; since these are the different ends which virtue and vice have a tendency to promote. Here therefore *reason* instructs us in the several tendencies of actions, and *humanity* makes a distinction in favour of those which are useful and beneficial.

This partition between the faculties of understanding and sentiment, in all moral decisions, seems clear from the preceding hypothesis. But I shall suppose that hypothesis false: it will then be requisite to look out for some other theory that may be satisfactory; and I dare venture to affirm that none such will ever be found, so long as we suppose reason to be the sole source of morals.

READING 7
Practical Rationality
Philippa Foot
(from *Natural Goodness*)

In the previous chapter I described what I believe to be the conceptual underpinnings of the ascription of "natural goodness," moving from plants and animals to human beings and suggesting that the same normative pattern is found in our evaluations of all three kinds of living things.

Now I come face to face with an apparently unanswerable objection, which is that human beings as rational creatures can ask why what has so far been said should have any effect on their conduct. For let us suppose that the normative pattern that I called "natural normativity" does govern our evaluations of human beings as human beings. Suppose that human beings are defective as human beings unless they do what is needed for human good, including such things as refraining from murder and keeping promises. The sceptic will surely ask "But what if I do not care about being a good human being?"

This is an objection to take seriously. For, after all, human beings are rational beings. It is part of the sea change that came at the point of transition from plants and animals on one side to human beings on the other that we can look critically at our own conduct and at the rules of behaviour that we are taught. The strange possibility seems even to arise that human beings could be as such defective in that they must sometimes either act badly, for example, in breaking a promise, or else act irrationally in keeping it where there is no reason so to do. If this were believed to be the case, our moral sceptic would probably point triumphantly to the irrelevance of a demonstration that there was human defect in promise-breaking, murder, and so on.

This is the difficulty with which the present chapter is concerned. I must, however, object to the precise way in which it was formulated. For the question is not whether we have reason to aim at being good human beings, but rather whether we have reason to aim at those things at which a good human being must aim, as for instance good rather than harm to others, or keeping faith. The problem is about the rationality of doing what virtue demands. And it has seemed to some to be an especially difficult problem for anyone who has an objective theory of moral evaluation as I do myself.

Gary Watson, a philosopher who is himself sympathetic to moral objectivism, posed this as a difficulty for someone like myself in the form of two questions:

1. Can an objective theory really establish that being a gangster is incompatible with being a good human being?
2. If it can, can it establish an intelligible connection between [this] appraisal and what we have reason to do as individuals?

I accept the challenge of answering question 1 in the affirmative, having already suggested the kind of ground on which a human being could be appraised as a bad—a defective—human being if, being a gangster, he goes in for robbery and murder. I therefore answer "Yes" to question 1 and now move on to question 2.

First, however, I want to say more about the idea that human beings are rational creatures, in being able to act on reasons, whereas even the higher animals, in many ways so like us, are different in that they cannot act rationally or irrationally because they do not act *on* reasons as we do.

It is easy to say this, but less easy to explain what we mean. The best way to understand it is, in my view, to consider what Aquinas said on the subject. That rational choice is possible for human beings is, of course, an ancient doctrine. Aristotle spends much time in expounding the idea of choice "on a rational principle" or *logos*. And Aquinas, following Aristotle as he so often does, explains this by contrasting animals and men. He says that animals, like small children, do not exercise choice *(electio)*. What does he mean by this? Do sheep not choose one patch of grass rather than another when they move to graze in a particular part of a field? Aquinas considers this example, and allows that such animal movements "partake of choice" in so far as they show "appetitive inclination" for one thing rather than another. He even stresses the fact that animals, having perception as plants do not, may do what they do for an apprehended end *(propter finem)*. Nevertheless he insists that in doing something for an end animals cannot apprehend *it as an end* (*non cognoscunt rationem finis*). A kind of knowledge is needed even for the "participation in the voluntary" that is possible for animals. However, Aquinas says, "Perfect knowledge of the end consists in not only apprehending the thing which is the end but also in knowing it under the aspect of end and the relation of the means to that end" ('sed etiam cognoscitur ratio finis, et proportio ejus quod ordinatur in finem ad ipsum'). And similarly he denies that animals have knowledge of the relation of means and ends *as humans do*. In a way they can be said to have this knowledge, since they go for one thing to get another. But here, too, Aquinas says that they do not have the *kind* of knowledge of the relation that human beings have . . . .

. . . Can it be the case that someone who does what is wrong *thereby* acts in a way that is contrary to reason? May we add considerations that are about right and wrong to the list of rationalizing considerations given above? I suggested in Chapter 1 that we can indeed do so, because one who acts badly *ipso facto* acts in a way that is contrary to practical reason.

. . . When Gary Watson issued the challenge described above, he was asking a question that belongs here, since he was wanting to know whether on an objective theory of moral goodness an "intrinsic link" could be established between moral goodness and *reasons for action*. My argument in the last few pages has been designed to show that there is such a link.

Earlier in the book, in Chapters 1–3, I gave reasons for believing propositions about natural goodness and badness in various plants, animals, and human beings; for instance, for believing that an individual oak tree with superficial, spindly roots was to be evaluated as defective, and, passing to human beings, gave reasons *of the same form* . . . [that] to break a promise was as such to act badly. Finally, supposing that doubts might be raised about the relevance of such considerations to moral philosophy, I argued for the extension of the concept of natural normativity to human beings, even to the moral evaluation of human action and will, and so argued for what Watson regarded as an objective theory of moral judgement. In the previous pages I have turned to the problem of practical reasons, and have gone on to answer "Yes" to his question 2.

Returning now to the beginning of the present chapter, to the sceptic who was supposed to have asked why he should do that which the good person must do, I would point out that there are two ways of understanding this question. If we understand the words "that which a good person must do" "transparently" (extensionally) as referring to, for example, keeping promises or refraining from murder, then our answer must consist in showing him why in doing *these things* he would act badly, and we are still in Chapters 1–3. But if his words are understood opaquely (intensionally) as referring to *bad actions* under that description, we must try to show him the conceptual connection between acting well and acting rationally; so that if he is to challenge us further, this is where the challenge must come. If the sceptic does not succeed in refuting us here, but still goes on saying that he has not been shown that there is reason for acting as a good person would act, it is no longer clear what he is asking for. To ask for a reason for acting rationally is to ask for a reason where reasons must a priori have come to an end.

READING 8
Abraham and "Breaking Through the Universal"
Søren Kierkegaard
(from *Fear & Trembling*)

The paradox of faith is this, that the individual is higher than the universal, that the individual (to recall a dogmatic distinction now rather seldom heard) determines his relation to the universal by his relation to the absolute, not his relation to the absolute by his relation to the universal. The paradox can also be expressed by saying that there is an absolute duty toward God; for in this relationship of duty the individual as an individual stands related absolutely to the absolute. So when in this connection it is said that it is a duty to love God, something different is said from that in the foregoing; for if this duty is absolute, the ethical is reduced to a position of relativity. From this, however, it does not follow that the ethical is to be abolished, but it acquires an entirely different expression, the paradoxical expression—that, for example, love to God may cause the knight of faith to give his love to his neighbor the opposite expression to that which, ethically speaking, is required by duty.

If such is not the case, then faith has no proper place in existence, then faith is a temptation (*Anfechtung*), and Abraham is lost, since he gave in to it.

This paradox does not permit of mediation, for it is founded precisely upon the fact that the individual is only the individual. As soon as this individual [who is aware of a direct command from God] wishes to express his absolute duty in [terms of] the universal [i.e. the ethical, and] is sure of his duty in that [i.e. the universal or ethical precept], he recognizes that he is in temptation [i.e. a trial of faith], and, if in fact he resists [the direct indication of God's will], he ends by not fulfilling the absolute duty so called [i.e. what here has been called the absolute duty]; and, if he doesn't do this, [i.e. doesn't put up a resistance to the direct intimation of God's will], he sins . . . So what should Abraham do? If he would say to another person, "Isaac I love more dearly than everything in the world, and hence it is so hard for me to sacrifice him"; then surely the other would have shaken his head and said, "Why will you sacrifice him then?"—or if the other had been a sly fellow, he surely would have seen through Abraham and perceived that he was making a show of feelings which were in strident contradiction to his act.

In the story of Abraham we find such a paradox. His relation to Isaac, ethically expressed, is this, that the father should love the son. This ethical relation is reduced to a relative position in contrast with the absolute relation to God. To the question, "Why?" Abraham has no answer except that it is a trial, a temptation (*Fristelse*)—terms which, as was remarked above, express the unity of the two points of view: that it is for God's sake and for his own sake. In common usage these two ways of regarding the matter are mutually exclusive. Thus when we see a man do something which does not comport with the universal, we say that he scarcely can be doing it for God's sake, and by that we imply that he does it for his own sake. The paradox of faith has lost the intermediate term, i.e. the universal. On the one side it has the expression for the extremest egoism (doing the dreadful thing it does for one's own sake); on the other side the expression for the most absolute self-sacrifice (doing it for God's sake). Faith itself cannot be mediated into the universal, for it would thereby be destroyed. Faith is this paradox, and the individual absolutely cannot make himself intelligible to anybody.

Chapter Three

The Moral Law

"LAW" IN ITS VARIOUS USES

Our constant use of the word *law* is an indication of how much our lives are in one way or another governed by it. We meet it in the physical universe whose activity is expressed in terms of *physical* laws, the law of gravity, or the laws of chemical reaction, or optics, or movement in space, and so on. Our public behavior is beholden to *civil* law, from stopping at a stop sign to the labyrinthine code for filing income tax. If *international* law is eventually realized, it will have been made possible by a developing sense of unity exhibited in the United Nations and the European Union. Even though it is a frustrating exercise, economists have been trying to discover consistent patterns in the ebb and flow of money that they would thankfully call the *laws* of economy governing economic health and stability. *Ecclesiastical* laws, for a community of coreligionists, direct them to certain ends for the good of their spiritual life. And so it goes, with our becoming more and more aware that the urgency of law touches every aspect of our existence, and none with greater urgency than the one referred to as the *moral law*.

Urgency is a function of moral climate which, at any given time and place, may record events difficult, or even impossible, to reconcile with a humanity seeking to deepen its own sense of compassion. What can be said of our time? In the past seventy-five years have we not seen tyrannies run amok, bringing about a desecration of human beings unmatched in human history? With genocide a tragic feature of the century? With the ever-widening gap between rich and poor? With religious tolerance buffeted beyond recognition? With the degradation of women rampant in many parts of the world? And in the day-by-day life of individuals, has there not been an erosion of sensitivity regarding what we, as individuals, owe one another, whether it be a matter of fidelity to a promise, help, sharing, thoughtfulness, or civility? And all of this in disregard of moral and civil laws intended to guide humans to their unique fulfillment. The philosopher Henri Bergson, whom we met earlier on, made this prophetic remark: "Mankind lies groaning, half crushed beneath the weight of its own progress. Men do not sufficiently realize that their future is in their own hands. Theirs is the task of determining first of all whether they want to go on living or not. Theirs the responsibility, then, for deciding if they want merely to live, or intend to make just the extra effort required for fulfilling, even on their refractory planet, the essential function of the universe, which is a machine for the making of gods."

In the interest of giving further attention to the urgent aspect of morality, the goal of this chapter is to consider *what the notion of "law" adds to the understanding of morality* we have thus far been developing. We can begin by asking, Is there a common element running through the various kinds of law mentioned earlier? Take an example from the inanimate world, say, the formation of crystals and the way they emerge from their matrix. It cannot be a haphazard confluence of forces that achieves this remarkable formation, but some kind of physical activity *necessarily* producing it, which can be referred to as the "law of crystallization." In the realm of living things, a plant reaches full development clearly in accordance with some built-in plan of growth. Animal life adds to these examples a range of activities that leaves us in a state of wonder as to both their variety and constancy. Yet a forced departure from their regular course can be dislocating, or even disastrous to animals, as in the case of the honeybee. These clever little insects ingeniously construct their honeycombs and then fill each cell with honey; should you prick the underside of a cell and let the honey run out, the bee, so clever in building it in the first place, never thinks of repairing it but keeps filling it up until it drops dead! On the other hand, you've never seen a squirrel miss a jump from roof to branch, so squirrels have got to be making some kind of judgment about negotiating the distance; dogs wag their tails in recognition of their masters; animals protect their young and, in a crowd, know which young are theirs. All marvelous and inscrutable actions destined to achieve some end.

The reason why we call living things "living" is found in the *spontaneous* activity they manifest, a movement from within, which increases in sophistication the higher you go on the scale of life until you reach the distinction that strikingly separates human beings from the nonhuman, *freedom of action.* As wonderful as the actions of nonhuman animals are, in being fitted to achieve their end, they are still significantly circumscribed so as to distinguish them from the higher levels of activity proper to human beings. Human activity is characterized by the use of intellect and will in the making of a *free* movement toward a chosen end; free in that it is not constrained to only one course of action, but open to more than one, as we saw in our discussion of freedom and necessity in Chapter 1. But in every instance of action, whether of living or nonliving beings, it is always action *toward an end.* The focus of law, then, pertains to action as it bears upon an end, and thus law can be defined as *a principle directing action toward an end.* Because nonliving beings are constituted entirely of matter, they observe the law of their nature in a physical way. Animals, as living beings acting out of an internal principle of movement, observe the law of their nature in a spontaneous way, yet not free. Human beings, acting out of properly human activities of intellect and will, observe the law of their nature freely (R #1).

Since we are addressing only the moral aspect of an act, not the morally neutral such as taking a walk or turning a door knob, we can apply the term *moral law* to the principle or principles that direct, guide and urge an action toward the achievement of an end befitting the moral context. Essentially this consideration ties in with the idea of "ought" discussed earlier, but it tends to draw out more decisively the "imperative" implied in it. In a sense, the moral *law* is the driving force behind the moral *ought,* already suggested in the Kantian "categorical imperative." If, for example, someone were to ask you why you should keep your promise, you could answer, depending on the gravity of the promise, it's the right thing to do, it's a matter of trust, it's a function of society, it's a question of respect, it's to be done out of love, and so on, all of which are subject to the driving force of the law called moral (R #2).

TOWARD A DEFINITION OF LAW: THOMAS AQUINAS

If we are looking for a concise, clear presentation of law, then it's hard to beat the treatise written by St. Thomas Aquinas (R #3). In it, he brings together the elements required for a definition of law and how this applies to the moral law for man. It is found in several articles of the *Summa Theologiae*, part one of the second part, questions 90 and 91. We have already seen in what sense we can speak of reason as the norm of morality, and here, in question 90, Thomas invokes reason as "the rule and measure of human activity, the first principle whose function it is to direct means to end." Our reason, or understanding, is able to hold together in a single function the end to be achieved and the means to achieve it, so that we can *reasonably* (according to our *understanding*) act to achieve it. Law does not become law merely because it is *willed* by legislative authority, but because it is *reasonably* willed; otherwise "it would be lawlessness rather than law." It is the proper ordering of means to end, whence Aquinas refers to it as an "ordinance of reason," which becomes the first part of his definition of law: *Law is an ordinance of reason made for the common good, and promulgated by the proper authority of the community.*

When he uses the term *common good*, as the second element of the definition, he is thinking of community as a totality of individuals, with emphasis on the good of the whole in which each individual shares. This supplies him with an effective definition of common good as *the perfection of the whole so that all, collectively and individually, share in it.* Law cannot be understood except in terms of actions undertaken toward a good that accrues to the whole community and to its individual members. The reason for the law is the good and happiness of all, as Aquinas puts it, "law is engaged mainly with the scheme of common happiness."

As to the third element of the definition, the *authority* for making laws, it is clear for St. Thomas that the good of the entire community has to be the aim of the law-making authority; thus the making of a law pertains "to the whole people or to the public authority having care of the whole people" and not to any private individual or group. He is not laying down any principle as to how an authority gets to be an authority but he is laying down the principle that the farther away a law gets from the common good, to that extent it is unreasonable. Private persons can offer advice that can indeed be reasonable, but if it is not taken, it has no compelling power as law.

Regarding the last element of the definition, *promulgation*, it's obvious that the law has to be made known to all who would be obliged to keep it. From a moral point of view, what is unknown cannot be willed, but from a legal point of view, you can only grit your teeth when in court the judge tells you that ignorance of the law is no excuse! How the law is made known to all will vary, of course, according to the circumstances of time, place, and culture.

This explanation of law in general, emphasizing its function in directing action to an end, is necessary for Aquinas as he leads into a discussion of the various kinds of law in the next question, whose first two articles are important in understanding how he situates the natural law for man in the eternal law of God. We recall from above how our understanding of any single thing increases as we see it in an increasingly larger context, so it is not surprising that Aquinas would try to insert human action into the widest context possible, the divine plan to move all creation toward a common end. God, whose existence Aquinas is taking as already established, is the creator of all else, and unless we allow that He acts unreasonably, or recklessly, or purposelessly. He has some ultimate end or purpose in mind for all created things and provides them with the means of achieving it. Inasmuch as law is reason's ordering of things, the design in the divine mind for directing all things toward their end can rightly be called the divine law, or the *eternal law*. "it is evident, granted that the world is ruled by divine providence, . . . that the whole community of the universe is governed by the divine reason . . . and has the nature of a law. And since the divine reason's conception of things is not subject to time, but is eternal . . . it must be called eternal."

So much for law on the side of the creator. Now let's look at the side of the created. All created things somehow share in the eternal plan and somehow are subject to the eternal law. Everything is directed to its end according to the kind of thing it is, so rational things, radically different from all others, are directed in a radically different way. They participate in the eternal law in a knowing and willing way and, insofar as they themselves have the experience of directing their actions to an end, they can also have an appreciation of law in its directive power. The basic notion of *natural law* for St. Thomas is *the rational creature's participation of the eternal law*. "Now among all others," he writes, "the rational creature is subject to divine providence in a more excellent way, in so far as it itself partakes of a share of providence, by being provident both for itself and for others. Therefore it has a share of the eternal reason, whereby it has a natural inclination to its proper act and end; and the participation of the eternal law in the rational creature is called the natural law." As it applies to the moral act, it is the *moral* law.

Finally, someone may insist that inasmuch as the natural law is a participation of the eternal law and covers every particular situation, there is no need for further lawmaking. Against this, Aquinas would point out that the natural law delivers principles of action and of itself does not cover every particular situation, so that application to singular cases has to be made by *practical wisdom*, which will often require a specific law made by humans. Such a law is referred to as *human law*, or positive law (not as opposed to negative, but as law put in place, or "posited," by human authority). So, for example, though "it may declare that criminals should be punished, the natural law does not settle the character of the penalty," which human law supplies.

MORE ON THE NATURAL LAW

There has been, often enough, some misunderstanding regarding the natural law, as though it were some kind of innate blueprint of behavior we can refer to at the time of moral decision making. Perhaps this misunderstanding is based on our experience of the way laws are promulgated. We are used to laws being communicated to us by a clear statement, in print, by voice, or by some other observable means and so all we have to do is compare our action with the directive to see whether it conforms or not. Or perhaps the "blueprint" is thought of as akin to Plato's world of forms, the world of perfection, which we are admonished to contemplate and reproduce in this world. Or, finally, perhaps the "blueprint" is already implanted in us by nature, and all we have to do is simply consult it and act accordingly: In any one of these cases, natural law is imagined to be a kind of template against which a person measures exactly the moral character of an action. As attractive as these descriptions may be, however, and as effective they may be as a style of speaking to suit the occasion, they fall quite short of the meaning of natural law as presented by St. Thomas. When they are used, therefore, it must be realized that (i) it is a popular use of metaphorical language and (ii) in individual cases, it is the details that make the difference between them, as Aquinas, cited in Chapter 2, put it: In individual cases, the details are "infinitely variable," so that one law does not necessarily fit all.

Actually how I know that my action is permitted or forbidden by the natural law comes about quite the other way around. If God directs humans to their end, as discussed earlier, he does so according to their *rational* nature, so that *human reason has a defining* role in natural law—what reason *understands* to be right or wrong *is* right or wrong and such understanding *is* the natural law. Examples *abound.* Through my experience, I come to understand that I must not use a fellow human being as a means to an end. Because I know it is wrong in the *human* scheme of things, I know it is *against the natural law.* I do not know it as wrong because God first declared it to me. No, I know it as wrong first, and in knowing it as wrong, I know it as against God's law. Or, another example stated in a different way: Because of my relationship with another, I know that she is in dire need. I know I ought to help her and I do. I know, from the very context, the act is good and therefore in accord with the natural law: I know it is God's will because I know it is right first.

Another popular way of speaking as to how to determine the right thing to do is that of a person who wants to see all things from God's viewpoint, or in classical terminology, under the viewpoint of eternity, *sub specie aeternitatis.* Such a person feels that if he knew what God wanted him to do, he would do it. It would give him a meaningful life. Both views, the more popular way of speaking and the more analytic way described earlier, speak to the notion of the God-centeredness of human action as the ultimate foundation of a meaningful life (R #4). This is what Kierkegaard had in mind when he exclaimed in his diaries, "What matters is to find a purpose, to see what it really is that God wills that I shall do; the crucial thing is to find a truth which is truth for me, to find the idea for which I am willing to live and die." Or, by framing it in the striking declaration of Ivan Karamazov, "If God does not exist, then anything is permissible," Dostoyevsky is forcing us to ask whether God's very existence establishes His law for man (re-read R #1, Chapter 2).

In a paradoxical way, we also find an answer in this discussion of law to the question, "Can an atheist be moral?" The process, already described, of our knowing the rightness or wrongness of an action from its context is open to both theist and atheist in the same way and there is no reason for denying that; in some instances, the latter can be more morally sensitive than the former. On the other hand, there is no reason for denying that the theist has an additional openness to moral sensitivity because he is called to invest interpersonal relationships with an awareness of the respect and love that comes from the image of God he sees in every fellow human being. Motivation of this kind is what we admire in those persons called saints, canonized or not, who are living examples of deep personal concern for others.

SOME REFLECTIONS ON MORAL LAW IN WESTERN PHILOSOPHY

This chapter deals with the moral law, but, in order to get a better grasp of law overall, we can expect to pass back and forth between moral law on the one hand and civil or positive law on the other; the former is the domain of moral philosophy, the latter is the domain of political philosophy or political science. So in the ensuing brief reflections, it is the moral law we have in mind while necessarily touching on civil law as they cross over each other in the busy intersections of human activity.

Freedom and law are among the great forces at work in human activity, sources for furthering human life; one detached from the other would lead to the worsening of life for all. The *abuse of freedom,* in the absolute sense that one can do whatever one wants with one's own, is inseparable from an individualistic view of humanity in that it disregards the social kinship a person has with others: It underscores "mine" as its predominant adjective. This holds true across the whole span of human behavior, from small private meannesses to the excesses of corporate business which have marred the financial scene for the past score of years. The *abuse of law* exhibits two dangers. One danger is to use law to repress individual freedoms, as world history of the past century testifies. The other danger is the possibility of generating a *legalistic frame of mind* which leans toward the letter of the law in its mere external observance, together with the impulse to believe that outward observance by itself makes one morally "better" than others.

This is poles apart from the meaning of law in its humanizing aspect as we find it in Western philosophy, beginning with the early Pre-Socratics in whose view the forces of nature were guided by law from a higher power. This is especially true of Heraclitus, in the sixth to fifth century, with whom the very word *law* came into common usage. Though the Greek term *logos* has a variety of meanings such as "word," "intelligence," "reason," "wisdom," and "structure," one of its prime meanings is "law." Heraclitus, likening the omnipresence of change in the world to a flowing river, rejects the inference that where there is nothing but change, no meaning at all can be found. On the contrary, he finds meaning in change because all change is directed toward a meaningful whole by the presiding Logos. He does not restrict the need for law to the physical world only, for he sees an unending flow of activity in the human world in sore need of direction too, but of another kind. There is an unmistakable *moral tone* in Heraclitus's admonition for humans to obey the Logos. The Logos as *Law* is also the Logos as *Word*, and it is this "word" that is spoken throughout the universe for us to hear, and to follow in shaping our lives toward a meaningful whole. When you hear the Logos, Heraclitus writes, "it is wise to agree that all things are one."

Socrates, Plato, and Aristotle, though they were never politicians, were committed to the notion of good government as the basis of society. Among other things, it was their way of insuring that every citizen would learn the meaning of virtue in pursuing the good life. One of the driving purposes for Plato's establishing the Academy was to educate young men in the art of governing. It was his firm belief that for a king to be a successful ruler, he must also be a philosopher, that is, inwardly disposed toward the Truth and Good of a higher realm, which in turn would inspire him to a genuine concern for cultivating these dispositions in the lower realm for every citizen in his community. The characterization of such a ruler has become famously known as the Philosopher-King, and so important was this role that without it, Plato felt, there would be "no cessation of troubles for our states, nor, I fancy, for the human race either."

The utopian side of Plato bends him toward the view that, in the best of all states, man would not need the dictates of law because he would have a clear grasp of what ought to be done and the unwavering character for doing it. But for all his utopian proclivities, he also shows a keen sense for things as they really are and a practical eye on life as it is actually lived. Having stated that the art of government "cannot be found in the world at all in its pure form," he goes on to give the reason: The law cannot be counted on to be the best for every individual in every circumstance. "The law," Plato has the Stranger explain in the *Statesman*, "does not perfectly comprehend what is noblest and most just for all and therefore cannot enforce what is best. The differences of men and actions, and the endless irregular movements of human beings, do not admit of any universal and simple rule. And no art whatsoever can lay down a rule which will last for all time" (294b). A bit later he adds that no lawgiver could possibly attend every act of an individual and "sit at his side, so to speak, all through his life and tell him just what to do." Yet, as he points out in the *Laws,* there is something we can do. As human beings we are aware of many tensions in our lives, like cords pulling us in opposite directions, but the one and only cord we must hold onto against all the others is the "sacred and golden cord of reason, called by us the common law of the State" (645a) (R #5).

On a different approach from Plato's, yet with the same goal in mind, Aristotle, operating out of a lifelong habit of observation, looked to the practical demands for shaping the best state achievable for each of the communities where goals and temperaments varied. This he did by studying the success or failure of present and past city-states, which then enabled him to draw up a new, practicable constitution for a particular city-state, which he was often called upon to do. It was, he felt, the only way that laws conducive to practical unity and harmony in a community could be brought about. But, for him, "law" had a much broader meaning than civil law. In speaking of what the meaning of "just" is, he writes, "The just, then, is the lawful and the fair; the unjust the unlawful and the unfair" (*Ethics*, V,1, 1129a32). Even now we use similar terminology, as when we praise someone's action as "fair," and another's "unfair," indicating the inherent justice or injustice of the action. He refines this by distinguishing different kinds of justice: "There is more than one kind of justice," he writes, and what he has to say about them can be put this way: An act can be "just" in two senses, each of which is described as acting in accordance with "law," but in the first instance it is in accordance with civil law, whereas the second is in accordance with another kind of law quite different from civil. He calls the second kind of law the *law of nature* in that it pertains to all human beings: "Universal law is the law of nature. For there really is, as everyone to some extent is aware of, a natural justice and injustice that is binding on all men . . . " (*Rhetoric*, I, 13, 1373b6–9).

For Aristotle, this "law of nature" has to be understood in the full context of his *Metaphysics* and *Ethics,* whose opening lines announce their guiding themes: "All men by nature desire to know" and "The good has rightly been declared to be that at which all things aim." Since there are many kinds of good, it is a sign of practical wisdom to discern what order obtains among them, which good is to be judged the highest, and the kinds of activity we should nurture to "possess" them. The activity signalized is not any kind of activity a human being is capable of, but the one that is significantly human, namely moral. And if the possession of any good renders happiness to some extent, the possession of the highest good renders happiness in its fullest extent; this is the ultimate goal of our moral life. Even though the notion of God is not developed by Aristotle as it will be by later Christian writers, he expands his insights on "the natural desire to know" and "the good at which all things aim," in the two great works already mentioned. For him, because true knowledge is knowledge of the good, our knowledge of God is heightened by the very goodness of the good things we choose in the course of life, which ultimately leads to the contemplation of God as the highest truth and the highest good: "Whatever choice among natural goods we make, or already possess—whether bodily goods, wealth, friends, or other things—will most conduce to the contemplation of God, that choice or possession is best" (*Eudemian Ethics*).

As hinted earlier, it would be a stretch to say that the term *God* as used by the pre-Christian Aristotle and the Christian Augustine has exactly the same meaning. The difference would seem to lie in the abstract character of the human–divine relationship as conceived by Aristotle, as against Augustine's fear that abstraction tends to de-personalize the relationship, making it extremely difficult, if not impossible, to speak of it as "love." It is true that God is almighty in power, omniscient in knowledge, and majestic in grandeur and that we are somehow related to all these attributes, but they cannot speak to the relationship that has the fullest meaning for man, the person-to-person relationship of *love*. It is this relationship that grounds Augustine's injunction, "Love, and do what you will." Though law has many levels of application for Augustine, its compelling moral feature is far less a matter of duty than it is an unfolding of the personal nature of man-in-the-divine.

What Augustine is implying is that, if our actions are to be judged according to some ultimate, then, strictly speaking, it cannot be a matter of law as we have been describing it, unless we re-think "moral law" as the "law of love." Only love can be the ultimate judge. Augustine must have had in mind the figure of Jesus inveighing against the Pharisees of his time who took the observance of the Mosaic Law purely in terms of externality, duty seen as a legal commitment, not personal. Duty for duty's sake deflates the personal. That's why Augustine can confidently maintain that anyone who acts out of love of God acts rightly. It would not be amiss to add that such love of God is diametrically opposed to religious righteousness and fanaticism, so much in evidence in our time, which can only be thought of as excesses mocking the silent strength of divine love.

St. Augustine and St. Thomas are both representatives of a tradition in philosophy holding that the notion of moral law befits human nature. But there are philosophers who, though for various reasons, are averse to using the term *moral law*, yet are not at all averse to speaking of duty or obligation. One of them is the Scottish philosopher David Hume, whose ideas we visited earlier. His moral presentation is not always easy to unravel but it's clear that he does center the goal of moral philosophy on the primacy of duty: "The end of all moral speculation is to teach us our duty; and, by proper representations of the deformity of vice and beauty of virtue, beget correspondent habits, and engage us to avoid the one, and embrace the other" (*Enquiry Concerning the Principles of Morals*, I, 136).

But the beauty of virtue and the deformity of vice are not, for Hume, qualities we reason to, or demonstrate by some kind of deduction. The moral awareness of virtue and vice is given directly and simply; reason, therefore, cannot be held to be the primary guide to morality. Reason is not what drives practical activity. On the contrary, "The hypothesis which we embrace is plain. It maintains that morality is determined by sentiment. It defines virtue to be *whatever mental action or quality gives to a spectator the pleasing sentiment of approbation*; and vice the contrary. We then proceed to examine a plain matter of fact, to wit, what actions have this influence. We consider all the circumstances in which these actions agree, and thence endeavour to extract some general observations with regard to these sentiments" (Enquiry Concerning the Principles of Morals, 239). It seems, though Hume does not use the term *moral law* in his account, that he entertains its equivalent—a state of affairs that dictates what action is to be taken.

In Chapter 2, in discussing the relationship of duty and freedom, we paid considerable attention to Kant's view as to how we are to make a moral judgment with the guidance of the "categorical imperative." Here something additional has to be said on how the notion of duty ties in with that of law. Most moralists who speak to the matter of duty or oughtness as characterizing human activity agree that duty entails freedom, but Kant speaks of it with an especially persuasive eloquence. If indeed the rest of reality is governed by necessity, the *will* is not. Its freedom is asserted by the "commonest reason," and cannot be argued away even by the "subtlest philosophy." The autonomy of the will is the signature of the human being; it is the real dignity of the human person.

If duty, for Kant, is given to me as an individual, it is no less given to *all*, in virtue of which it takes on the character of *law*, and observance of duty takes on the character of *fidelity to the law*. The inner meaning of *duty* becomes *the necessity of acting out of respect for the law*. Here, with several ideas flowing together, Kant proceeds to draw out the fullest implication of acting in accordance with the moral law or, as otherwise stated, out of fidelity to one's will. It is not only the condition for the rational being's *happiness*, it is happiness itself. Further, as though probing its inmost meaning, Kant identifies living one's life according to the moral law as *holiness*, a perfection that is inchoative here in this mortal life but, at the risk of contradiction, completed beyond.

We saw earlier how Aristotle tried to put together the notions of law and justice by appealing to an intuitive sense of fairness that people have, and it's interesting to note the similarity between Aristotle's project and that of John Rawls. Rawls is a recent American political philosopher whose main works, *A Theory of Justice* and *Justice as Fairness*, are highly influential. Any society, as an instance of the one and the many, must look to the balance between society seen as the one and the individual members seen as the many; no theory of society can be entertained that brings about the destruction of either dimension. Fairness as a mode of conduct naturally emerges when people interact with each other. It relates "to right dealing between persons who are cooperating with or competing against one another, as when one speaks of fair games, fair competition, and fair bargains." Based on this intuitive grasp of fairness and its moral implications, the rationality of man can construct whatever system of law it finds conducive for a society in which the common good of all is the personal good of each (R #6).

READINGS

READING 1
The Manual of Epictetus

1. There are things which are within our power, and there are things which are beyond our power. Within our power are opinion, aim, desire, aversion, and, in one word, whatever affairs are our own. Beyond our power are body, property, reputation, office, and, in one word, whatever are not properly our own affairs.

Now the things within our power are by nature free, unrestricted, unhindered; but those beyond our power are weak, dependent, restricted, alien. Remember, then, that if you attribute freedom to things by nature dependent and take what belongs to others for your own, you will be hindered, you will lament, you will be disturbed, you will find fault both with gods and men. But if you take for your own only that which is your own and view what belongs to others just as it really is, then no one will ever compel you, no one will restrict you; you will find fault with no one, you will accuse no one, you will do nothing against your will; no one will hurt you, you will not have an enemy, nor will you suffer any harm.

Aiming, therefore, at such great things, remember that you must not allow yourself any inclination, however slight, toward the attainment of the others; but that you must entirely quit some of them, and for the present postpone the rest. But if you would have these, and possess power and wealth likewise, you may miss the latter in seeking the former; and you will certainly fail of that by which alone happiness and freedom are procured.

Seek at once, therefore, to be able to say to every unpleasing semblance, "You are but a semblance and by no means the real thing." And then examine it by those rules which you have; and first and chiefly by this: whether it concerns the things which are within our own power or those which are not; and if it concerns anything beyond our power, be prepared to say that it is nothing to you.

5. Men are disturbed not by things, but by the views which they take of things. Thus death is nothing terrible, else it would have appeared so to Socrates. But the terror consists in our notion of death, that it is terrible. When, therefore, we are hindered or disturbed, or grieved, let us never impute it to others, but to ourselves—that is, to our own views. It is the action of an uninstructed person to reproach others for his own misfortunes; of one entering upon instruction, to reproach himself; and one perfectly instructed, to reproach neither others nor himself.

8. Demand not that events should happen as you wish; but wish them to happen as they do happen, and you will go on well.

9. Sickness is an impediment to the body, but not to the will unless itself pleases. Lameness is an impediment to the leg, but not to the will; and say this to yourself with regard to everything that happens. For you will find it to be an impediment to something else, but not truly to yourself.

13. If you would improve, be content to be thought foolish and dull with regard to externals. Do not desire to be thought to know anything; and though you should appear to others to be somebody, distrust yourself. For be assured, it is not easy at once to keep your will in harmony with nature and to secure externals; but while you are absorbed in the one, you must of necessity neglect the other.

19. You can be unconquerable if you enter into no combat in which it is not in your own power to conquer. When, therefore, you see anyone eminent in honors or power, or in high esteem on any other account, take heed not to be bewildered by appearances and to pronounce him happy; for if the essence of good consists in things within our own power, there will be no room for envy or emulation. But, for your part, do not desire to be a general, or a senator, or a consul, but to be free; and the only way to this is a disregard of things which lie not within our own power.

21. Let death and exile, and all other things which appear terrible, be daily before your eyes, but death chiefly; and you will never entertain an abject thought, nor too eagerly covet anything.

25. Is anyone preferred before you at an entertainment, or in courtesies, or in confidential intercourse? If these things are good, you ought to rejoice that he has them; and if they are evil, do not be grieved that you have them not. And remember that you cannot be permitted to rival others in externals without using the same means to obtain them.

26. The will of nature may be learned from things upon which we are all agreed. As when our neighbor's boy has broken a cup, or the like, we are ready at once to say, "These are casualties that will happen"; be assured, then, that when your own cup is likewise broken, you ought to be affected just as when another's cup was broken. Now apply this to greater things. Is the child or wife of another dead? There is no one who would not say, "This is an accident of mortality." But if anyone's own child happens to die, it is immediately, "Alas! how wretched am I!" It should be always remembered how we are affected on hearing the same thing concerning others.

30. Duties are universally measured by relations. Is a certain man your father? In this are implied taking care of him, submitting to him in all things, patiently receiving his reproaches, his correction. But he is a bad father. Is your natural tie, then, to a *good* father? No, but to a father. Is a brother unjust? Well, preserve your own just relation toward him. Consider not what *he* does, but what *you* are to do to keep your own will in a state conformable to nature, for another cannot hurt you unless you please. You will then be hurt when you consent to be hurt. In this manner, therefore, if you accustom yourself to contemplate the relations of neighbor, citizen, commander, you can deduce from each the corresponding duties.

31. Be assured that the essence of piety toward the gods lies in this—to form right

opinions concerning them, as existing and as governing the universe justly and well. And fix yourself in this resolution, to obey them, and yield to them, and willingly follow them amidst all events, as being ruled by the most perfect wisdom. For thus you will never find fault with the gods, nor accuse them of neglecting you. . . .

35. When you do anything from a clear judgment that it ought to be done, never shrink from being seen to do it, even though the world should misunderstand it; for if you are not acting rightly, shun the action itself; if you are, why fear those who wrongly censure you?

38. As in walking you take care not to tread upon a nail, or turn your foot, so likewise take care not to hurt the ruling faculty of your mind. And if we were to guard against this in every action, we should enter upon action more safely.

42. When any person does ill by you, or speaks ill of you, remember that he acts or speaks from an impression that it is right for him to do so. Now it is not possible that he should follow what appears right to you, but only what appears so to himself. Therefore, if he judges from false appearances, he is the person hurt, since he, too, is the person deceived. For if anyone takes a true proposition to be false, the proposition is not hurt, but only the man is deceived, Setting out, then, from these principles, you will meekly bear with a person who reviles you, for you will say upon every occasion, "It seemed so to him."

READING 2
The Starry Heavens Above and the Moral Law Within
Kant
(from *Critique of Pure Reason*)

Two things fill the mind with ever new and increasing awe and admiration the more frequently and continuously reflection is occupied with them: The starred heaven above me and the moral law within me. I ought not to seek either outside my field of vision, as though they were either shrouded in obscurity or were visionary. I see them confronting me and link them immediately with the consciousness of my existence. The first begins with the place I occupy in the external world of sense, and expands the connection in which I find myself into the incalculable vastness of worlds upon worlds, of systems within systems, over endless ages of their periodic motion, their beginnings and perpetuation. The second starts from my invisible self, from my personality, and depicts me as in a world possessing true infinitude which can be sensed only by the intellect. With this I recognize myself to be in a necessary and general connection, not just accidentally as appears to be the case with the external world. Through this recognition I also see myself linked with all visible worlds. The first view of a numberless quantity of worlds destroys my importance, so to speak, since I am an *animal-like being* who must return its matter from whence it came to the planet (a mere speck in the universe), after having been endowed with vital energy for a short time, one does not know how. The second view raises my value infinitely, as an *intelligence*, through my personality; for in this personality the moral law reveals a life independent of animality and even of the entire world of sense. This is true at least as far as one can infer from the purposeful determination of my existence according to this law. This is not restricted to the conditions and limits of this life, but radiates into the infinite.

READING 3
On Law
I-II (First Part of the Second Part)
Thomas Aquinas

(St. Thomas divides this work into Parts, Questions and Articles. Questions deal with larger headings subdivided into Articles which deal with individual topics. Each Article comprises introductory objections; the body, *corpus,* as his main statement; then replies to the objections. What follows is the body of each Article cited. The translation is that of the English Dominican Province, except where indicated.)

QUESTION 90: ON THE ESSENCE OF LAW

Article 1. Law is a matter of reason

Law is a rule and measure of acts, whereby man is induced to act or is restrained from acting: for *lex.* (law) is derived from *ligare* (to bind), because it binds one to act. Now the rule and measure of human acts is the reason, which is the first principle of human acts, as is evident from what has been stated above since it belongs to the reason to direct to the end, which is the first principle in all matters of action, according to the Philosopher [Aristotle]. Now that which is the principle in any genus, is the rule and measure of that genus: for instance, unity in the genus of numbers, and the first movement in the genus of movements. Consequently it follows that law is something pertaining to reason.

Article 2. Law is directed to the common good

As stated above, the law belongs to that which is a principle of human acts, because it is their rule and measure. Now as reason is a principle of human acts, so in reason itself there is something which is the principle in respect of all the rest: wherefore to this principle chiefly and mainly law must needs be referred.—Now the first principle in practical matters, which are the object of the practical reason, is the last end: and the last end of human life is bliss or happiness, as stated above.

Consequently the law must needs regard principally the relationship to happiness. Moreover, since every part is ordained to the whole, as imperfect to perfect; and since one man is a part of the perfect community, the law must needs regard properly the relationship to universal happiness. Wherefore the Philosopher, in the above definition of legal matters mentions both happiness and the body politic: for he says (*Ethic.* v. I) that we call those legal matters *just, which are adapted to produce and preserve happiness and its parts for the body politic:* since the state is a perfect community, as he says in *Polit.* i. I.

Now in every genus, that which belongs to it chiefly is the principle of the others, and the others belong to that genus in subordination to that thing: thus fire, which is chief among hot things, is the cause of heat in mixed bodies, and these are said to be hot in so far as they have a share of fire. Consequently, since the law is chiefly ordained to the common good, any other precept in regard to some individual work, must needs be devoid of the nature of a law, save in so far as it regards the common good. Therefore every law is ordained to the common good.

Article 3. Law is not a matter of only one person's reason

A law, properly speaking, regards first and foremost the order to the common good. Now to order anything to the common good, belongs either to the whole people, or to someone who is the vicegerent of the whole people. And therefore the making of a law belongs either to the whole people or to a public personage who has care of the whole people: since in all other matters the directing of anything to the end concerns him to whom the end belongs.

Article 4. A law, to be a law, must be promulgated

As stated above (A. I), a law is imposed on others by way of a rule and measure. Now a rule or measure is imposed by being applied to those who are to be ruled and measured by it. Wherefore, in order that a law obtain the binding force which is proper to a law, it must needs be applied to the men who have to be ruled by it. Such application is made by its being notified to them by promulgation. Wherefore promulgation is necessary for the law to obtain its force.

Thus from the four preceding articles, the definition of law may be gathered; and it is nothing else than an ordinance of reason for the common good made by him who has care of the community, and promulgated.

QUESTION 91: ON DIFFERENT KINDS OF LAW

Article 1. Eternal Law

As stated above a law is nothing else but a dictate of practical reason emanating from the ruler who governs a perfect community. Now it is evident, granted that the world is ruled by Divine Providence, as was stated in the . . . that the whole community of the universe is governed by Divine Reason. Wherefore the very Idea of the government of things in God the Ruler of the universe, has the nature of a law. And since the Divine Reason's conception of things is not subject to time but is eternal, according to Prov. viii. 23, therefore it is that this kind of law must be called eternal.

Article 2. Natural Law

As stated above, law, being a rule and measure, can be in a person in two ways: in one way, as in him that rules and measures; in another way, as in that which is ruled and measured,

since a thing is ruled and measured, in so far as it partakes of the rule or measure. Wherefore, since all things subject to Divine providence are ruled and measured by the eternal law, as was stated above (A. I); it is evident that all things partake somewhat of the eternal law, in so far as, namely, from its being imprinted on them, they derive their respective inclinations to their proper acts and ends. Now among all others, the rational creature is subject to Divine providence in the most excellent way, in so far as it partakes of a share of providence, by being provident both for itself and for others. Wherefore it has a share of the Eternal Reason, whereby it has a natural inclination to its proper act and end: and this participation of the eternal law in the rational creature is called the natural law. Hence the Psalmist after saying (Ps. iv. 6): *Offer up the sacrifice of justice,* as though someone asked what the works of justice are, adds: *Many say, Who showeth us good things?* in answer to which question he says: *The light of Thy countenance, O Lord, is signed upon us:* thus implying that the light of natural reason, whereby we discern what is good and what is evil, which is the function of the natural law, is nothing else than an imprint on us of the Divine light. It is therefore evident that the natural law is nothing else than the rational creature's participation of the eternal law.

Article 3. Human Law

As stated above, a law is a dictate of the practical reason. Now it is to be observed that the same procedure takes place in the practical and in the speculative reason: for each proceeds from principles to conclusions, as stated above. Accordingly we conclude that just as, in the speculative reason, from naturally known indemonstrable principles, we draw the conclusions of the various sciences, the knowledge of which is not imparted to us by nature, but acquired by the efforts of reason, so too it is from the precepts of the natural law, as from general and indemonstrable principles, that the human reason needs to proceed to the more particular determination of certain matters. These particular determinations, devised by human reason, are called human laws, provided the other essential conditions of law be observed, as stated above.

Wherefore Tully says in his *Rhetoric (De Invent. Rhet.* ii.) that *justice has its source in nature; thence certain things came into custom by reason of their utility; afterwards these things which emanated from nature and were approved by custom, were sanctioned by fear and reverence for the law.*

QUESTION 94: THE NATURAL LAW

Article 2. (selection) The first precept of the law

The first principle of practical reason is founded on the notion of the good, that is, the good is what all things seek. The first precept of the law, therefore, is that good is to be done and sought after, and evil to be avoided.

On this principle all other precepts of the natural law are founded so that all those things to be done or avoided, which practical reason naturally recognizes as human goods, are precepts of the natural law. [Translated by abh]

Article 4. How the natural law is universal and particular

As stated above, to the natural law belongs those things to which a man is inclined naturally: and among these it is proper to man to be inclined to act according to reason. Now the process of reason is from the common to the proper, as stated in *Phys.* i. The speculative reason, however, is differently situated in this matter, from the practical reason. For, since the speculative reason is busied chiefly with necessary things, which cannot be otherwise than they are, its proper conclusions, like the universal principles, contain the truth without fail. The practical reason, on the other hand, is busied with contingent matters, about which human actions are concerned: and consequently, although there is necessity in the general principles, the more we descend to matters of detail, the more frequently we encounter defects. Accordingly then in speculative matters truth is the same in all men, both as to principles and as to conclusions: although the truth is not known to all as regards the conclusions, but only as regards the principles which are called common notions. But in matters of action, truth or practical rectitude is not the same for all, as to matters of detail, but only as to the general principles: and where there is the same rectitude in matters of detail, it is not equally known to all.

It is therefore evident that, as regards the general principles whether of speculative or of practical reason, truth or rectitude is the same for all, and is equally known by all. As to the proper conclusions of the speculative reason, the truth is the same for all, but is not equally known to all: thus it is true for all that the three angles of a triangle are together equal to two right angles, although it is not known to all. But as to the proper conclusions of the practical reason, neither is the truth or rectitude the same for all, nor, where it is the same, is it equally known by all. Thus it is right and true for all to act according to reason: and from this principle it follows as a proper conclusion, that goods entrusted to another should be restored to their owner. Now this is true for the majority of cases: but it may happen in a particular case that it would be injurious, and therefore unreasonable, to restore goods held in trust; for instance if they are claimed for the purpose of fighting against one's country. And this principle will be found to fail the more, according as we descend further into detail, *e.g.,* if one were to say that goods held in trust should be restored with such and such a guarantee, or in such and such a way; because the greater the number of conditions added, the greater the number of ways in which the principle may fail, so that it be not right to restore or not to restore.

Consequently we must say that the natural law, as to general first principles, is the same for all in both rightness and knowability. But when it comes to individual cases, which are to be thought of as conclusions from the general principles, the natural law is the same for all only in the majority of cases, both in rightness and knowability. Still, in some few instances, it can fail both in rightness because of certain obstacles (just as any nature subject to change may be constrained by certain obstacles), and in knowability because reason itself is impeded by passion, or evil habit, or evil disposition of nature; for example, though thievery is expressly contrary to the natural law, it was not considered wrong by the Germans, as recounted by Julius Caesar in his *Gallic Wars* (VI, 23). [Translated by abh]

Article 5. Permanence and change in the natural law

Natural law may be understood to change in two ways. First, by way of addition, in which sense nothing prevents the natural law from being changed inasmuch as many things benefiting human life have been added over and above the natural law, by either divine law or human law.

Second, change in the natural law can be understood by way of subtraction, that is, what formerly was a matter of natural law ceases to be so, with the proviso that the natural law remains unchangeable in its first principles. Secondary principles (conclusions from first principles as they touch upon particular matters) are unchangeable in the sense that they hold true in the majority of cases, as already said. But the natural law may be changed in some few cases for particular reasons, because there may be some unique causes preventing the observance of such precepts, as said above.

READING 4
The Moral Law and the Highest Good
Immanuel Kant
(from *Critique of Practical Reason*)

The achievement of the highest good in the world is the necessary object of a will determinable by the moral law. In such a will, however, the complete fitness of intentions to the moral law is the supreme condition of the highest good. This aptness, therefore, must be just as possible as its object, because it is contained in the command that requires us to promote the latter. But complete fitness of the will to the moral law is holiness, which is a perfection of which no rational being in the world of sense is at any time capable. But since it is required as practically necessary, it can be found only in an endless progress to that complete fitness; on principles of pure practical reason, it is necessary to assume such a practical progress as the real object of our will.

This infinite progress is possible, however, only under the presupposition of an infinitely enduring existence and personality of the same rational being; this is called the immortality of the soul. Thus the highest good is practically possible only on the supposition of the immortality of the soul, and the latter, as inseparably bound to the moral law, is a postulate of pure practical reason. By a postulate of pure practical reason I understand

a theoretical proposition which is not as such demonstrable, but which is an inseparable corollary of an *a priori* unconditionally valid practical law.

The thesis of the moral destiny of our nature, viz., that it is able only in an infinite progress to attain complete fitness to the moral law, is of great use, not merely for the present purpose of supplementing the impotence of speculative reason, but also with respect to religion. Without it, either the moral law is completely degraded from its holiness, by being made out as lenient (indulgent) and thus compliant to our convenience, or our notions of our vocation and our expectation are strained to an unattainable destination, i.e., a hoped-for complete attainment of holiness of will, thus losing themselves in fanatical theosophical dreams which completely contradict our knowledge of ourselves. In either case, we are only hindered in the unceasing striving toward and precise and persistent obedience to a command of reason which is stern, unindulgent, truly commanding, really and not just ideally possible. Only endless progress from lower to higher stages of moral perfection is possible to a rational but finite being. The Infinite Being, to whom the temporal condition is nothing, sees in this series, which is for us without end, a whole conformable to the moral law; holiness, which His law inexorably commands in order to be true to His justice in the share He assigns to each in the highest good, is to be found in a single intellectual intuition of the existence of rational beings. All that can be granted to a creature with respect to hope for this share is consciousness of his tried character. And on the basis of his previous progress from the worse to the morally better, and of the immutability of intention which thus becomes known to him, he may hope for a further uninterrupted continuation of this progress, however long his existence may last, even beyond his life. But he cannot hope here or at any foreseeable point of his future existence to be fully adequate to God's will, without indulgence or remission which would not harmonize with justice. This he can do only in the infinity of his duration which God alone can survey.

READING 5
Following the Divine Law Is the Path of Justice, Virtue and Goodness
Plato
(from *Laws*)

ATHENIAN: "Friends," we say to them,—"God, as the old tradition declares, holding in His hand the beginning, middle, and end of all that is, travels according to His nature in a straight line towards the accomplishment of His end. Justice always accompanies Him, and is the punisher of those who fall short of the divine law. To justice, he who would be happy holds fast, and follows in her company with all humility and order; but he who is lifted up with pride, or elated by wealth or rank, or beauty, who is young and foolish, and has a soul hot with insolence, and thinks that he has no need of any guide or ruler, but is able himself to be the guide of others, he, I say, is left deserted of God; and being thus deserted, he takes to him others who are like himself, and dances about, throwing all things into confusion, and many think that he is a great man, but in a short time he pays a penalty which justice cannot but approve, and is utterly destroyed, and his family and city with him. Wherefore, seeing that human things are thus ordered, what should a wise man do or think, or not do or think?"

CLEINIAS: Every man ought to make up his mind that he will be one of the followers of God; there can be no doubt of that.

ATH: Then what life is agreeable to God, and becoming in His followers? One only, expressed once for all in the old saying that "like agrees with like, with measure measure," but things which have no measure agree neither with themselves nor with the things which have. Now God ought to be to us the measure of all things, and not man, as men commonly say (Protagoras): the words are far more true of Him. And he who would be dear to God must, as far as is possible, be like Him and such as He is. Wherefore the temperate man is the friend of God, for he is like Him; and the intemperate man is unlike Him, and different from Him, and unjust. And the same applies to other things; and this is the conclusion, which is also the noblest and truest of all sayings,—that for the good man to offer sacrifice to the Gods, and hold converse with them by means of prayers and offerings and every kind of service, is the noblest and best of all things, and also the most conducive to a happy life, and very fit and meet. But with the bad man, the opposite of this is true: for the bad man has an impure soul, whereas the good is pure; and from one who is polluted, neither a good man nor God can without impropriety receive gifts. Wherefore the unholy do only waste their much service upon the Gods, but when offered by any holy man, such service is most acceptable to them. This is the mark at which we ought to aim. But what weapons shall we use, and how shall we direct them? In the first place, we affirm that next after the Olympian Gods and the Gods of the State, honour should be given to the Gods below; they should receive everything in even numbers, and of the second choice, and ill omen, while the odd numbers, and the first choice, and the things of lucky omen, are given to the Gods above, by him who would rightly hit the mark of piety. Next to these Gods, a wise man will do service to the demons or spirits, and then to the heroes, and after them will follow the private and ancestral Gods, who are worshipped as the law prescribes in the places which are sacred to them. Next comes the honour of living parents, to whom, as is meet, we have to pay the first and greatest and oldest of all debts, considering that all which a man has belongs to those who gave him birth and brought him up, and that he must do all that he can to minister to them, first, in his property, secondly, in his person, and thirdly, in his soul, in return for the endless care and travail which they bestowed upon him of old, in the days of his infancy, and which he is now to pay back to them when they are old and in the extremity of their need. And all his life long he ought never to utter, or to have uttered, an unbecoming word to them; for of light and fleeting words the penalty is most severe; Nemesis, the messenger of justice, is appointed to watch over all such matters. When they are angry and want to satisfy their feelings in word or deed, he should give way to them; for a father who thinks that he has been wronged by his son may be reasonably expected to be very angry. At their death, the most moderate funeral is best, neither exceeding the customary expense, nor yet falling short of the honour which has been usually shown by the former generation to their parents. And let a man not forget to pay the yearly tribute of respect to the dead, honouring them chiefly by omitting nothing that conduces to a perpetual remembrance of them, and giving a reasonable portion of his fortune to the dead. Doing this, and living after this manner, we shall receive our reward from the Gods and those who are above us [i.e. the demons]; and we shall spend our days for the most part in good hope. And how a man ought to order what relates to his descendants and his kindred and friends and fellow-citizens, and the rites of hospitality taught by Heaven, and the intercourse which arises out of all these duties, with a view to the embellishment and orderly regulation of his own life—these things, I say, the laws, as we proceed with them, will acomplish, partly persuading, and partly when natures do not yield to the persuasion of custom, chastising them by might and right, and will thus render our state, if the Gods co-operate with us, prosperous and happy.

READING 6
Justice as Fairness
John Rawls
(from *Justice as Fairness*)

That the principles of justice may be regarded as arising in the manner described illustrates an important fact about them. Not only does it bring out the idea that justice is a primitive moral notion in that it arises once the concept of morality is imposed on mutually self-interested agents similarly circumstanced, but it emphasizes that, fundamental to justice, is the concept of fairness which relates to right dealing between persons who are cooperating with or competing against one another, as when one speaks of fair games, fair competition, and fair bargains. The question of fairness arises when free persons, who have no authority over one another, are engaging in a joint activity and among themselves settling or acknowledging the rules which define it and which determine the respective shares in its benefits and burdens. A practice will strike the parties as fair if none feels that, by participating in it, they or any of the others are taken advantage of, or forced to give in to claims which they do not regard as legitimate. This implies that each has a conception of legitimate claims which he thinks it reasonable for others as well as himself to acknowledge. If one thinks of the principles of justice as arising in the manner described, then they do define this sort of conception. A practice is just or fair, then, when it satisfies the principles which those who participate in it could propose to one another for mutual acceptance under the aforementioned circumstances. Persons engaged in a just, or fair, practice can face one another openly and support their respective positions, should they appear questionable, by reference to principles which it is reasonable to expect each to accept. . . .

Now if the participants in a practice accept its rules as fair, and so have no complaint to lodge against it, there arises a prima facie duty (and a corresponding prima facie right) of the parties to each other to act in accordance with the practice when it falls upon them to comply. When any number of persons engage in a practice, or conduct a joint undertaking according to rules, and thus restrict their liberty, those who have submitted to these restrictions when required have the right to a similar acquiescence on the part of those who have benefited by their submission. These conditions will obtain if a practice is correctly acknowledged to be fair, for in this case all who participate in it will benefit from it.

Chapter Four

The Meaning of Human Life

ASK "WHY?"

The first question we ask when we encounter a new thing is "what is it?" or "what's it for?" And we ask similar questions even of things we've lived with for a long time, and taken for granted, like a friend, a book, a place, and then suddenly, often at the moment of losing it, we ask why it meant so much to us, what purpose it served, and what it was for. Could this be the case with us as people who rush nonstop through life without giving serious attention to "what's it all about?" At what point in a person's life does he or she ask such a question? It may be asked sooner, it may be asked later, or it may be asked in different ways, but it finally has to be asked.

Literarily, in *Anna Karenina*, Leo Tolstoy describes his alter ego, the thoughtful and reflective landowner Levin, as "stricken with horror, not so much at death, as at life, without the least conception of its origin, its purpose, its reason, its nature." On a given day, though otherwise thoroughly occupied, "Levin's thoughts were busy with the one and only subject, outside his farming, that interested him at this time, and in everything he sought a bearing on his questions: 'What am I?' Where am I? And why am I here?' " Philosophically, Aristotle asks the same questions: "Have the carpenter, then, and the tanner certain functions or activities, and has man none? Is he born without a function? . . . What then can this be?" He lays out his project of inquiry in the first chapter of the *Ethics*, to seek for a "complete life" in which "human good turns out to be an activity of soul in accordance with virtue." Similarly our project in this chapter is to inquire whether man has a purpose, whether he has a "function," why he exists.

Aristotle, always bent on searching for ultimate explanations, serves as a good model to follow in trying to fix upon the highest explanation we can find to understand the "why" of our existence, else we run the risk of becoming mute on the most fundamental of all questions, like the students of Democritus who were advised against inquiring into the enigma of existence. We have to be careful in the way we think of "function" because the everyday notion of function, which helps us to understand the *raison d'être* of most things around us, doesn't help us to understand the meaning of human existence. The question "what's it for?" cannot be asked of man as it is of a hammer or a paint brush, for that would entail taking man to be an instrument in service of something else. But the human being is not an instrument, is not for something else, so the question of meaning pertains to the *very being* of man, to the nature of the human being. The question should really be put this way, "why man?" and the answer must lie in the deepest recesses of human life. There is no question but that life is a mystery, that life is a sea of activity into which we are summarily immersed, and that life cannot be sloughed off like a discarded carapace. As the theologian Romano Guardini, writing in the latter half of the last century, put it: "Life enjoys, abstains from, suffers, struggles, creates. It enfolds and permeates things, joins other life, resulting not in a mere sum, but in new and manifold vitality. Foremost and fundamental, it is and remains an inexplicable enigma" (R #1).

We really don't want to let questions about the purpose of life go unasked, and still less to go unanswered, at least as far as we can make it out. How does the story of man end? or this individual man? I may understand quite readily what *particular* acts are about: I turn the knob to open the door; I affix the stamp to mail the letter; I engage in this act to beget a child; I speak gently to offer solace to a disturbed friend. I can answer the question "why?" of the actions of my life as individual actions but the *why of my life as a whole* has still to be asked. Why life? If life has a purpose, an end, what is it? That I exist is a no-brainer. "Why?" is not.

The question has to be asked in a text of this kind because we are trying to fit the meaning of morality into the wider context in which the morality of an act is to be judged. From the very beginning, we settled on the notion that we know a thing primarily by how it's related to other things, and the more we grasp the thing-in-its-relatedness the more we know it. We understand the "why" of an acorn when we see the life of the tree as a whole. We would understand the "why" of a human being too if we were able to see human life as a whole, but we cannot, and that's the problem. Every conceivable answer has been given to the question, so there is a real temptation to throw one's hands up in a gesture of hopelessness, as exemplified in the Greek philosopher Epicurus, who denied that human life had any meaning whatsoever. In retrieving the philosophy of the Pre-Socratic atomists, Epicurus tried to find a way to allay the anxieties of life by presenting a physical universe in which every single thing was a configuration of atoms, and when the configuration ceased to be, so did the thing. When, therefore, the configuration called man ceases to be, so does man. Man then does not have to worry or be anxious about what he did in this life as the reason for suffering in the next, because there isn't any: "Death means nothing to us." Nor therefore does life.

THE MYSTERY OF EVIL

The futility of grasping the meaning of life as portrayed by Epicurus can readily be appreciated when we consider the many negatives pressing upon us. One dismal thing after another, tragedy upon tragedy, loss upon loss; so many sorrows, so much suffering; illness, pain, poverty, vulnerability; the trials of Job but without the happy ending. Angst. The farmer comes to the big city for the first time, walks down the street when a stone, just loosened from a lintel overhead, falls down and crushes him. Unbelievable. A boss so berates his well-meaning secretary that she goes into a catatonic stupor. Thoughtless. Death-dealing leukemia takes the life of a child. Tragic. The earthquakes, fires, floods, tsunamis, and other natural devastations wreak untold damage to life on the planet. Unspeakable. Thus, *evil*, as the antipathy of good, enters into human affairs and becomes the antipathy of life. Did the existentialists of several generations ago have it right, that life *is* absurd? and therefore meaningless?

The presence of evil in the world is, far and away, the most difficult problem a philosopher, or any thinking person, is called upon to face, for it squarely opposes the good around which human nature turns and has the power to nullify existence as the foundation for any human value. When we look at the awful aspect of events like those just mentioned, we may be well prone to say, "That's what life really *is*, why should I expect more?" But by the same token, we may well respond to the deeper promptings within us and say, "I know life is like that, but I also know it should *not be* like that, otherwise why do I call it awful, or sorrowful, or full of suffering?" We instinctively know that these events are *contrary to what human life should be.* The tragic visitations upon man by the force of nature are evils of a physical kind and are most frequently referred to by the term *natural evil.* But the deepest level of evil, that of iniquity, is the exercise of free will on the part of human beings against each other, to hate, defraud, deceive, injure, brutalize, despoil, belittle, ignore, burden, disrespect, marginalize; these are referred to as *moral evil.* We don't hesitate to call actions of this kind *inhuman;* they contravene the intuitive understanding we have of the value of human life. They are inimical to what *human* means. We comprehend them as evil precisely because they run contrary to the expectations we have as human beings.

Some philosophers, like the Scottish philosopher David Hume, have painted vivid verbal pictures of the evils afflicting human life. In his *Dialogues Concerning Natural Religion,* he writes: "Man [said Philo, usually speaking for Hume] is the greatest enemy of man. Oppression, injustice, contempt, contumely, violence, sedition, war, calumny, treachery, fraud; by these they mutually torment each other: And they would soon dissolve that society which they had formed, were it not for the dread of still greater ills, which must attend their separation. . . The disorders of the mind, continued Demea, though more secret, are not perhaps less dismal and vexatious. Remorse, shame, anguish, rage, disappointment, anxiety, fear, dejection, despair: who has ever passed through life without cruel inroads from these tormentors? Labour and poverty, so abhorred by everyone, are the certain lot of the far greater number. . . All the goods of life united would not make a very happy man: But all the ills united would make a wretch indeed." We'll see later how Hume tried to compromise the gap between the goodness of God and the evils of creation (R #2).

In the following century, John Henry Cardinal Newman, perhaps the most influential English divine of the nineteenth century and the direct religious opposite to Hume, painted a picture of evil in the world similar to Hume's, yet he, unlike Hume, wrote from the persuasion of an infinitely good God who created this world as a manifestation of that goodness. Newman, in a well-known quotation, collects the evils faced by human beings under the heading of original sin, taken as the rubric for the totality of evil: "To consider . . . the disappointments of life, the defeat of good, the success of evil, physical pain, mental anguish, the prevalence and intensity of sin, the pervading idolatries, the corruptions, the dreary hopeless irreligion, the condition of the whole race, so fearfully yet exactly described in the Apostle's words, 'having no hope without God in the world,'—all this is a vision to dizzy and appal; and inflicts upon the mind the sense of a profound mystery, which is absolutely beyond human solution . . . What shall be said to this heart-piercing, reason-bewildering fact? I can only answer that . . . the human race is implicated in some terrible aboriginal calamity. It is out of joint with the purposes of its Creator" (R #3).

Take a contemporary example on the same theme of the futility of life. In the section dealing with the meaning of life in his popular book *What Does It All Mean?* Thomas Nagel leaves off trying to furnish an answer because any answer is negated by a pervading pointlessness in life dominated, as it is, by absurdity. A mouse, says Professor Nagel in a complementary article entitled "The Absurd," never faces absurdity because it has no understanding and could never grasp the concept of transcendence and its link with the absurd as a human being can. But his statement that the concept of transcendence is linked to absurdity is troubling; it drains transcendence of any genuine meaning. Relationship and transcendence go hand in hand, for whatever is related to another transcends itself to the extent of its relatedness, and whatever transcends itself is to that extent related. To say that self "transcends itself" is not really saying it satisfactorily, for it suggests reaching out for something beyond the sum total of attributes already constituting the self. Its meaning is, rather, that *transcendence is a part of the self* but one that reaches out for fulfillment, which, if wanting, renders a self incomplete. When a person, for example, is related to another as a friend, he is going beyond himself, "transcending himself," to complete his very self by satisfying some *inward urgency for fulfillment*; friendship is not absurd; it touches the very meaning of humanity. Or, a totally different example: You have often heard it said that an artist, a musician let's say, can give himself so intimately to the music he's playing that he becomes one with it—he is creating himself anew while he plays. If transcendence refers to the natural tendency of reaching out for something beyond self for its fulfillment, then *transcendence is a link to meaning*, not absurdity. It is true that we can appreciate this more readily in *particular* instances, which we can see, than in human life *as a whole*, which we cannot. Perhaps this is what drives Nagel to a false dilemma regarding the handling of life: Either live with it, making the best of it by trying to lead a life "less absurd than most," or abandon life altogether. It's not entirely clear why Nagel insists that transcendence is a link to absurdity rather than fulfillment, for it is fulfillment that responds to the demands of our experience, not absurdity (in "The Absurd", *Journal of Philosophy*, 68, #20, Oct. 2003, p. 762).

In the last analysis, the term *absurd* is but one way of referring to the problem of evil which, as we have seen, is not a respecter of persons. Its afflictions attack everyone regardless of class, gender, age, office, habitat, wealth, ethnicity, or religion, but there is an aspect of evil that makes it a unique stumbling block for those who affirm the existence of God. They would ask, if creation is the act of an infinitely good God, how is it possible for evil to exist in the very world He created? A profoundly perplexing question for the theist, a dilemma that ultimately cannot be resolved. The theist can deny neither God nor evil. If the dilemma were to be expressed in terms of a cord held under tension, with God at one end and evil on the other, tension would be relieved if either end were to be denied, but such denial cannot take place. If the theist denies the existence of evil, he has lost faith in his experience. If he denies the existence of God, he has lost faith in his intellect. But he cannot deny either fidelity. Conclusion? He has to live with the tension, with the problem as to how the goodness of God and evil in the world are to be reconciled with each other. It's not my point here to review the arguments for God's existence, but it's very much to my point to recall that Thomas Aquinas himself, often cited for his formal presentation of those arguments, recognizes that the prime objection against them is the presence of evil in the world. In addressing the problem of evil, therefore, Thomas would lean toward defending God against the charge that He is ultimately responsible for the existence of evil, a posture philosophically referred to as *theodicy*. In its classical form, it was developed by St. Augustine, St. Thomas's predecessor by 800 years. Let's turn to Augustine to see how he managed a response.

Where, first of all, Augustine asks, is evil to be found? It cannot be a thing, as a dog is a thing, or a blade of grass, or a human being; that is, it is not a substance. Nor does it exist in the fashion of the color red, or the speed of light, or the weight of stone; that is, it is not a quality that attaches to a substance. Yet it is *there*. It's in the real world. Since evil cannot be understood as a "thing" in any ordinary sense, it must be understood in some other sense, and that other sense is that it exists as a *deprivation*, as a lack, or want of something that should be present: the lack of sight in a sighted being, or amnesia in a mature person, or the lack of rightness in a moral act. Evil is found in the good, not where good is, but where it is not. God, then, for Augustine, cannot be thought of as the cause of evil in the world, for whatever thing God creates, inasmuch as it is, is good: "All of nature is good, since the Creator of all nature is supremely good. But nature is not supremely and immutably good as is the Creator of it. Thus the good in created things can be diminished and augmented. For good to be diminished is evil . . . " If a thing is diminished, or corrupted, "its corruption is an evil because it is, by just so much, a privation of the good. Where there is no privation of the good, there is no evil." How, then, can God be faulted for creating things which, by definition, are imperfect, limited, and finite? Rather is He to be credited for the good they are. Should a painter, having colored his roses red, be blamed for not painting them white? Or should an author be blamed for the book he did not write? (R #4).

Augustine, of course, has uppermost in mind the evil that man can do by his *deliberate choice of evil,* by his free will, which we discussed in an earlier chapter. Once again, if God is responsible for the very being of human beings, it does not follow that He is responsible for the choices they make. No, the human being is free by nature; an unfree human being would be a contradiction; man is responsible for his actions. If evil in general cannot be attributed to God, then sin, the quintessential evil, cannot be attributed to Him either; it must be attributed to man as an abuse of the power for good the Creator gave him. "No man is ever blamed for what he has not been given, but he is justly blamed if he has not done what he should have done . . . When a man does not do what he ought, God the Creator is not at fault."

Though this is but a thumbnail sketch of Augustine's approach to the problem of evil, it is clear, as already mentioned, that it is an ingenious effort to absolve God from blame as the author of evil, the whole point of theodicy; but if, to any extent, it is unsatisfactory as a "solution" to the God-side of the problem, it is still less of a solution as far as the human-side is concerned. Mankind is still in the dark as to why human beings have to suffer the impersonal onslaught of nature and the unabated malevolence of fellow human beings.

For a moment, let's return to Hume's account of evil in the world. He does not follow Aquinas in the view that evil in the world is the strongest objection to the *existence* of God, but, he maintains, evil must be taken into account in our appraisal of the *nature* of God. It's not easy to discern a consistency in the thought of Hume at this point, but he does seem to allow, if not require, on the basis of design in nature, the existence of a being, not supreme nor all-powerful, but a god sufficiently proportioned to the unhappy condition of the world—a god, therefore, who is uncaring for the life of man, unconcerned about tragedy, and untouched by the human condition. A deist in one sense, a skeptic in another, Hume in any sense holds to a god morally indifferent to human activities, a "moral atheist" as one interpreter acutely puts it.

THE CENTRALITY OF THE GOOD

Accepting the fact that evil cannot be explained away, there is a response to it that unexpectedly comes from another quarter. Evil is evil, and there is no way of saying that good can come from evil as if it were the cause of good. Nothing good can come from evil *per se.* But evil can become the *occasion* of good when it compels us to see it as an epiphany of human meaning, as when we react to the afflictions of others by trying to reduce their suffering by our help or compassion. Examples are countless: The response of parents to their child's illness; compassion for the victims of catastrophe; solace offered to a friend in a personal tragedy; the kind word to a woman abused. In all these, there is a new expression of love that never existed before. Each example is an instance of evil being overcome by its opposite, namely, good. This is not at all suggesting that the existence of evil is justified by the good that comes about, but it is recognizing that *good is at the core of what it means to be a human being.* The kind of actions, then, we expect of human beings are those that are commensurate with humanity, those that fulfill and complete it, and reveal the dimensions of *goodness and love* as indispensable to human life. The entirety of life is not given in a single episode, but over the course of time in which we grow and develop. No one can say, at any particular time, that he or she is a perfect human being, for we know, by our experience, that life is unfinished and that growth-in-life is continual *movement toward a fuller meaning of life.* Does that movement have any direction? Ought we not ask what our growth culminates in? In what does human fulfillment eventually consist?

If a sense of direction in life can be found, then it's got to be found at the *highest point of our experience.* Unlike other living beings of our world, the human being possesses the attribute of *freedom,* recognized in our actions as spontaneous, voluntary, unconstrained, undetermined, and a matter of *free choice,* as described in an earlier chapter. If freedom is at the center of human life, it's there we should first look for an entrée into the meaning of life. Take a closer look at the choices we make and ask why we make them. We make a choice, do we not, because there is a fulfillment of some kind involved in the choice, some kind of completion, the satisfaction of some want, which is the first reason for placing the act? We choose what we choose precisely because it is *choosable.* This may sound redundant but, ask yourself, could it be otherwise? Wouldn't it be a contradiction to say that you are choosing something that's *not* choosable? It doesn't make any sense, for the very fact we choose it means it is choosable. And because the thing of our choice is seen as fulfillment, satisfaction, completion, we are wont to call it not only choosable but *good.* This is true of each and every act we could possibly place; every act of ours is centered on the good and thereby proclaims the **centrality of the good** for the human being.

A reasonable objection to this position may well be that a person chooses to do something horrible, and a horrible thing cannot be called good. However, that horrible thing, as perverse as it may be, is still choosable as far as the agent is concerned; the perversion lies in taking evil as good; what is evil is seen by the agent as good. Again, every human act of ours has a purpose, an end; a purposeless action is impossible; it is a contradiction. In other words, *the will is the faculty of the good*; the will and its choice of the good are inseparable—*every* choice is made for the good, or what appears to be good; it cannot be otherwise, for that's the nature of the will. In classical terminology, *good is the object of the will*; that's what the will is for. And I, the being that wills, am naturally oriented to the good—another way of saying that the human being in its very existence is centered on the good.

LOVE AS THE HIGHEST GOOD OF OUR EXPERIENCE

There are many good things in life: a pleasant day, a conversation, a delightful dinner, education, reading, art, money, and so on. Is there any good you can think of that would warrant being called the *highest good* of your experience? Suppose a person had any of the goods just mentioned to the nth degree, could that person still be unhappy? Put it this way: The possession of any one of these goods in no way guarantees a full human life (R #5). Not many years ago, one of the richest men in America, with all the money he could ever want at his fingertips, wound up his days sitting home alone in his private movie theater watching endless reruns of cowboy pictures! Or, what is a person, young or old, really saying when he or she cries out, "If I die tomorrow, who'll miss me?" It's the cry of loneliness, of despair, of a meaningless life, of being *unloved*: what is unrelated cannot be loved. A child, separated from its mother, yet given toys and comfort galore, will cry until restored to its mother and her love. "All those lonely people" said the song, and "Saturday night is the loneliest night of the week!" Many years ago, in the Port of New York Authority bus terminal, there was a mezzanine where travelers could rest a while. For whatever reason, the mezzanine was permanently closed and newspaper accounts spoke of the great inconvenience this created for hundreds of people. Tales were told of the particular sadness this meant for many of the elderly of the neighborhood, widows and widowers among them, who would go there every noontime just to be with someone, and even hold hands with people they barely knew!

It is only in the environment of person-to-person that we can speak of love, and to speak of it as the good beyond all other goods because it touches the deepest level of what it means to be human. Notice how much of the behavior we call good centers on the *other* person. Kindness, to an *other* person; respect, for an *other* person; and sympathy, for an *other* person. The self and the other, lover and beloved, as we've seen so often in bipolar relationships, are mutually self-defining: There is no self without the other, and no other without the self. This is what happens in the love relationship of person-to-person. One needs the other to be oneself. Such a need is not to be seen as a case of using the other, but rather the recognition that in each one of us there is a natural transcendence toward the other, a yearning or "desire" if you will for the fulfillment proper to being human.

A poignant instance of this need for an "other" is found in Viktor Frankl's *Man's Search for Meaning*, an extremely influential book of a generation ago. Frankl was an Austrian psychiatrist who, along with his family, was entrapped in the horrors of the Nazi Zeit and was able to endure the sufferings of an unspeakable episode in a concentration camp by thinking on the love that he and his wife had for each other. He was "transfixed" by the truth that love is the ultimate and highest goal that man can aspire to: "Then I grasped the meaning of the greatest secret that human poetry and human thought and belief have to impart: *The salvation of man is through love and in love*" (R #6).

LOVE AND DEATH IN PLATO'S *APOLOGY*

We may recall a remarkable adumbration of this aspect of our experience in the *Apology* when Socrates muses aloud for the men of Athens on what life after death may be like. In the beginning of the dialogue, Socrates says that he has no idea what death might be like, but as he comes toward the end of his defense, in Plato's literary account, he makes a fairly definitive assertion about his expectations. After rejecting other options, he states that there *is* life after death, and the most important ingredient of that life is, as it were, an extension of what is most important in this life, namely *friendship*. If we hope to uncover something of the future, it makes eminent sense to extrapolate from what we know now to a time ahead, of which we know nothing. So, from his experience of love in human friendship as the highest good this life can offer, Socrates looks for a yet higher level of this love in the life to come. Love of another is what the human heart seeks, and the passion with which Socrates says it bears a message of its own, "If death is the journey to another place, and there, as men say, all the dead abide, what good, O my friends and judges, can be greater than this? If indeed when the pilgrim arrives in the world beyond, . . . and finds the . . . sons of God who were righteous in their own life, that pilgrimage will be worth making. What would a man not give if he might converse with Orpheus and Musaeus and Hesiod and Homer? Nay, if this be true, let me die again and again" (R #7).

Socrates sews together into a seamless garment the three major factors of life we've been considering, *love, good,* and *happiness.* For him, who taught incessantly that ethical wisdom is the essential drive of the good person, the life of virtue is the truly human life; but it doesn't stand alone. It stands together with love for another around whom a moral life is framed and with whom the union, called *happiness,* is created. For the great teacher of Athens it is the fact of death that summons us to a constant renewal of this moral focus; if death is to be mastered, it can only be through a good life. Death paradoxically is a *life-revealing* event for it compels us to ask what life, every moment on the edge of being lost, is all about. And, for him, life is all about the good which, though enjoyed here, promises more as death opens up to a fuller dimension of life: "Wherefore, O judges, be of good cheer about death, and know of a certainty, that no evil can happen to a good man, either in life or after death" (R #8).

THE IN-GATHERING OF ALL LOVES

Extending this insight of Socrates suggests that it is the deep-seatedness of love that imparts a profound moral quality to our actions. There is a primordial sense in which every good act is an expression of love and every evil act an offense against it. Just as the soul gives life to the body, love gives life to the moral act. Love is the soul of the moral life. It doesn't follow from this that we must be conscious at every moment of the linkage between the moral act and the love that suffuses it, any more than we must be conscious at every moment of the linkage between the living body and the soul that animates it, but there must be a ready acknowledgment that love pertains to the essence of the human being lest we fail in understanding what being human really means.

But an interesting question arises. If love is the very substance of human life, how come we can't *define* it? Try defining it, and every time you think you have it in your grasp, it slips away. Why? Because, as discussed earlier on, what is utterly fundamental cannot be defined in terms of anything else—there's nothing left to define it with. To be known, then, love has to be known from within itself, like knowledge of our own existence: You know you exist; you don't explain it in terms of anything else, you do not prove it, for you know it directly. Similarly love. You know it on its own terms. You know that you love. And love invites you to express it in a thousand different ways, each a symbol of the reality: the box of candy, the rose, the thoughtful gesture, the sacrifice, the kiss, the making of love, the redress of hurt feelings. The poet exhibits a deep appreciation of how love shuns being defined when she asks, "How much do I love thee? Let me count the ways."

There are many goods and many loves in life, and the possession of one does not negate any other; the good experienced in seeing a work of art, for example, does not override the good experienced in the love spouses have for each other. It's not that these different kinds of good merely exist side-by-side, unconnected, but rather that they exist together as one in the person whose totality of life yearns for an *ordered relationship of the goods experienced* (R #9). Personal love as the highest good of our experience does not destroy the other goods of our experience; it gives them a new sense of wholeness. Should there be a still *higher dimension of personal love,* it would not destroy the other loves of our life, but in turn would give them a new sense of wholeness too. Think of it this way: If it is true that whatever is, is good, it is also true that what-ever *is* in the ultimate sense is also *good* in the ultimate sense. This can be said only of God, whose existence is not being argued for here but accepted as an established truth of enormous importance; as Ludwig Wittgenstein put it, "to believe in God means to see that life has meaning" (R #10). If we are wont to say of God, in order to secure attributes fitting his existence, that He is almighty and omniscient, we must be ready to say as well that they are meaningless as regards creation unless they are conjoined, first and foremost, with love, whence the gospel of John declares but one divine attribute, that "God is love." In his own mystical way, the French philosopher Henri Bergson, in reference to our effort to fathom the universal pervasiveness of love, avers that we must "push to the limit" the idea of a universe that is, above all, "the visible and tangible aspect of love and of the need for loving" (*Two Sources*, c.3).

That our actions take on a moral tone from this higher perspective is conveyed by Tolstoy's fictional character Levin, mentioned earlier, who finds an answer to the questions on the meaning of life that so agitated him across the years. It came as he "got talking" with one of his simple peasant workers, Fiodr, who chanced to say: "'Oh well, of course, folks are different. One man lives for his own wants and nothing else—take Mityuka, who only thinks of his belly . . . but Fokanich is an upright old man. He thinks of his soul. He does not forget God.' 'Not forget God? And how does he live for his soul?' Levin almost shouted. 'Why, that's plain enough: it's living rightly, in God's way.' The peasant's words had the effect of an electric spark, suddenly transforming and welding into one whole series of disjointed, impotent, separate ideas that never ceased to occupy his mind. . . . and Fiodr declares that . . . we must live for truth, for God, and a hint of it is enough to make me understand what he means!" (R #11).

It is the person-to-person love of our experience that shapes the humanness of our lives and looks to its continuity with the person-to-Person love that brings it to fulfillment. No other good, no other love, is lost or lessened in this new dimension but is subsumed into a transcendent whole while retaining its own identity: The flame of a match is not lost in the flame of the sun, for it burns with a new brightness. Every human being in this life is called to person-to-person love, and to person-to-Person love as well, and even though, as an unfortunate matter of fact, this may not be the experience of every individual, complete fulfillment can never be forfeited: It is the final unfolding of all humanity, and of each and every human being. The human condition, however, is such that the possession of *any* good in this life is subject to impermanence or losability out of human frailty, uncertainty, or death, so that the possession of the ultimate good must be achieved in a life that follows; the fullness of life after death has to be seen as the destiny of mankind. Were this not so, it would be a contradiction as blatant as a square circle or unequal justice (R #12).

We have been speaking of the *centrality of the good* in our lives and how this would be meaningless apart from *love* and *happiness*. It is in these three, good, love, and happiness, taken not as three separate ingredients combined for human fulfillment, but as one, that we find the answer to the questions we began with, why man? What is the meaning of man? That's why Aristotle could affirm that "we conceive happiness to be the most desir-able of all things and not merely as one among other good things . . . it is something final and self-sufficient, being the end of all action" (R #13). *Happiness* is the *love* of the *good* that human nature is ordered to. It invests our actions with a finality our nature calls for.

It's fitting to close this chapter by noting how Thomas Aquinas and Dante Alighieri present the triad of good, love, and happiness in the didactic words of the philosopher and the lyrical words of the poet. St. Thomas writes, "It is apparent that love, properly speaking, consists in the yearning one has to bind himself with another in some way; for which reason Dionysius describes love as a *unitive force* . . . Now, it is God's goodness, reflected in all things of his creation, that is exceedingly great and deep-seated, since he is himself his own goodness. Wherefore in God not only is there true love, but also perfect and abiding love" (R #14).

In a similar vein, in *The Divine Comedy*, Dante, renowned for translating philosophical and theological truths into poetry, asks hirgil, to counsel him as to the meaning of love:

> So I said, "Master, my seeing is so enlivened
> by your light that I am able to understand
> clearly the outlines of your explanation.
> Therefore, I pray you, gentle father,
> explain to me what love is, as you refer to it
> every good action and its opposite."
> "Turn toward me," he said, "the sharpened beams
> of your intelligence, and you will see
> the misleading way of the blind who say, 'Follow me.'
> The soul, as it is created quick to love,
> is drawn by everything that pleases it
> as soon as pleasure stirs to action in it
> Your apprehension takes from the real world
> an image and unfolds it within you
> so that it becomes what the soul turns to,
> and if the soul, so turned, inclines to it,
> that inclination is love, and it is nature,
> which is bound to you every time by pleasure.
> Then, as fire through its own form moves upward,
> born as it is to rise in the very place
> where it stays longest in its own matter,
> so the caught soul enters into desire,
> which is a movement of the spirit that never
> rests until what it loves brings joy to it"

> Purgatorio, xviii, 11–33
> (trans. W.S. Merwin)

READINGS

READING 1
Life and Death
Romano Guardini

(from *The Lord*)

What a strange phenomenon this thing called life! It is the *a priori* of everything, foundation of existence which, when threatened, responds with that unqualified reaction known as self-defense, which has its own laws. It is a miracle so precious that at times the sheer bliss of it is overwhelming. Life enjoys, abstains from, suffers, struggles, creates. It enfolds and permeates things, joins with other life, resulting not in a mere sum, but in new and manifold vitality. Foremost and fundamental, it is and remains an inexplicable enigma. For is it not strange that in order to possess one thing we must relinquish another? That in order to do anything of genuine value we must focus our attention on it and away from all else? That when we wish to do justice to one person we do injustice to all others, if only by not likewise accepting them into our range of heart, simply because there is not room enough for everyone? That when we experience any powerful sensation, then only in ignorance of what it is, the instant we try to understand it, the current is cut. Wakefulness is wonderful but tiring, and we long to lose ourselves in sleep. Sleep is pleasant, but how terrible to sleep away half our lives! Life is unity. It demands containment of things; demands that we preserve our entity in the superabundance around us, and yet that we throw the fullness of that entity into our slightest act. In all directions run the cracks. Everywhere we look we are faced with an either-or, this-or-that. And woe to us if we do not choose, for from the clean-cut choice of the one or the other, depends the decency of existence. The moment we attempt to grab everything, we have nothing properly. If we try to do justice to everyone, we are just to no one, only contemptible. As soon as we reach out to embrace the whole, our individuality dissolves into nothing. Thus we are forced to make clear decisions, and by so doing—woe again!—to cut into our existence. Really, life has something impossible about it! It is forced to desire what it can never have. It is as though from the very start some fundamental mistake had been made, as evinced by everything we do. And then the dreadful transitoriness of it all. Is it possible that things exist only through self-destruction? Doesn't to live mean to pass over? The more intensively we live, the swifter the passing? Doesn't death begin already in life? With desperate truth a modern biologist has defined life as the movement towards death. Yet what a monstrosity to define life only as part of death! Is death then better ordered? Must we surrender our deepest instinct to Biology? Research has pointed out that early man experienced death quite differently from us. He by no means considered it something self-understood, as the necessary antipode of life. Instinctively he felt that death was not only unnecessary, but wrong. Where it occurred it came as the result of a particular cause, of a spiritual power of evil—even in cases of accident, old age, or death in battle. Let us wait a moment with our smile and with an open mind try to accept the possibility of the primitive's being closer to the truth than the professor.

Is death self-understood? If it were, we should accept it with a sense, however heavy, of fulfillment. Where is there such a death? True, here or there we find someone who sacrifices his life for some great cause; or another who has grown weary of the burden of life and accepts death with a sense of relief. But does the man exist who from the very essence of his vitality, consents to death? I have never met him, and what I have heard of him was poppycock. Man's natural stand to death is one of defense and protest, both rooted deep in the core of his being. Death is not self-understood, and every attempt to make it so ends in immeasurable melancholy.

Nevertheless, this life and death of ours belong together. When the romanticists attempted to make them the opposite poles of existence, comparing them with light and dark, height and depth, ascent and decline, this was aesthetic thoughtlessness under which lay a demonic illusion. But on one point they were right: our present forms of living and dying do belong together.

READING 2
Evil: Disorder in an Ordered World
David Hume
(from *Dialogues Concerning Natural Religion*)

As to authorities, replied *Demea*, you need not seek them. Look round this library of *Cleanthes*. I shall venture to affirm, that, except authors of particular sciences, such as chemistry or botany, who have no occasion to treat of human life, there scarce is one of those innumerable writers, from whom the sense of human misery has not, in some passages or other, extorted a complaint and confession of it. At least, the chance is entirely on that side; and no one author has ever, so far as I can recollect, been so extravagant as to deny it.

. . .

And why should man, added he, pretend to an exemption from the lot of all other animals? The whole earth, believe me, *Philo,* is cursed and polluted. A perpetual war is kindled amongst all living creatures. Necessity, hunger, want stimulate the strong and courageous: fear, anxiety, terror agitate the weak and infirm. The first entrance into life gives anguish to the new-born infant and to its wretched parent: Weakness, impotence, distress attend each stage of that life: And it is at last finished in agony and horror.

Observe, too, says *Philo,* the curious artifices of nature, in order to embitter the life of every living being. The stronger prey upon the weaker, and keep them in perpetual terror and anxiety. The weaker too, in their turn, often prey upon the stronger, and vex and molest them without relaxation. Consider that innumerable race of insects, which either are bred on the body of each animal, or flying about infix their stings in him. These insects have others still less than themselves, which torment them. And thus on each hand, before and behind, above and below, every animal is surrounded with enemies, which incessantly seek his misery and destruction.

. . .

Besides, consider, *Demea:* this very society, by which we surmount those wild beasts, our natural enemies; what new enemies does it not raise to us? What woe and misery does it not occasion? Man is the greatest enemy of man. Oppression, injustice, contempt, contumely, violence, sedition, war, calumny, treachery, fraud; by these they mutually torment each other: And they would soon dissolve that society which they had formed, were it not for the dread of still greater ills, which must attend their separation.

. . .

And is it possible, *Cleanthes,* said *Philo,* that after all these reflections, and infinitely more,

which might be suggested, you can still persevere in your anthropomorphism, and assert the moral attributes of the deity, his justice, benevolence, mercy, and rectitude, to be of the same nature with these virtues in human creatures? His power we allow is infinite: Whatever he wills is executed: But neither man nor any other animal is happy: Therefore he does not will their happiness. His wisdom is infinite: He is never mistaken in choosing the means to any end: But the course of nature tends not to human or animal felicity: Therefore it is not established for that purpose. Through the whole compass of human knowledge, there are no inferences more certain and infallible than these. In what respect, then, do his benevolence and mercy resemble the benevolence and mercy of men?

. . .

But I will be contented to retire still from this retrenchment: For I deny that you can ever force me in it: I will allow, that pain or misery in man is *compatible* with infinite power and goodness in the deity, even in your sense of these attributes: What are you advanced by all these concessions? A mere possible compatibility is not sufficient. You must *prove* these pure, unmixed, and uncontrollable attributes from the present mixed and confused phenomena, and from these alone. A hopeful undertaking! Were the phenomena ever so pure and unmixed, yet, being finite, they would be insufficient for that purpose. How much more, where they are also so jarring and discordant? Here, *Cleanthes,* I find myself at ease in my argument. Here I triumph. Formerly, when we argued concerning the natural attributes of intelligence and design, I needed all my sceptical and metaphysical subtlety to elude your grasp. In many views of the universe, and of its parts, particularly the latter, the beauty and fitness of final causes strike us with such irresistible force that all objections appear (what I believe they really are) mere cavils and sophisms; nor can we then imagine how it was ever possible for us to repose any weight on them. But there is no view of human life or of the condition of mankind, from which, without the greatest violence, we can infer the moral attributes, or learn that infinite benevolence, conjoined with infinite power and infinite wisdom, which we must discover by the eyes of faith alone. It is your turn now to tug the labouring oar, and to support your philosophical subtleties against the dictates of plain reason and experience.

. . .

The disorders of the mind, said *Demea*, though more secret, are not perhaps less dismal and vexatious. Remorse, shame, anguish, rage, disappointment, anxiety, fear, dejection, despair: who has ever passed through life without cruel inroads from these tormentors? How many have scarcely ever felt any better sensations? Labour and poverty, so abhorred by everyone, are the certain lot of the far greater number: And those few privileged persons, who enjoy ease and opulence, never reach contentment or true felicity. All the goods of life united would not make a very happy man: But all the ills united would make a wretch indeed; and any one of them almost (and who can be free from every one) nay often the absence of one good (and who can possess all) is sufficient to render life ineligible.

Were a stranger to drop, on a sudden, into this world, I would show him, as a specimen of its ills, a hospital full of diseases, a prison crowded with malefactors and debtors, a field of battle strewed with carcasses, a fleet foundering in the ocean, a nation languishing under tyranny, famine, or pestilence. To turn the gay side of life to him, and give him a notion of its pleasures; whither should I conduct him? to a ball, to an opera, to court? He might justly think, that I was only showing him a diversity of distress and sorrow.

Dialogues concerning Natural Religion Part X

I shall further add, said *Cleanthes*, to what you have so well urged, that one great advantage of the principle of theism is, that it is the only system of cosmogony, which can be rendered intelligible and complete, and yet can throughout preserve a strong analogy to what we every day see and experience in the world. The comparison of the universe to a machine of human contrivance is so obvious and natural, and is justified by so many instances of order and design in nature, that it must immediately strike all unprejudiced apprehensions, and procure universal approbation. Whoever attempts to weaken this theory, cannot pretend to succeed by establishing in its place any other, that is precise and determinate: It is sufficient for him, if he starts doubts and difficulties; and by remote and abstract views of things, reach that suspense of judgement, which is here the utmost boundary of his wishes. But besides, that this state of mind is in itself unsatisfactory, it can never be steadily maintained against such striking appearances, as continually engage us into the religious hypothesis. A false, absurd system, human nature, from the force of prejudice, is capable of adhering to, with obstinacy and perseverance: But no system at all, in opposition to a theory, supported by strong and obvious reason, by natural propensity, and by early education, I think it absolutely impossible to maintain or defend.

So little, replied *Philo*, do I esteem this suspense of judgement in the present case to be possible, that I am apt to suspect there enters somewhat of a dispute of words into this controversy, more than is usually imagined. That the works of nature bear a great analogy to the productions of art is evident; and according to all rules of good reasoning, we ought to infer, if we argue at all concerning them, that their causes have a proportional analogy. But as there are also considerable differences, we have reason to suppose a proportional difference in the causes; and in particular ought to attribute a much higher degree of power and energy to the supreme cause than any we have ever observed in mankind. Here then the existence of a DEITY is plainly ascertained by reason; and if we make it a question, whether, on account of these analogies, we can properly call him a *mind* or *intelligence*, notwithstanding the vast difference, which may reasonably be supposed between him and human minds; what is this but a mere verbal controversy? No man can deny the analogies between the effects: To restrain ourselves from inquiring concerning the causes is scarcely possible: From this inquiry, the legitimate conclusion is, that the causes have also an analogy: And if we are not contented with calling the first and supreme cause a GOD or DEITY, but desire to vary the expression; what can we call him but MIND or THOUGHT, to which he is justly supposed to bear a considerable resemblance?

READING 3
The World Is Out of Joint
John Henry Newman
(from *Apologia*)

Starting then with the being of a God, (which, as I have said, is as certain to me as the certainty of my own existence, though when I try to put the grounds of that certainty into logical shape I find a difficulty in doing so in mood and figure to my satisfaction,) I look out of myself into the world of men, and there I see a sight which fills me with unspeakable distress. The world seems simply to give the lie to that great truth, of which my whole being is so full; and the effect upon me is, in consequence, as a matter of necessity, as confusing as if it denied that I am in existence myself. If I looked into a mirror, and did not see my face, I should have the sort of feeling which actually comes upon me, when I look into this living busy world, and see no reflexion of its Creator. This is, to me, one of those great difficulties of this absolute primary truth, to which I referred just now. Were it not for this voice, speaking so clearly in my conscience and my heart, I should be an atheist, or a pantheist, or a polytheist when I looked into the world. I am speaking for myself only; and I am far from denying the real force of the arguments in proof of a God, drawn from the general facts of human society and the course of history, but these do not warm me or enlighten me; they do not take away the winter of my desolation, or make the buds unfold and the leaves grow within me, and my moral being rejoice. The sight of the world is nothing else than the prophet's scroll, full of "lamentations, and mourning, and woe."

To consider the world in its length and breadth, its various history, the many races of man, their starts, their fortunes, their mutual alienation, their conflicts; and then their ways, habits, governments, forms of worship; their enterprises, their aimless courses, their random achievements and acquirements, the impotent conclusion of longstanding facts, the tokens so faint and broken of a superintending design, the blind evolution of what turn out to be great powers or truths, the progress of things, as if from unreasoning elements, not towards final causes, the greatness and littleness of man, his far-reaching aims, his short duration, the curtain hung over his futurity, the disappointments of life, the defeat of good, the success of evil, physical pain, mental anguish, the prevalence and intensity of sin, the pervading idolatries, the corruptions, the dreary hopeless irreligion, that condition of the whole race, so fearfully yet exactly described in the Apostle's words, "having no hope and without God in the world,"—all this is a vision to dizzy and appal; and inflicts upon the mind the sense of a profound mystery, which is absolutely beyond human solution.

What shall be said to this heart-piercing, reason-bewildering fact? I can only answer, that either there is no Creator, or this living society of men is in a true sense discarded from His presence. . . .

And so I argue about the world;—*if* there be a God, *since* there is a God, the human race is implicated in some terrible aboriginal calamity. It is out of joint with the purposes of its Creator. This is a fact, a fact as true as the fact of its existence; and thus the doctrine of what is theologically called original sin becomes to me almost as certain as that the world exists, and as the existence of God.

READING 4
The Problem of Evil
St. Augustine

(from *Confessions*)

III

But though I said and firmly held that the Lord God was incorruptible and unalterable and in no way changeable, the true God who made not only our souls but our bodies also, and not only our souls and bodies but all things whatsoever, as yet I did not see, clear and unravelled, what was the cause of Evil. Whatever that cause might be, I saw that no explanation would do which would force me to believe the immutable God mutable; for if I did that I should have been the very thing I was trying to find [namely a cause of evil]. From now it was with no anxiety that I sought it, for I was sure that what the Manichees said was not true. With all my heart I rejected them, because I saw that while they inquired as to the source of evil, they were full of evil themselves, in that they preferred rather to hold that Your substance suffered evil than that their own substance committed it.

So I set myself to examine an idea I had heard—namely that our free-will is the cause of our doing evil, and Your just judgment the cause of our suffering evil. I could not clearly discern this. I endeavoured to draw the eye of my mind from the pit, but I was again plunged into it; and as often as I tried, so often was I plunged back. But it raised me a little towards Your light that I now was as much aware that I had a will as that I had a life. And when I willed to do or not do anything, I was quite certain that it was myself and no other who willed, and I came to see that the cause of my sin lay there.

But what I did unwillingly, it still seemed to me that I rather suffered than did, and I judged it to be not my fault but my punishment: though as I held You most just, I was quite ready to admit that I was being justly punished.

But I asked further: "Who made me? Was it not my God, who is not only Good but Goodness itself? What root reason is there for my willing evil and failing to will good, which would make it just for me to be punished? Who was it that set and ingrafted in me this root of bitterness, since I was wholly made by my most loving God? If the devil is the author, where does the devil come from? And if by his own perverse will he was turned from a good angel into a devil, what was the origin in him of the perverse will by which he became a devil, since by the all-good Creator he was made wholly angel?" By such thoughts I was cast down again and almost stifled; yet I was not brought down so far as the hell of that error, where no man confesses unto You, the error which holds rather that You suffer evil than that man does it.

IV

I now tried to discover other truths, as I had already come to realise that incorruptible is better than corruptible, so that You must be incorruptible, whatever might be Your nature. For no soul ever has been able to conceive or ever will be able to conceive anything better than You, the supreme and perfect Good. Therefore since the incorruptible is unquestionably to be held greater than the corruptible—and I so held it—I could now draw the conclusion that unless You were incorruptible there was something better than my God. But seeing the superiority of the incorruptible, I should have looked for You in that truth and have learned from it where evil is—that is learned the origin of the corruption by which Your substance cannot be violated. For there is no way in which corruption can affect our God, whether by His will or by necessity or by accident: for He is God, and what He wills is good, and Himself is Goodness; whereas to be corrupted is not good. Not are You against Your will constrained to anything, for Your will is not greater than Your power. It would be greater, only if You were greater than Yourself: for God's will and God's power are alike God Himself. And what unlooked-for accident can befall You, since You know all things? No nature exists save because You know it. Why indeed should I multiply reasons to show that the substance which is God is not corruptible, since if it were, it would not be God?

V

I sought for the origin of evil, but I sought in an evil manner, and failed to see the evil that there was in my manner of enquiry. I ranged before the eyes of my mind the whole creation, both what we are able to see—earth and sea and air and stars and trees and portal creatures; and what we cannot see—like the firmament of the Heaven above, and all its angels and spiritual powers: though even these I imagined as if they were bodies disposed each in its own place. And I made one great mass of God's Creation, distinguished according to the kinds of bodies in it, whether they really were bodies, or only such bodies as I imagined spirits to be. I made it huge, not as huge as it is, which I had no means of knowing, but as huge as might be necessary, though in every direction finite. And I saw You, Lord, in every part containing and penetrating it, Yourself altogether infinite: as if Your Being were a sea, infinite and immeasurable everywhere, though still only a sea; and within it there were some mighty but not infinite sponge, and that sponge filled in every part with the immeasurable sea. Thus I conceived Your Creation as finite, and filled utterly by Yourself, and You were Infinite. And I said: "Here is God, and here is what God has created; and God is good, mightily and incomparably better than all these; but of His goodness He created them good: and see how He contains and fills them."

"Where then is evil, and what is its source, and how has it crept into the Creation? What is its root, what is its seed? Can it be that it is wholly without being? But why should we fear and be on guard against what is not? Or if our fear of it is groundless, then our very fear is itself an evil thing. For by it the heart is driven and tormented for no cause; and that evil is all the worse, if there is nothing to fear yet we do fear. Thus either there is evil which we fear, or the fact that we fear is evil."

"Whence then is evil, since God who is good made all things good? It was the greater and supreme Good who made these lesser goods, but Creator and Creation are alike good. Whence then comes evil? Was there perhaps some evil matter of which He made this creation, matter which He formed and ordered, while yet leaving in it some element which He did not convert into good? But why? Could He who was omnipotent be unable to change matter wholly so that no evil might remain in it? Indeed why did He choose to make anything of it and not rather by the same omnipotence cause it wholly not to be? Could it possibly have existed against His will? And if it had so existed from eternity, why did He allow it so long to continue through the infinite spaces of time past, and then after so long a while choose to make something of it? If He did suddenly decide to act, surely the Omnipotent should rather have caused it to cease to be, that He Himself, the true and supreme and infinite Good, alone should be. Or, since it was not good that He who was good should frame and create something not good, could He not have taken away and reduced to nothing that matter which was evil, and provided good matter of which to create all things? For He would not be omnipotent if He could not create something good without the aid of matter which He had not created."

Such thoughts I revolved in my unhappy heart, which was further burdened and gnawed at by the fear that I should die without having found the truth. But at least the faith of Your Christ, Our Lord and Saviour, taught by the Catholic Church, stood firm in my heart, though on many points I was still uncertain and swerving from the norm of doctrine. Yet my mind did not forsake it, but drank of it more deeply with every day that passed.

XII

And it became clear to me that corruptible things are good: if they were supremely good they could not be corrupted, but also if they were not good at all they could not be corrupted: if they were supremely good they would be incorruptible, if they were in no way good there would be nothing in them that might corrupt. For corruption damages; and unless it diminished goodness, it would not damage. Thus either corruption does no damage, which is impossible or—and this is the certain proof of it—all things that are corrupted are deprived of some goodness. But if they were deprived of all goodness, they would be totally without being. For if they might still be and yet could no longer be corrupted, they would be better than in their first state, because they would abide henceforth incorruptibly. What could be more monstrous than to say that things could be made better by losing all their goodness? If they were deprived of all goodness, they would be altogether nothing: therefore as long as they are, they are good. Thus whatsoever things are, are good; and that evil whose origin I sought is not a substance, because if it were a substance it would be good. For either it would be an incorruptible substance, that is to say, the highest goodness; or it would be a corruptible substance, which would not be corruptible unless it were good. Thus I saw and clearly realized that You have made all things good, and that there are no substances not made by You. And because all the things You have made are not equal, they have a goodness [over and above] as a totality: because they are good individually, and they are very good all together, for our God has made all things very good.

XIII

To You, then, evil utterly is not—and not only to You, but to Your whole creation likewise, evil is not: because there is nothing over and above Your Creation that could break in or derange the order that You imposed upon it. But in certain of its parts there are some things which we call evil because they do not harmonize with other things; yet these same things do harmonize with still others and thus are good; and in themselves they are good. All these things which do not harmonize with one another, do suit well with that lower part of creation which we call the earth, which has its cloudy and windy sky in some way apt to it. God forbid that I should say: "I wish that these things were not"; because even if I saw only them, though I should want better things, yet even for them alone I should praise You: for that You are to be praised, things of earth show—*dragons, and all deeps, fire, hail, snow, ice, and stormy winds, which fulfill Thy word; mountains and all hills, fruitful trees and all cedars; beasts and all cattle, serpents and feathered fowl; kings of the earth and all people, princes and all judges of the earth; young men and maidens, old men and young, praise Thy name*. And since from the heavens, O our God, *all Thy angels praise Thee in the high places, and all Thy hosts, sun and moon, all the stars and lights, the heavens of heavens, and the waters that are above the heavens, praise thy name*—I no longer desired better, because I had thought upon them all and with clearer judgment I realized that while certain higher things are better than lower things, yet all things together are better than the higher alone.

READING 5
Man's Ultimate Happiness Is not in this Life
Thomas Aquinas
(from *Summa Contra Gentes*)

If then human happiness does not consist in the knowledge of God, whereby He is commonly known by all or most men according to some vague estimate, nor again in the knowledge of God whereby He is known demonstratively in speculative science, nor in the knowledge of God whereby He is known by faith, as has been shown above; if again it is impossible in this life to arrive at a higher knowledge of God so as to know Him in His essence, or to understand other pure spirits, and thereby attain to a nearer knowledge of God; and still final happiness must be placed in some knowledge of God; it follows that it is impossible for the final happiness of man *to* be in this life.

2. The last end of man bounds his natural desire, so that, when that is reached, nothing further is sought: for if there is still a tendency to something else, the end of rest is not yet gained. But that cannot be in this life: for the more one understands, the more is the desire of understanding, natural to all men, increased.

3. When one gains happiness, he gains also stability and rest. All have this idea of happiness, that it involves stability as a necessary condition: hence the philosopher says that we do not take man for a chameleon. But in this life there is no stability: for however happy a man be called, sicknesses and misfortunes may always happen to debar him from that activity, whatever it is, wherein happiness consists.

4. It seems unfitting and irrational that the period of development should be great and the period of duration small: for it would follow that nature for the greater part of its time went without its final perfection. Hence we see that animals that live for a short time take a short time in arriving at maturity. But if human happiness consists in perfect activity according to perfect virtue, whether intellectual or moral, such happiness cannot accrue to man till after a long lapse of time; and this is especially apparent in speculative activity, in which the happiness of man is ultimately placed. For scarcely in extreme age can a man arrive a perfect view of scientific truth; and then for the most part there is little of human life left.

5. That is the perfect good of happiness, which is absolutely free from admixture of evil, as that is perfect whiteness, which is absolutely unmingled with black. But it is impossible for man in the state of this life to be altogether free from evils,—not to say bodily evils, as hunger, thirst, cold and heat, but even from evils of the soul. There is no man living who is not at times disturbed by inordinate passions, who does not at times overstep the mean in which virtue consists, or fall short of it, who is not in some things deceived, or ignorant of what he wishes to know, or driven to weak surmises on points where he would like absolute certainty.

6. Man naturally shrinks from death, and is sad at the thought of it. Yet man must die, and therefore cannot be perfectly happy while here he lives.

7. Happiness consists, not in habit, but in activity: for habits are for the sake of acts. But it is impossible in this life to do any act continually.

8. The more a thing is desired and loved, the greater grief and sadness does its loss bring. But if final happiness be to this world, it will certainly be lost, at least by death; and it is uncertain whether it will last till death, since to any man there may possibly happen in this life diseases totally debarring him from any virtuous activity, such as insanity. Such happiness therefore must always have a natural pendent of sadness.

But it may be replied that whereas happiness is the good of an intelligent nature, true and perfect happiness belongs to those in whom intelligent nature is found in its perfection, that is, in pure spirits; but in man it is found imperfectly by way of a limited participation. And this seems to have been the mind of Aristotle: hence, enquiring whether misfortunes take away happiness, after showing that happiness lies in virtuous activities, which are the most permanent things in this life, he concludes that they who enjoy such perfection in this life are "happy for men," meaning that they do not absolutely attain happiness, but only in a human way.

Now it is demonstrable that the aforesaid answer is not to the undoing of the arguments above alleged. For (*a*) though man is inferior in the order of nature to pure spirits, yet he is superior to irrational creatures; and therefore he must gain his final end in a more perfect way than they. But they gain their final end so perfectly as to seek nothing further. Thus the natural desire of dumb animals is at rest in the enjoyment of sensual delights. Much more must the natural desire of man be put to rest by his arrival at his last end. But that is impossible in this life: therefore it must be attained after this life.

(*b*) It is impossible for a natural desire to be empty and vain: for nature does nothing in vain. But the desire of nature (for happiness) would be empty and vain, if it never possibly could be fulfilled. Therefore this natural desire of man is fulfillable. But not in this life. Therefore it must be fulfilled after this life.

Alexander and Averroes laid it down that the final happiness of man is not in such knowledge as is possible to man through the speculative sciences, but in a knowledge gained by conjunction with a separately subsistent intelligence, which conjunction they conceived to be possible to man in this life. But because Aristotle saw that there was no other knowledge for man in this life than that which is through the speculative sciences, he supposed man not to gain perfect happiness, but a limited measure of happiness suited to his state. In all which investigation it sufficiently appears how hard pressed on this side and on that these fine geniuses (*praeclara ingenia*) were. From this stress of difficulty we shall find escape in positing, according to the proofs already given, that man can arrive at true happiness after this life, the soul of man being immortal. In this disembodied state the soul will understand in the way in which pure spirits understand. The final happiness of man then will be in the knowledge of God, which the human soul has after this life according to the manner in which pure spirits know Him.

Therefore the Lord promises us *reward in heaven* (Matt, v, 12), and says that the saints shall be *as the angels* (Matt, xxii, 30), who *see the face of God in heaven* (Matt, xviii, 10).

READING 6
Salvation Through Love
Victor Frankl
(from *Man's Search for Meaning*)

That brought thoughts of my own wife to mind. And as we stumbled on for miles, slipping on icy spots, supporting each other time and again, dragging one another up and onward, nothing was said, but we both knew: each of us was thinking of his wife. Occasionally I looked at the sky, where the stars were fading and the pink light of the morning was beginning to spread behind a dark bank of clouds. But my mind clung to my wife's image, imagining it with an uncanny acuteness. I heard her answering me, saw her smile, her frank and encouraging look. Real or not, her look was then more luminous than the sun which was beginning to rise.

A thought transfixed me: for the first time in my life I saw the truth as it is set into song by so many poets, proclaimed as the final wisdom by so many thinkers. The truth—that love is the ultimate and the highest goal to which man can aspire. Then I grasped the meaning of the greatest secret that human poetry and human thought and belief have to impart: *The salvation of man is through love and in love.* I understood how a man who has nothing left in this world still may know bliss, be it only for a brief moment, in the contemplation of his beloved. In a position of utter desolation, when man cannot express himself in positive action, when his only achievement may consist in enduring his sufferings in the right way—an honorable way—in such a position man can, through loving contemplation of the image he carries of his beloved, achieve fulfillment. For the first time in my life I was able to understand the meaning of the words, "The angels are lost in perpetual contemplation of an infinite glory."

READING 7
The Death of Socrates
(from *Phaedo*)

We will do our best, said Crito: And in what way shall we bury you?

In any way that you like; but you must get hold of me, and take care that I do not run away from you. Then he turned to us, and added with a smile:—I cannot make Crito believe that I am the same Socrates who has been talking and conducting the argument; he fancies that I am the other Socrates whom he will soon see, a dead body—and he asks, How shall he bury me? And though I have spoken many words in the endeavour to show that when I have drunk the poison I shall leave you and go to the joys of the blessed,—these words of mine, with which I was comforting you and myself, have had, as I perceive, no effect upon Crito. And therefore I want you to be surety for me to him now, as at the trial he was surety to the judges for me: but let the promise be of another sort; for he was surety for me to the judges that I would remain, and you must be my surety to him that I shall not remain, but go away and depart; and then he will suffer less at my death, and not be grieved when he sees my body being burned or buried. I would not have him sorrow at my hard lot, or say at the burial, Thus we lay out Socrates, or, Thus we follow him to the grave or bury him; for false words are not only evil in themselves, but they infect the soul with evil. Be of good cheer then, my dear Crito, and say that you are burying my body only, and do with that whatever is usual, and what you think best.

When he had spoken these words, he arose and went into a chamber to bathe; Crito followed him and told us to wait. So we remained behind, talking and thinking of the subject of discourse, and also of the greatness of our sorrow; he was like a father of whom we were being bereaved, and we were about to pass the rest of our lives as orphans. When he had taken his bath his children were brought to him—(he had two young sons and an elder one); and the women of his family also came, and he talked to them and gave them a few directions in the presence of Crito; then he dismissed them and returned to us.

Now the hour of sunset was near, for a good deal of time had passed while he was within. When he came out, he sat down with us again after his bath, but not much was said. Soon the jailer, who was the servant of the Eleven, entered and stood by him, saying:—To you, Socrates, whom I know to be the noblest and gentlest and best of all who ever came to this place, I will not impute the angry feelings of other men, who rage and swear at me, when, in obedience to the authorities, I bid them drink the poison—indeed, I am sure that you will not be angry with me; for others, as you are aware, and not I, are to blame. And so fare you well, and try to bear lightly what must needs be— you know my errand. Then bursting into tears he turned away and went out.

Socrates looked at him and said: I return your good wishes, and will do as you bid. Then turning to us, he said, How charming the man is: since I have been in prison he has always been coming to see me, and at times he would talk to me, and was as good to me as could be, and now see how generously he sorrows on my account. We must do as he says, Crito; and therefore let the cup be brought, if the poison is prepared: if not, let the attendant prepare some.

Yet, said Crito, the sun is still upon the hill-tops, and I know that many a one has taken the draught late, and after the announcement has been made to him, he has eaten and drunk, and enjoyed the society of his beloved; do not hurry—there is time enough.

Socrates said: Yes, Crito, and they of whom you speak are right in so acting, for they think that they will be gainers by the delay; but I am right in not following their example, for I do not think that I should gain anything by drinking the poison a little later; I should only be ridiculous in my own eyes for sparing and saving a life which is already forfeit. Please then to do as I say, and not refuse me.

Crito made a sign to the servant, who was standing by; and he went out, and having been absent for some time, returned with the jailer carrying the cup of poison. Socrates said: You, my good friend, who are experienced in these matters, shall give me directions how I am to proceed, The man answered: You have only to walk about until your legs are heavy, and then to lie down, and the poison will act. At the same time he handed the cup to Socrates, who in the easiest and gentlest manner, without the least fear or change of colour or feature, looking at the man with all his eyes, Echecrates, as his manner was, took the cup and said: What do you say about making a libation out of this cup to any god? May I, or not? The man answered: We only prepare, Socrates, just so much as we deem enough. I understand, he said: but I may and must ask the gods to prosper my journey from this to the other world—even so—and so be it according to my prayer. Then raising the cup to his lips, quite readily and cheerfully he drank off the poison. And hitherto most of us had been able to control our sorrow; but now when we saw him drinking, and saw too that he had finished the draught, we could no longer forbear, and in spite of myself my own tears were flowing fast; so that I covered my face and wept, not for him, but at the thought of my own calamity in having to part from such a friend. Nor was I the first; for Crito, when he found himself unable to restrain his tears, had got up, and I followed; and at that moment, Apollodorus, who had been weeping all the time, broke out in a loud and passionate cry which made cowards of us all. Socrates alone retained his calmness: What is this strange outcry? he said. I sent away the women mainly in order that they might not misbehave in this way, for I have been told that a man should die in peace. Be quiet then, and have patience. When we heard his words we were ashamed, and refrained our tears; and he walked about until, as he said, his legs began to fail, and then he lay on his back, according to the directions, and the man who gave him the poison now and then looked at his feet and legs; and after a while he pressed his foot hard, and asked him if he could feel; and he said, No; and then his leg, and so upwards and upwards, and showed us that he was cold and stiff. And he felt them himself, and said: When the poison reaches the heart, that will be the end. He was beginning to grow cold about the groin, when he uncovered his face, for he had covered himself up, and said—they were his last words—he said: Crito, I owe a cock to Asclepius; will you remember to pay the debt? The debt shall be paid, said Crito; is there anything else? There was no answer to this question; but in a minute or two a movement was heard, and the attendants uncovered him; his eyes were set, and Crito closed his eyes and mouth.

Such was the end, Echecrates, of our friend; concerning whom I may truly say, that of all the men of his time whom I have known, he was the wisest and justest and best.

READING 8
Fear of Death?
Plato
(from *Apology*)

Strange, indeed, would be my conduct, O men of Athens, if I who, when I was ordered by the generals whom you chose to command me at Potidaea and Amphipolis and Delium, remained where they placed me, like any other man, facing death—if now, when, as I conceive and imagine, God orders me to fulfil the philosopher's mission of searching into myself and other men, I were to desert my post through fear of death, or any other fear; that would indeed be strange, and I might justly be arraigned in court for denying the existence of the gods, if I disobeyed the oracle because I was afraid of death, fancying that I was wise when I was not wise. For the fear of death is indeed the pretence of wisdom, and not real wisdom, being a pretence of knowing the unknown; and no one knows whether death, which men in their fear apprehend to be the greatest evil, may not be the greatest good. Is not this ignorance of a disgraceful sort, the ignorance which is the conceit that man knows what he does not know? And in this respect only I believe myself to differ from men in general, and may perhaps claim to be wiser than they are:—that whereas I know but little of the world below, I do not suppose that I know: but I do know that injustice and disobedience to a better, whether God or man, is evil and dishonourable, and I will never fear or avoid a possible good rather than a certain evil. And therefore if you let me go now, and are not convinced by Anytus, who said that since I had been prosecuted I must be put to death (or if not that I ought never to have been prosecuted at all); and that if I escape now, your sons will all be utterly ruined by listening to my words—if you say to me, Socrates, this time we will not mind Anytus, and you shall be let off, but upon one condition, that you are not to enquire and speculate in this way any more, and that if you are caught doing so again you shall die;—if this was the condition on which you let me go, I should reply: Men of Athens, I honour and love you; but I shall obey God rather than you, and while I have life and strength I shall never cease from the practice and teaching of philosophy, exhorting any one whom I meet and saying to him after my manner: You, my friend,—a citizen of the great and mighty and wise city of Athens,—are you not ashamed of heaping up the greatest amount of money and honour and reputation, and caring so little about wisdom and truth and the greatest improvement of the soul, which you never regard or heed at all? And if the person with whom I am arguing, says: Yes, but I do care; then I do not leave him or let him go at once; but I proceed to interrogate and examine and cross-examine him, and if I think that he has no virtue in him, but only says that he has, I reproach him with undervaluing the greater, and overvaluing the less. And I shall repeat the same words to every one whom I meet, young and old, citizen and alien, but especially to the citizens, inasmuch as they are my brethren. For know that this is the command of God; and I believe that no greater good has ever happened in the state than my service to the God. For I do nothing but go about persuading you all, old and young alike, not to take thought for your persons or your properties, but first and chiefly to care about the greatest improvement of the soul. I tell you that virtue is not given by money, but that from virtue comes money and every other good of man, public as well as private. This is my teaching, and if this is the doctrine which corrupts the youth, I am a mischievous person. But if any one says that this is not my teaching, he is speaking an untruth.

Wherefore, O men of Athens, I say to you, do as Anytus bids or not as Anytus bids, and either acquit me or not; but whichever you do, understand that I shall never alter my ways, not even if I have to die many times.

. . .

Some one will say: Yes, Socrates, but cannot you hold your tongue, and then you may go into a foreign city, and no one will interfere with you? Now I have great difficulty in making you understand my answer to this. For if I tell you that to do as you say would be a disobedience to the God, and therefore that I cannot hold my tongue, you will not believe that I am serious; and if I say again that daily to discourse about virtue, and of those other things about which you hear me examining myself and others, is the greatest good of man, and that the unexamined life is not worth living, you are still less likely to believe me. Yet I say what is true, although a thing of which it is hard for me to persuade you. Also, I have never been accustomed to think that I deserve to suffer any harm.

. . .

Let us reflect in another way, and we shall see that there is great reason to hope that death is a good; for one of two things—either death is a state of nothingness and utter unconsciousness, or, as men say, there is a change and migration of the soul from this world to another. Now if you suppose that there is no consciousness, but a sleep like the sleep of him who is undisturbed even by dreams, death will be an unspeakable gain. For if a person were to select the night in which his sleep was undisturbed even by dreams, and were to compare with this the other days and nights of his life, and then were to tell us how many days and nights he had passed in the course of his life better and more pleasantly than this one, I think that any man, I will not say a private man, but even the great king will not find many such days or nights, when compared with the others. Now if death be of such a nature, I say that to die is gain; for eternity is then only a single night. But if death is the journey to another place, and there, as men say, all the dead abide, what good, O my friends and judges, can be greater than this? If indeed when the pilgrim arrives in the world below, he is delivered from the professors of justice in this world, and finds the true judges who are said to give judgment there, Minos and Rhadamanthus and Aeacus and Triptolemus, and other sons of God who were righteous in their own life, that pilgrimage will be worth making. What would not a man give if he might converse with Orpheus and Musaeus and Hesiod and Homer? Nay, if this be true, let me die again and again. I myself, too, shall have a wonderful interest in their meeting and conversing with Palamedes, and Ajax the son of Telamon, and any other ancient hero who has suffered death through an unjust judgment; and there will be no small pleasure, as I think, in comparing my own sufferings with theirs. Above all, I shall then be able to continue my search into true and false knowledge; as in this world, so also in the next; and I shall find out who is wise, and who pretends to be wise, and is not. What would not a man give, O judges, to be able to examine the leader of the great Trojan expedition; or Odysseus or Sisyphus, or numberless others, men and women too! What infinite delight would there be in conversing with them and asking them questions! In another world they do not put a man to death for asking questions: assuredly not. For besides being happier than we are, they will be immortal, if what is said is true.

Wherefore, O judges, be of good cheer about death, and know of a certainty, that no evil can happen to a good man, either in life or after death. He and his are not neglected by the gods; nor has my own approaching end happened by mere chance. But I see clearly that the time had arrived when it was better for me to die and be released from trouble; wherefore the oracle gave no sign. For which reason, also, I am not angry with my condemners, or with my accusers; they have done me no harm, although they did not mean to do me any good; and for this I may gently blame them.

READING 9
The Highest Love
Plato
(from *Symposium*)

Diotima of Mantineia, a woman wise in the knowledge of love, continued, saying

"He who has been instructed thus far in the things of love, and who has learned to see the beautiful in due order and succession, when he comes toward the end will suddenly perceive a nature of wondrous beauty (and this, Socrates, is the final cause of all our former toils)—a nature which in the first place is everlasting, not growing and decaying, or waxing and waning; secondly, not fair in one point of view and foul in another, or at one time or in one relation or at one place fair, at another time or in another relation or at another place foul, as if fair to some and foul to others, or in the likeness of a face or hands or any other part of the bodily frame, or in any form of speech or knowledge, or existing in any other being, as for example, in an animal, or in heaven, or in earth, or in any other place; but beauty absolute, separate, simple, and everlasting, which without diminution and without increase, or any change, is imparted to the evergrowing and perishing beauties of all other things. He who from these ascending under the influence of true love, begins to perceive that beauty, is not far from the end. And the true order of going, or being led by another, to the things of love, is to begin from the beauties of earth and mount upwards for the sake of that other beauty, using these as steps only, and from one going on to two, and from two to all fair forms, and from fair forms to fair practices, and from fair practices to fair notions, until from fair notions he arrives at the notion of absolute beauty, and at last knows what the essence of beauty is. This, my dear Socrates, is that life above all others which man should live, in the contemplation of beauty absolute . . . the divine beauty, I mean, pure and clear and unalloyed, not clogged with the pollutions of mortality and all the colours and vanities of human life—thither looking, and holding converse with the true beauty simple and divine? Remember how in that communion only, beholding beauty with the eye of the mind, he will be enabled to bring forth, not images of beauty, but realities (for he has hold not of an image but of a reality), and bringing forth and nourishing true virtue to become the friend of God and be immortal, if mortal man may. Would that be an ignoble life?"

READING 10
The Meaning of Happiness
Ludwig Wittgenstein
(from *Notebooks*)

And in this sense Dostoievsky is right when he says that the man who is happy is fulfilling the purpose of existence.

Or again we could say that the man is fulfilling the purpose of existence who no longer needs to have any purpose except to live. That is to say, who is content.

To believe in a God means to understand the question about the meaning of life.

To believe in a God means to see that the facts of the world are not the end of the matter.

To believe in God means to see that life has a meaning.

The world is *given* me, i.e. my will enters into the world completely from outside as into something that is already there.

(As for what my will is, I don't know yet.)

That is why we have the feeling of being dependent on an alien will.

However this may be, at any rate we *are* in a certain sense dependent, and what we are dependent on we can call God.

In order to live happily I must be in agreement with the world. And that is what "being happy" *means*.

I am then, so to speak, *in* agreement with that alien will on which I appear dependent. That is to say: "I am doing the will of God."

Fear in face of death is the best sign of a false, i.e. a bad, life.

When my conscience upsets my equilibrium then I am not in agreement with Something. But what is this? Is it *the world?*

Certainly it is correct to say: Conscience is the voice of God.

For example: it makes me unhappy to think that I have offended such and such a man. Is that my conscience?

Can one say: "Act according to your conscience whatever it may be?"

Live happy!

READING 11
To Live for God
Leo Tolstoy

(from *Anna Karenina*, Part 7)

XI

. . .

Levin got into conversation about that land with Fyodor and asked whether Platon, a wealthy and good muzhik from the same village, might rent it next year.

The price is too dear, Platon wouldn't make enough, Konstantin Dmitrich,' said the muzhik, picking ears of rye from under his sweaty shirt.

'Then how does Kirillov make it pay?'

'Mityukha' (so the muzhik scornfully called the innkeeper) 'makes it pay right enough, Konstantin Dmitrich! He pushes till he gets his own. He takes no pity on a peasant. But Uncle Fokanych' (so he called old Platon), 'he won't skin a man. He lends to you, he lets you off. So he comes out short. He's a man, too.'

'But why should he let anyone off?'

'Well, that's how it is—people are different. One man just lives for his own needs, take Mityukha even, just stuffs his belly, but Fokanych—he's an upright old man. He lives for the soul. He remembers God.'

'How's that? Remembers God? Lives for the soul?' Levin almost shouted.

'Everybody knows how—by the truth, by God's way. People are different. Now, take you even, you wouldn't offend anybody either . . .'

'Yes, yes, goodbye!' said Levin, breathless with excitement, and, turning, he took his stick and quickly walked off towards home.

A new, joyful feeling came over him. At the muzhik's words about Fokanych living for the soul, by the truth, by God's way, it was as if a host of vague but important thoughts burst from some locked-up place and, all rushing towards the same goal, whirled through his head, blinding him with their light.

XII

Levin went in big strides along the main road, listening not so much to his thoughts (he still could not sort them out) as to the state of his soul, which he had never experienced before.

The words spoken by the muzhik had the effect of an electric spark in his soul, suddenly transforming and uniting into one the whole swarm of disjointed, impotent, separate thoughts which had never ceased to occupy him. These thoughts, imperceptibly to himself, had occupied him all the while he had been talking about leasing the land.

He felt something new in his soul and delightedly probed this new thing, not yet knowing what it was.

'To live not for one's own needs but for God. For what God? For God. And could anything more meaningless be said than what he said? He said one should not live for one's needs— that is, one should not live for what we understand, for what we're drawn to, for what we want—but for something incomsprehensible, for God, whom no one can either comprehend or define. And what then? Didn't I understand those meaningless words of Fyodor's? And having understood, did I doubt their rightness? Did I find them stupid, vague, imprecise?

'No, I understood him, and in absolutely the same way that he understands, I understood fully and more clearly than I understand anything else in life, and never in my life have I doubted or could I doubt it. And not I alone, but everybody, the whole world, fully understands this one thing, and this one thing they do not doubt and always agree upon.

'Fyodor says that Kirillov the innkeeper lives for his belly. That is clear and reasonable. None of us, as reasonable beings, can live otherwise than for our belly. And suddenly the same Fyodor says it's bad to live for the belly and that one should live for the truth, for God, and I understand him from a hint! And I and millions of people who lived ages ago and are living now, muzhiks, the poor in spirit, and the wise men who have thought and written about it, saying the same thing in their vague language—we're all agreed on this one thing: what we should live for and what is good. I and all people have only one firm, unquestionable and clear knowledge, and this knowledge cannot be explained by reason—it is outside it, and has no causes, and can have no consequences.

'If the good has a cause, it is no longer the good; if it has a consequence—a reward—it is also not the good. Therefore the good is outside the chain of cause and effect.

'And I know it, and we all know it.

'But I looked for miracles, I was sorry that I'd never seen a miracle that would convince me. And here it is, the only possible miracle, ever existing, surrounding me on all sides, and I never noticed it!

READING 12
What Is the God I Love?
St. Augustine
(from *Confessions*)

But what is it that I love when I love You? Not the beauty of any bodily thing, nor the order of seasons, not the brightness of light that rejoices the eye, nor the sweet melodies of all songs, nor the sweet fragrance of flowers and ointments and spices: not manna nor honey, not the limbs that carnal love embraces. None of these things do I love in loving my God. Yet in a sense I do love light and melody and fragrance and food and embrace when I love my God—the light and the voice and the fragrance and the food and embrace in the soul, when that light shines upon my soul which no place can contain, that voice

sounds which no time can take from me, I breathe that fragrance which no wind scatters, I eat the food which is not lessened by eating, and I lie in the embrace which satiety never comes to sunder. This it is that I love, when I love my God.

And what is this God? I asked the earth and it answered: "I am not He"; and all things that are in the earth made the same confession. I asked the sea and the deeps and the creeping things, and they answered: "We are not your God; seek higher." I asked the winds that blow, and the whole air with all that is in it answered: "Anaximenes was wrong; I am not God." I asked the heavens, the sun, the moon, the stars, and they answered: "Neither are we God whom you seek." And I said to all the things that throng about the gateways of the senses: "Tell me of my God, since you are not He. Tell me something of Him." And they cried out in a great voice: "He made us." My question was my gazing upon them, and their answer was their beauty. And I turned to myself and said: "And you, who are you?" And I answered: "A man." Now clearly there is a body and a soul in me, one exterior, one interior. From which of these two should I have enquired of my God? I had already sought Him by my body, from earth to heaven, as far as my eye could send its beams on the quest. But the interior part is the better, seeing that all my body's messengers delivered to it, as ruler and judge, the answers that heaven and earth and all things in them made when they said: "We are not God," and, "He made us." The inner man knows these things through the ministry of the outer man: I the inner man knew them, I, I the soul, through the senses of the body. I asked the whole frame of the universe about my God and it answered me: "I am not He, but He made me."

Is not the face of the earth clearly seen by all whose senses function properly? Then why does it not give the same answer to all? Animals great and small see it, but cannot interrogate it. For reason does not preside in them to judge upon the evidence their senses bring. But man can interrogate it, and so should be able clearly to see *the invisible things of God understood by things which are made*; but they love these last too much and become subject to them, and subjects cannot judge. All these things refuse to answer those who ask, unless they ask with power to judge. If one man merely sees the world, while another not only sees but interrogates it, the world does not change its speech—that is, its outward appearance which speaks—in such a way as to appear differently to the two men; but presenting exactly the same face to each, it says nothing to the one, but gives answer to the other: or rather it gives its answer to all, but only those understand who compare its voice as it comes through their senses, with the truth that is within them. For truth says to me: "Your God is not heaven or earth or any corporeal thing." So their very nature tells us. For clearly there is less bulk in the part than in the whole. And I tell you, my soul, you are better, since *you* vivify the whole bulk of the body: you give the body life, which no body can give to a body. But your God is the Life of your life.

Late have I loved Thee, O Beauty so ancient and so new; late have I loved Thee! For behold Thou wert within me, and I outside; and I sought Thee outside and in my loveliness fell upon those lovely things that Thou hast made. Thou wert with me and I was not with Thee. I was kept from Thee by those things, yet had they not been in Thee, they would not have been at all. Thou didst call and cry to me and break open my deafness: and Thou didst send forth Thy beams and shine upon me and chase away my blindness: Thou didst breathe fragrance upon me, and I drew in my breath and do now pant for Thee: I tasted Thee, and now hunger and thirst for Thee: Thou didst touch me, and I have burned for Thy peace.

READING 13
Happiness and Man's Good
Aristotle
(from *Ethics*)

EVERY art and every scientific inquiry, and similarly every action and purpose, may be said to aim at some good. Hence the good has been well defined as that at which all things aim. But it is clear that there is a difference in the ends; for the ends are sometimes activities, and some- times results beyond the mere activities. Also, where there are certain ends beyond the actions, the results are naturally superior to the activities.

As there are various actions, arts, and sciences, it follows that the ends are also various. Thus health is the end of medicine, a vessel of ship-building, victory of strategy, and wealth of domestic economy. It often happens that there are a number of such arts or sciences which fall under a single faculty, as the art of making bridles, and all such other arts as make the instruments of horsemanship, under horsemanship, and this again as well as every military action under strategy, and in the same way other arts or sciences under other faculties. But in all these cases the ends of the architectonic arts or sciences, whatever they may be, are more desirable than those of the subordinate arts or sciences, as it is for the sake of the former that the latter are themselves sought after. It makes no difference to the argument whether the activities themselves are the ends of the actions, or something else beyond the activities as in the above mentioned sciences.

If it is true that in the sphere of action there is an end which we wish for its own sake, and for the sake of which we wish everything else, and that we do not desire all things for the sake of something else (for, if that is so, the process will go on *ad infinitum*, and our desire will be idle and futile) it is clear that this will be the good or the supreme good. Does it not follow then that, the knowledge of this supreme good is of great importance for the conduct of life, and that, *if we know it*, we shall be like archers who have a mark at which to aim, we shall have a better chance of attaining what we want? But, if this is the case, we must endeavour to comprehend, at least in outline, its nature, and the science or faculty to which it belongs.

5. But leaving this subject for the present let us revert to the good of which we are in quest and consider what its nature may be. For it is clearly this description, as we always desire happiness for its own sake and never as a means to something else, whereas we desire honour, pleasure, intellect, and every virtue, partly for their own sakes (for we should desire them independently of what might result from them) but partly also as being means to happiness, because we suppose they will prove the instruments of happiness. Happiness, on the other hand, nobody desires for the sake of these things, nor indeed as a means to anything else at all.

. . .

7. Again, we conceive happiness to be the most desirable of all things, and that not merely as one among other good things. If it were one among other good things, the addition of the smallest good would increase its desirableness; for the accession makes a superiority of goods, and the greater of two goods is always the more desirable. It appears then that happiness is something final and self-sufficient, being the end of all action.

READING 14
Love, the Divine Unifying Force
Thomas Aquinas
(from *Summa Contra Gentes*)

It is apparent that love, properly speaking, consists in the yearning one has to bind himself together with another in some way, for which reason, Dionysius describes love as a *unitive force*. Hence, as whatever it is that brings about the union between lover and beloved becomes more intense, so does love itself become more intense. That's why we have a greater love for those we are united to by birth or genuine friendship than for those we are united to by the common bond of nature. Again, love is stronger the more deeply-seated it is in the lover, which explains why sometimes a love that is brought about by passion is more intense than love brought about in any other way, though it is liable to be transitory. Now, God's goodness, which is reflected in all things, and which causes all things to be united in him, is measureless and deep-seated since he is himself his own goodness. Hence, in God there is true love, perfect and abiding.

Chapter Five

Society

That we live in the company of others, in *society*, is a truth made obvious to us on every side. We are born into a family, develop friendships, come to associate with others through school or workplace, and overall we experience life in a web of extended relationships. We are dependent on the other to the "nth" degree for education, for food and health requirements, for transportation, for communication, or for making a living. The same holds true for our activities in art and culture; for our involvements in industry, or economy and finance; in the pursuits of science; in the role of government; and in the exercise of religion. Without denying the isolating features of high technology, new aspects of the unity between individual and society have been dramatically disclosed by the advent of the Internet and the possibilities it provides for enlarging the parameters of human life. All of this testifies to the complementarity between the individual and society and certifies the fact that there is no individuality without society, nor society without the individual.

If, as we've seen many times, the context of an act is the key to its morality, then society itself becomes the context for a host of complex acts involving the community at large in relation to the individual and the individual to the community. An examination of the meaning of *society* will show how it generates that complex.

THE MEANING OF SOCIETY

The word *society* comes from the Latin word *socius*, with a variety of meanings like friend, ally, or the other whom we are in some way related to; its adjectival form *social* pertains to *other-relatedness*. Other-relatedness is a far-reaching concept, touching the very essence of all of our actions in society, drawing individuals together to work toward a common end (R #1).

The early Pre-Socratic philosophers were profoundly appreciative of the *cosmos*, the name they gave to the entire world as a single reality, a fantastic aggregate of countless separate entities, all working together in unity: the stars and the sun in their courses, water in its cycle of rarefaction and condensation, the coexistence and interdependence of plants and animals, all in awe-producing harmony. In Aristotle's phrase, the Pre-Socratics *wondered* at the balance nature achieved between the world's being *one* and *many* at the same time, and that neither pole surrenders itself to the other. As a relationship, unity and plurality pertain to *every* aspect of reality, the living body, the atom, the painting, the symphony, the clock, the play, the person—all of which are one but composed of many disparate elements. The polarity of the one and the many in balance with each other serves as a perfect template for the philosophy of society: society is one while the individual members are many; keeping the balance between them becomes the ground for rejecting any theory of society that brings about the destruction of either pole.

In a real sense, society exists for the sake of the individuals comprising it; and its actions must be for a common end that all may share; to the extent it fails to do so, it fails in its purpose. At the same time, any one individual in society must understand that society doesn't exist for him alone, but for the whole; all-out individualism will destroy not only the community but, in the long run, individuality itself. So, just as the community has obligations to the individual, the individual has obligations to the community. Or, to put it in terms of rights, society has rights to the inputs of the individual and the individual has rights to the inputs of society.

Literature is full of examples of the delicate dance necessary to maintain the balance between the individual and society, particularly in the destructiveness that follows when the balance is not honored. William Golding's *Lord of the Flies*, for example, shows how the characters, though youngsters, inflict damage on themselves in trying to save themselves as individuals, by not working out their salvation together. Or the works of poetry, drama, and fiction which are bitterly critical of society seen as crushing the individual—the novels, let's say, of Charles Dickens, or Flaubert's *Madame Bovary*, or any of the novels coming out of twentieth-century absolutist societies like Solzhenitzyn's *One Day in the Life of Ivan Denisovitch*.

Albert Camus' novel *The Stranger* is a powerful piece of literature that underscores the tragic failure of both society and individual to each other. The author, never an academic philosopher, lays out the existentialist themes of absurdity and meaninglessness. The opening line of *The Stranger* is a slashing revelation of the novel's main character, Meursault: "Maman died today, or was it yesterday, I can't be sure." We are immediately confronted with the *indifference* that dominates Meursault's view of the world, borne out in his unemotional behavior at his mother's wake, noted as "strange" by the French Christian society of Algiers. He has few, if any, genuine attachments. In a series of episodes with his girlfriend and people living in the same building, he is shown to be unconcerned and devoid of any real sense of values. By sheer fortuity Meursault kills a local Arab man, is brought to trial by a magistrate appalled by his lack of remorse and indifference to human life, is "defended" by a lawyer indifferent to the cause of his client, is convicted by a jury convinced of his guilt by his unfeeling deportment, and is condemned to death. In the dawning of the day of his execution, he hears outside the bustling activity in the harbor through his prison window and is keenly aware that life is going on about him, totally passing him by. He finally realizes that the *universe itself is indifferent* to him, and to everyone within it. All along he has been in tune with this cosmic indifference, and happy without being aware of it. The "stranger" is an alien in the very society that has made him so (R #2).

CHARACTERISTICS OF SOCIETY

As a term, *society* has a broad range of uses. In a *natural* sense, *society* can refer to mankind as a whole, as in *human* society; or to the family, as in *domestic* society; or to a community governed by law, as in *civil* society. In an *arbitrary* sense, it can refer to a religious ethos, as in the phrase used earlier, "the French Christian society of Algiers"; or to an epoch of manners, as in "Victorian society"; or to a cultural milieu, as the musical society of old Vienna. It can refer to any number of *conventional*, man-made societies such as trade unions, accrediting associations, the American Medical Society, and so on, all with varying degrees of rules and regulations for its members. By putting together the various elements essential to society—community, common good, collective goal—a workable definition of society is offered by Thomas Aquinas: *A union of persons acting together for the purpose of doing one thing in common.* This allows for both the *common good*, that is, the good of the whole, and the *individual* good, that is, the good required by each person for human well-being. The "one thing in common," for the most part, works out that a given measure may mean a hardship, or at least an inconvenience, for an individual, but is best overall as, for example, a traffic pattern that may compel an individual to go around a block to get to his house only a few yards away, but for the community as a whole the traffic pattern runs best. There is, however, a philosophical way of saying that all citizens can be thought of as "working together to do one thing," as John Rawls, the American philosopher we met earlier, put it, "namely to make sure every citizen has justice" (R #3).

With regard to the question as to whether domestic society and civil society are ordained by nature, that is, *natural societies*, it simply needs to be pointed out that domestic society is a natural coming together of man and woman creating the first instance of domestic society, and the advent of offspring creating the second instance, the family. As to civil society, it can be thought of, on one hand, as natural, insofar as people spontaneously gravitate together to solve common problems under some kind of direction while, on the other hand, it can be thought of as a human construction insofar as the laws governing it are of human devising. Either way, civil law can be defined by Aquinas as *a union of persons under one law for the pursuit of the common good.* The distinction between "society" and "civil society" is not at all firm, and we easily go back and forth between them. When we say "society must collect taxes," it's clear that civil society is meant. But when we say "society must take care of its poor" or "society must support the arts," we can be referring either to a social good wrought privately or to a good mandated by law. The context determines which is intended.

It would seem, then, that the question, whether man is a *social being by nature*, is a superfluous one, yet there are those who, for various reasons, would be prepared to deny it. The classical instance is the seventeenth-century Thomas Hobbes who, in his *Leviathan*, made the most out of combining the appeal of empiricism in England with the appeal of rationalism in France. He held it as obvious that man is individual at birth and *individualistic* by natural propensity, attested to by the fundamental passion of self-preservation. At the same time, however, man is possessed of the corrective power of *reason* and is able to appreciate the sad fact that, if no adjustment to life is made according to reason's dictates, he will lose even his individuality. That's why Hobbes famously concludes that there is a *natural state of man,* a "state of nature" which is not to be taken as an historical fact, yet not as a mere abstraction either, for it is that condition man would be reduced to were it not for the civilizing effects of organized society.

The state of nature is not a pretty one, and it is tellingly described by Hobbes in his often quoted paragraph: "In such condition, there is no place for industry; because the fruit thereof is uncertain; and consequently no culture of the earth; no navigation, nor use of the commodities that may be imported by sea; no commodious building; no instruments of moving, and removing such things as require much force; no knowledge of the face of the earth; no account of time; no arts; no letters; no society; and which is worst of all, continual fear, and danger of violent death; and the life of man, solitary, poor, nasty, brutish, and short." But man gets beyond this natural state by reasoning out to a society organized for protecting the individual, and the whole of the *Leviathan* shows how Hobbes would do it (R #4).

Contrary to the individualistic view of nature-in-itself propounded by Hobbes stands the main line of thinking on the subject in Western philosophy from Plato and Aristotle to the present day, in which society is seen as a natural relationship. "A social instinct," writes Aristotle, "is implanted in all men by nature," with the family as "the association established by nature for the supply of man's everyday wants," and when a single community becomes large enough, "the state comes into existence, originating in the bare needs of life and continuing for the sake of a good life" (R #5). The same holds for contemporary thinking as we see, for example, in John Rawls, who observes in his *A Theory of Justice,* "We need one another as partners in ways of life that are engaged in for their own sake, and the successes and enjoyments of others are necessary for and complementary to our own good." He contends that the essential ingredient of justice in society is an innately given sense of fairness, whence "justice as fairness" mutually binds society to its members, and its members to each other (R #6). In light of these remarks, particularly the notion of balance between society and its members, extreme collectivism as experienced in the last century can be seen as an utter tragedy for humanity.

There is no way of telling what the "best" society is or should be at any given time or place. The inexorable flow of human life, changing its pace in endless twists and turns, calls for an open understanding as to the shape of society in the unknowable future. But there are essentials to be striven for in any society worthy of the name. The term *a just society* immediately leaps forward as the primary claimant of what is essential to society. The word *justice* itself can be taken in two ways, coming from the Latin word *jus* which means both "right" and "law," suggesting that the *just* society is committed to doing what is right *in general*, and then *in particular* doing what is right as detailed by law.

Since there are many ways of distinguishing the role of justice in actual practice, each way warrants a different term. One author may distinguish two kinds of justice, another three, still another four or more. For our purposes, a distinction will be made along the simplest lines of relationship: whole to part, part to whole, and part to part. Three specific kinds emerge, therefore: distributive, contributive, and commutative. *Distributive justice* looks from the community to the individual in that it requires the equitable distribution of wealth and obligations, as, for example, an equitable assessment of taxes, equal opportunity for education, and fair access to health care. *Contributive justice,* sometimes referred to as *social justice,* looks from the individual to the community in that it pertains to what individuals or private groups can, or must, do for the community, such as the payment of taxes, caring for the homeless, and parent–teacher cooperation. It can also be interpreted in terms of the right and obligation each person has to *participate in the life of society,* that is, in the educational, cultural, recreational, political and economic life of the community, both in the sense of sharing that life and of adding to it the unique and valuable contributions an individual or group may make. *Commutative justice* looks from one individual to another, that is, private to private (nonpublic), and governs things we may owe one another such as keeping a promise or honoring a contract between employer and employee.

There is a sense, of course, in which we say that the terms of justice are to be satisfied in an impersonal way, as when we say that justice is not a respecter of persons, by which we mean a person's rights are not based on their state in life but on their humanity. In a deeper sense, therefore, justice is attached to the virtue of love, the guarantor of humanity and human dignity. Human dignity acknowledges each individual as a *person,* sacred and inviolable in his or her self, without regard to race, ethnicity, economic status, sex, or religion, and never to be used merely as a means to an end. Implied in the recognition of human dignity is the *freedom* or *liberty* each person has to engage in pursuits satisfying one's personal interests, to develop a style of life adapted to one's disposition, to enjoy mobility of location, and to undertake any personal direction as long as it does not impinge on the freedom of others—as has so often been said, one's freedom ends where another's begins. The United Nations notably tried to make the world conscious of the meaning of freedom in its *Universal Declaration of Human Rights* (R #7).

Human dignity is the immediate corollary of the value of human life, a value whose existence does not require proof or demonstration of any kind for it is known, as many truths are, intuitively. We do not have to prove that one's life is the ground of all meaning for the human being and is never to be transgressed. It is the one unarguable basis for the reality of one's selfhood. Respect for humanity, therefore, becomes the soil in which society grows and flourishes, and is able to move toward the good that is common to all and proper to everyone. But, despite the hopes of such a recipe for humanity, it is abstract, and abstractions, ideal in nature, have a difficult time in realizing themselves in the actual life of mankind with its history of war, enslavement, manipulation, abuse of power, and the unbelievable malevolence of individuals toward each other. Though these inhumanities have always been cankers on society, each has to be addressed by the human community as the occasion demands. There are two long-standing types of inhumanity that have been making claims on general consciousness during the past century or so, which now demand full public acknowledgment and political will for them to be eradicated: *racism* and *sexism*; both are destructive of equality, freedom, and justice seen earlier as the main ingredients of a truly human society.

The current use of the word *race* in this connection refers not so much to the archeologist's academic meaning of the word, but to the wider meaning which includes indigenous peoples and cultures, nationalities, or larger classes of people with shared identity even though they may be dispersed geographically. Differences among these various groups are the basis for *racism,* a view that differences manifest a hierarchy of human value, with those in possession being "superior" to those outside, giving them the right to suppress the "inferiors" by any means calculated to exercise or exhibit their "superiority." Thus, on a global scale, we find the massacre of Armenians in Turkey in the early twentieth century, the slaughter of the Jews in Nazi Germany out of a "purity of blood" fiction, the harassment of the Gypsies in central Europe, the genocide and exile of Bosnians by the Serbs in the 1990s, the enslavement of Negroes in the United States, the caste system in India, the instances of genocidal conflict throughout Africa, the forced migration of American Indians, or the expropriation of the small island of Diego Garcia in the Indian Ocean enacted against several thousand Chagossians by British and American authorities to make way for an American military fortress, a tightly kept secret even now. On a local scale, almost every country harbors cases of racism in matters of voting rights, health care, education, employment, upward mobility, and place of residence. There is no denying the huge gains made in these regards in the United States, while at the same time there is no denying that much remains to be done.

In line with racism, *sexism* too holds for the superiority of one segment of society over another. In practical terms "sexism" means "anti-feminism"—there never was a temptation to invent a neologism like "anti-masculinism"! All must acknowledge, of course, that the sexual distinction between male and female is made by nature, but the sexist goes further and holds that the biological, psychological, and social differences between male and female clearly signify the superiority of male over female. Speaking generally this view has been predominant in world history, with countless examples of keeping women "in their place": denial of education, severe dress codes lest immodesty entrap men, restricted movement in public, social immobility, exclusion from male-dominated activities or offices in the practice of religion, terms of address, unfair treatment in the workplace, years of political alienation, marginalization in the decision-making process, and so on. Women in certain countries have been, and still are, thoroughly degraded by human trafficking into domestic slavery or prostitution, victimized by rape, doubly victimized by rape and death in the endless ethnic wars in Africa. In the West there has been a forever bias against women as men's equal, the female being counted, even by Plato and Aristotle, as an "unfinished male." The mid-nineteenth century, however, saw an articulate upsurge against sexual inequality, especially among English writers like John Stuart Mill, Harriet Taylor, and Mary Wollstonecraft. In the United States, in the recent past, there has been remarkable deepening of sensitivity to feminist issues with a corresponding growth of practical consequences, not least of which is the enrichment of American society as a society.

It's in the nature of the case that, when looking at the ills of society, we are looking at them on a large scale, as with racism and sexism, and not on the actions of individuals involved in them. There is a political saying that "all politics are local" which means, of course, that good government at the top is possible only with good political sense at the bottom—the wise and practical decision making of individuals. In a similar sense, all morality is individual because actions themselves are singular. So, in the matter at hand, there can be no collective racism unless there are first individual racists, and no collective sexism unless first individual sexists. In as much as it's far easier to analyze problems and make judgments on an abstract level simply because they are impersonal, it falls to individuals themselves to put what they understand in the abstract into the actual practice of their daily lives.

THE ECONOMY

One of the great urgencies for society is to ensure that its members possess the resources to enjoy a human life—the basic necessities of food and shelter, and access to all the ingredients that make for a human life worth living. Such urgency begins with a call for the *distribution of wealth*, leaving no one so impoverished and constrained by circumstances beyond control that a decent life is out of reach. Nothing less than insistent care and commitment on the part of society will guarantee a prudent management of resources to satisfy the demands of distributive justice. Such management goes by the name of *economy*, which originally means "house management," with transferred usages to the management of a wide range of activity, like business economy, military economy, the economy of salvation, and so on. Here it refers to the *production and distribution of goods and services*, to the ebb and flow of money, because they are the key to acquiring the human necessities already mentioned.

Just as any question regarding society involves the reciprocal role of individual and community, the prime question at this point is, what is the role of society vis-à-vis the individual in the matter of the production and distribution of goods and services, and the movement of money attached thereto. Should private enterprise go without civil regulation? Completely? Somewhat? Should there not be laws governing economic activity, just as there are laws governing traffic patterns, collection of taxes, and educational opportunities? Extremes can, in the *abstract*, be thought of: *extreme individualism* and *extreme collectivism*. Extreme individualism would shred any meaningful concern for the common good, and extreme collectivism would destroy any vestige of individual good.

Insofar as extremes make any *historical* sense, the last two centuries offer us a picture of two systems, one at either end of a spectrum running from laissez-faire to communism. The first system, *laissez-faire* (let be, leave it alone) or *free market*, or *free enterprise*, calls for the government to "let be," keep "hands off" business, or at least to let it regulate itself with as few laws as possible. It therefore involves employing one's wealth to increase that wealth, to which the term *capitalism* is attached, and the societies where it predominates as *capitalist societies*. Its classical proponent is Adam Smith, the eighteenth-century English economist, author of *The Wealth of Nations*. He was no mean-spirited economist, and genuinely felt that the common interest would be served if private interests were protected. That's why he inveighed against the "mercantile monopoly" of his time and place because it was built upon the "mean rapacity" of merchants and manufacturers, and their solidarity with the government. This style economy, he felt, could only bring about human deterioration all along the line because it constrains individual initiative for enterprise abroad as well as at home, and renders competition, the key to quality and fair pricing, impossible or hard to come by. Adam Smith's bid for laissez-faire was, in the beginning, a bid for government *not* to tolerate such practices.

But the ease with which he at times talks of the primacy of the *self* leaves little room for regarding the *other* as an essential aspect of our life in society, as borne out in this oft-quoted passage: "It is not from the benevolence of the butcher, the brewer, or the baker that we expect our dinner, but from their regard for their own interest. We address ourselves, not to their humanity but to their self-love, and never talk to them of our own necessities, but of their advantages. Nobody but a beggar chooses to depend chiefly upon the benevolence of his fellows" (R #8).

In our day, the language of economy and business practice universally revolves around the term *profit*, the financial return made on an investment: Individuals launch into an enterprise to realize a gain, companies announce their success in percentage profit made, stocks are bought in the expectation of profits, and money is lent in view of percent interest returned. There is no reason to question or downplay the importance of the self-interest motive in making a profit, or the creative imagination it can stimulate, or the personal satisfaction following a successful venture. The free-market system, with the political superstructure it requires, has demonstrated its capacity to enhance human life physically, technologically, and culturally, but uncontrolled along its way, it has also wrought havoc in the lives of many as Marx passionately disclosed during the Industrial Revolution in England. So the question naturally arises as to whether an individual person, or a company acting as a "legal person," is morally free to make as much profit as possible without regard for any other considerations. This position was famously espoused by Milton Friedman, an American Nobel Prize winner for economics, as sampled in the following quotation: "In a free society . . . there is one and only one social responsibility of business—to use its resources and engage in activities designed to increase its profits so long as it stays within the rules of the game, which is to say, engages in open and free competition without deception or fraud . . . " (R #9).

At the other end of the spectrum is the second scheme, *communism*, which designates the collectivist style of economy derived from the anti-capitalist writings of Karl Marx. Marx himself was profoundly disturbed by what he saw as human alienation brought about by the expropriation of the laborer's work by that class of society whose only goal was amassing wealth, the class he referred to as the *capitalist class.* The working man, then, in order to regain a lost humanity, must be apportioned an equitable share in the wealth produced by his labor, under more humane working conditions. Committing his entire life toward achieving this goal, he developed a philosophy of history in which mankind was destined for a classless society without the domination of one class over another. This end was to be brought about, in Marx's personal view, only by peaceful means, though there were Marxists who believed that such a destiny should be brought about sooner, even if that meant violence and revolution.

Violence and revolution did indeed begin in early twentieth-century Russia and before the end of the century, with China's colossal communist enterprise, there was a huge percentage of mankind living under severe government domination, minutely directing the production and distribution of all goods and services, as well as the financial and social structure in those countries where communism took over, with dire consequences for human freedom in the world for the remainder of the century.

Even though the collectivist and capitalist doctrines each theoretically maintain that they hold for the well-being of both the individual and society, the historical working out of these doctrines could not but move toward the extremes just mentioned. We are then brought to the point of asking about a path between the two extremes, a middle path that would preserve the interests of the individual and the community in such a way as not to lose the role of the self in laissez-faire or the role of the community in collectivism. Such a middle path is offered in the economic doctrine of *socialism.* In one real sense, there is no such thing as socialist economic theory, for the mere fact that socialism lies "somewhere" between collectivism and capitalism announces that there can never be perfect clarity to such a theory, but it does mean some kind of public role in production and distribution, allowing a great latitude in what enterprises should be controlled as public utilities or flat-out owned and operated by the government. The words *socialism* or *socialistic* are not invasive words in most countries of the "first world," in Europe, Canada, Australia, and New Zealand, which are still referred to as "capitalist" countries, or countries embracing "democratic socialism." The only first-world country that is repelled by the idea of "socialism" is the United States, the capitalist country par excellence, where, ironically, a good number of "socialist" undertakings are already in place to some degree, such as the postal service, health care, social security, and public utilities. The socialist would have a profound problem with capitalism because in such a system it is virtually impossible to control the tendency to self-interest and the inclination to blame an individual who doesn't "make it" in such a society because "it's his own fault".

Further, stand back and take an impartial view of what's been happening in our own country. Not ignoring the many wonderful features of the American economy and the sensitivity of many of its adherents, the picture discloses features we cannot be proud of: so many unemployed; the yawning discrepancy of wealth between those who have and those who have not; the economic stagnation of large minority groups, especially Blacks and Hispanics; staggering greed; corporate circumvention of both law and morality in financial practices, always there, but coming traumatically to light in the early years of this century; the homelessness and miserable living conditions of many of our fellow citizens; the skyrocketing cost for healthcare and the unbelievable lack of even primary care for millions: all these are matters for a fresh wave of "social concern." When you consider the knee-jerk reaction attending the term *socialism*, perhaps the term *social concern* may prove more acceptable. The economist Paul Krugman puts it just right in observing that we cannot ignore "the reality that sometimes you can't have effective market competition without effective regulation" (*NY Times*, June 23, 2008).

In recent years, after long ignoring the problem, authors have come to recognize the importance of moral imperatives in the economy and have led the way for schools of business to offer courses and seminars in applied ethics, following the example of courses in medical ethics offered earlier in our schools of medicine. As the literature on ethics in the economy begins to abound, we can appreciate its impact from three instances deserving consideration: 1) *Economic Justice for All*, the pastoral letter of the American Catholic Bishops, 2) *On Ethics and Economics* by Amartya Sen, and 3) *On Globalization* by George Soros.

1. There is perhaps no other document today that covers the moral issues in economics more directly than *Economic Justice for All, 1986/1996*. Though it is written from a Christian perspective and addresses mainly the American state of affairs, its reasoned presentation of economic justice in the full context of social life is one that all can readily appreciate and accept. It is an appeal that, while recognizing the weakness and shortcomings of all members of the human family, is based on the love for humanity and the practice of justice that flows from it. Without attempting to establish what kind of economic system is best for any time or place, the document firmly insists that, inasmuch as human dignity can be realized only in community, society has a moral obligation to protect it for all its members. Though there are perfectly legitimate ways of measuring the economy, like gross national product, average income, stock market performance, the "vision of economic life looks beyond them all and asks, does economic life enhance or threaten our life *together* as a community?" All economic undertakings must be measured in that light.

The document underscores the notion of participation by insisting on every person's right to participate in the economic life of society. To exclude any person or group from participation in the economy, or contributing to it, is not only unfair but destructive of the very idea that society exists for the sake of the individual human beings composing it. People deprived of a job, for example, are by that fact deprived of the participation vital to human development and the acquisition of the material means necessary to live, and to live well. A large part of the bishops' pastoral letter, and certainly the most poignant, is devoted to the poorest segment of society, the segment standing at the short end of the fact that the wealthiest 500 people have the same income as the world's poorest 416,000,000! The poor, however, include not only the financially depressed, but also those who are homeless, vulnerable, undereducated, and in other ways marginalized. Poverty expresses itself in still other forms of vulnerability, spiritual as well as material: "All people face struggles of the spirit as they ask deep questions about their purpose in life. . . . material deprivation seriously compounds such sufferings of the spirit and heart." To all these, society has a unique obligation, a call "to have a special openness with the small and the weak, those that suffer and weep, those that are humiliated and left on the margin of society." The document refers to this obligation as the *fundamental option for the poor*, a phrase that has since become common currency (R #10).

2. It's a bit of irony that, in the early history of the emergence of economics as a discipline in Britain with John Stuart Mill and Adam Smith, economics was considered as a moral science right along with ethics and political science. But in the ensuing century economics became gradually separated from its moral beginnings, a point underscored by one of the world's leading economists *Amartya Sen*, who wrote in 1987, of the "self-consciously 'non-ethical' character of modern economics" and, further, "It is arguable that the importance of the ethical approach has rather substantially weakened as modern economics has evolved." However, as pointed out earlier, the gap between economics and morality has recently been closing, owing in great part to Sen himself.

He was born in India in 1933 and is now Professor of Economics and Policy at Harvard. He was awarded the Nobel Prize in Economics in 1998, cited "for his contributions to welfare economics." The phrase 'welfare economics' does not pertain to the narrow, popular usage as of a person relying on public funds, with a distinctly pejorative overtone. 'Welfare', as in 'welfare economics', has a broader human meaning because it touches on all the goods that a reasonable person would expect for a fundamentally human life, the 'well-being' sought for all members of society. Along with his efforts to refine the meaning of welfare economics, Sen has made a consistent attempt to determine ways of measuring social goods as indicators of the well-being of a society, whether it is improving, where it is wanting, and what recommendations might be made to policy-makers.

Take, as an example, the all-important question of poverty, treated earlier as urgent in the Bishops' pastoral letter. Sen does not get into practical details, indispensable as they are, as to how allocations to the poor are to be "engineered," any more than the Bishops do. His concern is that, if allocations to the poor are made *en bloc*, without any differentiation as to where the poor are in relation to the poverty line, then those who are far below will be helped far less: *Distribution* of the total is as important as the *total* to be distributed. Sen found that a mere "head count" is equivalent to an undifferentiated mass and gives no indication of the degree of severity afflicting individuals or groups for whom variations must be made; no allocation of goods can be "blind to distribution among the poor" (1981, p. 186).

Sen's approach to the distribution–poverty question is but one example of the meaning of justice he has been elaborating for years and which he has put into final shape in *The Idea of Justice* in 2009. While showing deep appreciation for economists who try to develop an idea of justice in the abstract and then use it to measure the justice involved in practical problems, Sen settles on the view that the case for justice is met best of all by comparing competing options against each other, not against an ideal that is too speculative to serve as a measuring device or by referring them to institutions too far detached from the scene of decision making. In the past several hundred years, those who espoused the "idealist" or "transcendentalist" view were thinkers like Thomas Hobbes, John Locke, Jean-Jacques Rousseau, Immanuel Kant, and John Rawls, while in the more pragmatic comparative camp were thinkers like Adam Smith, John Stuart Mill, the Marquis de Condorcet, Karl Marx, and Kenneth Arrow, with whom Sen aligns himself. Justice can only be advanced by making reason-based judgments after weighing options in a concrete situation, in which a speculative ideal can hardly be of much help. The aim of a theory of justice, Sen writes, "is to clarify how we can proceed to address questions of enhancing justice and removing injustice, rather than to offer resolutions of questions about the nature of perfect justice." The existential fact of the kinds of life people actually lead is indispensable in shaping the idea of justice. There is an echo here of the profound difference in the points of departure between the philosophies of Plato and Aristotle. Plato began with the idea of a perfect society as found in his world of ideas and then proceeded to deduce from it the characteristics of a perfect copy in the real world, whereas Aristotle began with the experience of societies as they actually existed and then assessed which worked best—that's why, we'll recall, Platonists are prone to write utopias while Aristotelians are prone to write politics!

But for our purposes here, the important point is to recognize Sen's position that matters of justice, far from being merely or only juridical, are matters of the highest moral concern and that economics can never be divorced from ethics, for in the last analysis every economic choice reduces to the profoundly human Socratic question, "How should one live?" On the whole notion of re-structuring economics on the basis of morality, Sen writes, "I would like to argue that the deep questions raised by the ethics-related view of motivation and of social achievement must find an important place in modern economics" (R #11).

3. In recent decades there has been an unmistakable rise in the consciousness of human beings as a worldwide society, an inchoative sense of community and common destiny, despite the fractiousness and bloodshed marring the landscape of life. There is international surveillance of human rights, international courts of justice, the hearing of cases against humanity, medical assistance without borders, common currency and acceptance of passports in most of Europe, talk of a "global village," and de facto economic globalization. On this last phenomenon much has been written over the past ten years, but the name of George Soros is of special importance. Though not an academic economist, he speaks from the position of a person who, despite having become a wealthy financier in the very markets he criticizes, has a profound sympathy for human society, which he has demonstrated by personal investment in areas where others fear to tread. He analyzes the enlarging phenomenon of a developing world society in his book On Globalization by considering the present direction of global markets and, in doing so, manifests his strong support of what he calls a "global civil society."

Globalization has a wide meaning inasmuch as it refers to any endeavor that transcends national boundaries and in doing so serves to bring the world closer together. It integrates activities in different parts of the world reaching out to become connected to each other, activities that pertain to culture, politics, religion, economy, markets, travel, transportation, and communication. Soros, in his short and unpretentious account, focuses on the question of *economic* globalization, defined as "the development of global financial markets, the growth of transnational corporations, and their increasing domination over national economies." He sees the need for an economy that is international and the implications it has for free markets, the creation of wealth, and the indispensability of international agencies like the World Trade Organization (WTO), the International Monetary Fund (IMF), the World Bank, and even the International Labor Organization (ILO). But he also sees that global capitalism, unfettered and unchecked, has brought about huge social problems that cry out for remedy lest the economically and socially deprived peoples of the world wind up worse off after a long run of global capitalism than they were before. The "deficiencies of global capitalism," as he calls them, are that 1) many have been hurt or marginalized by global markets, 2) the "heedless pursuit of profit" has resulted in a misallocation of resources between private and public goods: "Markets are good at creating wealth but are not designed to take care of social goods," and 3) financial markets are crisis prone, so that developing markets, notoriously infirm, are bound to be devastated.

What is the cause of this dark side of global capitalism? Though there is a concurrence of many reasons, the main one is the *nature of the free market economy itself.* Free markets, left to themselves, without a sense of moral direction, can indeed create wealth, but along with it the social destruction of poor or emerging economies: "Markets are amoral: They allow people to act in accordance with their interests, and they impose some rules on how those interests are expressed, but they pass no moral judgment on the interests themselves . . . " Further, by not taking account of what is right or wrong, people can "pursue their interests without let or hindrance." What Soros is underscoring as a shortcoming of *global* capitalism is nothing more or less than legitimate criticism of capitalism in lesser arenas.

To be sure, a number of measures have been taken by well-meaning people to remedy this tragic situation, but much more has yet to be done because the gap, simply put, between rich and poor on the world scale is growing wider. By and large Soros does not call for the dismantling of international institutions like the WTO and the IMF but for their overhaul, particularly in designing new ways to deploy capital to help recipient countries more effectively without increasing risk of drastic capital loss. The whole practice of foreign aid has to be revisited because, in so many cases, it has resulted in benefits to the donor rather than the recipient. Paradoxically, selfless interest is never at the expense of self-interest, witness the Marshall Plan for Europe at the end of World War II, which meant a healthy Europe *and* a healthy United States. Even ground swells among the public can bring about welcome changes. Soros cites the success of the Year of Jubilee 2000 movement which, inspired by Pope John Paul II, called for debt forgiveness for heavily indebted poor countries.

Free trade debates will continue, but this much is sure that there is no free trade agreement that would be up to distributing its benefits to all in the same way, whether globally among all the world's countries, or even within any given country, either because the gap between rich and poor gets wider, or the "developing" countries fail to "develop." Joseph E. Stiglitz, American Nobel Prize winner for economics, in full agreement with Soros, has consistently been against the kind of globalization that has been in effect for the past decade or more and has reiterated his position in a recently co-authored book *Fair Trade for All* in which he holds that radical changes have to be introduced by rich nations calibrated to the needs and abilities of poorer nations, while poorer nations have to be encouraged and assisted in building an infrastructure of roads, schools, banks, and other institutions to allow their own economies to flow more freely and equitably.

Soros offers several innovative financial recommendations which are not necessary to recite here, but his overall goal is to bring about, as much as possible in this imperfect world, an alleviation of the poverty and social deprivation of developing or underdeveloped peoples of the world. To do so, first-world countries must give up the "pursuit of narrow self-interest and give some thought to the future of humanity." What we need is "a reassertion of morality amid our amoral preoccupations. It would be naïve to expect a change in human nature, but humans are capable of transcending the pursuit of narrow self-interest. Indeed, they cannot live without some sense of morality. It is market fundamentalism, which holds that the social good is best served by allowing people to pursue their self-interest without any thought for the social good, . . . that is a perversion of human nature." The kind of society Soros has in mind was outlined in a prior book of his, *Open Society: Reforming Global Capitalism.*

It should be clear from the three samplings that the economy can be called robust when, far from the narrow sense of how easy it is to become a millionaire, all the members of society share it, first in the availability of the basics of life—food, shelter, and clothing—and then in access to those goods that are essential to, or contribute to, the development of one's humanity, like meaningful work, health care, education, art, music, drama, library facilities, exercise of religion, and so on. This does not mean that all these goals are the goals of government alone as much as they are the goals of a *total* society, government, and private alike, in achieving what is socially the right thing as a matter of *social justice* (R #12).

To deal with the economy in its larger issues and the moral questions concerning them does not mean to suggest that moral concerns do not extend as well to the business transactions that are part and parcel of our daily life. Every transaction of buying or selling, whether it is a huge company transaction or a simple individual one, involves the moral principles we've been discussing. Instances are countless and we fully expect, either as buyers or sellers, to treat or be treated by our counterparts in a fair and honest way. Let us say, that's normally so, but we also know that where there are opportunities for the unscrupulous, the unscrupulous will find them. It's possible for the seller of a house to conceal its defects, to discriminate on the basis of race or religion, to misinform on the assessed value of the house; and it's possible for the buyer to lie about the required assets, to be engaged in a swindle, or to supply false references. Or, in the time of tragedy, price gouging is a possibility whose particular sadness is that one's own *need* is for purchase—the lantern will cost you twice as much because you need it in a blackout. On a different tack, we have every right to be served by "truth in advertising"; again, that's normally so. But there are daily instances of dissimulation, of bait and switch, of con jobs, reminiscent of the wariness that Romans had of the furniture dealer who proudly proclaimed that *his* table was without blemish, "sincere," that is "without wax (*sine cera*)!" Good business does not need bad ethics, which is the reason why almost all business curricula in colleges today require some kind of course of ethics in business for their students.

The economy, in all its aspects, is in need of moral guidance, so a fitting way to end this section is to turn to a recent book by the preeminent economist, Duncan K. Foley, *Adam's Fallacy: A Guide to Economic Theology* in which "Adam" is not the biblical father of all but the "Adam" of Adam Smith, the father of laissez-faire, and "theology" has nothing to do with God, but everything to do with the traditional view since Adam Smith, that economic laws are universal and invariable, and contain within themselves a self-justifying system of moral guidance. But in this highly speculative atmosphere no allowance is made for the intractable ways of everyday life, nor for the common sense input that other than economists may have to guide the course of the economy. Left to itself, contemporary capitalism cannot "solve the problems of poverty and inequality."

POLITICAL ETHICS

We allow ourselves to make a distinction between politics and government, assigning to politics the practical skills to become or remain an important player in public affairs, and to government the actual art of leading a civic community; we don't, as it were, like to see our public officials get so involved in the nitty-gritty as to distract them from visions of the common good. We make that allowance even though we are fully aware that politics and government are inseparable and that a good governor, seeking a balance between vision and practical strategy, is also a consummate politician. Such a view goes as far back as Plato and Aristotle, for whom politics was seen as government-in-practice, as the practical side of political philosophy; both philosophers took politics to be one with the art of governing the *polis.* Despite their intense interest in the activities of the polis, neither became actively involved, preferring to commit themselves instead to the *philosophy* of politics/government.

There was a difference between them, however, in how they worked out their philosophy; Plato, as a rationalist thinker, would try to "think out," from the top down, what the best form of government might be, whereas Aristotle, more empirical, and working from the bottom up, would look to the realistic side of how successful communities actually got things done. That's why, it has been observed, Platonic thinkers have been given to writing utopias, while Aristotelians to writing politics. Aristotle himself, no slouch in shaping political practice, in addition to writing the *Politics*, also wrote 158 city-state constitutions! It's from his designation of the city-state as "polis" that the term *politics* derives. Plato and Aristotle bequeathed a rich legacy to future generations on the importance of political wisdom and, along with the revered Socrates, saw wisdom as driven by the ethical. For all three, the state loomed indispensable in the lives of its citizens; its rulers had an obligation to be adept at statecraft and a moral compulsion to exercise it.

Conceptually it may be possible to separate statecraft from morality but, just as the doctor, knowing the protocols of good health, is morally obliged to follow them, so the ruler who, knowing the protocols of governance, is morally obliged to follow them. Plato's admonition regarding the *philosopher-king* is as pressing today as when he first said "unless there be a blending of political power and philosophical intelligence . . . there can be no cessation of troubles for our states, nor, I fancy, for the human race either" (R #13). This would be roundly seconded by Aristotle in his view that the "polis" is the highest conceivable kind of community because "it aims at the highest good" (R #14).

When you are dealing with any civic entity, whether a nation, state, province, or municipality, you are dealing with a community of human beings who are bent on establishing a common approach to a labyrinth of laws, rules, regulations, and traditional practices so that each individual, for whom the entity exists, can safeguard his individuality while balancing it with the contributions he can make to the common good. Human beings are not, as we know only too well, precision instruments. They are wonderfully made, but imperfect withal, and subject to the goods, the ills and misfortunes that "man is heir to." They are generous, accommodating, compassionate, and good-willed, yet can be inconsiderate, greedy, spiteful, willful, and often intractable. It's from this variegated material that the community has to be fashioned, and moved toward the goals of justice and stability. How this is to be accomplished will vary according to the prevailing culture, the history of the people involved, and the kind of economy at stake. There is more than one way to develop a viable society, one in which the principles of human well-being can be effectively achieved.

It's readily understood that there is a moral imperative suffusing the role of the politician or office holder, vast in its demands and full of expectations, in which integrity is an indispensable virtue, diplomacy a prized skill, and a sense of priority a sine qua non. A competent politician will recognize that he is an arbiter of interests, both public and private, and that he or she has to evaluate the worthiness of projects and set budgets accordingly. Above all continual watch must be maintained over the legitimate use of power against the easy decline to its abuse, mindful of Lord Acton's dictum, now a truism, that "power corrupts, and absolute power corrupts absolutely."

The problems emerging from politics and government can reach dizzying proportions and in the most unsuspecting places. They are found at the interface between corporate and private concerns, between the need for taxation and its equitable distribution, between guilt and innocence in cases at court. They can be found in decisions affecting health care, poverty, housing, education, transportation, support for the arts, and the community library; in situations that range from common sense decision-making to the practically insoluble. It may be that many, if not most, instances offer no moral difficulty, but there also may be instances of such moral complexity that a course to follow is very difficult to disentangle.

Let's take just one example of the difficulties that arise in a constitutional democracy like the United States, where any number of political, cultural, religious, and moral differences have long existed side by side, an example which, for many citizens, demonstrates how civil and moral law can clash with each other—such as the current controversy on abortion. The morality of abortion will be taken up in a later chapter, but for now all we need to do is acknowledge the fact that, in our society, there are many millions who hold for abortion at any stage, and many millions against it at any stage. Let's further pinpoint the problem to that of a public official who is morally against abortion, yet is bound by the constitution to support access to it. Recall that the Supreme Court, in a carefully worded statement in the *Roe v. Wade* decision of 1973, declared that access to abortion, under various conditions, is a constitutional right (therefore legal) until the child is born. Now the dilemma the public official faces is this: How can he be true to the constitution and to his moral position at the same time? How can he hold that, for him, abortion is legally acceptable, yet morally unacceptable? Of course, it can be argued that it's a matter of conscience which way he chooses to go, but that solution would not be an objective one, for conscience is personal and subjective, not (necessarily) impersonal and objective.

Is there another way for the public official to solve the dilemma? Often enough light is shed on a problem by looking at a cognate case. Consider this: A doctor announces he is on his way to perform an abortion. May an anti-abortionist block his path, violently prevent him, and even, if necessary, take his life in order to protect the life of a defenseless human being, though unborn? There is an immediate, intuitive response that such an action on the part of the anti-abortionist is absolutely wrong; this is supported by the fact that there is no reputable moralist to be found for it. And if you ask why not, the answer can only lie in the profound social distress that would ensue by the anti-abortionist's taking the law into his own hands in a constitutionally founded democratic society. There is, then, an objectively valid argument to be made for the public official for morally defending his own personal anti-abortion stance while upholding the constitutional right to abortion.

The whole point of this section on political ethics is to stress the need for morality in the political arena, but it would be a mistake to think that political science is only a matter of morality. Following the rules of morality and goodwill are necessary for a good statesman, but of themselves they are not sufficient to make one, anymore than going to church makes a good lawyer. That's because governing is an art, that is, a skill for sorting out goals to aim at and the means to achieve them, in seeking advice and support from colleagues, in cultivating personal relationships to advance common purposes, and in negotiating differences among members of the community. All these are part and parcel of a political good, that is, the good of a society governed by prudent and practical public officials, characterized by John Rawls as "the good of free and equal citizens recognizing the duty of civility to one another: the duty to give citizens *public reasons* for one's political actions" (in *Collected Papers*, p. 622).

PROFESSIONAL ETHICS

Traditionally the word *profession* signified a skill based upon knowledge and experience acquired over a long period of time and respected for its being human centered to help one in the prime needs of life, those that turn to ministry, medicine, law, and education.

Priests and ministers had the obligation to lead their communities in spiritual matters, to develop a sense of sacred presence, and to inculcate the inestimable worth of every individual before God. Doctors were to insure the bodily health of their patients and to stay abreast of the latest medical techniques available. Lawyers were looked to for help in setting to rights the grievances one might have against another in acquiring the fairest judgment society can offer. And educators, thought by some to be engaged in the noblest of all professions, were entrusted with opening up eager minds to the truths of reality.

The characteristics identifying professions traditionally hold today as well, but they have a far greater range of application. Knowledge and practice have expanded into new horizons, spawning a multiplicity of new professions. The ramifications in health care, to take one example, have seen the growth of psychiatry, clinical psychology, nursing care, life-support expertise, X-ray and imaging techniques, transplant operations, noninvasive surgery, hospice care for the terminally ill, and so on. All of these, in their own way, are person-centered skills requiring learning and experience. And the caregivers must develop a moral sensitivity unique to their professions.

There is, however, in common usage today a meaning to the word *professional* that has nothing in common with tradition, namely, its use in distinguishing "professional" from the "amateur." Though this distinction is employed in many venues, it has particular relevance to athletics, where it is used to separate those who play for money and those who play for fun. Then there is a use of the word *profession* that empties it of all special meaning, when it is applied to whatever one does for a living!

Each of the established professions has its own special moral concerns, often spelled out in an appropriate code of ethics, but it is the intimate person-to-person feature found in them all that underscores the human dimension of the services they render to society. The priests or ministers who think more of their flocks than they do of their reputation as efficient administrators, the doctors who are gentle and unhurried with their patients, lawyers who are more client-conscious than they are golf-conscious, and educators who are attuned to the needs of their students, all win and deserve the gratitude and respect of those whom they are called to serve in their professions.

READINGS

READING 1
Closed and Open Society
Henri Bergson
(from *Two Sources of Morality and Religion*)

One of the results of our analysis has been to draw a sharp distinction, in the sphere of society, between the closed and the open. The closed society is that whose members hold together, caring nothing for the rest of humanity, on the alert for attack or defence, bound, in fact, to a perpetual readiness for battle. Such is human society fresh from the hands of nature.

. . . But if nature, and for the very reason that she has made us intelligent, has left us to some extent with freedom of choice in our type of social organization, she has at all events ordained that we should live in society. A force of unvarying direction, which is to the soul what force of gravity is to the body, ensures the cohesion of the group by bending all individual wills to the same end. That force is moral obligation. We have shown that it may extend its scope in societies that are becoming open, but that it was made for the closed society. And we have shown also how a closed society can live, resist this or that dissolving action of intelligence, preserve and communicate to each of its members that confidence which is indispensable, only through a religion born of the myth-making function. This religion, which we have called the static, and this obligation, which is tantamount to a pressure, are the very substance of closed society.

Never shall we pass from the closed society to the open society, from the city to humanity, by any mere broadening out. The two things are not of the same essence. The open society is the society which is deemed in principle to embrace all humanity. A dream dreamt, now and again, by chosen souls, it embodies on every occasion something of itself in creations, each of which, through a more or less far-reaching transformation of man, conquers difficulties hitherto unconquerable. But after each occasion the circle that has momentarily opened closes again. Part of the new has flowed into the mould of the old; individual aspiration has become social pressure; and obligation covers the whole . . .

This impetus is thus carried forward through the medium of certain men each of whom thereby constitutes a species composed of a single individual. If the individual is fully conscious of this, if the fringe of intuition surrounding his intelligence is capable of expanding sufficiently to envelop its object, that is the mystic life. The dynamic religion which thus springs into being is the very opposite of the static religion born of the myth-making function, in the same way as the open society is the opposite of the closed society. But just as the new moral aspiration takes shape only by borrowing from the closed society its natural form, which is obligation, so dynamic religion is propagated only through images and symbols supplied by the myth-making function. There is no need to go back over these different points. I wanted simply to emphasize the distinction I have made between the open and the closed society. . . .

Joy indeed would be that simplicity of life diffused throughout the world by an ever-spreading mystic intuition; joy, too, that which would automatically follow a vision of the life beyond attained through the furtherance of scientific experiment. Failing so throughgoing a spiritual reform, we must be content with shifts and submit to more and more numerous and vexatious regulations, intended to provide a means of circumventing each successive obstacle that our nature sets up against our civilization. But, whether we go bail for small measures or great, a decision is imperative. Mankind lies groaning, half crushed beneath the weight of its own progress. Men do not sufficiently realize that their future is in their own hands. Theirs is the task of determining first of all whether they want to go on living or not. Theirs the responsibility, then, for deciding if they want merely to live, or intend to make just the extra effort required for fulfilling, even on their refractory planet, the essential function of the universe which is a machine for the making of gods.

READING 2
The Price of Alienation
Albert Camus
(from *The Stranger*)

(In this story, set in Algeria, Camus portrays a young man, Meursault, as markedly individualistic and indifferent to the values and practices of the society he lives in. But indifference cuts two ways: Meursault shuns society, and society shuns him. After attending the funeral for his mother from a home for the elderly, and by an unfortunate set of circumstances involving both chance and misinterpretation, Meursault kills a man and is now on trial. He is condemned to death.)

(The judge. . . .) said that the trial proper was about to begin, and he need hardly say that he expected the public to refrain from any demonstration whatsoever. He explained that he was there to supervise the proceedings, as a sort of umpire, and he would take a scrupulously impartial view of the case. The verdict of the jury would be interpreted by him in a spirit of justice. Finally, at the least sign of a disturbance he would have the court cleared.

The day was stoking up. Some of the public were fanning themselves with newspapers, and there was a constant, rustle of crumpled paper. On a sign from the presiding judge the clerk of the court brought three fans of plaited straw, which the three judges promptly put in action.

My examination began at once. The judge questioned me quite calmly and even, I thought, with a hint of cordiality. For the nth time I was asked to give particulars of my identity and, though heartily sick of this formality, I realized that it was natural enough; after all, it would be a shocking thing for the court to be trying the wrong man.

The judge then launched into an account of what I'd done, stopping every two or three sentences to ask me, "Is that correct?" To which I always replied, "Yes, sir," as my lawyer had advised me. It was a long business, as the judge lingered on each detail. Meanwhile the journalists scribbled busily away. But I was sometimes conscious of the eyes of the youngest fixed on me; also those of the queer little robot woman. The jurymen, however, were all gazing at the red-robed judge, and I was again reminded of the row of passengers on one side of a tram. Presently he gave a slight cough, turned some pages of his file, and, still fanning his face, addressed me gravely.

He now proposed, he said, to touch on certain matters which, on a superficial view, might seem foreign to the case, but actually were highly relevant. I guessed that he was going to talk about Mother, and at the same moment realized how odious I would find this. His first question was: Why had I sent my mother to an Institution? I replied that the reason was simple; I hadn't enough money to see that she was properly looked after at home. Then he asked if the parting hadn't caused me distress. I explained that neither Mother nor I expected much of one another—or, for that matter, of any-

body else; so both of us had got used to the new conditions easily enough. The judge then said that he had no wish to press the point, and asked the prosecutor if he could think of any more questions that should be put to me at this stage.

The prosecutor, who had his back half turned to me, said, without looking in my direction, that, subject to His Honour's approval, he would like to know if I'd gone back to the stream with the intention of killing the Arab. I said "No." In that case, why had I taken a revolver with me, and why go back precisely to that spot? I said it was a matter of pure chance. The prosecutor then observed in a nasty tone: "Very good. That will be all for the present."

I couldn't quite follow what came next. Anyhow, after some palavering between the bench, the prosecutor and my counsel, the presiding judge announced that the court would now rise; there was an adjournment till the afternoon, when evidence would be taken.

Almost before I knew what was happening, I was rushed out to the prison van, which drove me back, and I was given my midday meal. After a short time, just enough for me to realize how tired I was feeling, they came for me. I was back in the same room, confronting the same faces, and the whole thing started again. But the heat had meanwhile much increased, and by some miracle fans had been procured for everyone; the jury, my lawyer, the prosecutor, and some of the pressmen, too. The young man and the robot woman were still at their places. But they were not fanning themselves and, as before, they never took their eyes off me.

I wiped the sweat from my face, but I was barely conscious of where or who I was until I heard the Warden of the Home called to the witness-box. When asked if my mother had complained about my conduct, he said "Yes," but that didn't mean much; almost all the inmates of the Home had grievances against their relatives. The judge asked him to be more explicit; did she reproach me with having sent her to the Home, and he said "Yes," again. But this time he didn't qualify his answer.

To another question he replied that on the day of the funeral he was somewhat surprised by my calmness. Asked to explain what he meant by "my calmness," the Warden lowered his eyes and stared at his shoes for a moment. Then he explained that I hadn't wanted to see Mother's body, or shed a single tear, and that I'd left immediately the funeral ended, without lingering at her grave. Another thing had surprised him. One of the undertaker's men told him that I didn't know my mother's age. There was a short silence; then the judge asked him if he might take it that he was referring to the prisoner in the dock. The Warden seemed puzzled by this, and the judge explained: "It's a formal question. I am bound to put it."

The prosecutor was then asked if he had any questions to put, and he answered loudly; "Certainly not! I have all I want." His tone and the look of triumph on his face, as he glanced at me, were so marked that I felt as I hadn't felt for ages. I had a foolish desire to burst into tears. For the first time I'd realized how all these people loathed me.

After asking the jury and my lawyer if they had any questions, the judge heard the door-keeper's evidence. On stepping into the box the man threw a glance at me, then looked away. Replying to questions, he said that I'd declined to see Mother's body, I'd smoked cigarettes and slept, and drunk *café au lait*. It was then I felt a sort of wave of indignation spreading through the courtroom, and for the first time I understood that I was guilty. They got the door-keeper to repeat what he had said about the coffee and my smoking. The prosecutor turned to me again, with a gloating look in his eyes. My counsel asked the door-keeper if he, too, hadn't smoked. But the prosecutor took strong exception to this. "I'd like to know," he cried indignantly, "who is on trial in this court. Or does my friend think that by aspersing a witness for the prosecution he will shake the evidence, the abundant and cogent evidence, against his client?" None the less, the judge told the door-keeper to answer the question.

The old fellow fidgeted a bit. Then, "Well, I know I didn't ought to have done it," he mumbled, "but I did take a fag from the young gentleman when he offered it—just out of politeness."

The judge asked me if I had any comment to make. "None," I said, "except that the witness is quite right. It's true I offered him a cigarette."

The door-keeper looked at me with surprise and a sort of gratitude. Then, after humming and hawing for a bit, he volunteered the statement that it was he who'd suggested I should have some coffee.

My lawyer was exultant. "The jury will appreciate," he said, "the importance of this admission."

The prosecutor, however, was promptly on his feet again. "Quite so," he boomed above our heads. "The jury will appreciate it. And they will draw the conclusion that, though a third party might inadvertently offer him a cup of coffee, the prisoner, in common decency, should have refused it, if only out of respect for the dead body of the poor woman who had brought him into the world."

(The last paragraph of *The Stranger* records Meursault's reflections on the last night before his execution.)

. . . But all this excitement had exhausted me and I dropped heavily on to my sleeping-plank. I must have had a longish sleep, for, when I woke, the stars were shining down on my face. Sounds of the countryside came faintly in, and the cool night air, veined with smells of earth and salt, fanned my cheeks. The marvellous peace of the sleepbound summer night flooded through me like a tide. Then, just on the edge of daybreak, I heard a steamer's siren. People were starting on a voyage to a world which had ceased to concern me, for ever. Almost for the first time in many months I thought of my mother. And now, it seemed to me, I understood why at her life's end she had taken on a "fiancé"; why she'd played at making a fresh start. There, too, in that Home where lives were flickering out, the dusk came as a mournful solace. With death so near, Mother must have felt like someone on the brink of freedom, ready to start life all over again. No one, no one in the world had any right to weep for her. And I, too, felt ready to start life over again. It was as if that great rush of anger had washed me clean, emptied me of hope, and, gazing up at the dark sky spangled with its signs and stars, for the first time, the first, I laid my heart open to the benign indifference of the universe. To feel it so like myself, indeed so brotherly, made me realize that I'd been happy, and that I was happy still. For all to be accomplished, for me to feel less lonely, all that remained was to hope that on the day of my execution there should be a huge crowd of spectators and that they should greet me with howls of execration.

READING 3
The Common Good in a Constitutional Democracy
John Rawls
(from *Collected Papers*)

BERNARD PRUSAK: . . . Your argument for respecting the dignity of the individual follows from the functioning of liberal constitutional democracy.

JOHN RAWLS: Liberal constitutional democracy is supposed to ensure that each citizen is free and equal and protected by basic rights and liberties. You see, I don't use other arguments since for my purposes I don't really need them and it would cause division from the start. Citizens can have their own grounding in their comprehensive doctrines, whatever they happen to be. I make a point in *Political Liberalism* of really not discussing anything, as far as I can help it, that will put me at odds with any theologian, or any philosopher.

BERNARD PRUSAK: How do you think, in your work, the idea of the common good is revised? Is there still a common good? How would we speak of it in a liberal constitutional democracy where pluralism is a fact? Is it thrown out, or is it reconceived?

JOHN RAWLS: Different political views, even if they're all liberal, in the sense of supporting liberal constitutional democracy, undoubtedly have some notion of the common good in the form of the means provided to assure that people can make use of their liberties, and the like. There are various ways you might define the common good, but that would be one way you could do it.

BERNARD PRUSAK: So the common good would be the good that is common to each citizen, each citizen's good, rather than an overarching good.

JOHN RAWLS: The point I would stress is this. You hear that liberalism lacks an idea of the common good, but I think that's a mistake. For example, you might say that, if citizens are acting for the right reasons in a constitutional regime, then regardless of their comprehensive doctrines they want every other citizen to have justice. So you might say they're all working together to do one thing, namely to make sure every citizen has justice. Now that's not the only interest they all have, but it's the single thing they're all trying to do. In my language, they're striving toward one single end, the end of justice for all citizens.

READING 4
Of the Natural Condition of Mankind
Thomas Hobbes
(from *Leviathan*)

Nature hath made men so equal, in the faculties of the body and mind; as that, though there be found one man sometimes manifestly stronger in body or of quicker mind than another, yet when all is reckoned together, the difference between man and man is not so considerable, as that one man can thereupon claim to himself any benefit, to which another may not pretend as well as he. For as to the strength of body, the weakest has strength enough to kill the strongest, either by secret machination or by confederacy with others that are in the same danger with himself.

And as to the faculties of the mind—setting aside the arts grounded upon words, and especially that skill of proceeding upon general and infallible rules, called science; which very few have, and but in few things; as being not a native faculty, born with us; nor attained, as prudence, while we took after somewhat else—I find yet a greater equality amongst men, than that of strength. For prudence is but experience which equal time equally bestows on all men, in those things they equally apply themselves unto. That which may perhaps make such equality incredible, is but a vain conceit of one's own wisdom, which almost all men think they have in a greater degree than the vulgar; that is, than all men but themselves, and a few others, whom by fame, or for concurring with themselves, they approve. For such is the nature of men, that howsoever they may acknowledge many others to be more witty, or more eloquent, or more learned, yet they will hardly believe there be many so wise as themselves; for they see their own wit at hand, and other men's at a distance. But this proveth rather that men are in that point equal, than unequal. For there is not ordinarily a greater sign of the equal distribution of anything, than that every man is contented with his share.

From this equality of ability, ariseth equality of hope in the attaining of our ends. And therefore if any two men desire the same thing, which nevertheless they cannot both enjoy, they become enemies; and in the way to their end, which is principally their own conservation, and sometimes their delectation only, endeavor to destroy, or subdue one another. And from hence it comes to pass that where an invader hath no more to fear than another man's single power; if one plant, sow, build, or possess a convenient seat, others may probably be expected to come prepared with forces united, to dispossess and deprive him, not only of the fruit of his labor, but also for his life or liberty. And the invader again is in the like danger of another.

And from this difference of one another, there is no way for any man to secure himself so reasonable as anticipation; that is, by force or wiles to master the persons of all men he can, so long, till he see no other power great enough to endanger him: and this is no more than his own conservation requireth, and is generally allowed. Also because there be some, that taking pleasure in contemplating their own power in the acts of conquest, which they pursue farther than their security requires; if others, that otherwise would be glad to be at ease within modest bounds, should not by invasion increase their power, they would not be able long time, by standing only on their defense, to subsist. And by consequence, such augmentation of dominion over men being necessary to a man's conservation, it ought to be allowed him.

Again, men have no pleasure, but on the contrary a great deal of grief, in keeping company, where there is no power able to overawe them all. For every man looketh that his companion should value him at the same rate he sets upon himself; and upon all signs of contempt, or undervaluing, naturally endeavors, as far as he dares (which amongst them that have no common power to keep them in quiet, is far enough to make them destroy each other), to extort a greater value from his contemners by damage, and from others by the example.

So that in the nature of man, we find three principal causes of quarrel. First, competition; second, difference; thirdly, glory.

The first maketh men invade for gain; the second, for safety; and the third, for reputation. The first use violence to make themselves masters of other men's persons, wives, children, and cattle; the second, to defend them; the third, for trifles, as a word, a smile, a different opinion, and any other sign of undervalue, either direct in their persons, or by reflection in their kindred, their friends, their nation, their profession, or their name.

Hereby it is manifest that during the time men live without a common power to keep them all in awe, they are in that condition which is called war: and such a war as is of every man against every man. For war consisteth not in battle only, or the act of fighting, but in a tract of time wherein the will to contend by battle is sufficiently known, and therefore the notion of time is to be considered in the nature of war, as it is in the nature of weather. For as the nature of foul weather lieth not in a shower or two of rain, but in an inclination thereto of many days together; so the nature of war consisteth not in actual fighting, but in the known disposition thereto, during all the time there is no assurance to the contrary. All other time is peace.

Whatsoever therefore is consequent to a time of war, where every man is enemy to every man; the same is consequent to the time, wherein men live without other security than what their own strength and their own invention shall furnish them withal. In such condition there is no place for industry, because the fruit thereof is uncertain: and consequently no culture of the earth: no navigation, nor use of the commodities that may be imported by sea; no commodious building; no instruments of moving, and removing, such things as require much force; no knowledge of the face of the earth; no account of time; no arts; no letters; no society; and which is worst of all, continual fear, and danger of violent death; and the life of man, solitary, poor, nasty, brutish, and short.

It may seem strange to some man that has not well weighed these things, that nature should thus dissociate, and render men apt to invade and destroy one another; and he may therefore, not trusting to this inference, made from the passions, desire perhaps to have the same confirmed by experience. Let him therefore consider with himself, when taking a journey, he arms himself and seeks to go well accompanied; when going to sleep, he locks his doors; when even in his house he locks his chests; and this when he knows there be laws, and public officers, armed, to revenge all injuries shall be done him; what opinion he has of his fellow-subjects, when he rides armed; of his fellow-citizens, when he locks his doors; and of his children, and servants, when he locks his chests. Does he not there as much accuse mankind by his actions, as I do by my words? But neither of us accuse man's nature in it. The desires, and other passions of man, are in themselves no sin. No more are the actions that proceed from those passions, till they know a law that forbids them; which till laws be made they cannot know; nor can any law be made, till they have agreed upon the person that shall make it.

It may peradventure be thought, there was never such a time nor condition of war as this; and I believe it was never generally so, over all the world; but there are many places where they live so now. For the savage people in many places of America, except the government of small families, the concord whereof dependeth on natural lust, have no government at all; and live at this day in that brutish manner, as I said before. Howsoever, it may be perceived what manner of life there would be, where there were no common power to fear; by the manner of life which men that have formerly lived under a peaceful government, use to degenerate into a civil war.

But though there had never been any time wherein particular men were in a condition of war one against another; yet in all times, kings, and persons of sovereign authority, because of their independency, are in continual jealousies, and in the state and posture of gladiators; having their weapons pointing, and their eyes fixed on one another; that is, their forts, garrisons, and guns upon the frontiers of their kingdoms; and continual spies upon their neighbors; which is a posture of war. But because they uphold thereby the industry of their subjects, there does not follow from it that misery which accompanies the liberty of particular men.

To this war of every man against every man, this also is consequent: *that nothing can be unjust.* The notions of right and wrong, justice and injustice, have there no place. Where there is no common power, there is no law; where no law, no justice. Force and fraud are in war the two cardinal virtues. Justice and injustice are none of the faculties neither of the body nor mind. If they were, they might be in a man that were alone in the world, as well as his senses and passions. They are qualities that relate to men in society not in solitude. It is consequent also to the same condition, that there be no propriety, no dominion, no *mine* and *thine* distinct; but only that to be every man's, that he can get; and for so long as he can keep it. And thus much for the ill condition which man by mere nature is actually placed in; though with a possibility to come out of it, consisting partly in the passions, partly in his reason.

The passions that incline men to peace are fear of death, desire of such things as are necessary to commodious living, and a hope by their industry to obtain them. And reason suggesteth convenient articles of peace, upon which men may be drawn to agreement. These articles are they which otherwise are called the Laws of Nature whereof I shall speak more particularly in the two following chapters.

READING 5
The Civil Society
Aristotle
(from *Politics*)

1. Every state is a community of some kind, and every community is established with a view to some good; for mankind always act in order to obtain that which they think good. But, if all communities aim at some good, the state or political community, which is the highest of all, and which embraces all the rest, aims at good in a greater degree than any other, and at the highest good.

Some people think that the qualifications of a statesman, king, householder, and master are the same, and that they differ, not in kind, but only in the number of their subjects. For example, the ruler over a few is called a master; over more, the manager of a household; over a still larger number, a statesman or king, as if there were no difference between a great household and a small state. The distinction which is made between the king and the statesman is as follows: When the government is personal, the ruler is a king; when, according to the rules of the political science, the citizens rule and are ruled in turn, then he is called a statesman.

But all this is a mistake; for governments differ in kind, as will be evident to any one who considers the matter according to the method which has hitherto guided us. As in other departments of science, so in politics, the compound should always be resolved into the simple elements or least parts of the whole. We must therefore look at the elements of which the state is composed, in order that we may see in what the different kinds of rule differ from one another, and whether any scientific result can be attained about each one of them.

2. He who thus considers things in their first growth and origin, whether a state or anything else, will obtain the clearest view of them. In the first place there must be a union of those who cannot exist without each other; namely, of male and female, that the race may continue (and this is a union which is formed, not of deliberate purpose, but because, in common with other animals and plants, mankind have a natural desire to leave behind them an image of themselves), and of natural ruler and subject, that both may be preserved. For that which can foresee by the exercise of mind is by nature intended to be lord and master, and that which can with its body give effect to such foresight is a subject, and by nature a slave; hence master and slave have the same interest. Now nature has distinguished between the female and the slave. For she is not niggardly, like the smith who fashions the Delphian knife for many uses; she makes each thing for a single use, and every instrument is best made when intended for one and not for many uses. But among barbarians no distinction is made between women and slaves, because there is no natural ruler among them: they are a community of slaves, male and female. Wherefore the poets say—

"It is meet that Hellenes should rule over barbarians";

as if they thought that the barbarian and the slave were by nature one.

Out of these two relationships between man and woman, master and slave, the first thing to arise is the family, and Hesiod is right when he says—

"First house and wife and an ox for the plough,"

for the ox is the poor man's slave. The family is the association established by nature for the supply of men's everyday wants, and the members of it are called by Charondas "companions of the cupboard," and by Epimenides the Cretan, "companions of the manger." But when several families are united, and the association aims at something more than the supply of daily needs, the first society to be formed is the village. And the most natural form of the village appears to be that of a colony from the family, composed of the children and grandchildren, who are said to be "suckled with the same milk." And this is the reason why Hellenic states were originally governed by kings; because the Hellenes were under royal rule before they came together, as the barbarians still are. Every family is ruled by the eldest, and therefore in the colonies of the family the kingly form of government prevailed because they were of the same blood. As Homer says:

> "Each one gives law to his children and to his wives."

For they lived dispersedly, as was the manner in ancient times. Wherefore men say that the Gods have a king, because they themselves either are or were in ancient times under the rule of a king. For they imagine, not only the forms of the Gods, but their ways of life to be like their own.

When several villages are united in a single complete community, large enough to be nearly or quite self-sufficing, the state comes into existence, originating in the bare needs of life, and continuing in existence for the sake of a good life. And therefore, if the earlier forms of society are natural, so is the state, for it is the end of them, and the nature of a thing is its end. For what each thing is when fully developed, we call its nature, whether we are speaking of a man, a horse, or a family. Besides, the final cause and end of a thing is the best, and to be self-sufficing is the end and the best.

Hence it is evident that the state is a creation of nature, and that man is by nature a political animal. And he who by nature and not by mere accident is without a state, is either a bad man or above humanity; he is like the

> "Tribeless, lawless, heartless one,"

whom Homer denounces—the natural outcast is forthwith a lover of war; he may be compared to an isolated piece at draughts.

Now, that man is more of a political animal than bees or any other gregarious animals is evident. Nature, as we often say makes nothing in vain, and man is the only animal whom she has endowed with the gift of speech. And whereas mere voice is but an indication of pleasure or pain, and is therefore found in other animals (for their nature attains to the perception of pleasure and pain and the intimation of them to one another, and no further), the power of speech is intended to set forth the expedient and inexpedient, and therefore likewise the just and the unjust. And it is a characteristic of man that he alone has any sense of good and evil, of just and unjust, and the like, and the association of living beings who have this sense makes a family and a state.

Further, the state is by nature clearly prior to the family and to the individual, since the whole is of necessity prior to the part; for example, if the whole body be destroyed, there will be no foot or hand, except in an equivocal sense, as we might speak of a stone hand; for when destroyed the hand will be no better than that. But things are defined by their working and power; and we ought not to say that they are the same when they no longer have their proper quality, but only that they have the same name. The proof that the state is a creation of nature and prior to the individual is that the individual, when isolated, is not self-sufficing; and therefore he is like a part in relation to the whole. But he who is unable to live in society, or who has no need because he is sufficient for himself, must be either a beast or a god: he is no part of a state. A social instinct is implanted in all men by nature, and yet he who first founded the state was the greatest of benefactors. For man, when perfected, is the best of animals, but, when separated from law and justice, he is the worst of all; since armed injustice is the more dangerous, and he is equipped at birth with arms, meant to be used by intelligence and virtue, which he may use for the worst ends. Wherefore, if he have not virtue, he is the most unholy and the most savage of animals, and the most full of lust and gluttony. But justice is the bond of men in states, for the administration of justice, which is the determination of what is just, is the principle of order in political society.

READING 6
Justice as Fairness
John Rawls
(from *A Theory of Justice*)

My aim is to present a conception of justice which generalizes and carries to a higher level of abstraction the familiar theory of the social contract as found, say, in Locke, Rousseau, and Kant. In order to do this we are not to think of the original contract as one to enter a particular society or to set up a particular form of government. Rather, the original idea is that the principles of justice for the basic structure of society are the object of the original agreement. They are the principles that free and rational persons concerned to further their own interests would accept in an initial position of equality as defining the fundamental terms of their association. These principles are to regulate all further agreements; they specify the kinds of social cooperation that can be entered into and the forms of government that can be established. This way of regarding the principles of justice I shall call justice as fairness.

Thus we are to imagine that those who engage in social cooperation choose together, in one joint act, the principles which are to assign basic rights and duties and to determine the division of social benefits. Men are to decide in advance how they are to regulate their claims against one another and what is to be the foundation charter of their society. Just as each person must decide by rational reflection what constitutes his good, that is, the system of ends which it is rational for him to pursue, so a group of persons must decide once and for all what is to count among them as just and unjust. The choice which rational men would make in this hypothetical situation of equal liberty, assuming for the present that this choice problem has a solution, determines the principles of justice.

In justice as fairness the original position of equality corresponds to the state of nature in the traditional theory of the social contract. This original position is not, of course, thought of as an actual historical state of affairs, much less as a primitive condition of culture. It is understood as a purely hypothetical situation characterized so as to lead to a certain conception of justice. Among the essential features of this situation is that no one knows his place in society, his class position or social status, nor does any one know his fortune in the distribution of natural assets and abilities, his intelligence, strength, and the like. I shall even assume that the parties do not know their conceptions of the good or their special psychological propensities. The principles of justice are chosen behind a veil of ignorance. This ensures that no one is advantaged or disadvantaged in the choice of principles by the outcome of natural chance or the contingency of social circumstances. Since all are similarly situated and no one is able to design principles to favor his particular condition, the principles of justice are the result of a fair agreement or bargain. For given the circumstances of the original position, the symmetry of everyone's relations to each other, this initial situation is fair between individuals as moral persons, that is, as rational beings with their own ends and capable, I shall assume, of a sense of justice. The original position is, one might say, the appropriate initial status quo, and thus the fundamental agreements reached in it are fair. This explains the propriety of the name "justice as fairness": it conveys the idea that the principles of justice are agreed to in an initial situation that is fair. The name does not mean that the concepts of justice and fairness are the same, any more than the phrase "poetry as metaphor" means that the concepts of poetry and metaphor are the same.

Justice as fairness begins, as I have said, with one of the most general of all choices which persons might make together, namely, with the choice of the first principles of a conception of justice which is to regulate all subsequent criticism and reform of institutions. Then, having chosen a conception of justice, we can suppose that they are to choose a constitution and a legislature to enact laws, and so on, all in accordance with the principles of justice initially agreed upon. Our social situation is just if it is such that by this sequence of hypothetical agreements we would have contracted into the general system of rules which defines it. Moreover, assuming that the original position does determine a set of principles (that is, that a particular conception of justice would be chosen), it will then be true that whenever social institutions satisfy these principles those engaged in them can say to one another that they are cooperating on terms to which they would agree if they were free and equal persons whose relations with respect to one another were fair. They could all view their arrangements as meeting the stipulations which they would acknowledge in an initial situation that embodies widely accepted and reasonable constraints on the choice of principles. The general recognition of this fact would provide the basis for a public acceptance of the corresponding principles of justice. No society can, of course, be a scheme of cooperation which men enter voluntarily in a literal sense; each person finds himself placed at birth in some particular position in some particular society, and the nature of this position materially affects his life prospects. Yet a society satisfying the principles of justice as fairness comes as close as a society can to being a voluntary scheme, for it meets the principles which free and equal persons would assent to under circumstances that are fair. In this sense its members are autonomous and the obligations they recognize self-imposed.

. . .

I shall now state in a provisional form the two principles of justice that I believe would be chosen in the original position. In this section I wish to make only the most general comments, and therefore the first formulation of these principles is tentative. As we go on I shall run through several formulations and approximate step by step the final statement to be given much later. I believe that doing this allows the exposition to proceed in a natural way.

The first statement of the two principles reads as follows.

> First: each person is to have an equal right to the most extensive basic liberty compatible with a similar liberty for others.

> Second: social and economic inequalities are to be arranged so that they are both (a) reasonably expected to be to everyone's advantage, and (b) attached to positions and offices open to alL. . . .

These principles primarily apply, as I have said, to the basic structure of society and govern the assignment of rights and duties and regulate the distribution of social and economic advantages. Their formulation presupposes that, for the purposes of a theory of justice, the social structure may be viewed as having two more or less distinct parts, the first principle applying to the one, the second principle to the other. Thus we distinguish between the aspects of the social system that define and secure the equal basic liberties and the aspects that specify and establish social and economic inequalities. Now it is essential to observe that the basic liberties are given by a list of such liberties. Important among these are political liberty (the right to vote and to hold public office) and freedom of speech and assembly; liberty of conscience and freedom of thought; freedom of the person, which includes freedom from psychological oppression and physical assault and dismemberment (integrity of the person); the right to hold personal property and freedom from arbitrary arrest and seizure as defined by the concept of the rule of law. These liberties are to be equal by the first principle.

The second principle applies, in the first approximation, to the distribution of income and wealth and to the design of organizations that make use of differences in authority and responsibility. While the distribution of wealth and income need not be equal, it must be to everyone's advantage, and at the same time, positions of authority and responsibility must be accessible to all. One applies the second principle by holding positions open, and then, subject to this constraint, arranges social and economic inequalities so that everyone benefits.

READING 7
The Universal Declaration of Human Rights

(On December 10, 1948 the General Assembly of the United Nations adopted and proclaimed this historic statement on human rights for all. It asked that it be "disseminated, displayed, read and expounded principally in schools and other educational institutions, without distinction based on the political status of countries or territories." The document is too long to include in its entirety, but its Preamble is given here. The full Declaration can be found online at un.org/Overview/rights. html.)

PREAMBLE

Whereas recognition of the inherent dignity and of the equal and inalienable rights of all members of the human family is the foundation of freedom, justice and peace in the world.

Whereas disregard and contempt for human rights have resulted in barbarous acts which have outraged the conscience of mankind, and the advent of a world in which human beings shall enjoy freedom of speech and belief and freedom from fear and want has been proclaimed as the highest aspiration of the common people.

Whereas it is essential, if man is not to be compelled to have recourse, as a last resort, to rebellion against tyranny and oppression, that human rights should be protected by the rule of law.

Whereas it is essential to promote the development of friendly relations between nations.

Whereas the peoples of the United Nations have in the Charter reaffirmed their faith in fundamental human rights, in the dignity and worth of the human person and in the equal rights of men and women and have determined to promote social progress and better standards of life in larger freedom.

Whereas Member States have pledged themselves to achieve, in co-operation with the United Nations, the promotion of universal respect for and observance of human rights and fundamental freedoms.

Whereas a common understanding of these rights and freedoms is of the greatest importance for the full realization of this pledge.

Now, Therefore THE GENERAL ASSEMBLY proclaims THIS UNIVERSAL DECLARATION OF HUMAN RIGHTS as a common standard of achievement for all peoples and all nations, to the end that every individual and every organ of society, keeping this Declaration constantly in mind, shall strive by teaching and education to promote respect for these rights and freedoms and by progressive measures, national and international, to secure their universal and effective recognition and observance, both among the peoples of Member States themselves and among the peoples of territories under their jurisdiction.

READING 8
Benefits of the Profit Motive
Adam Smith

(from *Wealth of Nations*)

. . . In almost every other race of animals each individual, when it is grown up to maturity, is entirely independent, and in its natural state has occasion for the assistance of no other living creature. But man has almost constant occasion for the help of his brethren, and it is in vain for him to expect it from their benevolence only. He will be more likely to prevail if he can interest their self-love in his favor, and show them that it is for their own advantage to do for him what he requires of them. Whoever offers to another a bargain of any kind, proposes to do this. Give me that which I want, and you shall have this which you want, is the meaning of every such offer; and it is in the manner that we obtain from one another the far greater part of those good offices which we stand in need of. It is not from the benevolence of the butcher, the brewer, or the baker, that we expect our dinner, but from their regard to their own interest. We address ourselves, not to their humanity but to their self-love, and never talk to them of our own necessities but of their advantages. Nobody but a begger chooses to depend chiefly upon the benevolence of his fellow-citizens. Even a beggar does not depend upon it entirely. The charity of well-disposed people, indeed, supplies him with the whole fund of his subsistence. But though this principle ultimately provides him with all the necessaries of life which he has occasion for, it neither does nor can provide him with them as he has occasion for them. The greater part of his occasional wants are supplied in the same manner as those of other people, by treaty, by barter, and by purchase. With the money which one man gives him he purchases food. The old clothes which another bestows upon him he exchanges for other old clothes which suit him better, or for lodging, or for food, or for money, with which he can buy either food, clothes, or lodging, as he has occasion.

. . .

Every individual is continually exerting himself to find out the most advantageous employment for whatever capital he can command. It is his own advantage, indeed, and not that of the society, which he has in view. But the study of his own advantage, naturally, or rather necessarily, leads him to prefer that employment which is most advantageous to the society . . . .

As every individual, therefore, endeavours as much as he can both to employ his capital in the support of domestic industry, and so to direct that industry that its produce may be of the greatest value, every individual necessarily labors to render the annual revenue of the society as great as he can. He generally, indeed, neither intends to promote the public interest, nor knows how much he is promoting it. By-preferring the support of domestic to that of foreign industry, he intends only his own security: and by directing that industry in such a manner as its produce may be of the greatest value, he intends only his own gain, and he is in this, as in many other cases, led by an invisible hand to promote an end which was no part of his intention. Nor is it always the worse for the society that it was no part of it. By pursuing his own interest he frequently promotes that of the society more effectually than when he really intends to promote it. I have never known much good done by those who affected to trade for the public good. It is an affectation, indeed, not very common among merchants, and very few words need be employed in dissuading them from it.

READING 9
Increasing Profits as Social Responsibility

Milton Friedman

(from *N.Y. Times,* Sept. 13, 1970)

[The businessmen who believe] that they are defending free enterprise when they declaim that business is not concerned "merely" with profit but also with promoting desirable "social" ends; that business has a "social conscience" and takes seriously its responsibilities for providing employment, eliminating discrimination, avoiding pollution and whatever else may be the catchwords of the contemporary crop of reformers. In fact they are—or would be if they or anyone else took them seriously—preaching pure and unadulterated socialism. Businessmen who talk this way are unwitting puppets of the intellectual forces that have been undermining the basis of a free society these past decades.

The discussion of the "social responsibilities of business" are notable for their analytical looseness and lack of rigor. What does it mean to say that "business" has responsibilities? Only people can have responsibilities. A corporation is an artificial person and in this sense may have artificial responsibilities, but "business" as a whole cannot be said to have responsibilities, even in this vague sense.

. . .

What does it mean to say that the corporate executive has a "social responsibility" in his capacity as businessman? If this statement is not pure rhetoric, it must mean that he is to act in some way that is not in the interest of his employers. For example, that he is to refrain from increasing the price of the product in order to contribute to the social objective of preventing inflation, even though a price increase would be in the best interests of the corporation. Or that he is to make expenditures on reducing pollution beyond the amount that is in the best interests of the corporation or that

is required by law in order to contribute to the social objective of improving the environment. Or that, at the expense of corporate profits, he is to hire "hardcore" unemployed instead of better qualified available workmen to contribute to the social objective of reducing poverty.

. . .

Whether blameworthy or not, the use of the cloak of social responsibility, and the nonsense spoken in its name by influential and prestigious businessmen, does clearly harm the foundations of a free society. I have been impressed time and again by the schizophrenic character of many businessmen. They are capable of being extremely far-sighted and clear-headed in matters that are internal to their businesses. They are incredibly short-sighted and muddle-headed in matters that are outside their businesses but affect the possible survival of business in general. This short-sightedness is strikingly exemplified in the calls from many businessmen for wage and price guidelines or controls or income policies. There is nothing that could do more in a brief period to destroy a market system and replace it by a centrally controlled system than effective governmental control of prices and wages.

. . .

But the doctrine of "social responsibility" taken seriously would extend the scope of the political mechanism to every human activity. It does not differ in philosophy from the most explicitly collectivist doctrine. It differs only by professing to believe that collectivist ends can be attained without collectivist means. That is why, in my book "Capitalism and Freedom," I have called it a "fundamentally subversive doctrine" in a free society, and have said that in such a society, "there is one and only one social responsibility of business—to use its resources and engage in activities designed to increase its profits so long as it stays within the rules of the game, which is to say, engages in open and free competition without deception or fraud."

READING 10
Economic Justice for All
Pastoral Letter 1986/1997 National Conference of Catholic Bishops

PRINCIPAL THEMES

13. *Every economic* decision *and institution must be judged in light of whether it protects or undermines the dignity of the human person.* The pastoral letter begins with the human person. We believe the person is sacred—the clearest reflection of God among us. Human dignity comes from God, not from nationality, race, sex, economic status, or any human accomplishment. We judge any economic system by what it does *for* and *to* people and by how it permits all to *participate* in it. The economy should serve people, not the other way around.

14. *Human dignity can be realized and protected only in community.* In our teaching, the human person is not only sacred but also social. How we organize our society—in economics and politics, in law and policy—directly affects human dignity and the capacity of individuals to grow in community. The obligation to "love our neighbor" has an individual dimension, but it also requires a broader social commitment to the common good. We have many partial ways to measure and debate the health of our economy: Gross National Product, per capita income, stock market prices, and so forth. The Christian vision of economic life looks beyond them all and asks, Does economic life enhance or threaten our life together as a community?

15. *All people have a right to participate in the economic life of society.* Basic justice demands that people be assured a minimum level of participation in the economy. It is wrong for a person or group to be excluded unfairly or to be unable to participate or contribute to the economy. For example, people who are both able and willing, but cannot get a job are deprived of the participation that is so vital to human development. For, it is through employment that most individuals and families meet their material needs, exercise their talents, and have an opportunity to contribute to the larger community. Such participation has a special significance in our tradition because we believe that it is a means by which we join in carrying forward God's creative activity.

16. *All members of society have a special obligation to the poor and vulnerable.* From the Scriptures and church teaching, we learn that the justice of a society is tested by the treatment of the poor. The justice that was the sign of God's covenant with Israel was measured by how the poor and unprotected—the widow, the orphan, and the stranger—were treated. The kingdom that Jesus proclaimed in his word and ministry excludes no one. Throughout Israel's history and in early Christianity, the poor are agents of God's transforming power. "The Spirit of the Lord is upon me, therefore he has anointed me. He has sent me to bring glad tidings to the poor" (Lk 4:18). This was Jesus' first public utterance. Jesus takes the side of those most in need. In the Last Judgment, so dramatically described in St. Matthew's Gospel, we are told that we will be judged according to how we respond to the hungry, the thirsty, the naked, the stranger. As followers of Christ, we are challenged to make a fundamental "option for the poor"—to speak for the voiceless, to defend the defenseless, to assess life styles, policies, and social institutions in terms of their impact on the poor. This "option for the poor" does not mean pitting one group against another, but rather, strengthening the whole community by assisting those who are most

vulnerable. As Christians, we are called to respond to the needs of *all* our brothers and sisters, but those with the greatest needs require the greatest response.

17. *Human rights are the minimum conditions for life in community.* In Catholic teaching, human rights include not only civil and political rights but also economic rights. As Pope John XXIII declared, "all people have a right to life, food, clothing, shelter, rest, medical care, education, and employment." This means that when people are without a chance to earn a living, and must go hungry and homeless, they are being denied basic rights. Society must ensure that these rights are protected. In this way, we will ensure that the minimum conditions of economic justice are met for all our sisters and brothers.

18. *Society as a whole, acting through public and private institutions, has the moral responsibility to enhance human dignity and protect human rights.* In addition to the clear responsibility of private institutions, government has an essential responsibility in this area. This does not mean that government has the primary or exclusive role, but it does have a positive moral responsibility in safeguarding human rights and ensuring that the minimum conditions of human dignity are met

for all. In a democracy, government is a means by which we can act together to protect what is important to us and to promote our common values.

19. These six moral principles are not the only ones presented in the pastoral letter, but they give an overview of the moral vision that we are trying to share. This vision of economic life cannot exist in a vacuum; it must be translated into concrete measures. Our pastoral letter spells out some specific applications of Catholic moral principles. We call for a new national commitment to full employment. We say it is a social and moral scandal that one of every seven Americans is poor, and we call for concerted efforts to eradicate poverty. The fulfillment of the basic needs of the poor is of the highest priority. We urge that all economic policies be evaluated in light of their impact on the life and stability of the family. We support measures to halt the loss of family farms and to resist the growing concentration in the ownership of agricultural resources. We specify ways in which the United States can do far more to relieve the plight of poor nations and assist in their development. We also reaffirm church teaching on the rights of workers, collective bargaining, private property, subsidiarity, and equal opportunity.

READING 11
Economic Behavior and Moral Sentiments
Amartya Sen
(from *On Ethics and Economics*)

. . . It is not altogether clear what congratulations are due to Political Economy for its alleged demand, to paraphrase Dante, "Abandon all friendliness, you who enter!" Perhaps the economist might be personally allowed a moderate dose of friendliness, provided in his economic models he keeps the motivations of human beings pure, simple and hard-headed, and not messed up by such things as goodwill or moral sentiments.

While this view of economics is quite widely held (and not without reason, given the way modern economics has evolved), there is nevertheless something quite extraordinary in the fact that economics has in fact evolved in this way, characterizing human motivation in such spectacularly narrow terms. One reason why this is extraordinary is that economics is supposed to be concerned with real people. It is hard to believe that real people could be completely unaffected by the reach of the self-examination induced by the Socratic question, "How should one live?" . . . Can the people whom economics studies really be so unaffected by this resilient question and stick exclusively to the rudimentary hard-headedness attributed to them by modern economics?

Another surprising feature is the contrast between the self-consciously "non-ethical" character of modern economics and the historical evolution of modern economics largely as an offshoot of ethics. Not only was the so-called "father of modern economics," Adam Smith, a Professor of Moral Philosophy at the University of Glasgow (admittedly, a rather pragmatic town), but the subject of economics was for a long time seen as something like a branch of ethics. The fact that economics used to be taught at Cambridge until fairly recently simply as a part of "the Moral Science Tripos" is no more than an instance of the traditional diagnosis of the nature of economics.

. . .

It is, in fact, arguable that economics has had two rather different origins, both related to politics, but related in rather different ways, concerned respectively with "ethics," on the one hand, and with what may be called "engineering," on the other. The ethics-related tradition goes back at least to Aristotle. At the very beginning of *The Nico-machean Ethics,* Aristotle relates the subject of economics to human ends, referring to its concern with wealth. He sees politics as "the master art," Politics must use "the rest of the sciences," including economics, and "since, again, it legislates as to what we are to do and what we are to abstain from, the end of this science must include those of the others, so that this end must be the good for man." The study of economics, though related immediately to the pursuit of wealth, is at a deeper level linked up with other studies, involving the assessment and enhancement of more basic goals. "The life of money-making is one undertaken under compulsion, and wealth is evidently not the good we are seeking; for it is merely useful and for the sake of something else." Economics relates ultimately to the study of ethics and that of politics, and this point

of view is further developed in Aristotle's *Politics.*

There is no scope in all this for dissociating the study of economics from that of ethics and political philosophy. In particular, it is worth noting here that in this approach there are two central issues that are particularly foundational for economics. First, there is the problem of human motivation related to the broadly ethical question "How should one live?" To emphasize this connection is not the same as asserting that people will always act in ways they will themselves morally defend, but only to recognize that ethical deliberations cannot be totally inconsequential to actual human behaviour. I shall call this "the ethics-related view of motivation."

The second issue concerns the judgement of social achievement. Aristotle related this to the end of achieving "the good for man," but noted some specially aggregative features in the exercise: "though it is worthwhile to attain the end merely for one man, it is finer and more godlike to attain it for a nation or for city-states." This "ethics-related view of social achievement" cannot stop the evaluation short at some arbitrary point like satisfying "efficiency." The assessment has to be more fully ethical, and take a broader view of "the good." This is a point of some importance again in the context of modern economics, especially modern welfare economics.

The first of the two origins of economics, related to ethics and to an ethical view of politics, does in this way point towards certain irreducible tasks of economics. I shall have to take on presently the question as to how well modern economics has been able to perform these tasks. But before that, I turn to the *other* origin of economics—related to the "engineering" approach. This approach is characterized by being concerned with primarily logistic issues rather than with ultimate ends and such questions as what may foster "the good of man" or "how should one live." The ends are taken as fairly straightforwardly given, and the object of the exercise is to find the appropriate means to serve them. Human behaviour is typically seen as being based on simple and easily characterizable motives.

. . .

It is arguable that the importance of the ethical approach has rather substantially weakened as modern economics has evolved. The methodology of so-called "positive economics" has not only shunned normative analysis in economics, it has also had the effect of ignoring a variety of complex ethical considerations which affect actual human behaviour and which, from the point of view of the economists studying such behaviour, are primarily matters of fact rather than of normative judgement. If one examines the balance of emphases in the publications in modern economics, it is hard not to notice the eschewal of deep normative analysis, and the neglect of the influence of ethical considerations in the characterization of actual human behaviour.

READING 12
The Deficiencies of Global Capitalism
George Soros
(from *George Soros on Globalization*)

Globalization is an overused term that can be given a wide variety of meanings. For the purposes of the present discussion, I shall take it to mean the development of global financial markets, the growth of transnational corporations, and their increasing domination over national economies. I believe that most of the problems that people associate with globalization, including the penetration of market values into areas where they do not traditionally belong, can be attributed to these phenomena.

. . .

The salient feature of globalization is that it allows financial capital to move around freely; by contrast, the movement of people remains heavily regulated. Since capital is an essential ingredient of production, individual countries must compete to attract it; this inhibits their ability to tax and regulate it. Under the influence of globalization, the character of our economic and social arrangements has undergone a radical transformation. The ability of capital to go elsewhere undermines the ability of the state to exercise control over the economy. . . .

The transformation that has occurred since the 1980s is not well understood. It is not even generally acknowledged. Capital has always been eager to avoid taxation and regulation, so it is easy to interpret the current tendency to reduce taxation and regulation as merely the manifestation of universally and timelessly valid economic laws. That is, in fact, the dominant view at least in the English-speaking world. I have called it *market fundamentalism*. It holds that the allocation of resources is best left to the market mechanism, and any interference with that mechanism reduces the efficiency of the economy. Judged by the criteria of market fundamentalism, globalization has been a highly successful project.

Globalization is indeed a desirable development in many ways. Private enterprise is better at wealth creation than the state. Moreover, states have a tendency to abuse their power; globalization offers a degree of individual freedom that no individual state could ensure. Free competition on a global scale has liberated inventive and entrepreneurial talents and accelerated technological innovations.

But globalization also has a negative side. First, many people, particularly in less-developed countries, have been hurt by globalization without being supported by a social safety net; many others have been marginalized by global markets. Second, globalization has caused a misallocation of resources between private goods and public goods. Markets are good at creating wealth but are not designed to take care of other social needs. The heedless pursuit of profit can hurt the environment and conflict with other social values. Third, global financial markets are crisis prone. People living in the developed countries may not be fully aware of the devastation wrought by financial crises because, for reasons that will be explained later, they tend to hit the developing economies much harder. All three factors combine to create a very uneven playing field.

. . .

Political processes generally speaking are less efficient than the market mechanism, but we cannot do without them. Markets are amoral: They allow people to act in accordance with their interests, and they impose some rules on how those interests are expressed, but they pass no moral judgment on the interests themselves. That is one of the reasons why they are so efficient. It is difficult to decide what is right and wrong; by leaving it out of account, markets allow people to pursue their interests without let or hindrance.

But society cannot function without some distinction between right and wrong. The task of making collective decisions about what is allowed and what is forbidden is left to politics—and politics suffers from the difficulties of reaching collective decisions in a world that lacks a strong moral code. Even the creation and maintenance of markets requires political action. This point is well understood by market fundamentalists. What is less well recognized is that the globalization of markets without a corresponding strengthening of our international political and social arrangements has led to a very lopsided social development.

. . .

The risks that confront us cannot be understood in terms of the disciplines we have relied on to establish our supremacy: market discipline and geopolitical realism. Both disciplines relate to power. But the responsibilities I am talking about are moral responsibilities. That is the missing ingredient in U.S. policy. It is of course not entirely missing; it is only shunted to the sidelines by the prevailing doctrines of market fundamentalism and geopolitical realism.

. . .

We have been so put off by the perversion of morality that we are trying to do without morality. The distinguishing feature of both market fundamentalism and geopolitical realism is that they are *amoral*—morality does not enter into the calculations. That is one of the reasons why they have been so successful. We have been seduced by their success into thinking that we can do without moral considerations. We have come to worship success. We admire businessmen who make a fortune and politicians who get themselves elected irrespective of how they have done it.

That is where we have gone wrong. No society can exist without morality. Even our amoral pursuits need a moral justification. Market fundamentalists claim that the untrammeled pursuit of self-interest serves the common interest; and the exercise of our geopolitical power appeals to our patriotism. The fact remains that these are amoral pursuits. If that is all we have to offer, our view of the world is liable to be rejected by more traditional societies where morality still plays a central role. That is the case in traditional Islamic societies where church and state have not even been separated. In the end, we may not find it satisfactory ourselves.

When I speak of morality . . . I mean accepting the responsibilities that go with belonging to a global community. Those responsibilities are not well defined at present. Our international arrangements are based on the sovereignty of states, and states are guided by their own interests that do not necessarily coincide with the interests of the people who live in those states and are even less likely to coincide with the interests of humanity as a whole. Those latter interests need to be better protected than they are at present.

READING 13
The Philosopher King
Plato
(from *Republic*)

Next, it seems, we must try to discover and point out what it is that is now badly managed in our cities, and that prevents them from being so governed, and what is the smallest change that would bring a state to this manner of government, preferably a change in one thing, if not, then in two, and, failing that, the fewest possible in number and the slightest in potency.

By all means, he said.

There is one change, then, said I, which I think that we can show would bring about the desired transformation. It is not a slight or an easy thing but it is possible.

What is that? he said.

I am on the very verge, said I, of what we likened to the greatest wave of paradox. But say it I will, even if, to keep the figure, it is likely to wash us away on billows of laughter and scorn. Listen.

I am all attention, he said.

Unless, said I, either philosophers become kings in our states or those whom we now call our kings and rulers take to the pursuit of philosophy seriously and adequately, and there is a conjunction of these two things, political power and philosophical intelligence, while the motley horde of the natures who at present pursue either apart from the other are compulsorily excluded, there can be no cessation of troubles, dear Glaucon, for our states, nor, I fancy, for the human race either. Nor, until this happens, will this constitution which we have been expounding in theory ever be put into practice within the limits of possibility and see the light of the sun. But this is the thing that has made me so long shrink from speaking out, because I saw that it would be a very paradoxical saying. For it is not easy to see that there is no other way of happiness either for private or public life.

READING 14
Wisdom and Virtue as the Basis of Society
Aristotle
(from *Politics*)

1. He who would duly inquire about the best form of a state ought first to determine which is the most eligible life; while this remains uncertain the best form of the state must also be uncertain; for, in the natural order of things, those may be expected to lead the best life who are governed in the best manner of which their circumstances admit. We ought therefore to ascertain, first of all, which is the most generally eligible life, and then whether the same life is or is not best for the state and for individuals.

Assuming that enough has been already said in discussions outside the school concerning the best life, we will now only repeat what is contained in them. Certainly no one will dispute the propriety of that partition of goods which separates them into three classes, viz.

external goods, goods of the body, and goods of the soul, or deny that the happy man must have all three. For no one would maintain that he is happy who has not in him a particle of courage or temperance or justice or prudence, who is afraid of every insect which flutters past him, and will commit any crime, however great, in order to gratify his lust of meat or drink, who will sacrifice his dearest friend for the sake of half-a-farthing, and is as feeble and false in mind as a child or a madman. These propositions are almost universally acknowledged as soon as they are uttered, but men differ about the degree or relative superiority of this or that good. Some think that a very moderate amount of virtue is enough, but set no limit to their desires of wealth, property, power, reputation, and the like. To whom we reply by an appeal to facts, which easily prove that mankind do not acquire or preserve virtue by the help of external goods, but external goods by the help of virtue, and that happiness, whether consisting in pleasure or virtue, or both, is more often found with those who are most highly cultivated in their mind and in their character, and have only a moderate share of external goods, than among those who possess external goods to a useless extent but are deficient in higher qualities; and this is not only matter of experience, but, if reflected upon, will easily appear to be in accordance with reason. For, whereas external goods have a limit, like any other instrument, and all things useful are of such a nature that where there is too much of them they must either do harm, or at any rate be of no use, to their possessors, every good of the soul, the greater it is, is also of greater use, if the epithet useful as well as noble is appropriate to such subjects. No proof is required to show that the best state of one thing in relation to another corresponds in degree of excellence to the interval between the natures of which we say that these very states are states:

so that, if the soul is more noble than our possessions or our bodies, both absolutely and in relation to us, it must be admitted that the best state of either has a similar ratio to the other. Again, it is for the sake of the soul that goods external and goods of the body are eligible at all, and all wise men ought to choose them for the sake of the soul, and not the soul for the sake of them.

Let us acknowledge then that each one has just so much of happiness as he has of virtue and wisdom, and of virtuous and wise action. God is a witness to us of this truth, for he is happy and blessed, not by reason of any external good, but in himself and by reason of his own nature. And herein of necessity lies the difference between good fortune and happiness; for external goods come of themselves, and chance is the author of them, but no one is just or temperate by or through chance. In like manner, and by a similar train of argument, the happy state may be shown to be that which is best and which acts rightly; and rightly it cannot act without doing right actions, and neither individual nor state can do right actions without virtue and wisdom. Thus the courage, justice, and wisdom of a state have the same form and nature as the qualities which give the individual who possesses them the name of just, wise, or temperate.

Thus much may suffice by way of preface: for I could not avoid touching upon these questions, neither could I go through all the arguments affecting them; these are the business of another science.

Let us assume then that the best life, both for individuals and states, is the life of virtue, when virtue has external goods enough for the performance of good actions. If there are any who controvert our assertion, we will in this treatise pass them over, and consider their objections hereafter.

Chapter Six

Integrity of Life Questions

VALUE AND THE INTEGRITY OF LIFE

The existence of values is a primary truth which, as with other primary truths, we know intuitively; we don't *argue* to the existence of *values*, we *recognize* them. Though value escapes definition, we comprehend it in and through our experience. On a trivial level, I choose one pair of shoes over another because they're my favorite color; or a Szechuan dinner over another, because it's spicier. But on a higher level we raise questions—significant ones—as to how things stand before us. How important is it for me? Do I cherish it? Is it worth something to me? Does it have meaning for me, or for anyone else? What would be the consequences if it were diminished, or done away with entirely? These questions touch a new dimension of reality, a dimension called *value*. Values are real; they are given; they cannot be suppressed. Whenever or wherever you try to push them down, they'll show up at another time or another place. Even the nineteenth-century philosopher Friedrich Nietzsche, widely considered as a "nihilist" because he weighed in so strongly against the accepted values of his time, knew that the notion of value could not be destroyed, only transformed, which is why he elaborated a vision for what he termed a "*transvaluation of values*," a program to do away with the "values" of the past that have brought us to the world's sorry state and to introduce a new set of values for rehumanizing humanity. Another way of putting it is found in Ludwig Wittgenstein, writing a generation or so later, who expressed a difference between what can be *said* and what can be *shown*; that is, among the things we know, there are some things that can be "said," or put into words; and there are other things that simply *show* themselves, which I can grasp or comprehend but cannot be put into words; they are unsayable, like life, soul, and God—these things "cannot be put into words. They *make themselves manifest*. They *are* what is mystical." It's in this category that values are located—values in general, but ethical values in particular—truths, so fundamental that they must be understood, not in terms of anything else but themselves (R #1).

At first, and for the most part, value strikes us as *relational*, or instrumental. For example, the chair has a value in relation to one's need for sitting down, or grandmother's wedding ring as a family heirloom, or a pair of right-fitting sneakers for running, or a palette of paints for the artist. We should ask, however, whether the value of a thing is always to be measured by its relation to something else, or is there a way of talking of the value of a thing *in itself*? There is a sense in which a thing has to *be* before it can be relational, and that fact touches upon a deeper reason, indeed the deepest reason, as to why a thing has any value at all, and why one thing can have a higher value than another: *its existential level.* When we say that a stone is a *being,* a rose is a *being,* a dog is a *being,* and a man is a *being,* the meaning of *being* is not the same in each case. It does not mean that a stone is a rose, is a dog, is a man; the stone-being is not the rose-being, nor is the dog-being the human-being. They are profoundly different because they differ in their *very existence.* One level is higher than the previous, and each higher level extends the boundary of meaning, until they open upon the human level, the level of intelligence and free will, of body and soul, of love and emotion, of art and creation, and of an interwoven tissue of relationships that can release the human spirit. That's what makes *human life valuable in itself* and, inasmuch as human life can only be lived in individuals, *every* individual human being is a *unique expression of human life and a value unto itself.* It is this fact that grounds moral concerns for the life of each human being and the obligation of everyone else to respect it. To the extent that the physical integrity of human life is lost or diminished, to that extent its value is lost or diminished as well.

There are many ways in which the integrity of human life can be diminished, as in a case of personal hurt, or loss of respect, or unrequited friendship, and so on, but the first palpable diminution of life is in its very physicality. This chapter will therefore consider some aspects of the *physical* life of human beings that are seriously threatened today—the life and death questions of abortion, euthanasia, physician-assisted suicide, and capital punishment.

ABORTION

In the United States, from the last generation to this, there has perhaps been no legal/moral question as hotly contested as abortion. It has stirred up emotions, fanned controversy, pitted legal minds against each other, divided politicians, created a breach between doctors who will or will not perform abortions, fueled the feminist movement, and provoked unexpected consequences like the assassination of abortion doctors and the demand for teenage privacy. There are those who maintain that abortion should never have entered the legal domain at all because, having done so, it again makes it appear that what is legal is thereby moral; civil law poaching upon the natural law. Legalists can argue among themselves as to whether or not the Supreme Court circumvented legal procedures in the *Roe v. Wade* decision of 1973, but it has become the *de facto* law of the country.

On January 22 of that year, the Supreme Court issued a landmark decision that has become the effective legal decision on abortion for the entire country. The case, *Roe v. Wade,* arose in Wade County, Texas, concerning a state statute that permitted abortion only when deemed necessary to save the woman's life. It was successfully argued that the state law was too restrictive. The Court was reluctant to refer to the developing fetus as having actual human life and thus referred to it as having "potential human life," thereby allowing the Court to decide that being a fetus does not qualify as being a "person" in the sense of the Constitution, and so is not covered by the Fourteenth Amendment. The Court saw the "interest of the state" increasing as the fetus developed toward birth and toward becoming a "person" in the Constitutional sense. Accordingly, the Court divided the time of pregnancy into three trimesters of an estimated three months each. During the first trimester, the state has no, or little, direct interest in the course of the pregnancy and so it may *not regulate abortion at* all. The abortion decision is left up to the medical judgment of the physician which, in practical terms, is abortion on request. During the second trimester the state's interest increases to that point where it may regulate, not the abortion itself, but the *abortion procedure*, where and how an abortion may be performed. During the third trimester, the state's interest is at its highest and the state, going beyond abortion procedure, may *regulate abortion itself* and even proscribe it, except in the case of the mother's health. Though *Roe v. Wade* has been under constant challenge, it remains the effective law of the land (R #2).

Even without *Roe v. Wade* there would still have been a profound controversy over the morality of abortion, for its morality lies beyond the law. But it's no way to settle a controversy by calling into question the good faith of the opposition with each side firing epithets at the other, the pro-life side calling its opponents "murderers" for attacking the unborn, and the pro-choice side calling its opponents "insensitive" to life because their stand on the unborn is mocked by their stand on the death penalty. After all, if half the country were to challenge the good faith of the other half on the question of abortion, then the whole country would be in bad faith! Some people display a callous disregard of human life, against which stands the vast majority of human beings who treasure its sanctity and for whom, as far as abortion is concerned, a decision is a painful and agonizing one to make (R #3). There is a remarkable social irony here in that the anonymous "Roe" of *Roe v. Wade* has since openly declared her name and personal history, and that today she is totally against abortion (R #4). It still remains true that discussing abortion thoroughly and presenting it sincerely is the only way to reach mutual understanding.

The definition of abortion given earlier as the *deliberate termination of a pregnancy* seems to be acceptable all around. But it's a matter of historical interest that in the not too distant past its definition was essentially "the removal of a living and non-viable fetus from the womb," which, by definition, would also mean the death of the fetus. This bygone definition of abortion can be ascertained by looking into any older encyclopedia or textbook in moral philosophy. Perhaps the universal acceptance of the current definition was all but guaranteed by the Supreme Court decision.

Innocent human life can never be taken deliberately, "innocent" (Latin: non-hurting) insofar as one is doing nothing to hurt another, either voluntarily or involuntarily. If human life is present before birth then that life is innocent and cannot directly be harmed. So the *key question* in deciding the morality of abortion is whether human life is present before birth: when does human life begin? when can we say there is a human being? at what point in the process of becoming human, sometimes called *humanization*, is there unquestionably a human being? It's clear that we are talking of the span of time running from the moment the male element (sperm) and the female element (ovum) unite in what is often called "conception," which biologists call "fertilization," to the moment of birth, when all, or almost all, admit that a human being is certainly present. To clarify a possible source of confusion it should be pointed out that, in everyday conversation, there is seldom a distinction made in the way the terms *human being* and *person* are used; they are used interchangeably. But during the years of abortion controversy, there has been a tendency to make a distinction between them. On one hand some distinguish between "human being" as a biological designation and "person" as a philosophical one inasmuch as a "person" is generated by intersubjective relationships which begin only after birth. Such a reason is, however, subject to challenge because, though it is true that a new set of relations opens up at birth, the unborn is already deeply related to its parents, for example, whose whole life has undergone a radical change by its very existence. The Supreme Court's use of "person" circumvents the biological meaning to the extent that the unborn is not yet a "person" in the sense of the Constitution. Normally, the context will clarify usage.

There are some moralists for whom the question about the beginning of human life makes no difference; it is *not* the key question because it is not at all relevant to the morality of abortion—aborting the fetus at any time may be defensible. So, for example, Judith Jarvis Thomson, whose views we'll consider later, holds that even if the fetus is human at the moment of conception, aborting it is still a defensible option.

There are *cultural* differences regarding the time in which human life begins. The Chinese and Japanese, for example, count the time of pregnancy as part of the child's first year, not that they say nine months plus three equal the first year, but that what they call the second birthday is what in the West would be called the *first*. Traditionally in the West some amount of time, without saying how much, was allowed for the *process* of humanization to take place. A recent and interesting study on sexual knowledge in nineteenth-century America points out that there was, in the earlier part of the century, no sure way of determining whether a woman was pregnant, but ordinary women, with a kind of secret female knowledge, knew how to bring an abortion about in the early stages of pregnancy, which is not as directly anti-life as it sounds, for "there was an understanding by both sexes that human life began not at conception but at quickening, the fetal movements at roughly twenty weeks into a pregnancy" (R #5).

Combining his *philosophical* point of view with the biological, Aristotle, in the fourth century B.C., maintained that, because a soul acts in and through a body, there could not be sufficient physical formation in the early stages to support the presence of a human soul, which would require, he felt, about three months; he offered no opinion as to how the soul was "generated." In this he was followed by St. Thomas Aquinas in the thirteenth century who believed that at the right moment of physical formation, God, in the process of "ensoulment," would "infuse" a human soul into the living, but not yet human, being to make it a human being. Finally others hold that, since we do not know the precise time of humanization, we must take the safer path and treat the first moment of fertilization as the first moment of human life.

The early two weeks or so in the *biological* process of human reproduction are very complicated in that there is persistent difficulty in interpreting the sequence of events leading to the formation of the embryo, particularly as to when it can be said for sure that the first phase of the continuing individuality of a human being (a person) is reached. By definition an individual organism is a whole being, living from within itself, so that it would be impossible to have one individual organism composed in turn of two or more individual organisms. The process of producing a human being, sometimes called humanization, takes time and precludes the expectation of a totally new and separate individual emerging immediately at the moment of fertilization. Biology tells us that shortly after fertilization, a one-celled entity, called a zygote, is produced and that development toward the status of embryo takes place by adding cells from without, with later division into separate cells for ultimate specific purposes in the body, or by recombining with other cells before it moves ahead. It's at this point where the biologist cannot say with any certitude that we are witnessing the emergence of the first phase of a unitary being ready to move on uninterruptedly to birth. Most biologists would seem to hold that the first phase is to be found in the fetus, or, put another way, that an individual human being can be traced back to the fetus. Some few would hold that we are not, with certainty, dealing with a human person until the cerebral cortex is formed, sometime between the twenty-fifth and fortieth day of pregnancy.

An interesting episode, called *twinning*, in these early events appears and gives some pause in arriving at certitude. The embryonic cell is considered at times to be able to divide into two individuals, therefore "twins," demonstrating that what can split in two is not yet a whole individual in itself. But others say "not so fast" because what we know today of cloning suggests that what takes place may not be a "division" into two but only the separation of a small part of the whole to be cultured into a whole in itself. The importance of a biological determination in this regard has an importance for moral determination as well, for if there is not yet *certainly* an individual, a unitary being, there cannot be an organism capable of being designated as human; in which case, it can be argued, the termination of the biological process would not *certainly* be the termination of a human life. But when the conditions for individuality are met, and there is a human organism, from that moment on there is also a destiny of *continuity* for that individual through the many stages of human life yet to come: gestation, birth, infancy, adolescence, adulthood, and old age, the same human being throughout. A biologist would be hard put to deny that at some point in its development, the unborn becomes a human being. Birth, then, cannot be considered as the dividing line between the not-as-yet human and the human, so the inviolability of life accorded those already born extends as well to the unborn life from the first moment it is humanized.

Regularly advanced in abortion discussion is an argument against individuality in that the *fetus is part of the woman's body* and therefore cannot be an individual strictly so called. It's inside of her; it's part of her life; its nutrition comes entirely from her; its growth and development and its very health depend on her; it's totally dependent on her, so there cannot be two lives, only one. How could it then not be part of her body? Implied, of course, is that the woman can do whatever she wants with her own body. The argument from total dependence, however, is hardly an argument at all when you realize that total dependence is also true of the newborn, and no one demonstrates this better than the newborn itself which, in a thousand different ways, asserts its need for attention. Total dependence of the infant does not argue against its individuality; it is simply a totally dependent individual, a totally dependent human being. Many of the old and infirm too are totally dependent on the care of others, but no one argues that they are not individual human beings. The same must be said of infants.

What then can be morally said of *abortion on demand*, that is, abortion for the asking? Surely this phrase is too simple a way of framing an important matter, for the fact is that no one asks for anything for without a reason; to do so would be impossible. But reasons can be multiple in number, if not countless. If the reasons are *frivolous*, they cannot be taken as morally justifying, such as distaste for appearing pregnant in public, or being unable to go horseback riding, or dancing. Can any reason be called a substantial reason when it comes to justifying an abortion? Note that the question is not to be answered by saying that it's a matter of conscience, which, of course, it is, as all moral matters are. It's whether the reason is founded objectively, whether there is, in the condition of pregnancy, sometime when it can be said that the living entity is not yet a human being. This possibility was explored earlier and we saw that becoming human is precisely that, a process; it takes time to become human; exactly when it is achieved cannot be stated with certainty, though it can be stated with certainty that the earlier the stage in question, the surer we can be that the entity is still in the process of becoming human. If the action terminating the pregnancy takes place before the entity becomes human, then it's arguable that it is morally justified by a substantial reason, such as signs of serious future abnormality, or profound complications for the mother. If the termination happens *after* becoming human, then no reason can be said to be substantial because no reason allows the taking of an innocent life.

It was pointed out earlier that Judith Jarvis Thomson is an abortion proponent of influence, so we should take a closer look at her argumentation, stressing one point in particular: the relation of the fetus to the woman's body. We saw that it is held by many pro-abortionists that the fetus is part of the woman's body. But Thomson's argument is quite different; for her there's no need to talk of the fetus as "part" of anything. She holds, from the viewpoint of rights and obligations, that the woman has no obligation to let the fetus *use* her body, nor has the fetus the right to that use, with perhaps some exceptions, because "no doubt the mother has a right to decide what shall happen in and to her body; everyone would grant that." But would everyone? That's precisely the problem that divides millions on either side of the abortion debate. To illustrate her point, Thomson proposes a hypothetical case which has become well known. Suppose you wake up one morning to the extraordinary event of your having been silently attached to an unconscious world-class violinist because you alone have the blood type necessary to relieve his kidney condition and rescue him from sure death. Now, if you ask yourself whether you have an obligation, or he a right, to let your body be used to save him, even if it takes a day, a week, a month, or nine months, clearly you would answer "no." Well, then, regardless of how the fetus got to where it is, the woman has no obligation to let it use her body, nor has it the reciprocal right. The conclusion, for Thomson, is obvious: to abort is not a moral problem.

To return to the position affirmed earlier, though no reason can be found to take an innocent life, some further consideration must be given when a pregnancy involving the mother's life is at stake. There is no moral dilemma if the death of a nonviable fetus is foreseen in the course of a medically required procedure, let's say, the removal of a cancerous uterus, which would be done even in the absence of pregnancy; the pregnancy, that is, has nothing to do with the cancerous condition. In such a case, the life of the fetus would not be terminated directly or deliberately, but would be the unintended result of a morally good medical procedure—an application of the *principle of the two-fold effect*, discussed in Chapter 2. However there is a moral dilemma if a pregnancy is allowed to continue and will pose *a serious threat* to the life of the mother. If the fetus is viable, it may be removed and then cared for in an artificial environment for the premature. What may be done, though, if the fetus is not viable and the doctor knows or is morally certain that the continuing pregnancy will be fatal to the mother? Here we have the dilemma at its highest point for, if the life of the fetus cannot be tampered with, and the situation is allowed to run its course, then the mother will die, or even both. May, then, the life of one be saved, at the expense of the other? If so, which one? Even if such a problem seldom occurs, and gynecologists have gone their entire lives without seeing one, it can still generate a strong passion against any moral doctrine that purports to "sacrifice the mother for the child."

We are dealing here with two precious lives and a decision is not easily arrived at, but another kind of analysis may offer some help. Several times we have seen the term *innocent* as the basic reason why a life cannot deliberately be taken, "innocent" meaning that no physical harm is gratuitously being done to another. But if one *is* doing such harm, then it may be repelled with as much force as is necessary to prevent it, even if death follows. Such a scenario presents a situation that is often called "unjust aggression," with the agent as the "unjust aggressor." If the aggressor is acting deliberately, that is, knowingly and willingly, then forceful repulsion is understandably justified. But even if the aggressor is not acting deliberately, forceful repulsion is still justified to defend life and integrity. A lifeguard, for example, called to help a man in distress swims out to help, but in doing so is overwhelmed by the man's manic strength, is taken down, and will certainly lose his life unless he does something. He is morally justified to use whatever force he has at his disposal to save himself, even if it results in the death of the drowning man. So, in the case of the difficult pregnancy given above, inasmuch as what the fetus is doing is threatening the life of the mother, though indeliberate, it is still an aggressor and whatever must be done to save the mother's life may justifiably be done. It cannot, however, be argued the other way around that, in threatening the life of the fetus, the mother's own life becomes forfeit: She has a prior right to life whatever her condition may be.

Those who favor abortion unconditionally will, of course, find the presentation given thus far unsupportable, but there are very few who would be willing to dismiss the *existential humanity* of the fetus so completely as *Peter Singer.* He is widely known for his forthright tackling of life issues and enjoys a well-deserved reputation in the matter of animal rights, as we shall see in a later section. His view on abortion is a radical departure from the path taken here. The point of departure rests on his assumption that the factor determining the value of life in a living being is not its existence, but the *degree of consciousness* it possesses. To determine the degree of consciousness in nonhuman animals that cannot articulate their self-awareness as humans can, Singer has recourse to other kinds of manifestation, particularly that of pain. On that basis the human fetus is shown to be far inferior to the calf, the pig, and the "much derided chicken"; even "a fish would show more signs of consciousness" than a human fetus less than three months old. The conclusion: " . . . we accord the life of a fetus no greater value than the life of a nonhuman animal at a similar level of rationality, self-consciousness, awareness, capacity to feel, etc." The fetus is not a person and does not have the same claim to life as a person. With some demurral in the case of late pregnancies, Singer writes: " . . . an abortion terminates an existence that is of no 'intrinsic' value at all." He ends this assertive paragraph by stating that our attitude toward an abortion even in late pregnancy, when some consciousness may be present, cannot be divorced from our attitude toward killing animals for meat: "Indeed, even an abortion late in pregnancy for the most trivial reasons is hard to condemn unless we also condemn the slaughter of far more developed forms of life for the taste of their flesh" (p. 151).

EUTHANASIA

Another life and death issue that has grown in recent years and will continue in years to come mainly because of increasing numbers of people reaching advanced age and developing technology is that of *euthanasia,* called "mercy killing" in times gone by. Any condition that prompts a person to ask for a release from life is one of profound poignancy for the person himself and those dear to him in an anguished *summary* of a lifetime of love, care, and concern. The action called for, misguided or not, that will bring an end to the useless suffering of a person in the state of terminal illness, is presumably done for his own good. A suitable definition of euthanasia, therefore, would be *an action, undertaken by another, that terminates, or allows the termination of, the life of a person already terminally ill or under intense physical suffering.* Any action outside this condition would simply be called murder. A distinction is often made between *active* (or *direct*) and *passive* (or *indirect*) euthanasia. *Active* euthanasia is had by a positive action that has the termination of life as its only end, for example, by lethal injection. *Passive* euthanasia is had, not by a positive action, but by "letting die," that is letting nature take its course, as, for example, in removing a life support system. The reason offered for this distinction is that those who favor euthanasia want to allow the patient to die without doing anything directly to kill him, therefore, letting "nature take its course." But this requires a second look. All of us, at times, speak of something we *should* have done, implying, of course, that some wrong has been done by *not doing* it. Thus a wrong can be done by *omission* as well as by *commission*: Just as we can *intend* to *do*, we can also *intend not to do*. So, from the moral viewpoint, it does not appear that there is any real distinction between active and passive euthanasia. In either case, it is the killing of an innocent person and against the inviolable character of human life, whether it is *voluntary* (willed by the person), *involuntary* (against the person's will), or *nonvoluntary* (beyond the person's will, as in the case of infants or the comatose).

Yet something more has to be said. An important distinction is made between *ordinary* and *extraordinary means.* In matters of health, "means" refer to any medication, procedure, or technology used to maintain health. *Ordinary means* (or proportionate) refers to any measures such as the average person would reasonably be expected to take; these measures will vary from time to time, and place to place—aspirin for a headache, an operation for appendicitis, a temporary life-support system for regaining one's own internal strength. *Extraordinary means* (or disproportionate) refer to those measures that are beyond what is normal and reasonable, or beyond what is averagely used. They are "extraordinary" by reason of their enormous expense, by their dubious efficacy, or by uncommon requirements for them to be successful; for example, the permanent use of a high-tech life-support system, the month-after-month need for special hospital and nursing services for the comatose elderly, or even an intense psychological aversion to a particular procedure. The application of this distinction is clear enough: In the name of reasonable and proportionate care, one is expected, or at times obliged, to use ordinary means. But as the means move toward the extraordinary, unreasonable, and disproportionate, therefore, the obligation becomes less and less to use them until no obligation at all remains. The distinction, it should be noted, is not based on whether technological intervention may be helpful *in the abstract, but whether relative to the patient* it is, with all things considered, proportionate or disproportionate intervention. One's refusal to use extraordinary care is not to be interpreted as intending one's own death, but only that death is foreseen and accepted as inevitable. If a person, let's say, in a permanent vegetative state as a result of a serious accident, is on a high-tech life-support system and after many months shows no chance of improvement, the system may be removed, though death is expected to follow.

The value of life demands that it not be treated cheaply, and that no measure affecting it should be taken without the person's consent. The freedom of the terminally ill is to be honored. If the person is an adult in the possession of his faculties, then there is no hindrance to his making his own choice regarding any extraordinary means to be taken; it is voluntary. If against his will, it is involuntary and wrongly administered. If the person is comatose, or otherwise incapable of making a decision, then some evidence of the choice he would have made if he were competent morally justifies the treatment; in such a case, the action is nonvoluntary. It is similarly nonvoluntary if the person is an infant or a child, and the decision for treatment is made by the parents or legally appointed guardians.

Moral decisions, as we've seen, are arrived at independently of legal decisions touching on the same matter, but it would be foolish to think that they never intersect, causing at times profound anxiety and frustration for everyone involved. One such case, and probably the one most widely known because it appeared when legal positions were in the process of being shaped, was the 1975 case of Karen Ann Quinlan. Karen, an adopted child, was a vigorous young adult and avid skier, twenty-one years of age, who, apparently because of some unforeseen consequences of medication, suddenly went into a comatose, vegetative state that was declared to be chronic and permanently irreversible. She never gave any signs of life, although she was never really brain dead. She was kept "alive" by means of a respirator. Upon consultation as to its morality, Karen's parents asked the authorities at Newton Memorial Hospital in Newton, New Jersey, to remove the respirator, which they felt they could not do without clear legal sanction. Mr. Quinlan then took steps to have himself declared Karen's legal guardian with the express purpose of legalizing the request made on her behalf. The case finally reached the Supreme Court of New Jersey whose decision was in favor of removing the respirator, which was then done. Despite the expectation of her dying shortly after that, she kept breathing on her own and lived for ten more years, eventually succumbing to pneumonia.

A second landmark case came in 1983. As a result of an accident Nancy Cruzan was cast into a persistent vegetative state, with only minimal brain activity, for seven years, fed by means of an abdominal tube. Her parents had been asking for the removal of the tube up until the time the case reached the U.S. Supreme Court, which denied the request because there was no "clear and convincing evidence" of her willingness to have it removed. Some time later, with new evidence submitted that she indeed would have rejected extraordinary treatment, the Missouri courts allowed the tube's removal in December 1990, and she died shortly thereafter.

Another recent event offers a third case in which the distinction between ordinary and extraordinary means in an end-of-life situation plays a decisive role—the case of Terri Schiavo who died March 31, 2005, at the age of forty-one. In February 1990, Terri suffered a heart attack, followed by a loss of oxygen to the brain and was in time declared to be in a permanent vegetative state. Ten years later, her husband asked for the feeding tubes to be removed. The Circuit Court judge agreed but the decision was directly challenged in a lengthy series of further court appeals and counter-appeals, and an endless chain of objections ranging from her parents' interventions to those put forward by parties with religious, political, ethical, and legal interests protracted over a five-year period. Finally the feeding tubes were removed and she died shortly afterward. There were clearly many complications to the case, but they all circled around the moral question of whether or not artificial nutrition and hydration (ANH) is mandatory in such instances, and if so, to withhold would be equivalent to murder, as some voices in the controversy maintained. But in the last analysis it's unwarrantable to dismiss a moral position on extraordinary or disproportionate means that is in agreement with a long-standing tradition and with the intuitive sense of the common person.

These three cases, each of which, in terms of extraordinary means, had an unclouded moral solution available, show the practical difficulties one has to work through at times to abide by the moral law and still not contravene civil law.

It's not unusual, in cases similar to those just presented, to hear something like "the person I knew is just not there . . . gone!" Could it be, by way of speculation, that there is a kernel of truth in such an exclamation? Early last century Dr. Alexis Carrell, if not the first, was one of the pioneers in demonstrating that an organ of the body, when separated from the body itself, can be kept alive indefinitely. This he demonstrated by keeping the heart of a chicken alive for fifteen years, that is, beating and even growing in a solution of nutrients. In a similar way, the famed biologist Jean Rostand, an expert in the biology of the frog, removed a muscle from the shinbone of a frog embryo which, in the course of time, grew and took its proper shape around a "phantom shinbone." Is it possible, and will science ever be able to show, that in some cases a human being, kept alive by high-tech ingenuity, is not really "alive" as one living organism, but is in reality an aggregate of many individual organs each living its own independent life? In which case, the termination of the aggregate would not be the termination of the life a human being.

PHYSICIAN-ASSISTED SUICIDE

Another contemporary problem alongside euthanasia, relating to end-of-life issues, is that of physician-assisted suicide, an issue in recent years dramatically moved to the forefront of America's consciousness not very long ago by the activity of Dr. Jack Kevorkian. It was he who, in order to publicize the plight of those suffering a terminal illness and genuinely wanting surcease, responded to a number of requests to assist them in taking their own lives. Thus, physician-assisted suicide and euthanasia together have made the issue of death by choice a hotly agitated one in moral circles, in legislative bodies, and in law courts, so that it is impossible to expect the emergence of any kind of consensus in the foreseeable future. They are spoken of in the same breath, use the same arguments, argue to the same end, and use the same appeals to humanity. Yet, though death by choice is shared by both, they differ in that the taking of one's life by one's own hand is the ultimate poignancy. And insofar as the suicide is assisted by a physician is concerned, there was a time when it would have been seen as chimerical. The physician, we have forever held, is called to protect life, to administer healing, to keep faith with the Hippocratic oath, and to share in the mythic life-giving power of the god Asclepius in restoring the sick to health. It's no wonder that a doctor's helping a person to take his life seems to have all the features of a glaring contradiction.

Yet the first question to be asked is not really about *physician*-assisted suicide, but about *suicide*. Once you answer that question on moral grounds, you can move on to the anomaly of its being physician assisted. That we have an innate tendency to safeguard our lives needs no elaboration and, since the possession of life is the prime value in living things, it generates the responsibility to protect and maintain it, with one's own individual life as the first instance of such care. In the cycle of birthing, nature has supplied a process for the appearance of a new human being, but it has not done the same for dying; there is *no cycle of dying*. The life of a child begins with the cooperation of a man and a woman, working its gradual, complicated, and wondrous way to the birth of a human being. No such process exists for dying. Death can come at any time, at any age, and for any cause; it is not a respecter of person, wealth, or power; it is not a barometer of moral stature or of religious persuasion. Yet coming-to-be and ceasing-to-be are principal human events and call for the human response of love and care more than at any other time in a person's life. We've discussed some of the issues of coming-to-be under the heading of abortion, and we are discussing now some of the issues of ceasing-to-be under the heading of suicide in the context of its being physician assisted.

Traditionally, as a tribute to the common sense of the plain man, homicide is seen as unjust killing and as the destruction of another person, the ultimate insult to reverence for life: "Cain attacked his brother Abel and murdered him. Then the

Lord said 'What have you done? Hark! Your brother's blood that has been shed is crying out to me from the ground.' " *Suicide* too is the destruction of life and shares the malice of homicide, but with the added tragic dimension that the murderer and the murdered are one and the same. For Aristotle, suicide is a failure in courage, an act of cowardice. St. Thomas Aquinas, speaking in the Christian tradition against the taking of one's own life, says: "It is altogether unlawful to kill oneself. . . . it is contrary to the inclination of nature, and to charity whereby every man should love himself." He goes on to add that it is against the community and is the desecration of God's gift of life. A supporting view on the wrongness of suicide comes unexpectedly from the existential philosophy of Albert Camus who, in his *Myth of Sisyphus*, holds that suicide is unacceptable because it is a repudiation of life's absurdity!

Yet, one may ask, just as there are moral exceptions to homicide as, for example, in the case of an unjust aggressor, may there not be *moral exceptions to suicide*? Socrates, whom we don't think of as having committing suicide, was firmly against it, but when he came closer to the end he justified drinking the lethal hemlock as an exception: "It is not unreasonable to say that we must not put an end to ourselves until God sends some compulsion like the one which we are facing now." With the later Stoics, both Greek and Roman, suicide was a permissible way of answering life's problems if they became unsupportable. Marcus Aurelius, for example, whose goal in life was a balanced temperament in harmony with nature, invites the person who cannot sustain the effort to be good, modest, or true, to consider departing " . . . from life, not in passion, but with simplicity and freedom and modesty, after doing the one laudable thing at least in thy life, to have gone out of it thus." Though Christianity has maintained an absolute prohibition against suicide, some individual Christians, like St. Thomas More, averred that there are understandable exceptions. In his *Utopia*, a book which, like Plato's *Republic*, is open to many interpretations, More suggested that suicide, in certain precise conditions, may be permissible and even laudable (Book II) (R #6).

Closer to our day, what are we to think of the military intelligence officer who, entrapped by the enemy, swallows a cyanide pill lest he be tortured into revealing knowledge that would mean the death of a thousand soldiers? What of the young Czech, Jan Palach, who immolated himself at the base of the statue of King St. Wenceslaus in Prague's Wenceslaus Square as a violent statement against further Russian occupation? Or the Vietnamese monks who did the same for the cause of world peace? Or of Maximilian Kolbe, a Catholic priest, who was imprisoned at Auschwitz and who, though not taking his life by his own hand, chose to forfeit his life in the place of another prisoner who had a wife and family? If the answer is "yes" to the question of whether suicide admits of any moral exceptions, it does not necessarily mean that life is being trivialized; it could mean the opposite, for suicide can be seen, as in the examples given, as an agonizing testimony to life in the desire to protect it for others. In that sense, it is not impossible, in an extraordinary way, to understand suicide as an event-sign of the deep appreciation of life. It is in this context, too, that the anomaly of calling on a physician, life's minister, to assist in its termination is to be understood.

CAPITAL PUNISHMENT

That there are so many different practices among the states regarding the death penalty, that there have been strong voices in the Supreme Court for and against it, that the United States is the only country in the first world still permitting it, that there are some countries refusing to extradite a high-profile criminal to this country precisely because he would be open to the death penalty here, that so many have been wrongfully executed, and that there are moralists who can be arrayed for and against it, all add up to a widespread testimony to the intense difference of opinion exhibited in America today. Those who defend the death penalty will admit it is violent, but say it is necessary to protect the life of the community. And those who oppose the death penalty will maintain that any violence against an individual is violence against society as well. But in recent years, sentiment in the United States against the death penalty has been growing, and it may not be too far in the future but that the death penalty will be nationally forbidden. In December 2007, New Jersey had the honor of being the first state in the union to outlaw capital punishment.

Any penalty is first of all a punishment. We can only dream of a human society in which all are saints and, out of reverential respect for each other, would never cross, defraud, or hurt one another. But, as it is, wrongdoing is never more than an eye blink away. Some wrongdoing is small and petty, but some is so horrendous as to make us cringe at the sight of humanity forsaking itself. Some wrongdoing is private, some public. When it is private, it can be personal, like greed, or it can be familial, like transgressing a parental rule, in which case it does not pertain to the public domain and is not subject to public law or punishment. When the wrongdoing is public, the common expectation is to look for society to mete out a fitting punishment, that is, for proper public authority to inflict some kind of pain or unpleasantness on the offender. A fitting punishment would be one calibrated to the seriousness of the offense, and includes the elements of *retribution* (restoring balance to society), *deterrence* (dissuading the wrongdoer or anyone else from doing it again), and *correction* (rehabilitating the wrongdoer as a law-abiding member of society).

Capital punishment is the penalty of death exacted of a criminal who has committed a serious crime, like murder or a comparably heinous act against society, and has therefore made his own life forfeit and liable to have it taken from him. As in all morally controverted questions, the views on the death penalty vary greatly: It is always justified; sometimes justified; or never justified. Those who hold to the first view maintain that the execution of the criminal is morally permissible in any case, principally because the offender has wounded society to such an extent that retribution has to exact an equivalent loss, namely, the offender's life. To commit the crime is an injustice to society; for society to deny the penalty is an injustice committed against itself. The eighteenth-century philosopher Immanuel Kant is the classical example of this view by his insisting that the death penalty not only may be exacted but must be; it is not only permissible but required. This is self-evident; it needs no proof. Kant writes: "Whoever has committed murder must die. There is, in this case, no juridical substitute or surrogate that can be given or taken for the satisfaction of justice. There is no likeness or proportion between life, however painful, and death, and therefore there is no equality between the crime of murder and the retaliation of it but what is judicially accomplished by the execution of the criminal" (Phil of Law, Part II tr. W. Hastie). This equivalent, literal, one-for-one kind of retribution is often referred to as "an eye for an eye, a tooth for a tooth," metaphors for returning like for like, or retaliation (from *lex talionis*, the law of like return). Such a view has obvious limitations since there is no penalty that has a like equivalence for selling drugs, insider trading, rape, or similar crimes. Nonetheless, the proponents of capital punishment cite the fact that the penalty of death is as far as punishment can go, for it is a "life for a life."

In addition to retribution, deterrence is regularly offered as a reason for the death penalty. It is based on the belief that the prospect of death as a penalty is enough to restrain a prospective killer. Is it not, we are asked, a matter of common sense that anyone would restrain himself in view of dire consequences? Though it appears, at least on the abstract level, to be perfectly clear, in practice it is an unknown quantity for there is no way of measuring how the human mind reacts, and how the will and emotions are moved, in planning and executing a capital crime.

The second view regarding the imposition of capital punishment is the one most commonly held, that is, capital punishment is justified in certain cases, such as repeated or multiple homicides. This position of the selective use of the death penalty has at least the merit of rejecting wholesale capital punishment while trying to allow penalties strong enough to protect society and to effect retribution, but it still insists that the penalty of death has of itself sufficient warrant to justify its being inflicted in some instances. The arguments employed here share the force of those given earlier but tailored down to fewer instances. But whatever argument is made for capital punishment, its proponents must recognize the possibility of putting innocents to death, which, they say, is a sad but unintended consequence that sometimes occurs in protecting the moral integrity of the community.

The third view, totally opposed to capital punishment, is that it is never justified. This is a moral position that has been growing in recent years and represents a radical departure from the position held for centuries, from the times in which capital punishment met with practically no resistance down to our own day when voices against it are strong and articulate. As mentioned earlier, all the countries in the First World have outlawed the death penalty except the United States. But even here, the sentiment against it is remarkably vigorous, demonstrating perhaps that capital punishment is on its way to its own demise. Why? It's not only because there have been so many horrible mistakes in executing innocent persons, or because the death penalty is meted out inequitably against minorities, the powerless, and the poor, but also because of seeing that it's wrong. It makes killing appear acceptable, it sanctions revenge, and it nourishes the belief that the first killing is cancelled out by the second. Society cannot help being affected by its dehumanizing influence.

This radical change across time from the total acceptability of capital punishment toward almost total unacceptability can only be explained by a deepening sensibility regarding the value of human life. This is clearly understandable in the recognition that development and growth are found in every human area. Our humanity is never a finished product; it is a process. The human community evolves on the strength of collective and shared experience so that practices like slavery, the subjugation of women, or the alienation of the poor slowly but surely fall away before a rising sense of a common humanity (R #7).

GUN CONTROL

The use of guns, inarguably beyond control, has become the center of legal and political frenzy, but it must first be seen as a moral question. Once the moral imperative is appreciated, then legal and political action will be seen as imperatives too. It's anomalous how seldom in the professional literature on gun control that *morality* is even mentioned; historians, criminologists, economists, medical experts, and constitutional experts make their views known, but little by the moralist. This omission, however, can be interpreted as an acknowledgment that the de facto violence following out-of-control gun use is such a savaging of humanity that its immorality is self-evident and the need for legal action is all too obvious. Time and again have we seen that life is the fundamental existential value of the human being whose inviolability commands our persistence in safeguarding it. Shakespeare's *Hamlet* says, "You cannot, sir, take from me anything that I will more willingly part withal; except my life, except my life, except my life." The violent taking of even one life is a desecration of life itself.

What then are we going to say about the thousands who are killed in the United States each year by firearms and triple that number who are injured, figures far and away ahead of any other first-world country? The statistics, as statistics, are depressing, but even more so is the gun *culture* that permits them. Statistics comparing one country with another, the relative increase or decrease of gun crimes, or evaluating costs to the nation have their importance, but they are secondary to the question of moral tolerability. Any life-threatening crime is, of course, horrendous, but those involving guns bear the special features of lawlessness, intimidation, power, finality, immediacy, precipitousness, and callousness. However you choose to frame the uniqueness of the human being— as the highest form of earthly life, as a rational animal, as a knowing and loving being, as a participant of the divine, as sacred, as a "little lower than the angels," as the image of God—taking a person down by gunfire is violent disregard for human life; it is contempt for humanity.

Every serious person is against violence, whether he is "for" or "against" gun control. Put another way, everyone is for gun control of some kind. Even the members of the National Rifle Association support laws restricting gun ownership based on age, sanity, criminal record, and so on, maintaining that laws already on the books are sufficient constraint against the reckless use of firearms. But why ignore the vagaries of human life, and the sad fact that human beings can act out of control? Doesn't this proclaim the need we have for a more responsive posture on gun control? Thomas Hobbes, the English philosopher of political science writing over three and a half centuries ago, had it just right in describing the dark side of human nature and warning of the relapse of mankind into the "state of nature" in which the elements of raw individualism would prevail. In such a state the rich potentialities for human growth would never be realized and, "worst of all" there would be, in a comment worthy of repetition, "continual fear, and danger of violent death; and the life of man, solitary, nasty, brutish, and short." The saving element for man is the gift of reason that nature has endowed him with. Man understands that society, while cherishing individuality, aims at peace and harmony but may still be obliged at times to restrict the activities of unrestrained individualism when they are seen as pitted against such harmony. The answer to those who raise their voices against gun control in the name of freedom is, as we have seen, that freedom is not the right to do as you please, but the right to do as you ought.

The part the government has to play in the matter of gun control is precisely here. The role of the moralist, psychologist, sociologist, or interested citizen is to weigh the state of affairs they live in and to discern goals for government action, but it's the role of government to engineer them. Laying aside the case for arms in the hands of the military or law enforcers, or for strictly controlled and harmless recreational targetry, for which some reasonable argument can be made, if we focus on the aspect of private ownership, we can ask, are we, even now, beyond the time for more explicit and meaningful control of the private ownership of guns? Despite the laws on purchasing and using them, they are still easily acquired, particularly at the so-called "gun shows" where background checks and waiting periods are literally nonexistent. If, for any reason they cannot be got legally, they are notoriously easy to get illegally, and it requires no special gift of prophecy to foresee that guns procured unlawfully will be used unlawfully. And they will work their way into the hands of those who revel in gang culture or those who, in pursuing their victims, will indirectly kill or injure innocents too. Or they will become weapons for those who are so alienated from society that they fantasize retribution in other Columbines or Virginia Techs. With these observations in mind, no social solace can be had in pronouncing the mantra, "guns don't kill people, people do," for the whole notion of control is that when guns are not available they cannot be used. Whatever curtailment of private ownership of guns is required, in this time and place it is a small price to pay for the gain it would bring to a society yearning for peace, or at least a reduction of violence.

READINGS

READING 1
Reverence for Life
Albert Schweitzer
(from *The Teaching of Reverence for Life*)

I cannot but have reverence for all that is called life. I cannot avoid compassion for everything that is called life. That is the beginning and foundation of morality. Once a man has experienced it and continues to do so—and he who has once experienced it will continue to do so—he is ethical. He carries his morality within him and can never lose it, for it continues to develop within him. He who has never experienced this has only a set of superficial principles. These theories have no root in him, they do not belong to him, and they fall off him. The worst is that the whole of our generation had only such a set of superficial principles. Then the time came to put the ethical code to the test, and it evaporated. For centuries the human race had been educated with only a set of superficial principles. We were brutal, ignorant, and heartless without being aware of it. We had no scale of values, for we had no reverence for life.

It is our duty to share and maintain life. Reverence concerning all life is the greatest commandment in its most elementary form. Or expressed in negative terms: "Thou shalt not kill." We take this prohibition so lightly, thoughtlessly plucking a flower thoughtlessly stepping on a poor insect, thoughtlessly, in terrible blindness because everything takes its revenge, disregarding the suffering and lives of our fellow men, sacrificing them to trivial earthly goals.

Much talk is heard in our times about building a new human race. How are we to build a new humanity? Only by leading men toward a true, inalienable ethic of our own, which is capable of further development. But this goal cannot be reached unless countless individuals will transform themselves from blind men into seeing ones and begin to spell out the great commandment which is: Reverence for Life. Existence depends more on reverence for life than the law and the prophets. Reverence for life comprises the whole ethic of love in its deepest and highest sense. It is the source of constant renewal for the individual and for mankind.

READING 2
Roe v. Wade Supreme Court Decision on Abortion, January 22, 1973

(*The Supreme Court, hearing a challenge against the constitutionality of the State of Texas criminal abortion laws, decided as follows*)

State criminal abortion laws, like those involved here, that except from criminality only a life-saving procedure on the mother's behalf without regard to the stage of her pregnancy and other interests involved violate the Due Process Clause of the Fourteenth Amendment, which protects against state action the right to privacy, including a woman's qualified right to terminate her pregnancy. Though the State cannot override that right, it has legitimate interests in protecting both the pregnant woman's health and the potentiality of human life, each of which interests grows and reaches a "compelling" point at various stages of the woman's approach to term.

(a) For the stage prior to approximately the end of the first trimester, the abortion decision and its effectuation must be left to the medical judgment of the pregnant woman's attending physician.
(b) For the stage subsequent to approximately the end of the first trimester, the State, in promoting its interest in the health of the mother, may, if it chooses, regulate the abortion procedure in ways that are reasonably related to maternal health.
(c) For the stage subsequent to viability the State, in promoting its interest in the potentiality of human life, may, if it chooses, regulate, and even proscribe, abortion except where necessary, in appropriate medical judgment, for the preservation of the life or health of the mother.

READING 3
Charlie's Ghost
Bill Keller
(from *N.Y. Times*, June 29, 2002)

(*This op-ed article describes the agony of conscientious parents, facing an extremely complicated pregnancy, in finally deciding for abortion.*)

Two years ago this summer, my wife and I lost a baby. I say "lost," as if we had misplaced it. There is nothing like abortion to make you appreciate the solace of euphemism. Lord knows the zealots who have occupied the field and mined it with moral explosives have left little room for comfort.

Let's begin with what happened. At 17 weeks, we went to Mount Sinai Hospital in New York City to view ultrasound pictures of our future child and have amniotic fluid drawn for testing. The ultrasound image showed that the fetus was not growing as fast as expected, and before long we had a couple of specialists puzzling over the pictures. Why was there so little fluid? Why was the placenta so large? Was there a defective chromosome? Were the kidneys missing?

They rushed the tests, but the chromosomes revealed nothing more about our stunted fetus, except—except that he was male. This is the double-edged scalpel of reproductive science. The technology that informs you your future baby is mysteriously endangered also makes him real, a boy-like creature swimming in utero. (And this was before the new, hyper-realistic sonography that, judging by General Electric's TV commercials, portrays your fetus as a mesmerizing little 3-D merman.)

Yes, I know how shamelessly the anti-abortion lobby has exploited this illusion to give tadpole-sized fetuses the poster appeal of full-grown infants. But no amount of reasoning about the status of this creature can quite counteract the portrait that begins to form in your heart with the poetry of the first heartbeats. Sentimental fools, we gave him a name, Charlie, maybe imagining it would help him put up a fight.

For the next five weeks Emma was examined by the best minds at one of the best hospitals. She was screened for viruses, blood disorders, hereditary indicators — all normal. She had weekly sonograms by virtuosos of the machine. There were momentary highs (kidneys were functioning after all; a dissenting sonogram reader even thought the amniotic fluid was on the rise) and dispiriting lows (bad blood flow to the fetus, which meant organs were probably not developing properly), but no definite answers. Something was clearly, badly wrong.

The doctors assumed that, of course, we would want to abort, as soon as possible. "We know you can get pregnant easily," Emma's obstetrician said. "Why risk an unhappy outcome?" She urged us to schedule quickly, because it would be difficult to line up a surgeon around the July 4 holiday. Appalled by the rush, Emma changed doctors, but we never quite escaped the feeling that by holding out, week after week, hoping for better odds, we were being more than a little eccentric.

My wife clings more firmly to her faith than I, so she called the hospital's Catholic chaplain for counseling and left tear-choked voicemails explaining the predicament. He never called back. She found some consolation outside official channels, from a nun she's known since school. "Think about what God would want, not what the church would want," the nun advised, with a wisdom that would surely disqualify her from Vatican office. "They are not always necessarily the same thing."

As we approached 24 weeks, the legal deadline for abortions in New York, the most explicit prognosis we could wheedle from the experts was that chances were high — one was willing to say over 90 percent — that the baby would be born dead or in a vegetative state. And carrying the child to term would pose some danger to Emma's health. Facing the prospect of a greater heartbreak, watching a child die or suffer inconsolably, or exhausting the emotional resources needed for two other children, we decided to end it. The last thing Emma was aware of before surrendering to the anesthetic was Charlie kicking madly.

Two years later, past the mourning and the guilt and into the precarious hope of a new pregnancy, our experience at the intersection of science and parenthood haunts my thinking in ways I did not anticipate. Among other things it has deepened my suspicion of moral clarity, and also of disembodied rationalism, both of which seem to otter a kind of ethics without human beings. The ideologues on both sides, those who view abortion as an absolute wrong and those who view it as an inalienable right, too often treat these decisions as if they were clear-cut and pain-free.

If you'd asked me before that summer, I'd have told you reflexively that I was pro-choice. As a matter of law and politics, that is still my position, for this is not a decision I would entrust to courts and legislatures, even given that some parents will make choices I would find repugnant. But like a lot of parents who have lived through it, I have come to see "choice" as a mixed blessing.

I've often wondered what we'd have done if the decision had been less stark — if the doctor had said 50–50, or if the gamble had been on something known, on Down syndrome or one of the severe crippling diseases. Would we have had the strength to ride it out? The fact that I think of this as something to aspire to is itself a change of heart.

Science is rapidly chipping away at biological uncertainty. In addition to the growing sophistication of pregnancy testing — amnio and chorionic villus sampling and sonograms and specialized blood screens — some fertile couples now spend the money for in vitro fertilization, accompanied by genetic analysis before the embryo is implanted, to screen for abnormalities that may not kick in for 20 years. It is already possible to check embryos for a gene that will show a predisposition for Alzheimer's. Scientists anticipate tests that will predict whether your child is likely to be homosexual, or unusually aggressive.

There is astonishingly little good research on what parents do with this proliferating prenatal information (the subject of abortion is too much of a political minefield to get the research funded), but it is fair to say that the reproductive industrial complex grinds in favor of "perfection." For some parents, the abortion threshold is multiple sclerosis. For some, it's a cleft palate. Counselors who specialize in this say there are prospective parents who end pregnancies because they had their hearts set on the other gender.

"You get questionable news and you make the abortion decision," said Adrienne Asch, a Wellesley bioethicist who argues that prenatal screening and selective abortion have become too routine. "Anything else you do is viewed as stupid by your educated friends, by your doctors, by your genetic counselors."

No one mandates prenatal testing, although it is such an automatic part of the regimen that many expectant mothers believe it is obligatory, and few fight it. My wife is a testing skeptic. She is convinced that if we had just let nature take its course, without sonograms and amniocentesis, "we would have lost that baby, but we would not have killed that baby." All the same, the next time around we tested. Emma says she didn't have the energy to defend her "right to be ignorant"—to doctors, friends and a husband who can't bear not knowing.

It seems to me a plausible fear that eventually these decisions will slip more and more from our hands. In a world of market-driven health care, I can imagine insurers refusing to cover a costly childhood disability that could have been detected in advance and "prevented" by aborting. Wouldn't that be an infringement of choice as surely as outlawing abortion?

This is not a subject with much of a middle ground, but one reasonable alternative to reducing parents' choices is to make their choices more educated. Adrienne Asch, for example, advocates better counseling of prospective parents at the time of testing, including some informed discussion of what life is like for children born disabled—to present that as a choice rather than an unthinkable horror. Glenn McGee, a University of Pennsylvania ethicist who is more sympathetic to prenatal screening, agrees with her that the system offers too little support for parents who might want to keep an "imperfect" baby. Most parents who reach the second trimester, when the most intensive testing takes place, have already made a place in their hearts for a child. But the counseling they get when something wrong shows up is cursory, not covered by insurance and geared to avoiding the burden of abnormality. Perhaps Planned Parenthood would like to live up to its name by taking this on.

As for our story, it has, if not a happy ending, at least a happy new beginning: Our daughter Alice was born 11 days ago.

READING 4
"Roe" of Roe v. Wade
Norma McCorvey
(from *Won by Love*)

In April 1996 I returned to the Supreme Court where, in 1972, Sarah Weddington had argued on my behalf that women should be able to obtain a legal abortion.

A soft, steady rain was falling as I approached the marble steps of the Supreme Court. A video of my conversion, *Reversing Roe: The Norma McCorvey Story*, had just been released, and I was there to take complementary copies to members of the United States Supreme Court.

I couldn't unsign the affidavit the justices had already argued and decided upon, but perhaps I could, through the video, help them see the lies behind that fateful decision. And then, perhaps, they would decide to hear a case in which *Roe v. Wade* might be overturned.

Nothing would please me more than to have *Roe* wiped off the books.

After delivering the videos to a courier, I went back outside. A steady drizzle continued to fall. My business was not done, however. I had something even more important to do. Before I became a Christian, I thought political action was the most important thing. Now I realized there was a much more powerful activity available to those who desire change: prayer.

At a news conference earlier in the day, I had explained my visit to the Supreme Court and the purpose of the *Reversing Roe* video. Now I wished the reporters would just go away. What I had to do next was not about getting my name in the newspapers or my picture on television—it was about fulfilling a personal mission.

I started to kneel down on the steps, when a police officer came up and said such an action would not be allowed. Not to be defeated, I walked down the steps to the sidewalk, and there I knelt in the rain, praying that what I had done might be overturned.

My prayer went something like this: "Lord, please let these justices come to know the truth about abortion. Let them understand in their hearts that it's wrong, and that they need to reconsider their decision."

Rain fell on my back and head as I knelt there. It seemed as if heaven itself were crying. My own tears fell on an already wet sidewalk.

"Please, God" I pleaded, "please, open their eyes as you opened mine. Help them to see the truth."

One of the "truths" I wanted people to see involved an admission I had made many years before. As Sarah Weddington presented my case, she used the fact that I had claimed to have become pregnant through a gang rape. The public had certain misgivings about abortion in the early seventies, but there was much greater acceptance of abortion in cases of rape, so even though I wasn't really raped, I thought saying so would garner greater public support.

This means that the abortion case that destroyed every state law protecting the unborn was based on a lie.

READING 5
Abortion and Viability in Mid-nineteenth Century America
Helen Lefkowitz Horowitz
(from *Rereading Sex*)

Aristotle's Master-piece is again a guide. Judging from its locations in western Massachusetts households, the work was a book owned by common people and kept in their houses, hidden from view. Nicknamed the "Granny Book" in Northampton and elsewhere, it purported to be for midwives. Such a man as Jonathan Edwards may have regarded it as a book "unclean to be read" but this phrase needs to be qualified by the words "by men." Edwards never questioned the book's appropriateness for female readers.

Despite its likely male authorship, *Aristotle's Master-piece* contained much of interest to women, including a drawing of a fetus in utero, information on pregnancy and childbirth, and discussion of menstruation. The latter emphasized the need for menstrual regularity, congruent with humoral theory, which sought the balance of fluids in the body. This was the section in which a woman might learn about abortion, for it stated, in guarded language, that a woman might go to her doctor for "a strong enthartical Potion," to restore her monthly flow. Translated, this meant that a woman might seek from a physician a medicine enabling her to abort a fetus. As other historians have demonstrated, ordinary women knew ways of inducing abortion in the early stages of pregnancy and could resort to these means when they did not want to bear a child. These practices can be best understood as part of the secret vernacular culture of women. Although they were deeply disapproved of by Christian authorities, until the nineteenth century they were tolerated under common law.

. . .

Behind these hidden practices lay an understanding by both sexes that human life began not at conception but at quickening, the fetal movements at roughly twenty weeks into a pregnancy. In the eighteenth and early nineteenth centuries, there was no way to determine with certainty if a woman was pregnant. Again, *Aristotle's Master-piece* offered to women a description of some of the important symptoms of pregnancy, such as changes in the breasts. But since no one, neither a woman nor her physician, could be sure, it was reasonable to assume that a woman who missed her menstrual flow was experiencing an "obstruction" of her menses, dangerous in the light of, humoral theory. To restore her menses, a woman might take cathartics and purgatives, strong medicines to induce vomiting and evacuation of the bowels. If she needed knowledge or specific herbs or chemicals, she might apply to a woman friend or a midwife, or possibly a physician. Men who treated women were their confidants and were trusted to respect female secrets.

. . .

The line between clearing up an obstruction and inducing a miscarriage was a blurred one, and it was important to keep it so. If ingesting "remedies" failed, a woman might seek to dislodge the fetus by injuring herself through falling or blows to the abdomen. If she remained pregnant, a woman might request intervention from her physician. By the early nineteenth century, physicians had the knowledge necessary to terminate pregnancy. Along with pulling out a tooth to incur sympathetic bleeding, a doctor would dilate a woman's cervix to induce contractions to cause a miscarriage or, especially, in the later stages, would rupture the amniotic sac to achieve the same end. In more complicated cases, a physician would intervene surgically to destroy the fetus. When these efforts involved abortion after quickening, they posed problems of medical ethics and conscience. They were violations of common law—abortion after quickening was a misdemeanor—and thus required concealment.

READING 6
On Taking One's Life
Thomas More
(from *Utopia*)

As I've already said, they take care of the sick with great affection, omitting no medicine or nutrition necessary to restore their health. They do everything they can to comfort the incurably ill by sitting and talking with them. If the disease holds fast and the pain excruciating, the priests and civil magistrates come to tell the suffering person that he is now not able to face up to the duties of life, and has become a burden to himself and irksome to others by overliving his time to die. They exhort him not to let the painful and unremitting torment transfix him any longer, and not to hold out against dying but hope for relief by taking his own life or allowing another to do it for him: In this way, they tell him, he would be acting prudently because he will lose nothing but the pain. Besides, he will be following the counsel of the priests who are, after all, the interpreters of God's will and give him the assurance that the act would be holy and pious.

Those who have been persuaded as described starve themselves to death of their own accord, or else die in their sleep without the sensation of dying. But the caretakers do not force anyone against his will, nor do they lessen their care of anyone who refuses. But if a man were to take his own life before the priests and the council permit it, he is considered unworthy of burial or cremation, and they cast his body, disgraced, into a foul pit.

READING 7

The Execution of the Non-Guilty

Sister Helen Prejean

(from *The Death of Innocents*)

As in *Dead Man Walking*, this is my eyewitness account of accompanying two men to execution—but with one huge difference: I believe that the two men I tell about here— Dobie Gillis Williams and Joseph Roger O'Dell—were innocent. The courts of appeal didn't see it that way. Once the guilty verdicts were pronounced and death sentences imposed, every court in the land put their seal of approval on the death sentences of these two men without once calling for thorough review of their constitutional claims. The tragic truth is that you as a reader of this book have access to truths about forensic evidence, eyewitnesses, and prosecutorial maneuvers that Dobie's and Joseph's jurors never heard. Not surprisingly, Dobie and Joseph were indigent. It's also no surprise that their defenses at trial were abysmal. In fact, Joseph O'Dell defended himself.

As of September 2004, 117 wrongfully convicted persons have been released from death row. Citizen Innocence Projects, staffed mainly by college student volunteers, have ferreted out evidence and eyewitnesses that liberated the wrongly accused, sometimes only hours away from execution. Dobie and Joseph were not so lucky. And I—my soul seared from watching state governments kill these men—entrust these stories to you. Brace yourself. These stories are going to break your heart. And learning about the court system that allowed the injustices at trial to remain in place might upset you even more.

I used to think that America had the best court system in the world. But now I know differently. Why is it that southern states are (and have always been) the most fervent practitioners of government killing, accounting for over 80 percent of U.S. executions? Why is it that Texas alone accounts for one third of the total number of U.S. executions and, in the latest tally, accounts for fully one half of all state killings in 2004 (as of September 27), while the Northeast, supposedly guided by the same Constitution and Supreme Court guidelines, accounts for only 1 percent of executions? What explains the dramatic regional disparity in the way the death penalty is implemented?

I urge you to stick with me when we come to the constitutional arguments in the third and fourth chapters of this book. It's vitally important that We the People assume ownership of our Constitution and do not leave its interpretation and application solely to attorneys and jurists, even Supreme Court justices. The justices are as prone to ideological bias as anyone else. What's behind Chief Justice Rehnquist's drive to speed up executions ("Let's get on with it!") despite growing evidence of a seriously flawed system? What motivates Justice Antonin Scalia to declare, without shame, that he is a willing part of the "machinery of death"?

When I started out as a young Catholic nun, I had no idea that I would walk this path into America's death chambers. My Catholic faith has been the catalyst to inspire me to follow the way of Jesus, who sided with the poor and dispossessed and despised. In these pages I tackle head-on the spirit of vengeance—a wrongful death can be set right only by killing the perpetrator—that has dominated the religious, political, and legal discourse of our country during the past twenty-five years.

I especially reach out to readers who experience fierce ambivalence about the death penalty (almost everybody): who are outraged at the murder of innocents and want to see their killers pay with their lives, but who also recognize that government bureaucrats can scarcely be trusted to get potholes in the streets filled, much less be allowed to decide who should live and who should die.

This book is only the beginning of the dialogue. At its end you'll find a page of resources, which offers ways to continue the dialogue and—if you're ready—to engage in public action to transform our society.

To young people I say: As you see what happened to Dobie Williams and Joseph O'Dell and see what is going on in our courts, may you be impassioned to devote your lives to soul-size work. I hope what you learn here sets you on fire.

Chapter Seven

The Environment

There are many ways we employ the word *environment*: the "residential environment," the complex of houses and infrastructure built in view of commodious living; the "educational environment," the various institutions established for the education of the community; the "economic environment," the organs of finance that control the ebb and flow of money; the "cultural environment," the atmosphere in which poetry, drama, music, art, and dance can flourish as activities of human enjoyment. But in this chapter "environment" is used for *nature*—the world that ancient Greek philosophers wondered at, American Indians worshipped, the biblical God created in six days, and, above all, the world in which life exists. So a good, working definition of *environment* is *the natural surrounding in which life exists*. During the past half century, rising concerns for the environment have made it a significant part of the moral horizon of our time.

NATURE AND LIFE

The purpose of the first part of this chapter, before speaking of practical matters concerning the environment, is to consider what there is about nature that should command our respect, love, and care. It's hardly possible to think of nature as just being "there," as though it's indifferent to us whether it's there or not. It's where we exist, where we live. It has a history, especially the history of the evolution of living beings trying to secure a "more complex and supple adaptation . . . to the conditions of existence that are made for them" (Bergson, *Creative Evolution*). There can be, therefore, no separation between nature and life: the respect we have for nature is the respect we have for life, and the respect we have for life is the respect we have for nature.

Care for the environment, known by the scientific term *ecology*, has its scientific, political, and economic aspects, but they all depend on the appreciation we humans have for nature which is so hospitable to life as to be indistinguishable from it. Not only does nature define our physical life but, on a deeper reading, our spiritual life as well, beginning with a renewed understanding of what "self" means as "self-in-nature," a reading that often goes by the name of "deep ecology," a phrase coined by the Swedish ecologist Arne Naess a generation ago. It is a kind of wisdom that grows out of respect for the earth. As such, it is an appeal to trust our basic intuition regarding the relationship between nature and living things, especially for humans in search of self-understanding (R #1). Though we do not often deliberately focus on the unity of life and nature, we intuitively resonate to the way nature expresses herself in the world about us, as a kaleidoscope of living things. Socrates knew this. Retreatants seeking spiritual insight know this. Monks, whose chapel walls are made of glass to let nature pour in, know this. Imagine what kind of world it would be if it were suddenly stripped of life, rendering it barren, impersonal, and meaningless, poles apart from the world of nature we exult in. It is not as though nature is given to us as the first segment of reality, and then life as a second. They are one reality, identified with each other; when you think "nature," you think "life": nature is life, and life is nature. This is borne out in the very language we use, in phrases like "Mother Earth" or "Mother Nature," employed by humans from the time we first began to acknowledge nature as the source of all the bounty for maintaining life. The Latin term for Mother Nature is *Mater Natura*, whence *mater* is cognate with *materia* (matter, material), while *natura* derives from a form of the verb "to be born" (natal, natal day), so even etymology touches on the mystery of nature as life-giving force (R #2).

Everyone of us has experienced the feeling of being closed-in, cooped-up, afflicted with cabin fever, spiritual ennui, emptiness, simply waiting to break out into the open, to see the sky, to warm to the sun, to wonder at the night stars, to exhilarate on the forest trail, to float our thoughts on the flowing stream, to amble on the beach at the edge of the sea, or simply to take a quiet walk on a country road. Experiences such as these are so many instances of our "coming alive" by re-connecting with nature, not only for its inspiration, but also for its being the very source of life we are a part of. They are experiences of a deeper meaning of human existence. This was poignantly expressed by Anne Frank in her diary, having just turned fifteen, after several desperate years of hiding during the Nazi occupation of Amsterdam. "Is it," she wrote, "because I haven't been outdoors for so long that I've become so smitten with nature?" On a given night, when she was able to peer out of a window fortuitously left open, she continued, "It's not just my imagination—looking at the sky, the clouds, the moon and the stars really does make me feel calm and hopeful. . . . Nature makes me feel humble and ready to face every blow with courage!" She tragically died of typhus a few months later at the concentration camp at Bergen-Belsen.

Poets of the naturalist cast weave these experiences into reverential imagery, as William Wordsworth does in his well-known nature poem "Lines Composed a Few Miles above Tintern Abbey":

> (I am still . . .)
> A lover of the meadows and the woods,
> And mountains; and of all that we behold
> From this green earth; of all the mighty world
> Of eye and ear; what they half-create,
> And what perceive; well pleased to recognize
> In nature and the language of the sense,
> The anchor of my purest thoughts, the nurse,
> The guide, the guardian of my heart, and soul
> Of all my moral being. (R #3)

Or, from "Inversnaid" by Gerard Manley Hopkins:

> What would the world be, once bereft
> Of wet and of wildness? Let them be left,
> O let them be left, wildness and wet;
> Long live the weeds and the wilderness yet.

The experiences recounted here speak out of a long tradition in which the unity of the world was accepted without question, and to be separated from it was seen as being out of joint. The Pre-Socratic Parmenides, for example, pleaded for a higher understanding of what existence meant by warning us not to let ourselves get trapped in the manifold of discrete things about us, but to seek the realm above, in which the being of things in the "lower" world share the Being of the "higher." For many of the ancients, the unity between life and nature was so much accepted that life was attributed to the world as a whole, the *cosmos* as a living thing. If you first see a vast horizon of individuals, and then see them harmoniously meshed together as one, then you have seen an organized entity, and where there is an organized entity, there must be a principle making it so, the principle the ancients called *soul*. Plato, for example, in speaking of creation, writes, " . . . using the language of probability, we may say that the world came into being as a living creature truly endowed with soul and intelligence by the providence of God" (Tim, 30b). Aristotle wrote at great length about the soul and, though he agreed with Plato that the togetherness of the physical and nonphysical, or material and immaterial, is necessary for our understanding of man as a living being, he insisted that body and soul are constituents of *one living entity*, as against his teacher's view that body and soul are *two separate entities* merely functioning together. So, for Aristotle, nature and life are *intrinsically* bound to each other in that every living thing is matter enlivened by soul, and from this it was a logical transition to the conclusion, made by others if not explicitly by Aristotle, that an organized world demanded a world-soul.

If some scientific minds today find the word *soul*, meaning the principle of life in animals, too elusive to handle, then "world-soul" would have zero chance of acknowledgment. Ironically the thrust to understand the physical unity of the cosmos has never been greater, when physicists are coming closer and closer to what they feel is the ultimate unifying principle of cosmic activity. Perhaps something similar can be said of the universe of living things. For several decades, James Lovelock, eminent English scientist, inventor, and environmentalist, has been developing a view of the world, which Aristotle himself would have embraced, called the *Gaia hypothesis* (named after the Greek goddess Gaia), that the earth is a "self-regulating entity" comprising the totality of organisms, rocks, bodies of water, and the atmosphere, all bearing upon the regulation of the earth's "surface conditions so as always to be favourable as possible for contemporary life." In the last few years, however, Lovelock has been profoundly disturbed for the fate of humanity because "we have driven Earth to a crisis state" (R #4).

The names of Pythagoras, Plato, and Aristotle enjoy renown not only for their philosophic wisdom but also for their commitment to teaching and learning. Each of them established a community in which education played an indispensable part. That of Pythagoras, often called the *Pythagorean Society*, aimed at a total life style, in which the role of learning was an essential ingredient. Pythagoras himself was a mathematician and mystic for whom life had a profound meaning inasmuch as it was a journey leading to the ultimate reunion with the One, a kind of salvation. The *Academy* of Plato and the *Lyceum* of Aristotle were two distinguished communities of learning and were the forerunners of the university as we know it today. Each of these communities was built with a closeness to nature in mind—easily accomplished given the peacefulness of the natural geography of ancient Greece—which was to nurture the life of learning along with the cultivation of friendship. So it was with the later philosopher *Epicurus*, fourth and third centuries B.C., whose school/community in Athens was referred to simply as the "Garden." Here, for thirty-five years until his death, he lived a simple, communal life with like-minded followers, apart from the distracting bustle of the city, trying to develop a sense of genuine friendship for the sake of mutual support in a life of learning. The goal of each of these communities was peace of mind, a quiet atmosphere for reflection, mutual friendship, conversation, and the development of an ambience for nourishing a meaningful life. Living close to nature—light and color and growth and nearness to living things—was the most attractive feature of these garden retreats.

Whether they were styled after the Garden of Epicurus, or arose spontaneously, such garden retreats proliferated in the West. To such a place, the philosopher Siro's garden in Naples, the twenty-something Virgil went seeking the peace and meditative solace he needed to compose the works that gave them pride of place in Latin literature, among them the famed *Aeneid*. One of his other works, the *Georgics*, was destined to become an influential book, in point of style and content, for centuries following, and to work its way toward becoming the favorite study of nature for the young American nature-writer Henry Thoreau. The orientation of the *Georgics* is found in its name—*geo* is the Greek word for "earth," thus *Georgics* is "things of the earth." On the face of it, the poem deals with life on the farm, presenting the details of coaxing life out of the soil, but it is not a didactic tract on how to farm; it is a literary device showing one how to live and make the everyday world as beautiful as possible. In that sense, the farmer is everyman. Thus,

> First, before all else, may the sweet Muses,
> For whom I have been struck by a great love
> And whose rites I perform,
> Receive me . . .
> But if the blood around my heart doesn't warm up
> To the subtle workings of nature,
> Then may I love the rivers and woods
> In a simpler way . . .
> Yes, happy is he who is able to know the reasons for things,
> But happy too is he who knows the gods
> Of forest and field. (Book 2)

St. Augustine, fourth and fifth centuries, often referred to as the Christian mirror image of Plato, exemplifies this tradition of reading nature as a pathway to the spiritual values that disclose human meaning. As with the Greek philosophers, Augustine and his companions chose to live, study, write, and pray in a garden retreat, there to cultivate the human spirit. This is clear, for example, from Augustine's commentary on the verses in the book of Genesis which speak of Adam and Eve in their own lovely garden: "What more marvelous sight can there be, or more aptly describe the conformity between the way the human mind works and the way nature works when seeds are sown, cuttings are planted, shrubs transplanted, and shoots engrafted? (*De Gen. ad Litt.*, VIII, 16)

Again, in his *City of God*, after praising the wonderful structure of the human body, Augustine writes,

> How can I tell of the rest of creation, in all its beauty and usefulness,
> that the divine goodness has given to man to please his eye and
> serve his purposes? . . . Shall I speak of the manifold and ever-changing
> loveliness of sky, and earth, and sea; of the plentiful supply and
> wonderful qualities of the light; of sun, of moon, and stars; of the

shade of trees; of the colors and perfume of flowers; of the multitude
of birds, all differing in plumage and in song; of the variety of animals,
of which the smallest in size are often the most wonderful? . . . Shall I
speak of the sea, which itself is so grand a spectacle, when it arrays
itself as it were in vestures of various colors, running through
every shade of green, and again becoming purple or blue?

What was being said by these early philosophers was being said on a far simpler level, on an affective, emotional, and personal level, by the thirteenth-century saint who rejoiced in the wonders of nature (R #5). It was not as though St. Francis of Assisi was trying to follow some established plan to nature mysticism, for his rejoicing was simply a spontaneous outpouring of gratitude for the world about him. Stories are told about his love of animals. He spoke with the birds, gently reminding them, as they alighted on the palms of his hands, that the beauty of their song and the color of their plumage were gifts of God. A group of swallows that had flown into church while Francis was preaching, stopped their swooping flights and chattering so as not to interfere with his sermon. He would remove an earthworm from the path so as not to crush it. A fish that Francis returned to the water showed its gratitude by following him across the lake and, when he left the boat, stayed there until he returned. He had pets, a lamb, a pheasant, a rabbit, a cicada, a dog, happy to have them as his friends. And then there is the well-known story of the bad wolf of Gubbio, bent on terrorizing the town, that was quieted by the hand of the saint signing it with the sign of the cross, after which the wolf accompanied Francis on his walks about town, greeted by the very people it would have terrorized (R #6). All of creation was a marvel, and all of it to be praised. In a poem called the "Canticle of the Sun," Francis proclaims praise for the sun as his brother: "Brother Sun, who, in his splendor, brings the light of day"; and for moon as his sister: "Sister Moon and Stars, bright and precious, and fair." Likewise, praise for Brothers Wind, Air, and Fire; and for Sisters Water and Earth; and praise even for Sister Death (R #7).

For St. Francis whatever is of life is of nature, and whatever is of nature is of life. If nature is alive for the Plato in one sense, and for Aristotle in another, it is alive for Francis in still another—for him nature proclaims life, nature means life, and nature is life. And while the scientist lays down the physical structures for ecological integrity, the visionary, like St. Francis, sees ecological integrity as the integrity of humanity itself. That's why he is the patron saint of ecology.

A downturn in this tradition of nature-as-life occurred when Descartes, in the seventeenth century, took on the problem of certitude and laid prime emphasis on the view that all knowledge was initiated from within the mind, before any kind of sense experience, concluding therefore that the mind, or soul, was in essence separate from the body. Such a conclusion encouraged others to go on to say that no activities of the animal whatsoever were more than physical, mechanical activities; there was no need for a "soul," which was an hypothesis from the past deconstructed by the advent of science. But when soul has no meaning, neither has life. Without soul, the cosmos could never again be held, as it was with the ancients, to be living in any sense. That's why, in this line of thinking, it would be nonsense to speak of a deeper meaning of man, of reaching out for something higher to enlarge man's self-understanding, of transcendence that would put man in touch with the rest of reality, of man's oneness with living nature.

The sciences of themselves are immensely fruitful in investigating the secrets of the natural world, and mankind is indebted to scientists for their commitment to research and their ingenuity in translating their findings into practical service for humanity. But not all scientists can resist the blandishments of a thoroughgoing physical world, unyielding to the intellectual warrants for a reality beyond the physical. Whence the term "scientism" is often used of science when it's taken to be the sole source of our knowledge of reality, when the empirical circumvents the rational, when sense knowledge is given exclusive rights to truth. LaMettrie, an early eighteenth-century physician, was confident in writing his book, *Man a Machine*, that all human activity is mechanical in nature and that, for example, just as we have "walk muscles" we have "thought muscles" as well. Cross the centuries to our own time, and we find the Nobel Prize winner Steven Weinberg who is given to the view that the more we know about the universe, the more pointless it becomes.

The lure of pan-mechanism emerges in a fascinating way in our technological age, when there seems to be no limit to the astonishing things computer versatility can generate. One almost feels the need to apologize when sitting before a computer, knowing that the machine can always do more than he knows what to do with it. It's captivating. An outstanding name in the complete capitulation to computer wizardry is one we've seen earlier, Ray Kurzweil, whose inventive skill and profound grasp of computer possibilities launch him into staggering, off-the-wall, predictions for human life. Even the title of his main work in this connection gives pause: *The Age of Spiritual Machines: When Computers Exceed Human Intelligence.* Machines can "know." Never mind that they are not living entities, they still can "know." In time they will be able "to read and understand" written documents. Further, "Once a computer achieves a human level of intelligence, it will necessarily roar past it." We will be able to duplicate ourselves and put our second selves on a shelf, to be activated when the first self peters out. We will be able to store, in the memory system of the computer, our experiences, our sensations, our love-life, to produce them on command. In a bold time-line of events, Kurzweil predicts that by the year 2099 there will be "no clear distinction between humans and computers." This, then, is the scenario left us in a universe in which soul is denied a place, a lifeless mass in which the role of humanity is zeroed out and nature is at an end (R #8).

Although there have been scientists who have bent the method proper to science to serve as the method for interpreting all reality, thus limiting the activities of nature to the parameters of mechanistic necessity, there are others who feel that a science of life demands a different kind of understanding, one that allows the forces of life a creative power not found in the mechanistic conception of nature. Charles Darwin, after his lengthy scientific analysis of variations, natural selection, instinct and the struggle for existence, and despite "the war of nature, famine and death," concludes that the "production of the higher animals" is "the most exalted object which we are capable of conceiving." The last sentence of *The Origin of Species* is a hymn to the vision he labored so long to portray: "There is a grandeur in this view of life, with its several powers, having been originally breathed into a few forms or into one; and that, whilst this planet has gone cycling on according to the fixed law of gravity, from so simple a beginning endless forms most beautiful and most wonderful have been, and are being, evolved."

Darwin, not a philosopher himself, opened up a vast field of reality for the philosopher, called to think out the implications of evolution on another level. Such a philosopher was the French professor, peace advocate, and Nobel Prize winner Henri Bergson, who lived at the turn of the nineteenth century into the twentieth. He was the model philosopher in how he handled the discoveries of bio-logical science and how he expressed his ideas in stunning writing style. In his

Creative Evolution, concerned that the biologist deals only with discrete entities like organs, cells, tissues and such like, and not with life itself, Bergson envisions the whole of life as an elemental stratum of nature, an *élan vital*, a *life impulse*, pushing its way through the world of matter, trying to find different ways to exist in new environments. From that viewpoint, Bergson is the quintessential philosopher of nature-as-life, which is why he writes, "All the living hold together, and all yield to the same tremendous push. The animal takes its stand on the plant, man bestrides animality, and the whole of humanity, in space and time, is one immense army galloping beside and before and behind each of us in an overwhelming charge able to beat down every resistance and clear the most formidable obstacles, perhaps even death."

The nature-as-life tradition never really died out in America where the mid-nineteenth century witnessed a resurgence of interest in man's relation to nature, commonly referred to as *transcendentalism*, found mainly in the New England states. It was not so much a "movement" as it was a coalescence of common interest on the part of those who felt that somehow contemporary man had become lost in the search for authentic meaning. It tended, therefore, to spiritualize, or romanticize, the union of man with nature so that the life of man was seen as one with the realm of nature, from which it would follow that a deeper appreciation of nature was a deeper appreciation of man, and that the love of nature would nurture the love of humanity. The central figure of this style of thought was Ralph Waldo Emerson and alongside him Henry David Thoreau, his younger contemporary. In the introduction to his essay on *Nature*, in his studied prose style, Emerson writes,

> The lover of nature is he whose inward and outward
> senses are still truly adjusted to each other; who has
> retained the spirit of infancy into the era of manhood.
> . . . In the woods . . . .a man casts off his years as the snake
> his slough, and at what period soever of life is always a
> child. In the woods is perpetual youth . . . In the woods
> we return to reason and faith. There I feel that nothing
> can befall me in life,—no disgrace, no calamity . . .
> which nature cannot repair. Standing on the bare ground
> . . . the currents of the Universal Being circulate through
> me; I am part or parcel of God. (R #9)

The world-soul, mentioned above as occupying an indispensable role in the worldview of the ancients, re-emerges in Emerson as the concept of the "over-soul" which, once again, testifies to the fundamental unity of all things, in particular, the unity of man with nature. In his essay entitled *The Over-Soul*, he writes,

> The Supreme Critic on the errors of the past and the
> present, and the only prophet of that which must be, is
> that great nature in which we rest as the earth lies in
> the soft arms of the atmosphere; that Unity, that
> Over-Soul, within which every man's particular
> being is contained and made one with all others; . . . to
> which all right action is submission; . . . which evermore
> tends to pass into our thought and hand and become
> wisdom and virtue and power and beauty, to which
> every part and particle is equally related; the eternal ONE.

Henry David Thoreau was a friend of Emerson's and shared kindred sentiments regarding the natural world. Today he is known chiefly through two works, *Civil Disobedience* and *Walden*. The first is a short work on pacifism that subsequently became very influential, as we'll see in a later chapter. The second has relevance for this chapter, inasmuch as Thoreau's love for the earth was a forerunner of contemporary ecology. The earth, he wrote, is not a mere fragment of dead history, but living poetry like the leaves of a tree, "not a fossil earth, but a living earth." The only way to discover whether nature would share its secrets for a meaningful life, Thoreau thought, was to accept its invitation to live as close to the earth as he could:

> I went to the woods because I wanted to live deliberately, to
> front only the essential facts of life, and see if I could not
> learn what it had to teach, and not, when I came to die,
> discover that I had not lived. I did not wish to live what was
> not life, living is so dear; nor did I wish to practise resignation,
> unless it was quite necessary.

Accordingly, Thoreau lived for over a year in the woods at Walden Pond and left us a treasury of reflections on the ways of nature, on a life in solitude, on building a small house for oneself, on woodland sounds, on working a garden, on the growth of plants, on animals, on the pond in winter, on the coming of the spring—all reminiscent of the sentiments expressed in Virgil's *Georgics*, as we've seen. No wonder he recommended that, before it was too late, that every town should set aside no fewer than 500 acres of woodland to preserve the sanity of its citizens. In a broad sense, in *Walden's* concluding chapter, Thoreau tells us what he learned from his time immersed in nature:

> I learned this, at least, by my experiment; that as one advances
> confidently in the direction of his dreams, and endeavors to
> live the life which he has imagined, he will meet with a success
> unexpected in common hours. He will put some things behind,
> will pass an invisible boundary; new, universal, and more
> liberal laws will begin to establish themselves around and within him . . .
> in proportion as he simplifies his life, the laws of the
> universe will appear less complex, and solitude will not be
> solitude, nor poverty poverty, nor weakness weakness. (R #10 and #11)

While Emerson and Thoreau were well-known devotees of nature on the east coast, John Muir (1831–1914), an American of Scottish origin, was falling in love with the wilderness in California. He was a peripatetic naturalist, having visited the great forests in Canada, Alaska, Russia, Brazil, and Africa, even though he was "settled" in the Yosemite Valley. Nature was an inspiration to Muir; it was more than a "place" for him. It was a state, an atmosphere, a life, a paradise, so much so that nature was the true revelation of divinity, God's only gospel. Of a given evening, with the glow created by the sun's setting and the moon's rising at Cathedral Peak in Yosemite, he wrote, "This was the alpenglow, to me one of the most impressive of all the terrestrial manifestations of God." He was the right person at the right time to respond to a national disquiet over the recklessness with which the nation's natural heritage was being despoiled. Muir raised the national consciousness to the imperative of sequestering huge tracts of wilderness as national parks, exemplified in his plans for establishing Yosemite, already a state park, as a national park in 1890.

The environmentalist who today falls within the nature-as-life tradition we have been describing, and most akin to the spirit of Henry Thoreau, is the nature-writer Bill McKibben, who has lived for years in the midst of natural surroundings and is in love with the wilderness. His way of life is not as a primitive but, as a man of his times, welcomes whatever science and industry produce to make life more livable, yet is fearful of the assaults man has made on nature in the recent past. Some of these assaults will be long-lasting, some irreversible, thus reducing or destroying the life-enhancing character of nature. "Soon," he writes, "Thoreau will make no sense. And when that happens, the end of nature—which began with our alteration of the atmosphere, and continued with the responses to our precarious situation of the 'planetary managers' and the 'genetic engineers'—will be final. The loss of memory will be the loss of meaning" (p. 213). Although he issues a stern warning that there may be "no future in loving nature," it is all the more reason for us "to act in every way possible, and immediately . . . The choice of doing nothing . . . is not a choice" (p. 146).

THE NEED FOR ECOLOGY

The term *ecology*, though in its earlier usage it had a strict biological meaning, has come to be used regularly to express *care for the environment*. The earth, as we've seen, has always been an inspiration and a source of wonder, but from the viewpoint of *care* it was certainly more, in earlier ages, that somehow the earth should care for humans, since, despite its harshness on life in the raw, it could be counted on to be hospitable to human dwelling; that *we* should care for *it*, so awesome and overwhelming, would never even have occurred to the earlier mind. So, in our day, given our headlong exploitation of the earth's abundance, we have now to reverse our speed of destruction, and reshape our understanding of the role we play in using the earth's plenitude.

All of us are aware of vulgar abuses of the environment like tossing the empty soda bottle into the stream, or leaving the empty McDonald's hamburger box on the park bench, or strewing trash on the walkway. Contrariwise it's enheartening to see the occasional person pick up the out-of-place beer can from the sidewalk or the plastic cup from the trail just because they are blemishes on the environment. But in recent decades, we have become more and more aware of a larger despoliation of nature instigated by humans creating pollutants all around us, taking their toll of flora and fauna alike. This is not a charge of guilt against those who earlier on developed and used chemicals designed for beneficent purposes, but now, having been introduced and their disastrous effects known, their indiscriminate and unregulated use can no longer be tolerated. The ancient Greeks were insightful in using the terms *earth, air, fire*, and *water* to designate the four elements of nature necessary to sustain its life-giving destiny, so it's a testimony to our common interest in nature across the ages that we can meaningfully employ the same terminology of 2500 years ago to speak of environmental concerns today. Even though there are good reasons for speaking of one element of nature separately, we realize that we are speaking of nature as a whole, for what affects one affects all; what advances understanding of one, advances understanding of all; what supports one, supports all; and what damages one damages all.

Earth, the terrestrial element, shapes our dwelling place, maintains the plants and animals for food and clothing, supplies the raw wood and stone for housing, stores chemicals for a thousand human uses, and conceals deep energies for the unpredictable engines of life in time to come. Still, nature has substances within itself, such as certain poisonous chemicals or sources of radiation, that are inimical to life, yet life has endured. But human assaults are another matter entirely: they are man-made, man-tested, and man-used. Some assaults are momentous and sudden, like the meltdown of the notorious atomic reactor at Chernobyl, Ukraine, 1986, and the radioactive fallout whose disastrous effects will be felt for centuries, or the titanic oil spill from the tanker *Exxon Valdez* off the shores of Alaska. Other assaults take place over time and are recognized belatedly. When, in recent memory, chemicals were spread on the earth's green mantle as a help to the environment, their ultimate consequences were never foreseen, but now we know how long-lasting and devastating they can be. Gradually measures have been taken to discontinue, or at least restrict, their use. Take one early example, DDT, whose discovery by Paul Muller won him the Nobel Prize in 1939, "was hailed as a means of stamping out insect-borne disease and winning the farmers' war against crop destroyers overnight." But it proved to be so potent that, through the food chain, it ravaged every aspect of life, from chicks dying because of the impotent eggs out of which they were hatched to the poisoning of vital organs in human beings. The metastasis of destruction caused by these pollutants was passionately described by Rachel Carson in her book *Silent Spring* in 1962, which was hugely influential in making the public aware of what was scientifically known for some time. She writes, for example,

> We poison the caddis flies in a stream and the salmon runs dwindle and die. We poison the gnats in a lake and the poison travels from link to link of the food chain and soon the birds of the lake margins become its victims. We spray our elms and the following springs are silent of robin song, not because we sprayed the robins directly but because the poison traveled, step by step, through the now familiar elm leaf-earthworm-robin cycle. These are matter of record, observable, part of the visible world around us. They reflect the web of life—or death—that scientists know as ecology. (*Silent Spring*, ch. 12) (R #12)

Air, always acknowledged to be the main life-essential element, refreshes the body, renews the soul and, in some mysterious way, keeps the stars and planets aloft to remind humans that they are terrestrial and extraterrestrial at the same time. But air can be saturated by gas emissions from factories, engines, and a vast variety of human activities which, taken separately, may not cause apprehension, but collectively are cause for alarm. Certain of these gases, the CFCs (chlorofluorocarbon gases), are responsible for *ozone depletion*, the thinning out of the layer of ozone in the stratosphere which serves as a filter to moderate the sun's ultraviolet rays; in excess they have the potential to annihilate life by damaging the food chain and producing a vast array of illnesses like cancer of the skin, as corroborated by two American scientists, Sherry Rowland and Mario Molina, both of whom won the Nobel Prize in 1995 for their work.

This scenario on ozone depletion, together with *global warming*, has been repeated many times over in scientific journals and in the popular media, with none perhaps more influential than Al Gore's film and book on climate change, *An Inconvenient Truth*, in making the public actively aware of the huge problems facing the planet unless drastic steps are taken. The raising of the globe's average temperature by the increase of carbon dioxide in the atmosphere increases the amount of heat on the surface of the earth by entrapping it through the greenhouse effect. Its results can be disastrous in the rising of sea levels throughout the world, in the drought wrought inland, and in the huge disruption in food production. All this is made unequivocally clear in the latest report of the International Panel on Climate Change, under the aegis of the United Nations, in February 2007. Even now we know that animals and plants survive only in specific zones, and there is much evidence that certain animals have already migrated to different zones because of climate change, and even plants are spoken of as "migrating." A humorous cartoon on global warming was printed in the *New Yorker* of Eskimos exiting, let's say, at the subway station at 52,333rd Street! Not so humorous are the constant assurances we get from the scientific community that global warming is the most pressing environmental problem on the planet today, making it imperative for national and international bodies to summon up the political will to halt the otherwise inevitable advent of calamity. One of the country's best-known climatologists James Hansen of NASA has this to say as a measured statement of catastrophe:

> If human beings follow a business-as-usual course, continuing to exploit fossil fuel resources without reducing carbon emissions or capturing and sequestering them before they warm the atmosphere, the eventual effects on climate and life may be comparable to those at the time of mass extinctions. Life will survive, but it will do so on a transformed planet. For all foreseeable generations, it will be a far more desolate world than the one in which civilization developed and flourished during the past several thousand years. (*NY Times*, 7/13/06)

Fire, the third of the four classic elements, was thought by the Greeks to be a substance somehow locked up in physical things and which, in the process of being released, caused them to become hot and sometimes to burst into flames. This view was traditionally held for many centuries, clear down to the eighteenth, when the "substance" called "fire" began to be called "caloric." Fire then, in all its power, ideally lends itself to be taken as a symbol for any kind of energy in the vast storehouse of nature that is there to be recognized, discovered, released, and finally harnessed for the good of life on the planet. By the same token, such energies are to be controlled and prevented from becoming agents of environmental pollution. If fire was first looked upon as a gift from the gods, a source of energy to be used to enhance human life, then other sources of energy, whether in plain sight or buried deep in their subatomic fastnesses, are waiting to be tapped for the same end.

Among the many meanings associated with the word *energy*, the definition that pertains to the environment is *the ability* or *power to do work*, from the Greek word for work, *ergon*; it involves the activity in going from one physical state to another. Thus, it takes energy to row the boat, to raise the temperature of water, to grow plants, to drive to Chicago, to launch a mission to Mars. There are many different kinds of energy: mechanical, wind, aquatic (hydropower from rivers, falls, ocean tides), chemical, thermal, solar, electrical, magnetic, light (radiant energy), nuclear, all of which are life-enhancing but still require adequate *control* to prevent possible injury to the environment. The phrase *clean energy* is the current buzzword for the scientific search for the safe use of the planet's sources of power. There may come a time when the supply of energy is endless, a possibility that lies within the atomic structure of matter. But now the great demand is for the conservation of the sources we already possess, for alternate fuels for combustion engines, and for the efficient and financially feasible deployment of wind and solar power.

For many years now, as we have seen, scientific associations have warned of the foreseeable and unimaginable destruction of the earth's environment, and it's arguable that the bottom line of the earth's fate is the reckless use of energy. That's why the international community, which has already implemented some measures of worldwide environmental significance, must find the political will to turn away from the trajectory of disaster by taking practical action. The Kyoto Protocol, for one example, has been actively advanced by the United Nations since 1997 with the goal of reducing gas emissions responsible for global warming, and almost all the world's countries have accepted it. The United States, the world's leader in those emissions, was a signatory to the original protocol, but it has never ratified it.

It's an irony of modern history that the discovery of the planet's greatest potential source of power, the atom, should have found its first use as an engine of destruction in World War II, which we'll address in the next chapter. Here, nuclear energy has to be welcomed as the most abundant source of power ever discovered, and along with it, the need for the most exacting control, as tragically demonstrated in the Chernobyl disaster mentioned above. It's more than a problem of polluting the environment, it's destroying it altogether. But its benefits are enormous, especially in the production of electricity in areas bereft of natural resources, so it's a problem of how to use it without hurting the environment. Currently the problem has been magnified politically—how to keep nuclear energy to peaceful purposes without yielding to the temptation of using it for political domination. The nuclear energy available today is by way of fission, the breaking apart of subnuclear particles with the release of tremendous energy. The next advance will be by way of fusion, the coming together of the same particles with the release of still more power, duplicating in a reactor the same process taking place in the sun; when that happens, the way is open to limitless energy in support of life on earth, with still more ecological concern required of mankind.

Water is the fourth and last element of the classic Greek elements of nature and, with the other three, structures the observable world. For the Greek mind, water is full of mystery and power, respected and feared at the same time, as we find it, for example, dramatically presented in the gods and heroes of Homer's epic in playing out their strategies for good or evil among mortals. But the basic Greek reverence for water is unmistakably centered in *Thales*, the first philosopher in Western thought. From his observation of the all-pervading presence of water in the growth and nourishment of living things, and that seeds are lifeless until they are made moist, and from his belief that the earth rests on water, Thales concluded that water was the underlying principle of life in all living things. The cycle of water is also the cycle of life, for as water evaporates from the earth, rarefies into the air, condenses and then falls back to earth, it nourishes living things lest they die of dryness. Life originates with water. Is this ancient view different from that of today's biologists? They too give first-place honors to the sea for the emergence of life on earth when they refer to the vast, secret-laden mixture of chemicals as the "primal soup" which generated and nourished primitive life, a view captured poetically in the saying that "the sea is the mother of all living things." As much as water is an agent of life anew, it is also an agent of life renewed; it has the ability to clean what is soiled and to refresh what is weary. In a more than physical sense, water is a symbol of interior life, as for example, in the rite of baptism or its equivalent in the religions of the world, or in the image of the "living water" that flows from the temple in the prophet Ezekiel, "Wherever it flows, there shall be teeming life again." Or, time over time, water symbolizes the washing away of guilt, as when Lady Macbeth says to her husband after the murder of Duncan, "a little water clears us of this deed" (II, 2).

The need for water on the part of the planet's living things is so obvious that it's unnecessary to draw up a list to establish it, though it is less obvious that the nonliving, physical structure of the earth requires water too inasmuch as many chemicals do not react unless they are first dissolved in water. So let's simply recall that an assault on any one of the elements of nature is an assault on them all; what pollutes water pollutes the total environment. Water can be polluted from the air by acid rain, rain saturated by sulfur dioxide and nitrogen dioxide from power plants, decaying trees and other vegetative life. Dissolved in water, or carried atmospherically, these gases can affect human health by inducing asthma or lung infection, or contribute to the erosion of building structures. Water can be polluted from the soil by industrial waste, by fallout from insecticides and herbicides, by agricultural fertilizers and animal waste, by domestic waste, and radioactive fallout; often these are in the form of synthetic chemicals, unknown in nature, and therefore not easily broken down. We are perhaps still prone to think that if a pollutant goes underground, it's safe. But this is wishful thinking, as Rachel Carson reminds us—all the running water on the surface of the earth was at one time underground. Potable water is thus a rare commodity in certain parts of the world, and an estimated five million human beings die each year as result of waterborne diseases.

All running water runs to the sea. Once again, we can be gulled into believing that the sea, so vast and deep, would harmlessly swallow up anything thought injurious. But on the way there the waters can dissolve or carry poisons or harmful metals, like mercury, that can easily be absorbed by small organisms, and then by fish or larger animals potentially destroying them and the food chain as well. It is not so much the liquid mercury itself, which kids used to be so fascinated with, that is poisonous, but the compound form of methyl mercury which, in humans, can cause damage to the nervous system, bone joints, brain, and to the newly born. The seas can also be invaded by tanker oil spills, malfunctioning drilling rigs, human waste and debris, industrial carelessness. Plastic debris alone accounts for Texas size areas on the surfaces of the ocean, and pieces of plastic have been found in the stomachs of birds and animals.

ECOLOGY AS A MATTER OF SOCIAL JUSTICE

The impact of deliberate environmental damage is a matter of social justice, incumbent therefore on society as a whole and on each individual, that our natural surroundings be made, or kept, as welcoming as possible for the life it is meant to sustain. Carelessness, recklessness, unconcern for a wholesome human habitation and for nonhuman animal life as well must all be recognized for what they are, signs of disregard for the value of life.

There have been hopeful signs of restoring some kind of balance between human needs and natural resources, witness worldwide undertakings to reverse air and water pollution, and in the United States the preservation of species act, the restoration of waterways and clean air via industrial emissions controls and cigarette smoking restrictions. But there have also been signs, and far too many, of retrenchment of interest and commitment. No one should minimize the huge effort necessary to bring changes about, including formidable costs, technological know-how, widespread popular support, and the solution of practical problems, not least of which is the political will to do so. The judgment made over thirty years ago in the report commissioned by the United Nations, *Only One Earth*, is still true: "The planet is not yet a center of loyalty for all mankind," and after pointing out that, despite the planet's waywardness and vulnerability it is still beautiful and enriching, the report concludes, " . . . is this not a precious home for all of us earthlings? Is it not worth our love? Does it not deserve all the inventiveness and courage and generosity of which we are capable to preserve it from degradation and destruction and by doing so, to secure our own survival?"

Care for the environment as *a moral matter* is hardly questionable, but what does remain a question, at least in certain aspects, is whether some things have a greater claim to our concern than others? If everything were of equal value then of course the answer would be "no." From time to time you may hear the assertion to the effect that only humans are arrogant enough to believe they are of higher value than other living things of nature. But common sense rebels against the idea. There's no way a tiger's claw can be the equal of Einstein's brain, or, as John Stuart Mill said, he'd rather be "Socrates dissatisfied than a pig satisfied!" It's clear that there is a *valuation* among things in nature, that there are things of higher value than others. This is seen in the broad distinction between living things and nonliving, the former clearly of higher value because they have a higher existential level. Likewise, within the vast range of living things, the three-fold tier of vegetative, animal, and rational life gives an order of increasing perfection so that *human* life has the highest existential level and the highest value among the things of nature, and therefore invoke the highest concern.

To speak of an ordered whole makes sense only if you are speaking of a harmony of *different* things—a symphony cannot be a mere togetherness of similar notes, but of different notes brought together in a harmony of music. Likewise, the cosmos. It is a harmony of different things, radically different from each other in their individuality, yet coming together in an overall unity; a *unified whole* of its individual members ranging through the entire chain of being from the inanimate to plants, to animals, to humans. And if we are only a stage now in the evolving transit of the universe, the future unity-in-difference will be marvelous to behold. And following through on the idea that whatever is, is good (*omne ens est bonum*), then the entire cosmos is good because it is, and every individual thing is good because it is. Thus "being-real" is "being-good," and "being-good" is "being-loved," whence the biblical God saw that every created thing was good.

This gives the background to the *focus* we ought to adopt regarding the demands of ecology. There is first the long-standing view in which man is situated at the center of environmental concern, the traditional or anthropocentric view, so that the rest of nature is there to serve him. Then there is the recently emerging view that sees nature itself as the center of concern. Let's call the first view *human-centered ecology* and the second view *nature-centered ecology*.

HUMAN-CENTERED ECOLOGY

The most striking feature of the first view is that it is obvious. Without considering the moral merit of any of their activities and speaking in general terms, humans tend use nature as its sole beneficiary. As we saw at length above, the terms *earth, air, fire,* and *water*, designated by the Greeks as the four elements of nature, refer to the natural elements that sustain human life and make it livable. But only human beings can make nonhuman nature yield its secrets and put them to use for the well-being of human life, which is the main reason for asserting that human dominion over the nonhuman world is obvious. It was part of Descartes' dream, in support of this contention, that, inasmuch as he felt he had "proven" that the "living" body was actually an entity operating on physical laws only, he also felt he had "freed" the powers of the physical world to be used in the service of humanity. This view resonates with the first chapter of Genesis in which God, having created male and female, blessed them and said to them, "Be fruitful and multiply, and fill the earth and subdue it; and have dominion over the fish of the sea and over the birds of the air and over every living thing that moves upon the earth."

However, it's an abuse of nature to follow the misguided notion of "absolute dominion"—that man has unqualified control over nature permitting him to dispose of it any way he wants, without at all being held accountable. Such unconstrained authority invalidates the true meaning of human-centered ecology, which looks to the prudent use of nature for human welfare and must be understood in light of the remarkable admonition of the Book of Revelations, "Do not harm the earth or the sea or the trees." Though the word *dominion* has traditionally been used in this regard, it doesn't seem to be the most appropriate one to use in today's lexicon because it carries with it overtones of selfish and individualistic dealings with nature's resources, whence the word *stewardship* seems to be a more suitable term. The key to stewardship is the reasonable and prudent use of nature, taking care of the incredible abundance nature offers for the well-being of man. In the same vein, particular mention can be made of our behavior toward animals, noting that gratuitous infliction of hurt has always been rejected by the sensitive person; kindness to animals is the only human response to the value of life wherever it is found. Touchingly instructive is the ritual expression of gratitude on the part of the Peruvian Indians toward the llama for providing them with the essentials for life, signifying a sense of unity among all living things. Human-centered ecology, by its very definition, is centered on the quality of human life for one's self and one's neighbor, not just to meet the goals of physical health but also, through nature, to meet the goals of personal and spiritual growth for the present generation and for generations to come.

NATURE-CENTERED ECOLOGY

As already alluded to, it should come as no surprise that in the course of time new philosophical questions arise as life adapts to changes in working its way from age to age. In talking of human-centered ecology, we acknowledged the gradation of life as all too obvious to deny; it would take extraordinary mental acrobatics to deny the fact that the human being is the fullest expression of life as we know it. Saying so is not saying that lesser than human forms of animal life have no value in themselves and are not to be respected for what they are. Even those who maintain the tradition on the valuation of life are bound to maintain that human beings must not maltreat animal life and must take all reasonable measures to respect it.

There is always a danger in categorizing things or ideas or persons for, in the last analysis, it's uncertain where the boundaries between them lie. But in any list of environmentalists in America the name of Aldo Leopold, writing in the Midwest in the first half of the last century, holds a top place among the early contributors to nature-centered ecology. Though as a young man he was in favor of "controlling" the "imbalance" of nature by, for example, hunting down predatory mountain wolves to save the deer, he finally came to see how this freed the deer to savage the rest of the mountain and to lead to the starvation of countless numbers of the very deer he wanted to save (R #13). This led him to a gradual change from hunting and game management to become an ardent apostle of environmental "holism," the view that the "land" is a "biotic community" whose self-control we should respect:

> Land, then, is not merely soil; it is a fountain of energy flowing
> through a circuit of soils, plants, and animals. Food chains are
> the living channels which conduct energy upward; death and
> decay return it to the soil. (*Sand County Almanac*, p. 253)

Clearly this is a plea for keeping hands off artificial control of nature as much as humanly possible, a kind of environmental laissez-faire attitude favored by many environmentalists since Leopold's time. It doesn't follow, with the environmentalism of Leopold and others subscribing to it, that they are necessarily signaling an equality of rights among all natural things so that, outrageously, the life of a tree and the life of a human are of the same value. But problems emerging like this force us to think harder on the role we have in caring for the environment.

The main question, then, with regard to nature-centered ecology has to do with nonhuman animal life, or, simply, "animal" life. The notion that animals, or at least some, have "rights," hitherto attributed only to human beings, is a comparatively recent notion that has given the question of animal life a new urgency and, though there have been many who have long supported undertakings for animal rights, there is no name better known in this regard than Peter Singer, whose views on abortion we discussed in an earlier chapter. His views on animal life can collectively be referred to as *animal liberation.*

Animal liberation is an ethical stance holding that an open, fresh look at the life of animals reveals sentient life as a compelling call for the "liberation" of animals from the traditional view of the keystone value of human life, and for the recognition of the "rights" animals have as *conscious* beings. The key, according to Singer, to determining whether a being is conscious or not is its sentiency, that is, the ability to feel, or to sense, pleasure and pain; to sense pleasure or pain entails an *awareness* or *consciousness* of what is happening. Pain especially, because it is an unequivocal sign of suffering that cannot be verbalized by the animal any more than by an inarticulate child; this leads to but one conclusion, that the animal is conscious of itself hurting. To permit, or to tolerate, suffering in animals is self-evidently wrong and without any moral justification. So, no scheme requiring the subservience of animal life to human life is acceptable, despite the claim of supposed needs on the part of human beings as a higher species. Singer is adamant in his belief that human superiority has to be challenged: the human species is not a higher species than any other species possessing consciousness. For this purpose, he invents a new name signifying this denial of equality: *speciesism.* The name, modeled after *racism,* stands for the wrongness involved in evaluating one conscious species as lower than any other and in justifying actual practices against a lower whose natural role is presumed to be to serve the purposes of a higher. Speciesism is to species as racism is to race.

This flattening out of the difference between humans and animals leads to some terrifying consequences which Singer unflinchingly supports. The word *person,* for example, traditionally used to designate a special feature of the human being, can be used, Singer suggests, of any self-conscious animal: to be conscious is to be a person. It can, of course, be used of human beings, but not all; the unborn, infants, the hopelessly deranged, are not persons because they are not conscious. It can also be used of some animals, but not all, for example, chimpanzees, gorillas, orangutans, since they are conscious, are persons. One cannot categorically affirm, then, that it is always worse to kill humans who are not persons than animals who are! "So," he writes, "it seems that killing, say, a chimpanzee is worse than killing a human being who, because of a congenital intellectual disability, is not and can never be a person."

Above, we cautioned ourselves against thinking that the traditional human-centered ecology precludes human concern for animals, not because animals have rights but because showing concern for animals is the *human* thing to do. A different view is emerging in nature-centered ecology. In the human-to-animal relationship of the traditional view, the question of *rights* pertains only to the human side, with respectful treatment of animals being the expected human thing to do. In the emerging view of nature-centered ecology, however, it is *animal life itself* that generates the human obligation of respectful treatment of animals. In this transferred sense, then, the term *animal rights* has come to be used as a meaningful term. That's why there are animal rights lawyers today, a designation unheard of before, and why there has been any number of cases of animal cruelty taken to court. Not long ago, animal rights had a simple test when a gentleman, caught up in an angry dispute on a corner in New York City, hurled a little dog into oncoming traffic, for which he had to spend time in jail. These facts indicate how far public awareness of animal rights has come.

It's not as though no adjustment can be made to accommodate the essential meaning of both human-centered and nature-centered ecology because they both address the one and same nature, and can do so together by reining in the extremes that each exhibits. It would be foolish to hold that any being other than human can do anything about the environment as a whole. Humans have at their disposal the power to envision, to plan, and to execute projects for the sake of enhancing life on earth. Theirs is the power of *stewardship*, an expressive word introduced above, which directs those guardian hands into which nature is given to keep and shape it into a loving habitation.

In edging his way toward extremes, there is a remarkable consistency in the way Singer views the use of animals for human consumption, necessarily involving a turn in favor of vegetarianism. To kill animals for food is wrong, except in the case of sheer survival: " . . . it would be better to reject altogether the killing of animals for food unless one must do so to survive . . . To foster the right attitude of consideration for animals, including non-self-conscious ones, it may be best to make it a simple principle to avoid killing them for food." Singer's case for vegetarianism has been persuasive for a lot of people, including fellow-philosophers.

As a last note, how are we to make any kind of ecological sense of the activity that makes a mockery of the ecology of animal life? Hunting, not for food which can arguably be its own self-justification, but hunting for entertainment, for fun? It has been engaged in for centuries, clear down to our own time, and embraced as a sport for rugged men—it's outdoors, it's bracing, it's braving the elements, it's heroic, it has risks. Nevertheless, however one talks about it, it still comes down to killing animals for mere pleasure, for the "sport" of it, and it is this feature of hunting that makes it impossible to square with kindness to animals. The travesty is aggravated by the trophy complex of deer head and antlers commanding the hunter's rec room. Or consider the moneyed hunter who is able to buy his share of trouble-free, big game "hunting" in a private wild in northern Minnesota—how this kind of assault on innocent animal life can be morally justified would take an awful lot of explaining to do.

READINGS

READING 1

A Platform of the Deep Ecology Movement

Arne Naess

(from *Ecology, Community and Lifestyle*)

(1) The flourishing of human and non-human life on Earth has intrinsic value. The value of non-human life forms is independent of the usefulness these may have for narrow human purposes.

(2) Richness and diversity of life forms are values in themselves and contribute to the flourishing of human and non-human life on Earth.

(3) Humans have no right to reduce this richness and diversity except to satisfy vital needs.

(4) Present human interference with the non-human world is excessive, and the situation is rapidly worsening.

(5) The flourishing of human life and cultures is compatible with a substantial decrease of the human population. The flourishing of non-human life requires such a decrease.

(6) Significant change of life conditions for the better requires change in policies. These affect basic economic, technological, and ideological structures.

(7) The ideological change is mainly that of appreciating *life quality* (dwelling in situations of intrinsic value) rather than adhering to a high standard of living. There will be a profound awareness of the difference between big and great.

(8) Those who subscribe to the foregoing points have an obligation directly or indirectly to participate in the attempt to implement the necessary changes.

READING 2

Earth as Mother

Rupert Sheldrake

(from *Rebirth of Nature*)

Although the conquest of nature for the sake of human progress is the official ideology of the modern world, the old intuition of nature as Mother still affects our personal responses and gives emotional force to phrases such as "nature's bounty," "the wisdom of nature," and "unspoiled nature." It also conditions our response to the ecological crisis. We feel uncomfortable when we recognize that we are, polluting our own Mother; it is easier to rephrase the problem in terms of "inadequate waste management." But today, with the rise of the green movement, Mother Nature is reasserting herself, whether we like it or not. In particular, the acknowledgment that our planet is a living organism, Gaia, Mother Earth, strikes a responsive chord in millions of people; it reconnects us both with our personal, intuitive experience of nature and with the traditional understanding of nature as alive.

. . .

One of the primary meanings of nature is an inborn character or disposition, as in the phrase *human nature*. This in turn is linked to the idea of nature as an innate impulse or power. On a wider scale, nature is the creative and regulative power operating in the physical world, the immediate cause of all its phenomena. And hence *nature* comes to mean the natural or physical world as a whole. When nature in this sense is personified, she is Mother Nature, an aspect of the Great Mother, the source and sustainer of all life, and the womb to which all life returns.

In archaic mythologies, the Great Mother had many aspects. She was the original source of the universe and its laws, and the ruler of nature, fate, time, eternity, truth, wisdom, justice, love, birth, and death. She was Mother Earth, Gaia, and also the goddess of the heavens, the mother of the sun, the moon, and all heavenly bodies-like Nut, the Egyptian sky-goddess or Astarte, the goddess of heaven, queen of the stars. She was Natura, the goddess of Nature. She was the world soul of Platonic cosmology, and she had many other names and images as the mother and matrix and sustaining force of all things.

These feminine associations play an important part in our thinking; our conception of nature is intertwined with ideas about the relations between women and men, between goddesses and gods, and between the feminine and the masculine in general. If we prefer to reject these traditional sexual associations, what are the alternatives to the idea of nature as organic, alive, and motherlike? One is that nature consists of nothing but inanimate matter in motion. But in this case we only deny the mother principle by being unaware of it; the very word for matter is derived from the same root as *mother*—in Latin, the corresponding words are *materia* and *mater*—the whole ethos of materialism is permeated with maternal metaphors.

READING 3
Nature and the Moral Sense
William Wordsworth
(from *Lines Written a Few Miles above Tintern Abbey*)

I have learned

To look on nature, not as in the hour
Of thoughtless youth; but hearing oftentimes
The still, sad music of humanity,
Nor harsh nor grating, though of ample power
To chasten and subdue. And I have felt
A presence that disturbs me with the joy
Of elevated thoughts; a sense sublime
Of something far more deeply interfused,
Whose dwelling is the light of setting suns,
And the round ocean and the living air,
And the blue sky, and in the mind of man:
A motion and a spirit, that impels
All thinking things, all objects of all thought,
And rolls through all things. Therefore am I still
A lover of the meadows and the woods,
And mountains; and of all that we behold
From this green earth; of all the mighty world
Of eye, and ear,—both what they half create,
And what perceive; well pleased to recognise
In nature and the language of the sense
The anchor of my purest thoughts, the nurse,
The guide, the guardian of my heart, and soul
Of all my moral being.

READING 4
The Fate of Gaia, the Living Earth
James Lovelock
(from *The Revenge of Gaia*)

Like the Norns in Wagner's *Der Ring des Nibelungen*, we are at the end of our tether, and the rope, whose weave defines our fate, is about to break.

Gaia, the living Earth, is old and not as strong as she was two billion years ago. She struggles to keep the Earth cool enough for her myriad forms of life against the ineluctable increase of the sun's heat. But to add to her difficulties, one of those forms of life, humans, disputatious tribal animals with dreams of conquest even of other planets, has tried to rule the Earth for their own benefit alone. With breathtaking insolence they have taken the stores of carbon that Gaia buried to keep oxygen at its proper level and burnt them. In so doing they have usurped Gaia's authority and thwarted her obligation to keep the planet fit for life; they thought only of their own comfort and convenience.

Some time towards the end of the 1960s I walked along the quiet back lane of Bowerchalke village with my friend and near neighbour William Golding; we were talking about a recent visit I had made to the Jet Propulsion Laboratory in California and the idea of searching for life on other planets. I told him why I thought that both Mars and Venus were lifeless and that the Earth was more than just a planet with life, and why I saw it somehow in certain ways alive. He immediately said, "If you intend to put forward so large an idea you must give it a proper name, and I suggest that you call it Gaia." I was truly grateful to have his gift of this simple, powerful name for my ideas about the Earth. I gladly accepted it then as a scientist acknowledging an earlier literary reference, just as others in previous centuries referred to Gaia when naming the Earth sciences geology, geography and so on. At that time I knew little of Gaia's biography as a Greek goddess and never imagined that the New Age, then just beginning, would take Gaia as a mythic goddess again. In a way, however harmful this has been to the acceptance of the theory in science, the New Agers were more prescient than the scientists. We now see that the great Earth system, Gaia, behaves like the other mythic goddesses, Khali and Nemesis; she acts as a mother who is nurturing but ruthlessly cruel towards transgressors, even when they are her progeny.

I know that to personalize the Earth System as Gaia, as I have often done and continue to do in this book, irritates the scientifically correct, but I am unrepentant because metaphors are more than ever needed for a widespread comprehension of the true nature of the Earth and an understanding of the lethal dangers that lie ahead.

After forty years living with the concept of Gaia I thought I knew her, but I realize now that I underestimated the severity of her discipline. I knew that our self-regulating Earth had evolved from those organisms that left a better environment for their progeny and by the elimination of those who fouled their habitat, but I never realized just how destructive we were, or that we had so grievously damaged the Earth that Gaia now threatens us with the ultimate punishment of extinction.

I am not a pessimist and have always imagined that good in the end would prevail. When our Astronomer Royal, Sir Martin Rees, now President of the Royal Society, published in 2004 his book *Our Final Century*, he dared to think and write about the end of civilization and the human race. I enjoyed it as a good read, full of wisdom, but took it as no more than a speculation among friends and nothing to lose sleep over.

I was so wrong; it was prescient, for now the evidence coming in from the watchers around the world brings news of an imminent shift in our climate towards one that could easily be described as Hell: so hot, so deadly that only a handful of the teeming billions now alive will survive. We have made this appalling mess of the planet and mostly with rampant liberal good intentions.

READING 5
St. Francis
G.K. Chesterton
(from *The Common Man*)

There is something about peasant traditions, and even about peasant legends, which knows how to keep close to the earth. It is a mark of true folklore that even the tale that is evidently wild is eminently sane. We see this in the most extravagant stories of the saints, if we compare them with the extravagant theories of the sophists and the sentimentalists. Take, for instance, that most beautiful attribute for which St. Francis is rightly loved throughout the modern world: his tenderness towards the lower animals. It is illustrated in medieval folklore by fancies but not by fads. It is impossible to imagine any fable more fabulous, in the sense of fantastic and frankly incredible, than the story of St. Francis making a business bargain with a very large and dangerous wolf; drawing up a legal document with carefully numbered promises and concessions from the party of the first part and the party of the second part; the wild beast solemnly lodging a legal affidavit by the number of times he nodded his head. And yet there is in that fairy-tale a rustic and realistic sagacity that comes from real relations with animals, and is therefore perhaps called by the picturesque name of horse-sense. It was not written by the modern monomaniac animal-worshipper. It is a pleasant story because the saint is considering the peasants as well as the wolf.

St. Francis was not the sort of man to agree with the hypothetical Hindoo who would be slowly devoured by a Bengal tiger, and remain in a state of philosophical absent-mindedness, because tigers are quite as cosmic as Hindoos. The Christian common sense of St. Francis, even in this wild fable, seized on the vital fact; that men must be saved from wolves as well as wolves from hunger, or even more so, and that this could only be done by some sort of definite arrangement. And it does put its finger upon the difficulty; in the absence of communication and therefore of contract between men and beasts. It realises that a moral obligation must be a mutual obligation. St. Francis contemplating the mountain wolf, hits on the same point as Job contemplating the monstrous Leviathan: "Will he make a pact with thee?" That is a sort of solid popular instinct, which was never lost by the really popular saint, in spite of anything which strangers might stare at as his antics or his agonies. Men remembered that he had been a good friend to them as well as to birds and beasts; and the fact is still apparent in the most remote and extravagant rumours of him. It is in this that he differs from some of the rather unbalanced and unnatural humanitarians of modern times.

READING 6
How St. Francis Converted the Very Fierce Wolf of Gubbio
(from *The Little Flowers*)

At the time that Saint Francis was staying in the city of Gubbio, in the district of Gubbio there appeared a very big wolf, fearsome and ferocious, which devoured not only animals but even human beings, so that all the citizens were in great fear, because many times he came near the city. All would go armed when they went out of the city as if they were going to combat, yet with all this, those who were alone and encountered him could not defend themselves from him. And out of fear of this wolf it came to the point that no one dared to leave that town.

For this reason Saint Francis had compassion on the people of the town, and decided to go out to this wolf, even though all the citizens advised against it. Making the sign of the most holy cross, he went out of the town, he and his companions, placing all his confidence in God. As the others hesitated to go any further, Saint Francis took the road toward the place where the wolf was. Then that wolf, seeing many citizens who had come to see this miracle, ran toward Saint Francis with his mouth open. Drawing close to him, Saint Francis made the sign of the most holy cross on him and called him to himself and said this: "Come here, Brother Wolf. I command you on behalf of Christ that you do no harm to me or to anyone." An amazing thing to say! Immediately, when Saint Francis had made the sign of the cross, the fearsome wolf closed his mouth and stopped running; and once the command was given, it came meekly as a lamb, and threw itself to lie at the feet of Saint Francis.

And Saint Francis spoke to him thus: "Brother Wolf, you do much harm in this area, and you have done great misdeeds, destroying and killing the creatures of God without His permission. And not only have you killed and devoured beasts, but you have dared to kill *people, made in the image of God.* For this reason you are worthy of the gallows as a thief and the worst of murderers. And all the people cry out and complain against you, and all this town is your enemy. But I, Brother Wolf, want to make peace between you and these people, so that you do not offend them any more, and they may pardon you every past offense, and so neither the people nor the dogs will persecute you any more. And after these words were said, the wolf showed that he accepted what Saint Francis said and wanted to observe it, by movement of his body and tail and ears and by bowing his head. Then Saint Francis said, "Brother Wolf, since it pleases you to make this pact of peace and keep it, I promise that I will have food given to you constantly, as long as you live, by the people of this town, so that you will no longer suffer hunger, since I know very well that you did all

this harm because of hunger. But in order for me to obtain this grace for you, I want you, "Brother Wolf, to promise me that you will never harm any human person nor any animal. Do you promise me this?" And the wolf, bowing his head, made a clear sign that he promised it. And Saint Francis said this: "Brother Wolf, I want you to guarantee this promise, so that I can truly trust it." Saint Francis reached out his hand to receive his guarantee, the wolf lifted his right paw in front of him, and tamely placed it on top of the hand of Saint Francis, giving the only sign of a guarantee that he was able to make.

Then Saint Francis said, "Brother Wolf, *I command you in the name of Jesus Christ:* come with me now without any hesitation, and we will go to seal this peace-pact in the name of God." And the obedient wolf went with him like a tame lamb; and the citizens, seeing this, were greatly amazed. Immediately this news was known throughout the whole city; and because of it all the people, men and women, great and small, young and old, poured into the piazza to see the wolf with Saint Francis. And once all the people were fully assembled Saint Francis got up and preached to them, saying, among other things, that God allows such things and pestilences because of sins; and the flame of hell, which lasts forever for the damned, is much more dangerous than the fierceness of the wolf, which *can* only *kill the body.* "How much should the mouth of hell be feared when the mouth of a little animal holds such a great multitude in fear! Dear people, return to God, therefore, and do fitting penance for your sins, and God will free you from the wolf in the present, and from hell's fire in the future."

When he finished the sermon, Saint Francis said. "Listen my brothers! Brother Wolf, who is here before you, has promised me, and given me his guarantee, to make peace with you, and never to offend you in anything, if you promise him to give him every day the things he needs. And I make myself trustee for him that he will firmly observe the peace-pact." Then all the people with one voice promised to feed him regularly. And Saint Francis, in front of them all, said to the wolf: "And you, Brother Wolf, do you promise to observe the peace-pact with these people, that you will not harm the people, the animals, nor any creature?" And the wolf knelt down and bowed his head and with gentle movements of his body and tail and ears showed, as much as possible, that he wished to observe every part of the pact with them. Saint Francis said: "Brother Wolf, as you gave me a guarantee of this promise outside the gate, I also want you to give me in front of all the people a guarantee of your promise, that you will not deceive me in my promise and the guarantee that I gave for you." Then the wolf, lifting his right paw, placed it in the hand of Saint Francis. Because of this action, and the others mentioned above, there was such rejoicing and wonder among all the people, both for the devotion of the Saint and for the novelty of the miracle and for the peace of the wolf, that they all began to cry out to heaven, *praising and blessing* God who sent Saint Francis to them who, through his merits, had freed them from the jaws of the cruel beast.

Afterwards that same wolf lived in Gubbio for two years, and he tamely entered the houses, going from door to door, without doing harm to anyone and without any being done to him; and he was kindly fed by the people, and as he went this way through the town and the houses, no dog barked at him. Finally after two years Brother Wolf died of old age, at which the citizens grieved very much, because when they saw him going through the city so tamely, they better recalled the virtue and holiness of Saint Francis.

READING 7
The Canticle of Brother Sun
St. Francis of Assisi

Most high, all-powerful, all good Lord!
    All praise is yours, all glory, all honour
    And all blessing.
To you, alone, Most High, do they belong.
    No mortal lips are worthy
    To pronounce your name.
All praise be yours, my Lord, through all that you have made,
    And first my lord Brother Sun,
    Who brings the day; and light you give to us through him.
How beautiful is he, how radiant in all his splendour!
    Of you, Most High, he bears the likeness.
All praise be yours, my Lord, through Sister Moon and Stars;
    In the heavens you have made them, bright
    And precious and fair.
All praise be yours, my Lord, through Brothers Wind and Air,
    And fair and stormy, all the weather's moods,
    By which you cherish all that you have made.
All praise be yours, my Lord, through Sister Water,
    So useful, lowly, precious and pure.
All praise be yours, my Lord, through Brother Fire,
    Through whom you brighten up the night.
    How beautiful is he, how gay! Full of power and strength.
All praise be yours, my Lord, through Sister Earth, our mother,
    Who feeds us in her sovereignty and produces
    Various fruits with coloured flowers and herbs.
Praise and bless my Lord, and give him thanks,
    And serve him with great humility.

READING 8
Transition to the Twenty-First Century
Ray Kurzweil

(from *Age of Spiritual Machines*)

Computers today exceed human intelligence in a broad variety of intelligent yet narrow domains such as playing chess, diagnosing certain medical conditions, buying and selling stocks, and guiding cruise missiles. Yet human intelligence overall remains far more supple and flexible. Computers are still unable to describe the objects on a crowded kitchen table, write a summary of a movie, tie a pair of shoelaces, tell the difference between a dog and a cat (although this feat, I believe, is becoming feasible today with contemporary neural nets—computer simulations of human neurons),[3] recognize humor, or perform other subtle tasks in which their human creators excel.

One reason for this disparity in capabilities is that our most advanced computers are still simpler than the human brain—currently about a million times simpler (give or take one or two orders of magnitude depending on the assumptions used). But this disparity will not remain the case as we go through the early part of the next century. Computers doubled in speed every three years at the beginning of the twentieth century, every two years in the 1950s and 1960s, and are now doubling in speed every twelve months. This trend will continue, with computers achieving the memory capacity and computing speed of the human brain by around the year 2020.

Achieving the basic complexity and capacity of the human brain will not automatically result in computers matching the flexibility of human intelligence. The organization and content of these resources—the software of intelligence—is equally important. One approach to emulating the brain's software is through reverse engineering—scanning a human brain (which will be achievable early in the next century)[4] and essentially copying its neural circuitry in a neural computer (a computer designed to simulate a massive number of human neurons) of sufficient capacity.

There is a plethora of credible scenarios for achieving human-level intelligence in a machine. We will be able to evolve and train a system combining massively parallel neural nets with other paradigms to understand language and model knowledge, including the ability to read and understand written documents. Although the ability of todays computers to extract and learn knowledge from natural-language documents is quite limited, their abilities in this domain are improving rapidly. Computers will be able to read on their own, understanding and modeling what they have read, by the second decade of the twenty-first century. We can then have our computers read all of the world's literature—books, magazines, scientific journals, and other available material. Ultimately, the machines will gather knowledge on their own by venturing into the physical world, drawing from the full spectrum of media and information services, and sharing knowledge with each other (which machines can do far more easily than their human creators).

Once a computer achieves a human level of intelligence, it will necessarily roar past it. Since their inception, computers have significantly exceeded human mental dexterity in their ability to remember and process information. A computer can remember billions or even trillions of facts perfectly, while we are hard pressed to remember a handful of phone numbers. A computer can quickly search a database with billions of records in fractions of a second. Computers can readily share their knowledge bases. The combination of human-level intelligence in a machine with a computers inherent superiority in the speed, accuracy, and sharing ability of its memory will be formidable.

Mammalian neurons are marvelous creations, but we wouldn't build them the same way. Much of their complexity is devoted to supporting their own life processes, not to their information-handling abilities. Furthermore, neurons are extremely slow; electronic circuits are at least a million times faster. Once a computer achieves a human level of ability in understanding abstract concepts, recognizing patterns, and other attributes of human intelligence, it will be able to apply this ability to a knowledge base of all human-acquired—and machine-acquired—knowledge.

A common reaction to the proposition that computers will seriously compete with human intelligence is to dismiss this specter based primarily on an examination of contemporary capability. After all, when 1 interact with my personal computer, its intelligence seems limited and brittle, if it appears intelligent at all. It is hard to imagine one's personal computer having a sense of humor, holding an opinion, or displaying any of the other endearing qualities of human thought.

But the state of the art in computer technology is anything but static. Computer capabilities are emerging today that were considered impossible one or two decades ago. Examples include the ability to transcribe accurately normal continuous human speech, to understand and respond intelligently to natural language, to recognize patterns in medical procedures such as electrocardiograms and blood tests with an accuracy rivaling that of human physicians, and, of course, to play chess at a world-championship level. In the next decade, we will see translating telephones that provide real-time speech translation from one human language to another, intelligent computerized personal assistants that can converse and rapidly search and understand the world's knowledge bases, and a profusion of other machines with increasingly broad and flexible intelligence.

In the second decade of the next century, it will become increasingly difficult to draw any clear distinction between the capabilities of human and machine intelligence. The advantages of computer intelligence in terms of speed, accuracy, and capacity will be clear. The advantages of human intelligence, on the other hand, will become increasingly difficult to distinguish.

The skills of computer software are already better than many people realize. It is frequently my experience that when demonstrating recent advances in, say, speech or character recognition,

observers are surprised at the state of the art. For example, a typical computer user's last experience with speech-recognition technology may have been a low-end freely bundled piece of software from several years ago that recognized a limited vocabulary, required pauses between words, and did an incorrect job at that. These users are then surprised to see contemporary systems that can recognize fully continuous speech on a 60,000-word vocabulary, with accuracy levels comparable to a human typist.

Also keep in mind that the progression of computer intelligence will sneak up on us. As just one example, consider Gary Kasparov's confidence in 1990 that a computer would never come close to defeating him. After all, he had played the best computers, and their chess-playing ability—compared to his—was pathetic. But computer chess playing made steady progress, gaining forty-five rating points each year. In 1997, a computer sailed past Kasparov, at least in chess. There has been a great deal of commentary that other human endeavors are far more difficult to emulate than chess playing. *This is true.* In many areas—the ability to write a book on computers, for example—computers are still pathetic. But as computers continue to gain in capacity at an exponential rate, we will have the same experience in these other areas that Kasparov had in chess. Over the next several decades, machine competence will rival—and ultimately surpass—any particular human skill one cares to cite, including our marvelous ability to place our ideas in a broad diversity of contexts.

Evolution has been seen as a billion-year drama that led inexorably to its grandest creation: human intelligence. The emergence in the early twenty-first century of a new form of intelligence on Earth that can compete with, and ultimately significantly exceed, human intelligence will be a development of greater import than any of the events that have shaped human history. It will be no less important than the creation of the intelligence that created it, and will have profound implications for all aspects of human endeavor, including the nature of work, human learning, government, warfare, the arts, and our concept of ourselves.

This specter is not yet here. But with the emergence of computers that truly rival and exceed the human brain in complexity will come a corresponding ability of machines to understand and respond to abstractions and subtleties. Human beings appear to be complex in part because of our competing internal goals. Values and emotions represent goals that often conflict with each other, and are an unavoidable by-product of the levels of abstraction that we deal with as human beings. As computers achieve a comparable—and greater—level of complexity, and as they are increasingly derived at least in part from models of human intelligence, they too, will necessarily utilize goals with implicit values and emotions, although not necessarily the same values and emotions that humans exhibit.

A variety of philosophical issues will emerge. Are computers thinking, or are they just calculating? Conversely, are human beings thinking, or are they just calculating? The human brain presumably follows the laws of physics, so it must be a machine, albeit a very complex one. Is there an inherent difference between human thinking and machine thinking? To pose the question another way, once computers are as complex as the human brain, and can match the human brain in subtlety and complexity of thought, are we to consider them conscious? This is a difficult question even to pose, and some philosophers believe it is not a meaningful question; others believe it is the only meaningful question in philosophy. This question actually goes back to Plato's time, but with the emergence of machines that genuinely appear to possess volition and emotion, the issue will become increasingly compelling.

For example, if a person scans his brain through a noninvasive scanning technology of the twenty-first century (such as an advanced magnetic resonance imaging), and downloads his mind to his personal computer, is the "person" who emerges in the machine the same consciousness as the person who was scanned? That "person" may convincingly implore you that "he" grew up in Brooklyn, went to college in Massachusetts, walked into a scanner here, and woke up in the machine there. The original person who was scanned, on the other hand, will acknowledge that the person in the machine does indeed appear to share his history, knowledge, memory, and personality, but is otherwise an impostor, a different person.

Even if we limit our discussion to computers that are not directly derived from a particular human brain, they will increasingly appear to have their own personalities, evidencing reactions that we can only label as emotions and articulating their own goals and purposes. They will appear to have their own free will. They will claim to have spiritual experiences. And people—those still using carbon-based neurons or otherwise—will believe them.

One often reads predictions of the next several decades discussing a variety of demographic, economic, and political trends that largely ignore the revolutionary impact of machines with their own opinions and agendas. Yet we need to reflect on the implications of the gradual, yet inevitable, emergence of true competition to the full range of human thought in order to comprehend the world that lies ahead.

READING 9
Nature and Man
Ralph Waldo Emerson
(from *Nature*)

To go into solitude, a man needs to retire as much from his chamber as from society. I am not solitary whilst I read and write, though nobody is with me. But if a man would be alone, let him look at the stars. The rays that come from those heavenly worlds will separate between him and what he touches. One might think the atmosphere was made transparent with this design, to give man, in the heavenly bodies, the perpetual presence of the sublime.

Seen in the streets of cities, how great they are! If the stars should appear one night in a thousand years, how would men believe and adore; and preserve for many generations the remembrance of the city of God which had been shown! But every night come out these envoys of beauty, and light the universe with their admonishing smile.

The stars awaken a certain reverence, because though always present, they are inaccessible; but all natural objects make a kindred impression, when the mind is open to their influence. Nature never wears a mean appearance. Neither does the wisest man extort her secret, and lose his curiosity by finding out all her perfection. Nature never became a toy to a wise spirit. The flowers, the animals, the mountains, reflected the wisdom of his best hour, as much as they had delighted the simplicity of his childhood.

When we speak of nature in this manner, we have a distinct but most poetical sense in the mind. We mean the integrity of impression made by manifold natural objects. It is this which distinguishes the stick of timber of the wood-cutter from the tree of the poet. The charming landscape which I saw this morning is indu-bitably made up of some twenty or thirty farms. Miller owns this field, Locke that, and Manning the woodland beyond. But none of them owns the landscape. There is a property in the hori-zon which no man has but he whose eye can integrate all the parts, that is, the poet. This is the best part of these men's farms, yet to this their warranty-deeds give no title.

To speak truly, few adult persons can see nature. Most persons do not see the sun. At least they have a very superficial seeing. The sun illuminates only the eye of the man, but shines into the eye and the heart of the child. The lover of nature is he whose inward and outward senses are still truly adjusted to each other; who has retained the spirit of infancy even into the era of manhood. His intercourse with heaven and earth becomes part of his daily food. In the presence of nature a wild delight runs through the man, in spite of real sorrows. Nature says,—he is my creature, and maugre all his impertinent griefs, he shall be glad with me. Not the sun or the summer alone, but every hour and season yields its tribute of delight; for every hour and change corresponds to and authorizes a different state of the mind, from breathless noon to grimmest midnight. Nature is a setting that fits equally well a comic or a mourning piece. In good health, the air is a cordial of incredible virtue. Crossing a bare common, in snow puddles, at twilight, under a clouded sky, without having in my thoughts any occurrence of special good fortune, I have enjoyed a perfect exhilaration. I am glad to the brink of fear. In the woods, too, a man casts off his years, as the snake his slough, and at what period soever of life is always a child. In the woods is perpetual youth. Within these plantations of God, a decorum and sanctity reign, a perennial festival is dressed, and the guest sees not how he should tire of them in a thousand years. In the woods, we return to reason and faith. There I feel that nothing can befall me in life,—no disgrace, no calamity (leaving me my eyes), which nature cannot repair. Standing on the bare ground,— my head bathed by the blithe air and uplifted into infinite space,—all mean egotism vanishes. I become a transparent eyeball; I am nothing; I see all; the currents of the Universal Being circulate through me; I am part or parcel of God. The name of the nearest friend sounds then foreign and accidental: to be brothers, to be acquaintances, master or servant, is then a trifle and a disturbance. I am the lover of uncontained and immortal beauty. In the wilderness, I find something more dear and connate than in streets or villages. In the tranquil landscape, and especially in the distant line of the horizon, man beholds somewhat as beautiful as his own nature.

The greatest delight which the fields and woods minister is the suggestion of an occult relation between man and the vegetable. I am not alone and unacknowledged. They nod to me, and I to them. The waving of the boughs in the storm is new to me and old. It takes me by surprise, and yet is not unknown. Its effect is like that of a higher thought or a better emotion coming over me, when I deemed I was thinking justly or doing right.

Yet it is certain that the power to produce this delight does not reside in nature, but in man, or in a harmony of both. It is necessary to use these pleasures with great temperance. For nature is not always tricked in holiday attire, but the same scene which yesterday breathed perfume and glittered as for the frolic of the nymphs is overspread with melancholy to-day. Nature always wears the colors of the spirit. To a man laboring under calamity, the heat of his own fire hath sadness in it. Then there is a kind of contempt of the landscape felt by him who has just lost by death a dear friend. The sky is less grand as it shuts down over less worth in the population.

READING 10
Morning in the Woods
Henry David Thoreau
(from *Walden*)

Every morning was a cheerful invitation to make my life of equal simplicity, and I may say innocence, with Nature herself. I have been as sincere a worshipper of Aurora as the Greeks. I got up early and bathed in the pond; that was a religious exercise, and one of the best things which I did. They say that characters were engraven on the bathing tub of king Tching-thang to this effect: "Renew thyself completely each day; do it again, and again, and forever again." I can understand that. Morning brings back the heroic ages. I was as much affected by the faint hum of a mosquito making its invisible and unimaginable tour through my apartment at earliest dawn, when I was sitting with door and windows open, as I could be by any trumpet that ever sang of fame. It was Homer's requiem; itself an Iliad and Odyssey in the air, singing its own wrath and wanderings. There was something cosmical about it; a standing advertisement, till forbidden, of the everlasting vigor and fertility of the world. The morning, which is the most memorable season of the day, is the awakening hour. Then there is least somnolence in us; and for an hour, at least, some part of us awakes which slumbers all the rest of the day and night. Little is to be expected of that day, if it can be called a day, to which we are not awakened by our Genius, but by the mechanical nudgings of some servitor, are not awakened by our own newly-acquired force and aspirations from within, accompanied by the undulations of celestial music, instead of factory bells, and a fragrance filling the air—to a higher life than we fell asleep from; and thus the darkness bear its fruit, and prove itself to be good, no less than the light. That man who does not believe that each day contains an earlier, more sacred, and auroral hour than he has yet profaned, has despaired of life, and is pursuing a descending and darkening way. After a partial cessation of his sensuous life, the soul of man, or its organs rather, are reinvigorated each day, and his Genius tries again what noble life it can make. All memorable events, I should say, transpire in morning time and in a morning atmosphere. The Vedas say, "All intelligences awake with the morning." Poetry and art, and the fairest and most memorable of the actions of men, date from such, an hour. All poets and heroes, like Memnon, are the children of Aurora, and emit their music at sunrise. To him whose elastic and vigorous thought keeps pace with the sun, the day is a perpetual morning. It matters not what the clocks say or the attitudes and labors of men. Morning is when I am awake and there is a dawn in me, Moral reform is the effort to throw off sleep. Why is it that men give so poor an account of their day if they have not been slumbering? They are not such poor calculators. If they had not been overcome with drowsiness they would have performed something. The millions are awake enough for physical labor; but only one in a million is awake enough for effective intellectual exertion, only one in a hundred millions to a poetic or divine life. To be awake is to be alive. I have never yet met a man who was quite awake. How could I have looked him in the face?

We must learn to reawaken and keep ourselves awake, not by mechanical aids, but by an infinite expectation of the dawn, which does not forsake us in our soundest sleep. I know of no more encouraging fact than the unquestionable ability of man to elevate his life by a conscious endeavor. It is something to be able to paint a particular picture, or to carve a statue, and so to make a few objects beautiful; but it is far more glorious to carve and paint the very atmosphere and medium through which we look, which morally we can do. To affect the quality of the day, that is the highest of arts. Every man is tasked to make his life, even in its details, worthy of the contemplation of his most elevated and critical hour. If we refused, or rather used up, such paltry information as we get, the oracles would distinctly inform us how this might be done.

READING 11
Elected Solitude
Henry David Thoreau
(from *Walden*)

There is commonly sufficient space about us. Our horizon is never quite at our elbows. The thick wood is not just at our door, nor the pond, but somewhat is always clearing, familiar and worn by us, appropriated and fenced in some way, and reclaimed from Nature. For what reason have I this vast range and circuit, some square miles of unfrequented forest, for my privacy, abandoned to me by men? My nearest neighbor is a mile distant, and no house is visible from any place but the hill-tops within half a mile of my own. I have my horizon bounded by woods all to myself; a distant view of the railroad where it touches the pond on the one hand, and of the fence which skirts the woodland road on the other. But for the most part it is as solitary where I live as on the prairies. It is as much Asia or Africa as New England. I have, as it were, my own sun and moon and stars, and a little world all to myself. At night there was never a traveller passed my house, or knocked at my door, more than if I were the first or last man; unless it were in the spring, when at long intervals some came from the village to fish for pouts—they plainly fished much more in the Walden Pond of their own natures, and baited their hooks with darkness—but they soon retreated, usually with light baskets, and left "the world to darkness and to me," and the black kernel of the night was never profaned by any human neighborhood. I believe that men are generally still a little afraid of the dark, though the witches are all hung, and Christianity and candles have been introduced.

Yet I experienced sometimes that the most sweet and tender, the most innocent and encouraging society may be found in any natural object, even for the poor misanthrope and most melancholy man. There can be no very black melancholy to him who lives in the midst of Nature and has his senses still. There was never yet such a storm but it was Aeolian music to a healthy and innocent ear. Nothing can rightly compel a simple and brave man to a vulgar sadness. While I enjoy the friendship of the seasons I trust that nothing can make life a burden to me. The gentle rain which waters my beans and keeps me in the house today is not drear and melancholy, but good for me too. Though it prevents my hoeing them, it is of far more worth than my hoeing. If it should continue so long as to cause the seeds to rot in the ground and destroy the potatoes in the low lands, it would still be good for the grass on the uplands, and, being good for the grass, it would be good for me. Sometimes, when I compare myself with other men, it seems as if I were more favored by the gods than they, beyond any deserts that I am conscious of; as if I had a warrant and surety at their hands which my fellows have not, and were especially guided and guarded. I do not flatter myself, but if it be possible they flatter me. I have never felt lonesome, or in the least oppressed by a sense of solitude, but once, and that was a few weeks after I came to the woods, when, for an hour, I doubted if the near neighborhood of man was not essential to a serene and healthy life. To be alone was something unpleasant. But I was at the same time conscious of a slight insanity in my mood, and seemed to foresee my recovery. In the midst of a gentle rain while these thoughts prevailed, I was suddenly sensible of such sweet and beneficent society in Nature, in the very pattering of the drops, and in every sound and sight around my house, an infinite and unaccountable friendliness all at once like an atmosphere sustaining me, as made the fancied advantages of human neighborhood insignificant, and I have never thought of them since. Every little pine needle expanded and swelled with sympathy and befriended me. I was so distinctly made aware of the presence of something kindred to me, even in scenes which we are accustomed to call wild and dreary, and also that the nearest of blood to me and humanest was not a person nor a villager, that I thought no place could ever be strange to me again.

“Mourning unti.mely consumes the sad;
Few are their days in the land of the living,
Beautiful daughter of Toscar.”

Some of my pleasantest hours were during the long rain storms in the spring or fall, which confined me to the house for the afternoon as well as the forenoon, soothed by their ceaseless roar and pelting; when an early twilight ushered in a long evening in which many thoughts had time to take root and unfold themselves. In those driving north-east rains which tried the village houses so, when the maids stood ready with mop and pail in front entries to keep the deluge out, I sat behind my door in my little house, which was all entry, and thoroughly enjoyed its protection. In one heavy thunder shower the lightning struck a large pitch-pine across the pond, making a very conspicuous and perfectly regular spiral groove from top to bottom, an inch or more deep, and four or five inches wide, as you would groove a walking-stick. I passed it again the other day, and was struck with awe on looking up and beholding that mark, now more distinct than ever, where a terrific and resistless bolt came down out of the harmless sky eight years ago. Men frequently say to me, “I should think you would feel lonesome down there, and want to be nearer to folks, rainy and snowy days and nights especially.” I am tempted to reply to such—This whole earth which we inhabit is but a point in space. How far apart, think you, dwell the two most distant inhabitants of yonder star, the breadth of whose disk cannot be appreciated by our instruments? Why should I feel lonely? is not our planet in the Milky Way? This which you put seems to me not to be the most important question. What sort of space is that which separates a man from his fellows and makes him solitary? I have found that no exertion of the legs can bring two minds much nearer to one another. What do we want most to dwell near to? Not to many men surely, the depot, the post office, the barroom, the meeting-house, the school-house, the grocery, Beacon Hill, or the Five Points, where men most congregate, but to the perennial source of our life, whence in all our experience we have found that to issue, as the willow stands near the water and sends out its roots in that direction.

READING 12
A Fable for Tomorrow
Rachel Carson
(from *Silent Spring*)

THERE WAS ONCE a town in the heart of America where all life seemed to live in harmony with its surroundings. The town lay in the midst of a checkerboard of prosperous farms, with fields of grain and hillsides of orchards where, in spring, white clouds of bloom drifted above the green fields. In autumn, oak and maple and birch set up a blaze of color that flamed and flickered across a backdrop of pines. Then foxes barked in the hills and deer silently crossed the fields, half hidden in the mists of the fall mornings.

Along the roads, laurel, viburnum and alder, great ferns and wildflowers delighted the traveler's eye through much of the year. Even in winter the roadsides were places of beauty, where countless birds came to feed on the berries and on the seed heads of the dried weeds rising above the snow. The countryside was, in fact, famous for the abundance and variety of its bird life and when the flood of migrants was pouring through in spring and fall people traveled from great distances to observe them. Others came to fish the streams, which flowed clear and cold out of the hills and contained shady pools where trout lay. So it had been from the days many years ago when the first settlers raised their houses, sank their wells, and built their barns.

Then a strange blight crept over the area and everything began to change. Some evil spell had settled on the community: mysterious maladies swept the flocks of chickens; the cattle and sheep sickened and died. Everywhere was a shadow of death. The farmers spoke of much illness among their families. In the town the doctors had become more and more puzzled by new kinds of sickness appearing among their patients. There had been several sudden and unexplained deaths, not only among adults but even among children, who would be stricken suddenly while at play and die within a few hours.

There was a strange stillness. The birds, for example—where had they gone? Many people spoke of them, puzzled and disturbed. The feeding stations in the backyards were deserted. The few birds seen anywhere were moribund; they trembled violently and could not fly. It was a spring without voices. On the mornings that had once throbbed with the dawn chorus of robins, catbirds; doves, jays, wrens, and scores of other bird voices there was now no sound; only silence lay over the fields and woods and marsh.

On the farms the hens brooded, but no chicks hatched. The farmers complained that they were unable to raise any pigs—the litters were small and the young survived only a few days. The apple trees were coming into bloom but no bees droned among the blossoms, so there was no pollination and there would be no fruit.

The roadsides, once so attractive, were now lined with browned and withered vegetation as though swept by fire. These, too, were silent, deserted by all living things. Even the streams were now lifeless. Anglers no longer visited them, for all the fish had died.

In the gutters under the eaves and between the shingles of the roofs, a white granular powder still showed a few patches; some weeks before it had fallen like snow upon the roofs and the lawns, the fields and streams.

No witchcraft, no enemy action had silenced the rebirth of new life in this stricken world. The people had done it themselves.

This town does not actually exist, but it might easily have a thousand counterparts in America or elsewhere in the world. I know of no community that has experienced all the misfortunes I describe. Yet every one of these disasters has actually happened somewhere, and many real communities have already suffered a substantial number of them. A grim specter has crept upon us almost unnoticed, and this imagined tragedy may easily become a stark reality we all shall know.

What has already silenced the voices of spring in countless towns in America? This book is an attempt to explain.

READING 13
Thinking Like a Mountain
Aldo Leopold
(from *Sand County Almanac*)

A deep chesty bawl echoes from rimrock to rimrock, rolls down the mountain, and fades into the far blackness of the night. It is an outburst of wild defiant sorrow, and of contempt for all the adversities of the world.

Every living thing (and perhaps many a dead one as well) pays heed to that call. To the deer it is a reminder of the way of all flesh, to the pine a forecast of midnight scuffles and of blood upon the snow, to the coyote a promise of gleanings to come, to the cowman a threat of red ink at the bank, to the hunter a challenge of fang against bullet. Yet behind these obvious and immediate hopes and fears there lies a deeper meaning, known only to the mountain itself. Only the mountain has lived long enough to listen objectively to the howl of a wolf.

Those unable to decipher the hidden meaning know nevertheless that it is there, for it is felt in all wolf country, and distinguishes that country from all other land. It tingles in the spine of all who hear wolves by night, or who scan their tracks by day. Even without sight or sound of wolf, it is implicit in a hundred small events: the midnight whinny of a pack horse, the rattle of rolling rocks, the bound of a fleeing deer, the way shadows lie under the spruces. Only the ineducable tyro can fail to sense the presence or absence of wolves, or the fact that mountains have a secret opinion about them.

My own conviction on this score dates from the day I saw a wolf die. We were eating lunch on a high rimrock, at the foot of which a turbulent river elbowed, its way. We saw what we thought was a doe fording the torrent, her breast awash in white water. When she climbed the bank toward us and shook out her tail, we realized our error: it was a wolf. A half-dozen others, evidently grown pups, sprang from the willows and all joined in a welcoming mêlée of wagging tails and playful maulings. What was literally a pile of wolves writhed and tumbled in the center of an open flat at the foot of our rimrock.

In those days we had never heard of passing up a chance to kill a wolf. In a second we were pumping lead into the pack, but with more excitement than accuracy: how to aim a steep downhill shot is always confusing. When our rifles were empty, the old wolf was down, and a pup was dragging a leg into impassable slide-rocks.

We reached the old wolf in time to watch a fierce green fire dying in her eyes. I realized then, and have known ever since, that there was something new to me in those eyes—something known only to her and to the mountain. I was young then, and full of trigger-itch; I thought that because fewer wolves meant more deer, that no wolves would mean hunters' paradise. But after seeing the green fire die, I sensed that neither the wolf nor the mountain agreed with such a view.

* * *

Since then I have lived to see state after state extirpate its wolves. I have watched the face of many a newly wolfless mountain, and seen the south-facing slopes wrinkle with a maze of new deer trails. I have seen every edible bush and seedling browsed, first to anaemic desuetude, and then to death. I have seen every edible tree defoliated to the height of a saddlehorn. Such a mountain looks as if someone had given God a new pruning shears, and forbidden Him all other exercise. In the end the starved bones of the hoped-for deer herd, dead of its own too-much, bleach with the bones of the dead sage, or molder under the high-lined junipers.

I now suspect that just as a deer herd lives in mortal fear of its wolves, so does a mountain live in mortal fear of its deer. And perhaps with better cause, for while a buck pulled down by wolves can be replaced in two or three years, a range pulled down by too many deer may fail of replacement in as many decades.

So also with cows. The cowman who cleans his range of wolves does not realize that he is taking over the wolf's job of trimming the herd to fit the range. He has not learned to think like a mountain. Hence we have dustbowls, and rivers washing the future into the sea.

* * *

We all strive for safety, prosperity, comfort, long life, and dullness. The deer strives with his supple legs, the cowman with trap and poison, the statesman with pen, the most of us with machines, votes, and dollars, but it all comes to the same thing; peace in our time. A measure of success in this is all well enough, and perhaps is a requisite to objective thinking, but too much safety seems to yield only danger in the long run. Perhaps this is behind Thoreau's dictum: In wildness is the salvation of the world. Perhaps this is the hidden meaning in the howl of the wolf, long known among mountains, but seldom perceived among men.

Chapter Eight

War and Peace

WAR VERSUS PEACE

War has never been a stranger to mankind. From the earliest days of recorded history to the present day, you find it wherever you look; the histories of Europe, Asia, the Americas, and Africa cannot be told without stories of war. Wherever peoples emerge, so does violence, and so do the weapons of violence that trace a sad trajectory from primitive combat with club and spear to the touch of a computer keyboard capable of destroying the living substance of the planet. Even in times of peace, weapons of violence have always been at the edge—in early ages with sling shots, bows, arrows, lances, catapults, and incendiary engines, to the guns, bombs, cannon, torpedoes, gases, chemicals, poisons, diseases, missiles, and atomic and nuclear devices of modern times. The complex nature of man does not guarantee that yearning for peace will prevail for long over the insatiable urging for violence, with the tragic conclusion that, according to the logic implied in possessing weapons, using them will inevitably follow. Cries for peace, so strongly voiced in a time or threat of war, will remain just that, cries, as the prophet Jeremiah laments, *"Peace, when there is no peace."*

This chapter deals with the question of war *and* peace, directly acknowledging how difficult it is to talk of one without the other, or to think that the absence of one is the definition of the other: war is the absence of peace, and peace is the absence of war. It is true that where there is war, there is the absence of peace, but it is also true that where there is peace, the absence of war is just the beginning, for the wider meaning of peace is the fulfillment of all human needs required by the dignity of human life. Therefore, though this chapter mostly deals with the problem of war, its primary tone is the wider meaning of peace. It's far easier to write about war than about peace, for war is so much upon us, so impressive and reportable, that volume after volume can be written about it. The same cannot be said of peace, for it does not lend itself to the graphic and sensational portraiture available in a world at war. This point is underscored by a line in Alexis de Tocqueville's *Democracy in America*: "No kind of greatness is more pleasing to the imagination of a democratic people than military greatness, a greatness of vivid and sudden luster, obtained without toil, by nothing but the risk of life."

There are many contexts in which the word *peace* is used, and in all of them there is a fundamental reality trying to find expression, a harmony seeking to assert its rightful place among disparate elements, among people of different dispositions and temperaments, among those who have divergent sets of value or visions of life. Inasmuch as peace pertains both to individuals and the public at large, a useful distinction may be made between *personal peace* and *public peace.*

PERSONAL PEACE

All of us have experienced those times when we can truly say we are at peace with ourselves. We know, for example, the calmness settling over us when we've resolved an ugly state of affairs, or when we've come to terms with a difficult individual, or when we've worked our way through a moral dilemma in good conscience, which moved even Shakespeare's ill-fated Cardinal Wolsey to declare: "I know myself now, and I feel within me/a peace above all earthly dignities/a still and quiet conscience." The individual person's own peace of mind was the main concern of Stoic ethics over an 800-year period whose key theme was to put anxiety aside, and not to worry about things beyond our control: The principal rule, says Epictetus, is to examine what is "unpleasing" to you and then to determine "whether it concerns anything which is within your power or not; if it concerns anything beyond your power, be prepared to say that it is nothing to you."

But personal peace requires a broad spectrum of essential and practical features beginning, in a sense, with family life in which intimate relationships and household activity furnish each family member with the daily personal experience of the joys and anxieties of togetherness, and the need for harmony in personal interaction. Personal peace further includes a complex of indispensables such as the availability of sufficient food and shelter, a share in the economy through employment, health care, space for rest and leisure, support in old age, the opportunity to enjoy the cultural life of the community, and access to education. No one can be at peace without the assurance of the freedom to practice their religion, of unhampered association with others, and of giving voice to their opinions. As part and parcel of one's personal sense of peace is the acceptance of one's duties and the responsibility of discharging them, at which point personal peace goes beyond the individual and tends to spread upward and outward touching others at the farthest edge. Peace at any level is impossible unless there is peace at the personal level first, a sentiment captured in the hymn, "Let there be peace on earth, and let it begin with me."

PUBLIC PEACE

Personal peace opens up to public peace, the harmony that seeks its rightful place among communities at every level—local, national, and international—each of which has the obligation to insure peace for its members. Recall the analysis made earlier in the chapter on society: There is a mutual relationship between the individual members of a community and the community itself, and among the goals of this relationship is the achievement of public peace. In a sense, public peace is a twofold challenge to the community, one to secure its members from violence, and second to respond to the human needs of all.

With regard to the first challenge, violence against a person, whether it is physical or spiritual, is a bold attack against the very humanity of the individual. All the crimes, including the killings, the shootings, the arsons, the thefts, and the assaults, and all the concealed violations of integrity are blights in human relationships that society must find measures to protect against in the name of the common good. For a political philosopher like Thomas Hobbes, the whole purpose of the state, or the commonwealth (that which secures the common weal), is to ensure peace which, on the large scale, is the only antidote to war. It is the first "general rule of reason" that "every man ought to endeavor peace," the elaboration of which is the purpose of the next section.

With regard to the second challenge, considering that local levels offer a unique immediacy between the authorities and the people in their day-by-day lives, they become the first place where the human needs of its members are to be met. There can be no harmony without a reasonable structure of taxation, without practical concern for education, health, food, and shelter; for care for the elderly; for transportation; and for the unexpected exigencies that can occur at any time. All these concerns are obligations on the national level too where the national community, through its federal authority, can execute oversight and supply funding when required throughout the nation's cities and states. Even though an international community of nations is beyond our present vision, there is an ever-growing consciousness for the need of international organizations, like the United Nations, to enhance a peaceful quality of life for all mankind. Peace is the rightful patrimony of every human being, which is the subtext of the profoundly sensitive encyclical letter Peace on Earth of Pope John XXIII, 1963, in which he states that all human societies must accept as their foundation principle, "that every human being is a person; his nature is endowed with intelligence and free will. By virtue of this, he has rights and duties of his own, flowing directly and simultaneously from his very nature, which are therefore universal, inviolable and inalienable."

CAN WAR EVER BE JUSTIFIED?

Given humanity's profound yearning for peace, we have to answer the question whether war is ever justified. Do human beings *ever* have the *right* to engage in war? Isn't the devastation of war, tragic and long-standing in its consequences, horrible enough to deny its ever being called "right"? Over 1,500 years ago, St. Augustine, a north African Roman citizen, bitterly complained about the imperial ambitions of Rome, observing that even though Rome had brought some benefits of civilization to conquered countries, the human cost was huge: "True, but think of the cost of this achievement! Consider the scale of those wars, with all that slaughter of human beings, all the human blood that war has shed! . . . everyone who reflects with sorrow on such grievous evils, in all their horror and cruelty, must acknowledge the misery of them" (R #1).

Sharing Augustine's burning sense of the misery of war can be found abundantly in war literature—poetry, fictional narrative, drama, and unadorned journalism— particularly in the last century whose wartime history has properly been described as "straight from hell." Stephen Spender, one among many soul-searching antiwar poets, asks, "Why cannot the one good/Benevolent feasible/Final dove, descend?" (R #2). The most scathing poem coming out of World War I by Wilfred Owen who, after calling to mind the gas, the guns, and the fire that ended with blood-soaked, knock-kneed, sleepless soldiers, writes, "My friend, you would not tell with such high zest/To children ardent for some desperate glory,/The old Lie: Dulce et decorum est/Pro patria mori." (It is sweet and honorable to die for one's country.)

(R #3). And W. H. Auden's sobering stanzas on how humanity is undermined by ideology of war:

> Here war is simple like a monument:
> A telephone is speaking to a man;
> Flags on a map assert that troops were sent;
> A boy brings milk in bowls. There is a plan
>
> For living men in terror of their lives,
> Who thirst at nine who were to thirst at noon,
> And can be lost and are, and miss their wives,
> And, unlike an idea, can die too soon.
>
> But ideas can be true although men die,
> And we can watch a thousand faces
> Made active by one lie:
>
> And maps can really point to places
> Where life is evil now:
> Nanking; Dachau. (*In Time of War*, XVI)

Erich Maria Remarque's *All Quiet on the Western Front* tells the story of several German friends taken into the army as young men who become disillusioned by the horrors and the personal tragedy of World War I (R #4). The newspaper reports made by Ernie Pyle during World War II, in a style that was both plain and human, made him one of the most respected journalists of the war (R #5). Iris Chang's book *The Rape of Nanking* was written years after the events in 1937 during the Sino-Japanese war because they were, for all political considerations, an untold story, the story of the utterly inhuman atrocities committed by the Japanese soldiery on the people of this beloved city (R #6). The novel *Citadel in Spring* by the Japanese author Hiroyuki Agawa is a fictional account of the lives of several young adults in Hiroshima just before the dropping of the atomic bomb and the drastic consequences for them right after (R #7). *Night,* by Elie Wiesel, Nobel Prize winner for literature, is still the most poignant account of the Holocaust as experienced by a young Jew (R #8).

The human cost of war requires nothing less than the scrupulous satisfaction of the moral demands for engaging in it. What those moral demands are, though we may be able to determine them in an abstract way, seldom prove to be available with absolute moral certitude. The living, practical, concrete world in which motives, goals, and decisions are intertwined with human fallibility and recklessness, make such certitude difficult, if not impossible, to achieve. Indeed, some rightly feel that the public reasons offered to justify going to war often mask the underlying lust for power and greed for wealth. "What are nations," St. Augustine again asks, "but great thieves?" A classical exemplification of this rhetorical question reaches back to the Peloponnesian War between Athens and Sparta in the fifth century B.C. as presented in the writings of the Athenian soldier-turned-historian *Thucydides*. In a particular event, when the Athenians invaded the small island-nation Melos as an ally of Sparta, an historically unusual discussion, called the Melian Dialogue, took place between representatives of both sides on the justification for going to war. The Athenians, facing a much weaker foe, maintained that "might is right" is its own justification and, having thus turned morality upside down, went forward to "kill all the grown men they captured, enslaved the children and women" and proceeded to colonize the island (p. 1).

The prospect of war has always generated a desire for peace on the part of the more sensitive members of society. There were, for example, pacifists and lovers of peace in Hebrew, Greek, and Roman antiquity. The great prophet Isaiah expressed his longing in the words, "They shall beat their swords into plowshares and their spears into pruning hooks; nation shall not lift up sword against nation, neither shall they learn war any more" (pp. 2, 4). In *Lysistrata* Aristophanes has the women declaiming to the magistrate, "Where are the sons we sent to your battlefields . . . and the husbands who can never approach their wives." Or Seneca, the Roman Stoic: "Shameful it is that men should delight in mutual bloodshed." The early Christian church stood against war, and its opposition was urgent enough to persuade some young men, anticipating the prophetic role conscientious objectors have in our times, by refusing to join the military. Such was the case of the twenty-one-year-old Maximilianus of Tabessa who, in the year 295, refused to be inducted into the Roman army with the words, "I cannot serve in the military, I am a Christian," and he was forthwith executed. A hundred years later we hear St. Augustine decrying the glory associated with war that for centuries enthralled the popular emotion, when he writes, "it is a higher glory to slay war itself with the word than men with the sword, and to procure and maintain peace by peace, not by war" (Ramsey, p. 151). He felt, as Aristotle did before him, that all men desire peace, which is their goal even at war: "every man, even when he makes war, longs for peace—no one makes peace to engage in war." But the reason they go to war is not that they hate peace but that they want the kind of peace that suits them.

With so much having been said on the misery of war, and at the same time acknowledging the deep-seated human desire for peace, we still have to answer the question, "Is war ever justified?" Or, if it is ever to be called "right," can we at least say that war must be a defensive engagement only, and never aggressive? It would be helpful to think of violence on a war-size scale if we first think of violence on an individual scale; that is, the response we give as individuals in certain particular instances. Even though we may be repelled by violence, we would tend to agree that an individual, having a right to his own life, also has the right to defend it. That is, he has the right to defend himself against anyone who would try to take his life, or those things pertaining to the integrity of life, such as freedom, health, and property. Thus a person has the right to defend himself against aggression even if it may, as a last resort, require the use of violence.

In a similar sense, the state, though not a physical person, is a moral person—a collective life-unity—and may defend itself against any attempt to despoil it, even by the use of violent means as a last resort. Just as the individual may rightly defend himself against aggression, so the state, as a collective person, may defend itself against aggression. Since the nation-state is the de facto highest legitimate political authority in our time, no individual province or state can engage in war on its own authority, and it will be a long time, if ever, until an international authority arises which, as the central world authority for adjudicating disputes between member nation-states, would absorb the war-making authority of its member-states.

It was the same Augustine, whom we have seen as declaiming against the specter of war, who considered what the "wise man" would do who, hating war, still felt that defending life by violent means would sometimes be necessary. He was trying to tame the passion for war, inherited from earlier Roman times, with a sense of justice which, ironically, was also inherited from Roman law, by laying out principles to be followed in order for a war to be called "just." He is often referred to as the progenitor of just-war thinking prevalent today.

JUST WAR THEORY

There are those, perhaps of a more liberal type, who feel that war can hardly ever be justified, so, for them, the phrase "just war" is difficult to accept because it seems to speak in favor of war; they prefer, considering war to be a human tragedy, to speak of a "presumption against war," which terminology tends to narrow the limits within which a war can be called just. There are others, of the more conservative type, who feel that such a position ignores the injustice against which a war is fought and, therefore, prefer to speak of a "presumption for justice." As we go on in this discussion of the conditions of a just war, it becomes clear that the author aligns himself with the first category because, despite the historical proclivity of nations to go to war, and despite the readiness of citizens to applaud their government's engagement in war, the presumption against war best reflects the humane aspects of the tradition favoring peace. In any case, if war is justifiable, it must be on the basis of morally unambiguous premises. These premises are referred to as *conditions* to be met for the justification of war, and together they are called the *Just War Theory*. Depending on how they are broken down, the conditions can be presented in any number, but they can conveniently be listed as four:

1. just cause
2. rightful authority
3. last resort
4. proportionate means

(1) A *just cause* is the weightiest condition of all. A cause cannot be founded on issues that can be settled diplomatically, like honor, credibility, disrespect, territorial disputes, and ethnic or religious differences. It has to touch on the very life of the nation—aggression against its population, the rape of its land, and the destruction of its freedom—that truly call for self-defense. (2) A nation, as a whole, possesses a government in charge of the common good and possesses, in its own style of government, the *rightful authority* to declare war. In the United States this authority is constitutionally vested in Congress. Where rightful authority resides in the case of a justified rebellion is not at all clear, and only becomes so in sorting itself out as the rebellion coalesces. (3) To be called a *last resort*, war can never be undertaken until every peaceful measure is exhausted, until no stone is left unturned. Mediation, arbitration, treaties, and moratoriums must all be tried to avoid a headlong rush into preventable chaos. (4) Since the ultimate goal of war is peace, it follows that no more violence than is necessary to restore peace can morally be used. The utter crushing of an enemy people, unconditional surrender, the demand for extreme reparation, or vindictive retribution go beyond the limits of *proportionate means*. Under this condition is also included the all-important requirement of the *probability of success*, which some authors list as a separate condition. But it seems reasonable to hold that if there is no probability of success, then "proportionate means" has no significance, for this particular war would never satisfy the reason for undertaking it in the first place. Further, success is not a scorecard approach to war, we win, you lose, for it is conceivable that, if the war results in extremely dire consequences for the victor, then the victor "wins" the war but loses the peace. The conditions for a just war are not to be considered apart from each other; they interlock so that the absence of one condition would vitiate the collective impact of all.

It should be clear that Just War Theory can be presented as though it is a straightforward guide to decision making when in fact it is totally abstract; that is, it is not directly connected with facts on the ground. Applying principles to practice is always a delicate activity, especially in the matter of committing an entire population to the horrors of war and its irretrievable consequences. To give ourselves some insight as to the enormous difficulties in evaluating the fulfillment of the conditions outlined above, let's give attention to some of the practical, historical problems pertaining to each of the conditions.

In the matter of whether a cause is a *just cause* or not, we can point out that during the time leading up to war when a decision has to be made as to its rightfulness, the very fact that you have to *decide* whether the cause is just is in itself an indication of the inherent, agonizing difficulty involved. And even if the cause is just, it doesn't stand alone as the sole factor in going to war, for the other conditions must also be satisfied. There could hardly be a more dramatic example of a just cause for war than that of a small country aggressively invaded by a super power, but even a case like this becomes dubious when you realize that the probability for success is zero. Czechoslovakia first lost its independence under Nazi Germany, and then later under the Soviets, but for a short time before 1968, while still under Soviet surveillance, it was like a fledgling trying to find a cautious path to democratize politics, to decentralize authority, to introduce a wider range of freedom for its citizens, and it did so successfully enough to lift the spirit of the beleaguered country so as to refer to it as the "Prague Spring." In the late summer of 1968, however, Russian troops, always present but hidden, rolled into Wenceslaus Square to restore their authoritarian rule. The Czechs saw the futility of armed resistance and retreated into nonviolent resistance to hold out for a brighter day. The feeling of depression on the part of the Czechoslovakian people was memorialized in the tragic demonstration of a young man, Jan Palach (mentioned earlier), who immolated himself at the base of the statue of St. Wenceslaus in the Square that bears his name.

In right-ordered societies, there is normally no problem as to where *rightful authority* lies, although there could be a huge problem as to the actual use of that authority. For example, it will always be contested whether the U.S. Congress abandoned its constitutional authority and obligation in the decision to invade Iraq in 2003, and whether the president exceeded his authority in committing the country to a de facto war without formal congressional approval. In this regard, we are living in interesting times. Legitimate authority has been vested for centuries in the nation-state, but with the emergence of more and more internationalization, politically as well as economically, some people have a fond dream that war-making authority will eventually be vested in an international authority, instead.

War as a *last resort* demands that every peaceful means has been taken to resolve the conflict and has failed, yet diplomatic avenues should never be closed off, nor communications terminated, no matter what. The Cuban missile crisis of 1962 is a stunning example. For several years preceding, relations between the United States and the Soviet Union were frightfully strained, especially on the issue of nuclear missiles which the Soviets began deploying in Cuba, along with a significant number of troops. A cataclysm was in the making, but both President Kennedy and President Khrushchev never let communications between them stop, and the confrontation was resolved with a peaceful outcome.

Just War Theory applies, first and foremost, to a country bound to defend itself, but we can ask whether there are times when a country may use force against another, not to defend its own interests, but the interests of a third? Two general categories can be distinguished: *intervention* and *prevention*, both of which are fraught with moral complications. Observing all the safeguards against a war's being unjust, there may be times when an intervention may be legitimate, as in the case of helping a country defend itself when it cannot do so on its own. Considering all things, there was a general feeling that Truman's intervention to defend South Korea in 1950 was right, and, contrariwise, there are many who feel that, in view of Eisenhower's proclamations regarding the independence of Hungary, his failure to intervene to help them against the Russians in 1956, was wrong.

As far as defending one's country is concerned, an important distinction has come to the fore today between *preemptive war* and *preventive war*. Preemption is easier to describe in that it refers to a country's military action against another whose threat is seen as immediate, imminent, or certain, whereas prevention means military action based on the mere possibility of an attack at some indefinite time in the future. It's conceivable that a preemptive war, with all the conditions for a just war satisfied, could stake out a claim for its being a just one, but a preventive war, never. The importance of the distinction today was not lost on the Bush administration as it gave it cover to legitimate the war in Iraq as preemptive, not preventive.

Granting that a particular war is just, it does not follow that each and every activity to prosecute the war is also just, which different moralists refer to as a distinction between a "right to war" (*jus ad bellum*) and a "right in war" (*jus in bello*). That is, "proportionate means" refers not only to the amount and kind of violence used, but also to activities like the use of internationally banned weapons, treatment of prisoners, and torture; or measures that infringe upon the rights of others as, for example, threatening the children of an escaped prisoner to force him to give up. The need to drop two atom bombs over Japan still remains a highly questionable decision, it having been known before the event that Japan was already on its knees.

Among a number of international efforts to contain the horrors of war, the Geneva Conventions occupy an influential and honorable place. The first Convention was held as a result of a Red Cross initiative in 1864, with three more to follow until 1949. Almost all the countries of the world are signatories to some portion or other of the articles of the Conventions which touch on every conceivable way to ameliorate life for military personnel and for civilians in the time of war: humane treatment of prisoners, anti-discrimination, safeguards for hospitals and medics, medical care for civilians and military, care of the wounded, condemnation of torture, treatment for those shipwrecked or injured at sea, and the rejection of gas warfare—are all spelled out in hundreds of provisions that could fittingly serve as the foundation for international humanitarian laws in general.

Restraints against war as embodied in the conditions of Just War Theory are almost impossible to find in the catalogue of wars in mankind's history. Just to mention a few, what restraints are to be found in Homer's *Iliad* whose warriors were honored for destroying cities, taking slaves, disemboweling the enemy, and rejecting pleas for mercy? (R #9). No restraints appear in the battle of Kleidion, Bulgaria, in 1014, when the Byzantine forces, under Basil II, entrapped the Bulgarian forces of Czar Samuel and then, after rounding up the prisoners in groups of a hundred, gouged out the eyes of ninety-nine but left the last soldier of each group with one eye to lead them back to their commander who, at the sight of the blinded horde, collapsed and died the following day. What image of restraint can we possibly conjure up of World War I, fought in the trenches, in which the human physical cost alone was over eight and a half million men killed and over twenty-one million wounded or maimed? And how to evaluate the many wars of rebellion, some of which were sheer opportunism, while others were a genuine strike against tyranny and oppression? It's hard to escape the conclusion that, despite the raising of prophetic voices against war, human beings have unfailingly accustomed themselves to the insane slaughter of each other and, out of necessity, have had to honor its dead warriors as heroes lest their lives be thought of as wasted or their deaths be deemed in vain. After completing his huge work *War and Peace* culminating in the slaughter between the Russians and the French in 1812, Tolstoy could not find any satisfactory answer to the question "Why did millions of people kill one another when it has been known since the world began that it is physically and morally bad to do so?" How could he? Rather than say that man would *freely* choose his own self-destruction, Tolstoy settled on an inevitable necessity by calling war an "elemental biological law" or "zoological" as he termed it.

In American history there has never been a generation that has not experienced war or its after-effects, a sad commentary on how prone to militancy the American psyche seems to be, but at the same time all wars have been subject to some kind of opposition. The war with the least opposition was World War II. After the long, valiant, and uncertain struggle of the Allies in Europe, the United States came to see its entry into the war justified in the absolute need to defeat the Nazi threat to civilization, and any doubt subsided with the outrageous act of war in the Japanese attack on Pearl Harbor. In general, however, opposition to American involvement in war has been vocal and strong, but never enough to deter military action. The War of 1812 was, in the opinion of the respected historian Samuel Eliot Morison, "the most unpopular war that this country ever waged, not even excepting the Vietnam conflict." The Mexican War precipitated a resolution on the part of the Massachusetts legislature calling it "wanton, unjust and unconstitutional," and Henry Thoreau wrote *The Duty of Civil Disobedience* to oppose it, ringing with the words, "What I have to do is to see, at any rate, that I do not lend myself to the wrong which I condemn" (R #10). Intense criticism was directed against President William McKinley for the Spanish-American War and the struggle for independence of the Philippine Islands. Though Woodrow Wilson was credited with keeping the country out of the conflagration in Europe, in 1917 he called for a declaration of war against Germany and then tried to keep criticism at bay with laws criminalizing any language that would bring "into contempt, scorn . . . or disrepute" either the government or its institutions. The Vietnam War, gradually intensifying over its long duration, saw a new level of opposition to a government whose credibility was worn threadbare even before the infamous Gulf of Tonkin Resolution and whose prosecution of the war drove thousands of young men into conscientious objection or into expatriation by moving up to Canada. Of the two Gulf Wars, the first was hyped up into acceptance by Congress, and the second has met opposition unlike any other war in American history: its legality will be questioned for years to come, and its consequences in human and financial costs, overwhelming in every respect, will haunt generations yet to come. There was ample reason for the quintessential American, Benjamin Franklin, to say, "There never was a good war or a bad peace."

NUCLEAR WARFARE

The conditions for a just war make sense in judging the morality of war historically down to the present day, but with the advent of weaponry so powerful we have to ask whether a "just war" still makes sense. The problem we have to address is whether Just War Theory has application to warfare across the board in today's world. An indispensable and clarifying distinction, touched on above, must be made between war in the *conventional* (traditional) sense and war in the *nuclear* (contemporary) sense. In the conventional sense, which becomes clearer the farther back you go, there is a marked delineation between soldiery and people, between combatants and noncombatants, and between fighters and innocents. The battle was between the forces on either side designated by authority to fight for their respective countries, and every effort was made to keep the ordinary citizens out of harm's way. Citizens kept their distance from the fighting, news of which had to be brought back to the community. From time to time, citizens were able to come close to the fighting, to become spectators of the fracas. In the early battles of our own Civil War, there were occasions when ladies and gentlemen went out to watch, and in such numbers as to block the passage of the wounded being brought back to the city. But as we come closer to the present day, the distinction between combatants and noncombatants has become blurred or lost entirely so that events, in World War II, like the rocket bombing of London or the fire bombing of Dresden, were attacks on total populations.

Whole cities were bombed too at Hiroshima and Nagasaki, but the difference this time was that the obliteration was wrought with new-age weaponry, the atom bomb, which brought with it the unleashing of power never before witnessed by human beings, and with technology that would soon lead to the nuclear bomb. In turn, the nuclear bomb would spring free the vast energy of the cosmos trapped in the nucleus of the hydrogen atom, the humblest of them all. The power meant to serve mankind became its unspeakable master. There is no way, then, that the conditions for a just war could possibly apply to nuclear war. The delimiting categories of soldiery and people, and of combatants and noncombatants have been erased and the notion of "innocents" has become meaningless in the struggle of all against all. Without trying to detail the numbing horrors scientists tell us would befall the world in a nuclear exchange, what sane mind would think that war with weapons capable of destroying life on the planet earth is morally permissible? What "just" cause can be assigned or imagined for total destruction? What rightful authority, what last resort, and what proportionate means? What kind of macabre accounting, as some analysts did during the cold war, would draw the conclusion that, in a nuclear exchange, we would "prevail" against the Soviets because sixty-four million Americans would still be left to a handful of Russians? There are *absolutely no conditions that would justify nuclear war.*

Though it is clear that nuclear war must be rejected, and that there can be no initiation of nuclear war nor retaliation, still, in the words of the morally sensitive 1983 letter *The Challenge of Peace* of the American Catholic bishops, it remains "much less clear how we translate a 'no' to nuclear war into the personal and public choices which can move us in a new direction" (R #11). Would it be morally permissible to produce nuclear bombs and to stockpile them? May such bombs be possessed if they cannot be used? It might be expected that questions like these would be answered with an unequivocal "no" in a letter that strongly condemns nuclear war but that would let dangling the moral problems associated with the policy of *deterrence*, the policy of dissuading a potential enemy from the first use of nuclear weaponry under threat of overwhelming, destructive retaliation, which has been the U.S. policy since the end of World War II. If the use of nuclear bombs is immoral, how can possessing them be justified? This is a tough question to answer. It was tough even when there were only two powers, Russia and the United States, which had the capability of producing and delivering them. But this bilateral equation has been nullified by a half dozen other nations that have already built them or are on their way to doing so. And there is still the possibility, however remote, of rogue groups commandeering their acquisition.

The Bishops' letter does not skirt the problem of deterrence, but after a careful analysis of its elements, especially at the time when the letter was issued, there were "two dimensions of the contemporary dilemma of deterrence": the danger of nuclear war and the danger to the freedom of "entire peoples." "Thus," the letter states, "a balance of forces, preventing either side from achieving superiority, can be seen as a means of safeguarding both dimensions." The letter, in keeping with the position of every sane person, is adamant in rejecting nuclear war as a moral option, so, with this understanding, the bishops caution that their grudging acceptance of deterrence should not be seen as anything more than support for continued pressure for arms reduction and a comprehensive and effective test ban treaty, pressure that is as imperative today as it ever was.

TERRORISM AND TORTURE

Just War Theory, as we have seen, makes sense when the conflict involves nation-states or large identifiable areas as in our own Civil War, but not when the conflict goes beyond nation-states to cultures and civilizations without borders. The historian Samuel Huntington shook up academia a number of years ago with his writings on the *Clash of Civilizations* which presaged a conflict of global dimensions, not out of geopolitical concerns, but out of ethnic or cultural/religious concerns. The fighting, the war, would not take place within well-defined geographical spaces, or along battle lines, or with uniformed battalions but in strike and hide tactics that would make military pursuit extremely difficult, if not impossible. Ironically much of the turmoil, in view of serious studies on the tragic events in the Mid-east, has been fueled by an intense religious imagination, which holds out the prospect for divine approval of violence to secure God's dominion and to remedy real or perceived injustices among their people.

In this light, terrorism, not at all unknown in human history, has displayed a new dimension in our time in that it is an organized and sophisticated attack on innocent people for political purposes. It takes unprecedented advantage of the innate idealism of young people to welcome martyrdom by witnessing to God's judgment through indiscriminate acts of violence. An immediate consequence of terrorism is torture; that is, physical, psychological, and spiritual assaults on a human being for any purpose, be it for punishment or sadism or, as in the case of terrorism, for eliciting information supposedly possessed by the victim and presumably revealable under personal violence. It's an all too understandable reaction in trying to combat terrorism to get information out of real or suspected terrorists by using any and all possible means, including torture, but, even putting aside the question of the veracity of extorted information, torture, of which Abu Ghraib is a constant reminder, stands against the basic tenets of democracy and the ideals of true morality.

PACIFISM AND CONSCIENTIOUS OBJECTION

There is a blunt irony, then, to the question, is war ever just? Is the killing, the slaughter, the maiming, the burning, the radiation, the physical and spiritual destruction, and the endless insecurity of postwar consequences, ever morally acceptable? Should the causes of war, even though proposed in the name of religion, society, or economy, be honored at all costs? The *pacifist* says no. For many years the pacifist was ridiculed as a coward, unpatriotic, or guilty of rejecting the dictates of conscience, totally unlike the soldiers who put their lives on the line for their country every day. But the pacifist puts his life on the line in a different way. In good conscience, he sees his country, and indeed every human being, in a far wider context—war, in all its horror, is inhumane and destructive of the peace and love to which all human beings are called. The role of the pacifist is akin to that of a prophet, a teacher, whose testimony, though it can be misunderstood, is indispensable in keeping alive mankind's ultimate aspirations. Among the many and varied voices trying to be heard on the preciousness of life, pitiably lost in the time of war, was that of the Nobel Laureate Hermann Hesse in praising those who, in 1919 after the Great War, "staunchly rejected the duty of murdering and hating."

There is a kinship between *conscientious objection* and pacifism in that both are a matter of conscience which, as we have seen, is the last arbiter of morality for an individual and, out of the uniqueness of that conscience, an individual may find himself outside the general view in favor of war. It is an individual's sincere judgment as to his place in the world. Conscience must always be respected, this side of an action that would infringe the known rights of others. A conscientious objector may be against all war, and thus is not practically different from a pacifist. But he is more likely to be against a particular one, and as such is referred to as a *selective* conscientious objector. Either way, vis-a-vis the draft in American history, conscientious objection has undergone a profound change in acceptability in the past generation or so. It was almost unheard of at the draft boards during World War I, and in World War II, exemptions were granted with great reluctance, and then with the stipulation of serving in a noncombative capacity. But often enough, there were peculiar twists. For instance, a Catholic young man pleading for C.O. status could have been turned down by the local draft board with the fatuous question, "your Church is not against war, so how can you be?"

Selective conscientious objection reached its peak during the Vietnam War, when thousands of young men, though not against war per se, were against this particular one as unjust. It was a somber, depressing time for them, with some finally accepting office jobs or medical assignments, but hundreds of others, feeling that to agree to a noncombative position would still make room for someone else to take up arms, chose rather to escape to Canada. A dean in an eastern university tells the story of a young man who was a "gung ho" member of the ROTC and won all sorts of awards as the outstanding student cadet in the summer camp between his junior and senior year. But at camp he had an unbelievable change of heart about the military, and upon returning to school requested an honorable discharge from the Corps. The officers of the ROTC formed a tribunal, with the captain as foreman, to hear his case and turned him down. When asked by the Dean why he was turned down, the captain responded, "Well, Dean, this case was too hot for us to handle here, so we had to send it on to Washington!"

A great deal of courage in the cause of peace, and in the name of conscience, has been exhibited by an impressive number of people, usually inspired by their religious belief—people like Mahatma Gandhi, Dietrich Bonhoeffer, Martin Luther King, Dan and Phil Berrigan, Dorothy Day, and the legendary boxing icon, Muhammed Ali. An interesting linkage obtains between conscientious objection and nonviolence beginning with Henry David Thoreau's essay on the justification of civil disobedience, which influenced the Russian novelist Leo Tolstoy, and in turn the Indian Mahatma Gandhi, and in turn the American Martin Luther King, thus returning to the country where it began.

READINGS

READING 1
The Misery of War
St. Augustine
(from *The City of God*)

I shall be told that the Imperial City has been at pains to impose on conquered peoples not only her yoke but her language also, as a bond of peace and fellowship, so that there should be no lack of interpreters but even a profusion of them. True; but think of the cost of this achievement! Consider the scale of those wars, with all that slaughter of human beings, all the human blood that was shed!

Those wars are now past history; and yet the misery of these evils is not yet ended. For although there has been, and still is, no lack of enemies among foreign nations, against whom wars have always been waged, and are still being waged, yet the very extent of the Empire has given rise to wars of a worse kind, namely, social and civil wars, by which mankind is more lamentably disquieted either when fighting is going on in the hope of bringing hostilities eventually to a peaceful end, or when there are fears that hostilities will break out again. If I were to try to describe, with an eloquence worthy of the subject, the many and multifarious disasters, the dour and dire necessities, I could not possibly be adequate to the theme, and there would be no end to this protracted discussion. But the wise man, they say, will wage just wars. Surely, if he remembers that he is a human being, he will rather lament the fact that he is faced with the necessity of waging just wars; for if they were not just, he would not have to engage in them, and consequently there would be no wars for a wise man. For it is the injustice of the opposing side that lays on the wise man the duty of waging wars; and this injustice is assuredly to be deplored by a human being, since it is the injustice of human beings, even though no necessity for war should arise from it. And so everyone who reflects with sorrow on such grievous evils, in all their horror and cruelty, must acknowledge the misery of them. And yet a man who experiences such evils, or even thinks about them, without heartfelt grief, is assuredly in a far more pitiable condition if he thinks himself happy simply because he has lost all human feeling.

READING 2
The War God
Stephen Spender
(from *The War of God*)

Why cannot the one good
Benevolent feasible
Final dove, descend?

And the wheat be divided?
And the soldiers sent home?

And the barriers torn down?
And the enemies forgiven?
And there be no retribution?

Because the conqueror
Is victim of his own power

Hammering his will
Out of fear of former fear:
Remembering yesterday
When those he now vanquishes
Destroyed his hero-father
And surrounded his cradle
With fabled anguishes.

Today his sun of victory
Hides the night's anxiety
Lest children of the slain
Prove dragon teeth sown
By their sun going down,
To rise up tomorrow
In sky and sea all blood
And avenge their fathers again.

Those who surrender
On the helpless field
May dream the pious reasons
Of mercy, but alas
They know what they did
In their own sun-high season.

For the world is the world
And not the slain
Nor the slayer forgive
And it writes no histories
That end in love.

Yet under the waves'
Chains chafing despair
Love's need does not cease.

READING 3
Dulce et Decorum Est
Wilfred Owen

Bent double, like old beggars under sacks,
Knock-kneed, coughing like hags, we cursed through sludge,
Till on the haunting flares we turned our backs
And towards our distant rest began to trudge.
Men marched asleep. Many had lost their boots
But limped on, blood-shod. All went lame; all blind;
Drunk with fatigue; deaf even to the hoots
Of tired, outstripped Five-Nines that dropped behind.

Gas! Gas! Quick, boys!-An ecstasy of fumbling,
Fitting the clumsy helmets just in time;
But someone still was yelling out and stumbling
And flound'ring like a man in fire or lime. . .
Dim, through the misty panes and thick green light,
As under a green sea, I saw him drowning.

In all my dreams, before my helpless sight,
He plunges at me, guttering, choking, drowning.

If in some smothering dreams you too could pace
Behind the wagon that we flung him in,
And watch the white eyes writhing in his face,
His hanging face, like a devil's sick of sin;
If you could hear, at every jolt, the blood
Come gargling from the froth-corrupted lungs,
Obscene as cancer, bitter as the cud
Of vile, incurable sores on innocent tongues,—
My friend, you would not tell with such high zest
To children ardent for some desperate glory,
The old Lie: Dulce et decorum est
Pro patria mori.

READING 4
All Quiet on the Western Front
Erich Maria Remarque

(*World War I*)

The silence spreads. I talk and must talk. So I speak to him and to say to him: "Comrade, I did not want to kill you. If you jumped in here again, I would not do it, if you would be sensible too. But you were only an idea to me before, an abstraction that lived in my mind and called forth its appropriate response. It was that abstraction I stabbed. But now, for the first time, I see you are a man like me. I thought of your hand-grenades, of your bayonet, of your rifle; now I see your wife and your face and our fellowship. Forgive me, comrade. We always see it too late. Why do they never tell us that you are poor devils like us, that your mothers are just as anxious as ours, and that we have the same fear of death, and the same dying and the same agony—Forgive me, comrade; how could you be my enemy? If we threw away these rifles and this uniform you could be my brother just like Kat and Albert. Take twenty years of my life, comrade, and stand up—take more, for I do not know what I can even attempt to do with it now."

"I will write to your wife," I say hastily to the dead man, "I will write to her, she must hear it from me, I will tell her everything I have told you, she shall not suffer, I will help her, and your parents too, and your child—"

His tunic is half open. The pocket-book is easy to find. But I hesitate to open it. In it is the book with his name. So long as I do not know his name perhaps I may still forget him, time will obliterate it, this picture. But his name, it is a nail that will be hammered into me and never come out again. It has the power to recall this forever, it will always come back and stand before me.

Irresolutely I take the wallet in my hand. It slips out of my hand and falls open. Some pictures and letters drop out. I gather them up and want to put them back again, but the strain I am under, the uncertainty, the hunger, the danger, these hours with the dead man have made me desperate, I want to hasten the relief, to intensify and to end the torture, as one strikes an unendurably painful hand against the trunk of a tree, regardless of everything.

There are portraits of a woman and a little girl, small amateur photographs taken against an ivy-clad wall. Along with them are letters. I take them out and try to read them. Most of it I do not understand, it is so hard to decipher and I scarcely know any French. But each word I translate pierces me like a shot in the chest;—like a stab in the chest.

My brain is taxed beyond endurance. But I realize this much, that I will never dare to write to these people as I intended. Impossible. I look at the portraits once more; they are clearly not rich people. I might send them money anonymously if I earn anything later on. I seize upon that, it is at least something to hold on to. This dead man is bound up with my life, therefore I must do everything, promise everything in order to save myself; I swear blindly that I mean to live only for his sake and his family, with wet lips I try to placate him—and deep down in me lies the hope that I may buy myself off in this way and perhaps even get out of this; it is a little stratagem: if only I am allowed to escape, then I will see to it. So I open the book and read slowly:—Gérard Duval, compositor.

With the dead man's pencil I write the address on an envelope, then swiftly thrust everything back into his tunic.

I have killed the printer, Gérard Duval. I must be a printer, I think confusedly, be a printer, printer—

***

By afternoon I am calmer. My fear was groundless. The name troubles me no more. The madness passes. "Comrade," I say to the dead man, but I say it calmly, "to-day you, to-morrow me. But if I come out of it, comrade, I will fight against this, that has struck us both down; from you, taken life—and from me—? Life also. I promise you, comrade. It shall never happen again."

READING 5
After a Battle
Ernie Pyle
(from *Ernies War*)

(*One of the most respected correspondents of World War II*)

DEBRIS, SUNSHINE AND UTTER SILENCE

ON THE WESTERN FRONT, *August 21, 1944*—When you're wandering around our very far-flung front lines—the lines that in our present rapid war are known as "fluid"—you can always tell how recently the battle has swept on ahead of you.

You can sense it from the little things even more than the big things—

From the scattered green leaves and the fresh branches of trees still lying in the middle of the road.

From the wisps and coils of telephone wire, hanging brokenly from high poles and entwining across the roads.

From the gray, burned-powder rims of the shell craters in the gravel roads, their edges not yet smoothed by the pounding of military traffic.

From the little pools of blood on the roadside, blood that has only begun to congeal and turn black, and the punctured steel helmets lying nearby.

From the square blocks of building stone still scattered in the village street, and from the sharp-edged rocks in the roads, still uncrushed by traffic.

From the burned-out tanks and broken carts still unremoved from the road. From the cows in the fields, lying grotesquely with their feet to the sky, so newly dead they have not begun to bloat or smell.

From the scattered heaps of personal debris around a gun. (I don't know why it is, but the Germans always seem to take off their coats before they flee or die.)

From all these things you can tell that the battle has been recent—from these and from the men dead so recently that they seem to be merely asleep.

And also from the inhuman quiet. Usually battles are noisy for miles around. But in this recent fast warfare a battle sometimes leaves a complete vacuum behind it.

The Germans will stand and fight it out until they see there is no hope. Then some give up, and the rest pull and run for miles. Shooting stops. Our fighters move on after the enemy, and those who do not fight, but move in the wake of the battles, will not catch up for hours.

There is nothing left behind but the remains—the lifeless debris, the sunshine and the flowers, and utter silence.

An amateur who wanders in this vacuum at the rear of a battle has a terrible sense of loneliness. Everything is dead—the men, the machines, the animals—and you alone are left alive.

READING 6
The Rape of Nanking
Iris Chang

THE MURDER OF CIVILIANS

After the soldiers surrendered en masse, there was virtually no one left to protect the citizens of the city. Knowing this, the Japanese poured into Nanking on December 13, 1937, occupying government buildings banks, and warehouses, shooting people randomly in the streets, many of them in the back as they ran away. Using machine guns, revolvers, and rifles, the Japanese fired at the crowds of wounded soldiers, elderly women, and children who gathered in the North Chungshan and Central roads and nearby alleys. They also killed Chinese civilians in every section of the city: tiny lanes, major boulevards, mud dugouts, government buildings, city squares. As victims toppled to the ground, moaning and screaming, the streets, alleys, and ditches of the fallen capital ran rivers of blood, much of it coming from people barely alive, with no strength left to run away.

The Japanese systematically killed the city dwellers as they conducted house-to-house searches for Chinese soldiers in Nanking. But they also massacred the Chinese in the nearby suburbs and countryside. Corpses piled up outside the city walls, along the river (which had literally turned red with blood), by ponds and lakes, and on hills and mountains. In villages near Nanking, the Japanese shot down any young man who passed, under the presumption that he was likely to be a former Chinese soldier. But they also murdered people who could not possibly be Chinese soldiers—elderly men and women for instance—if they hesitated or even if they failed to understand orders, delivered in the Japanese language, to move this way or that.

During the last ten days of December, Japanese motorcycle brigades patrolled Nanking while Japanese soldiers shouldering loaded rifles guarded the entrances to all the streets, avenues, and alleys. Troops went from door to door, demanding that the doors be opened to welcome the victorious armies. The moment the shopkeepers complied, the Japanese opened fire on them. The imperial army massacred thousands of people in this manner and then systematically looted the stores and burned whatever they had no use for.

TORTURE

The torture that the Japanese inflicted upon the native population at Nanking almost surpasses the limits of human comprehension. Here are only a few examples:

* **—Live burials:** The Japanese directed burial operations with the precision and efficiency of an assembly line. Soldiers would force one group of Chinese captives to dig a grave and a second group to bury the first, and then a third group to bury the second and so on. Some victims were partially buried to their chests or necks so that they would endure further agony, such as being hacked to pieces by swords or run over by horses and tanks.
* **—Mutilation:** The Japanese not only disemboweled, decapitated, and dismembered victims but performed more excruciating varieties of torture. Throughout the city they nailed prisoners to wooden boards and ran over them with tanks, crucified them to trees and electrical posts, carved long strips of flesh from them, and used them for bayonet practice. At least one hundred men reportedly had their eyes gouged out and their noses and ears hacked off before being set on fire. Another group of two hundred Chinese soldiers and civilians were stripped naked, tied to columns and doors of a school, and then stabbed by *zhuizi*—special needles with handles on them—in hundreds of points along their bodies, including their mouths, throats, and eyes.
* **—Death by fire:** The Japanese subjected large crowds of victims to mass incineration. In Hsiakwan a Japanese soldier bound Chinese captives together, ten at a time, and pushed them into a pit, where they were sprayed with gasoline and ignited. On Taiping Road, the Japanese ordered a large number of shop clerks to extinguish a fire, then bound them together with rope and threw them into the blaze. Japanese soldiers even devised games with fire. One method of entertainment was to drive mobs of Chinese to the top stories or roofs of buildings, tear down the stairs, and set the bottom floors on fire. Many such victims committed suicide by jumping out windows or off rooftops. Another form of amusement involved dousing victims with fuel, shooting them, and watching them explode into flame. In one infamous incident, Japanese soldiers forced hundreds of men, women, and children into a square, soaked them with gasoline, and then fired on them with machine guns.
* **—Death by ice:** Thousands of victims were intentionally frozen to death during the Rape of Nanking. For instance, Japanese soldiers forced hundreds of Chinese prisoners to march to the edge of a frozen pond, where they were ordered to strip naked, break the ice, and plunge into the water to go "fishing." Their bodies hardened into floating targets that were immediately

riddled with Japanese bullets. In another incident, the Japanese tied up a group of refugees, flung them into a shallow pond, and bombarded them with hand grenades, causing "an explosive shower of blood and flesh."

• **—Death by dogs:** One diabolical means of torture was to bury victims to their waist and watch them get ripped apart by German shepherds. Witnesses saw Japanese soldiers strip a victim naked and direct German shepherds to bite the sensitive areas of his body. The dogs not only ripped open his belly but jerked out his intestines. . . .

THE RAPES

If the scale and nature of the executions in Nanking are difficult for us to comprehend, so are the scale and nature of the rapes.

Certainly it was one of the greatest mass rapes in world history. . . . The Japanese raped Nanking women from all classes: farm wives, students, teachers, white-collar and blue-collar workers, wives of YMCA employees, university professors, even Buddhist nuns, some of whom were gang-raped to death. And they were systematic in their recruitment of women. In Nanking Japanese soldiers searched for them constantly as they looted homes and dragged men off for execution. Some actually conducted door-to-door searches, demanding money and *hua gu niang*—young girls. . . .

Chinese women were raped in all locations and at all hours. An estimated one-third of all rapes occurred during the day. Survivors even remember soldiers prying open the legs of victims to rape them in broad daylight, in the middle of the street, and in front of crowds of witnesses. No place was too sacred for rape. The Japanese attacked women in nunneries, churches, and Bible training schools. Seventeen soldiers raped one woman in succession in a seminary compound. "Every day, twenty-four hours a day," the *Dagong Daily* newspaper testified of the great Rape of Nanking, "there was not one hour when an innocent woman was not being dragged off somewhere by a Japanese soldier." . . .

One of the most notorious stories of such a slaughter was recorded in detail by American and European missionaries in Nanking. On December 13, 1937, thirty Japanese soldiers came to the Chinese home at 5 Hsing Lu Kao in the southeastern part of Nanking. They killed the landlord when he opened the door, and then Mr. Hsia, a tenant who had fallen to his knees to beg them not to kill anyone else. When the landlord's wife asked why they murdered her husband, they shot her dead. The Japanese then dragged Mrs. Hsia from under a table in the guest hall where she had tried to hide with her one-year-old baby. They stripped her, raped her, then bayoneted her in the chest when they were finished. The soldiers thrust a perfume bottle in her vagina and also killed the baby by bayonet. Then they went into the next room, where they found Mrs. Hsia's parents and two teenage daughters. The grandmother, who tried to protect the girls from rape, was shot by revolver; the grandfather clasped the body of his wife and was killed immediately.

The soldiers then stripped the girls and took turns raping them: the sixteen-year-old by two or three men, the fourteen-year-old by three. The Japanese not only stabbed the older girl to death after raping her but rammed a bamboo cane into her vagina. The younger one was simply bayoneted and "spared the horrible treatment meted out to her sister and mother," a foreigner later wrote of the scene. The soldiers also bayoneted another sister, aged eight, when she hid with her four-year-old sister under the blankets of a bed. The four-year-old remained under the blankets so long she nearly suffocated. She was to endure brain damage for the rest of her life from the lack of oxygen. . . .

But not all of the victims were women. Chinese men were often sodomized or forced to perform a variety of repulsive sexual acts in front of laughing Japanese soldiers. At least one Chinese man was murdered because he refused to commit necrophilia with the corpse of a woman in the snow. The Japanese also delighted in trying to coerce men who had taken lifetime vows of celibacy to engage in sexual intercourse. A Chinese woman had tried to disguise herself as a man to pass through one of the gates of Nanking, but Japanese guards, who systematically searched all passing pedestrians by groping at their crotches, discovered her true sex. Gang rape followed, at which time a Buddhist monk had the misfortune to venture near the scene. The Japanese tried to force him to have sex with the woman they had just raped. When the monk protested, they castrated him, causing the poor man to bleed to death.

Some of the most sordid instances of sexual torture involved the degradation of entire families. The Japanese drew sadistic pleasure in forcing Chinese men to commit incest—fathers to rape their own daughters, brothers their sisters, sons their mothers. Guo Qi, a Chinese battalion commander stranded in Nanking for three months after the city fell, saw or heard of at least four or five instances in which the Japanese ordered sons to rape their mothers; those who refused were killed on the spot. His report is substantiated by the testimony of a German diplomat, who reported that one Chinese man who refused to rape his own mother was killed with saber strokes and that his mother committed suicide shortly afterwards.

READING 7
Hiroshima and the Death of a Young Woman
Hiroyuki Agawa
(from *Citadel in Spring*)

The all-clear notwithstanding, a lone B-29 bomber flew westward past clouds high up and directly overhead, the metallic roar of its engines trailing behind it. As she walked along she would now and again look up, head back, and watch it. Suddenly three small parachutes were floating in the sky. That struck her as curious. At that moment there was an urgent change in the sound of the plane's engines. The aircraft sped quickly out of sight, a thin vapor trail following behind it. Then all at once a flash like arcing electric current flared across the sky.

Startled, Chieko dashed toward a large boulder for cover. She heard a dull sound of things giving way and in the same instant was lifted up and slammed down on the huge rock, and her face and arms and legs were peppered all over with something hot and stinging like burning sand.

It was suddenly pitch black all around her and deathly quiet, as though movie film had abruptly broken in its projector. Her baggy black *mompe* had burst into flames at the knees. She immediately ripped them off as she lay there, leaving only her white bloomers. But now she was paralyzed with embarrassment at the thought of being so exposed.

Suddenly she heard a girl wailing nearby. As the darkness around her gradually lifted, visions presented themselves to her: a school girl, her face deathly white and her eyebrows burned away; a soldier, the skin of his face peeling off and dangling in the air like a dust mop turned on end; a woman, her face scorched charcoal black, vomiting blood.

Looking towards the city through the abating darkness, she could see an indistinct column of smoke rising into the air. It quickly swelled into the shape of a gigantic question mark, the middle of which was a vivid crimson, and as this thunderhead-like column billowed upward through the sky, she could see a red ball of fire at its core. The earth below was enshrouded in a sheet of fire, a dust storm, a chaotic commingling of red, ocher and brown. . . .

Chieko got to her feet gingerly, testing her footing as she rose.

I must get home immediately.

Her shoes were gone, blown off her feet. Her white blouse was torn, but as she looked at those around her she realized she was in relatively good shape. Her embarrassment vanished when she saw that everyone else was naked.

The dead and dying lay everywhere. One man lay dead in a pool of blood, his eyeballs, blown from their sockets, hanging at least five inches down his face, each the thickness of a thumb. He had bled profusely from the nose and mouth. . . .

The huge mushroom cloud that stood high over the city was gradually changing shape, swelling and growing as it vigorously sucked up smoke from below.

As she walked along, Chieko could not fathom why everyone should be naked, yet there was no doubt that almost all these people running about in confusion had no clothes. While some people had quickly had their wounds treated and bandaged, Chieko saw others whose peeling skin was hanging in shreds all over their bodies, people injured so badly you could not tell the front of their bodies from the back. It was the bodies of the dead that still wore their scorched clothing. . . .

Suddenly she felt pain throughout her body. She put her hand to her forehead. Her palm came away sticky with blood.

"My face is injured, isn't it."

"Yes, it's bad," the girl replied, then immediately averted her eyes as though she had said something rude.

Chieko felt the blood drain from her head. She dropped weakly to her knees, then fell to the ground. . . .

She spent the night there on the grass. A dozen or so people who had been unable to flee had somehow drawn together, and now lay next to one another. . . .

Hours passed. As evening drew near the force of the fires in the city seemed, little by little, to spend itself at last. Chieko tossed and turned on the grass, her mind intent on her parents: were they safe? But there was nothing she could do. . . .

The sun rose, and the mountains of white bones where the bodies had been burned the night before looked like fish bones heaped high, yet even from a distance Chieko could see heads and arms and legs the fire had not consumed lying strewn around the mounds.

Chieko's body was racked with pain and she felt an intense lassitude that robbed her of the will to stand, so she stayed where she lay. From time to time someone looking for a relative would peer into her face, then move on. Each time this happened she would try to cover her naked breasts, her hands moving wearily. All was still, as though everything had been exterminated; no insects moved in the grass.

Some time had passed since daybreak. Chieko was wondering if it might not be around noon, when she realized that someone was calling her name.

"Chieko Ibuki! Is Chieko Ibuki here?"

She raised herself up and saw her father shouting out her name as he walked in a half stoop along the road that wandered gently down from where she was lying. She tried to cry out to him, but her voice was too weak. She raised her hand and waved, and this he saw. He came running up the slope.

"Chieko? Are you Chieko?"

In the space of a day her face had darkened and swelled to melon size and her lips were swollen and puffy. Only her eyes and nose were normal, almost lost in the middle of this polished round face of ebony.

"I can't believe you survived!" her father exclaimed. "Well, let's go. We'll evacuate to Kinu's place in Shinjo,"

"What about Mother?"

"Your mother is dead."

Her father told her what had happened. Her mother had been pinned under a collapsing lintel, her pelvis and legs crushed, and the flames had reached the house before he could pull her free. Half-mad, he had tried to cut off her legs to get her out, but Mrs. Ibuki urged her husband to flee alone to the village of Shinjo outside the city, to the home of a former maid. He plucked some hair from her head, held her hand for the last time, then made his escape. . . .

Chieko's father was carrying her to Shinjo. And there on his back she let the tears stream down her blackened cheeks.

Her father, out of breath, had to set her down and rest many times along the way. Each time he would tell her a little more of what had happened since the previous day and ask her questions in turn. A bag filled with bones hung from his waist. Early that morning he had gone to where their house had been and dug out his wife's bones from the burned-out ruins. . . .

Late in the afternoon the two of them at last arrived at the Kinu's house in Shinjo. . . . They could see clearly she was beginning to weaken. Her father brought in his dear friend, who had been evacuated to the countryside, yet it was obvious that even this doctor, who had come five miles on foot to the examination, could do little for her. . . . All the symptoms of what would be called the atomic disease began to manifest themselves developed spots over her body, her face didn't regain its normal shape, and she immediately vomited whatever she ate.

A week after, the holocaust, when the doctor friend came to examine her, Chieko's father called him into another room.

"I'm sure absolutely nothing can be done to save her, but do *you* think, frankly speaking?"

"The nature of this condition differs from that of ordinary and external injuries," the doctor began. "This is the first time I've seen anything like it, and diagnosis is difficult. But to be completely honest with you, whatever its nature, Chieko has only a day or two to live. Even if she were to survive longer than that, recovery barring some kind of miracle—would be out of the question. That's my opinion."

Her father was silent, his arms folded, briefly lost in thought. Then he spoke.

"Well, if she's going to die no matter what is done—I can't stand to see her suffer. I'd like to make it easy for her. I don't suppose I could get an anesthetic from you."

"I've got it ready," the doctor said, choosing his words carefully, "but—and you may think this cowardly of me—it's not possible for me, as a doctor, to inject it and euthanatize your daughter."

"It's all right if I do it, isn't it?"

The doctor did not answer.

Chieko's father, his face ashen, wordlessly drew his friend's satchel to him and took out the syringe and narcotic. His hands were shaking.

When the first injection took effect Chieko's pain-contorted face became tranquil and she fell into a peaceful sleep.

She slept soundly until evening, then suddenly opened her eyes languorously, like a child after a good night's sleep.

"I had a good sleep," she said, seeing her father by her side. Moments later she spoke again. "How odd. Has Koji come home?"

"You want to see Koji?" her father asked, bending over her. Chieko turned her face away from him and nodded.

"Don't worry. Koji will be here soon. So will your brother and Ikuko."

Chieko accepted this and closed her eyes.

"You're not in any pain, are you?" her father asked. She shook her head and opened her eyes.

"Water, please."

Kinu immediately drew some cool water from the well and brought it to her. Kinu was weeping.

Chieko drank half a glass of water.

"It tastes so good," she said, and closed her eyes once more.

Shortly afterward, her father gave her another injection, a large dose. She died.

READING 8
The Unanswering
Elie Wiesel
(from *Night*)

"Poor devils, you're going to the crematory."

He seemed to be telling the truth. Not far from us, flames were leaping up from a ditch, gigantic flames. They were burning something. A lorry drew up at the pit and delivered its load—little children. Babies! Yes,

I saw it—saw it with my own eyes . . . those children in the flames. (Is it surprising that I could not sleep after that? Sleep had fled from my eyes.)

So this was where we were going. A little farther on was another and larger ditch for adults.

I pinched my face. Was I still alive? Was I awake? I could not believe it. How could it be possible for them to burn people, children, and for the world to keep silent? No, none of this could be true. It was a nightmare. . . . Soon I should wake with a start, my heart pounding, and find myself back in the bedroom of my childhood, among my books. . . .

My father's voice drew me from my thoughts:

"It's a shame . . . a shame that you couldn't have gone with your mother. . . . I saw several boys of your age going with their mothers. . . ."

His voice was terribly sad. I realized that he did not want to see what they were going to do to me. He did not want to see the burning of his only son.

My forehead was bathed in cold sweat. But I told him that I did not believe that they could burn people in our age, that humanity would never tolerate it. . . .

"Humanity? Humanity is not concerned with us. Today anything is allowed. Anything is possible, even these crematories. . . ."

His voice was choking.

"Father," I said, "if that is so, I don't want to wait here. I'm going to run to the electric wire. That would be better than slow agony in the flames."

He did not answer. He was weeping. His body was shaken convulsively. Around us, everyone was weeping. Someone began to recite the Kaddish, the prayer for the dead. I do not know if it has ever happened before, in the long history of the Jews, that people have ever recited the prayer for the dead for themselves.

"*Yitgadal veyitkadach shmé raba.* . . . May His Name be blessed and magnified. . . ." whispered my father.

For the first time, I felt revolt rise up in me. Why should I bless His name? The Eternal, Lord of the Universe, the All-Powerful and Terrible, was silent. What had I to thank Him for?

We continued our march. We were gradually drawing closer to the ditch, from which an infernal heat was rising. Still twenty steps, to go. If I wanted to bring about my own death, this was the moment. Our line had now only fifteen paces to cover. I bit my lips so that my father would not hear my teeth chattering. Ten steps still. Eight. Seven. We marched slowly on, as though following a hearse at our own funeral. Four steps more. Three steps. There it was now, right in front of us, the pit and its flames. I gathered all that was left of my strength, so that I could break from the ranks and throw myself upon the barbed wire. In the depths of my heart, I bade farewell to my father, to the whole universe; and, in spite of myself, the words formed themselves and issued in a whisper from my lips: *Yitgadal veyitkadach shmé raba.* . . . May His name be blessed and magnified. . . . My heart was bursting. The moment had come. I was face to face with the Angel of Death. . . .

No, Two steps from the pit we were ordered to turn to the left and made to go into a barracks.

I pressed my father's hand. He said:

"Do you remember Madame Schächter, in the train?"

Never shall I forget that night, the first night in camp, which has turned my life into one long night, seven times cursed and seven times sealed. Never shall I forget that smoke. Never shall I forget the little faces of the children, whose bodies I saw turned into wreaths of smoke beneath a silent blue sky.

Never shall I forget those flames which consumed my faith forever.

Never shall I forget that nocturnal silence which deprived me, for all eternity, of the desire to live. Never shall I forget those moments which murdered my God and my soul and turned my dreams to dust. Never shall I forget these things, even if I am condemned to live as long as God Himself. Never.

READING 9
Battle Scene: Trojan War between Menelaus (Greek) and Pisander (Trojan)
Homer
(from *Iliad*)

And now Pisander rushed Menelaus famed in arms
but a grim fate was rushing *him* to the stroke of death—
to be crushed in this hell of war by you, Menelaus.
Just as the two men closed, heading into each other,
Atrides missed—his spearshaft hooking off to the side—
Pisander stabbed his shield but the bronze could not bore through—
the huge hide blocked it, the shaft snapped at the socket.
Still the Trojan exulted, wild with hopes of triumph
as Menelaus, drawing his sword with silver studs,
leapt at Pisander, who clutched beneath his shield
his good bronze ax with its cleaving blade
set on a long smooth olive haft—

        A clash!

Both fighters at one great stroke
chopped at each other—Pisander hacked the horn
of the horsehair-crested helmet right at its ridge,
lunging as Menelaus hacked Pisander between the eyes,
the bridge of the nose, and bone cracked, blood sprayed
and both eyes dropped at his feet to mix in the dust—
he curled and crashed. Digging a heel in his chest
Menelaus stripped his gear and vaunted out in glory,
"So home you'll run from our racing ships, by god,
all as corpses—see, you death-defying
Trojans? Never sated with shattering war cries, are you?
Nor do you lack the other brands of outrage,
all that shame you heaped on me, you rabid dogs!
No fear in your hearts for the quaking rage of Zeus,
the thundering god of host and welcome stranger—
one day he'll raze your lofty city for you.
You Trojans who stole away my wedded wife
and hoards of riches too—for no reason, none—
my queen of the realm who hosted you with kindness.
And now you rampage on among our deep-sea ships,
wild to torch our hulls and kill our heroes—well,
you'll be stopped, somewhere, mad as you are for combat!

READING 10
Civil Disobedience
Henry Thoreau

(*Thoreau wrote this short work to express his deep felt anxiety against the Mexican War, slavery, or any kind of dehumanization which he saw as tantamount to slavery.*)

Unjust laws exist: shall we be content to obey them, or shall we endeavor to amend them, and obey them until we have succeeded, or shall we transgress them at once? Men generally, under such a government as this, think that they ought to wait until they have persuaded the majority to alter them. They think that, if they should resist, the remedy would be worse than the evil. But it is the fault of the government itself that the remedy *is* worse than the evil. *It* makes it worse. Why is it not more apt to anticipate and provide for reform? Why does it not cherish its wise minority? Why does it cry and resist before it is hurt? Why does it not encourage its citizens to be on the alert to point out its faults, and *do* better than it would have them? Why does it always crucify Christ, and excommunicate Copernicus and Luther, and pronounce Washington and Franklin rebels?

One would think, that a deliberate and practical denial of its authority was the only offence never contemplated by government; else, why has it not assigned its definite, its suitable and proportionate, penalty? If a man who has no property refuses but once to earn nine shillings for the State, he is put in prison for a period unlimited by any law that I know, and determined only by the discretion of those who placed him there; but if he should steal ninety times nine shillings from the State, he is soon permitted to go at large again.

If the injustice is part of the necessary friction of the machine of government, let it go, let it go: perchance it will wear smooth—certainly the machine will wear out. If the injustice has a spring, or a pulley, or a rope; or a crank, exclusively for itself, then perhaps you may consider whether the remedy will not be worse than the evil; but if it is of such a nature that it requires you to be the agent of injustice to another, then, I say, break the law. Let your life be a counter-friction to stop the machine. What I have to do is to see, at any rate, that I do not lend myself to the wrong which I condemn.

. . .

I have paid no poll-tax for six years. I was put into a jail once on this account, for one night; and, as I stood considering the walls of solid stone, two or three feet thick, the door of wood and iron, a foot thick, and the iron grating which strained the light, I could not help being struck with the foolishness of that institution which treated me as if I were mere flesh and blood and bones, to be locked up. I wondered that it should have concluded at length that this was the best use it could put me to, and had never thought to avail itself of my services in some way. I saw that, if there was a wall of stone between me and my townsmen, there was a still more difficult one to climb or break through before they could get to be as free as I was. I did not for a moment feel confined, and the walls seemed a great waste of stone and mortar. I felt as if I alone of all my townsmen had paid my tax. They plainly did not know, how to treat me, but behaved like persons who are underbred. In every threat and in every compliment there was a blunder; for they thought that my chief desire was to stand the other side of that stone wall. I could not but smile to see how industriously they locked the door on my meditations, which followed them out again without let or hindrance, and *they* were really all that was dangerous. As they could not reach me, they had resolved to punish my body; just as boys, if they cannot come at some person against whom they have a spite, will abuse his dog. I saw that the State was half-witted, that it was timid as a lone woman with her silver spoons, and that it did not know its friends from its foes, and I lost all my remaining respect for it, and pitied it.

· · ·

I have never declined paying the highway tax, because I am as desirous of being a good neighbor as I am of being a bad subject; and as for supporting schools, I am doing my part to educate my fellow-countrymen now. It is for no particular item in the tax bill that I refuse to pay it. I simply wish to refuse allegiance to the State, to withdraw and stand aloof from it effectually. I do not care to trace the course of my dollar, if I could, till it buys a man or a musket to shoot one with—the dollar is innocent—but I am concerned to trace the effects of my allegiance. In fact, I quietly declare war with the State, after my fashion, though I will still make what use and get what advantage of her I can, as is usual in such cases.

If others pay the tax which is demanded of me, from a sympathy with the State, they do but what they have already done in their own case, or rather they abet injustice to a greater extent than the State requires. If they pay the tax from a mistaken interest in the individual taxed, to save his property, or prevent his going to jail, it is because they have not considered wisely how far they let their private feelings interfere with the public good.

This, then, is my position at present. But one cannot be too much on his guard in such a case, lest his action be biased by obstinacy or an undue regard for the opinions of men. Let him see that he does only what belongs to himself and to the hour.

READING 11
The Challenge of Peace

Excerpts from the pastoral letter
U.S. Catholic Bishops, 1983

126. At the center of the new evaluation of the nuclear arms race is a recognition of two elements: the destructive potential of nuclear weapons, and the stringent choices which the nuclear age poses for both politics and morals.

127. The fateful passage into the nuclear age as a military reality began with the bombing of Nagasaki and Hiroshima, events described by Pope Paul VI as a "butchery of untold magnitude." Since then, in spite of efforts at control and plans for disarmament (e.g., the Baruch Plan of 1946), the nuclear arsenals have escalated, particularly in the two superpowers. The qualitative superiority of these two states, however, should not overshadow the fact that four other countries possess nuclear capacity and a score of states are only steps away from becoming "nuclear nations."

128. This nuclear escalation has been opposed sporadically and selectively but never effectively. The race has continued in spite of carefully expressed doubts by analysts and other citizens and in the face of forcefully expressed opposition by public rallies. Today the opposition to the arms race is no longer selective or sporadic, it is widespread and sustained. The danger and destructiveness of nuclear weapons are understood and resisted with new urgency and intensity. There is in the public debate today an endorsement of the position submitted by the Holy See at the United Nations in 1976: the arms race is to be condemned as a danger, an act of aggression against the poor, and a folly which does not provide the security it promises.

134. We see with increasing clarity the political folly of a system which threatens mutual suicide, the psychological damage this does to ordinary people, especially the young, the economic distortion of priorities—billions readily spent for destructive instruments while pitched battles are waged daily in our legislatures over much smaller amounts for the homeless, the hungry, and the helpless here and abroad. But it is much less clear how we translate a "no" to nuclear war into the personal and public choices which can move us in a new direction, toward a national policy and an international system which more adequately reflect the values and vision of the kingdom of God.

137. The political paradox of deterrence has also strained our moral-conception. May a nation threaten what it may never do? May it possess what it may never use? Who is involved in the threat each superpower makes: government officials? or military personnel? or the citizenry in whose defense the threat is made?

138. In brief, the danger of the situation is clear; but how to prevent the use of nuclear weapons, how to assess deterrence, and how to delineate moral responsibility in the nuclear age are less clearly seen or stated. Reflecting the complexity of the nuclear problem, our arguments in this pastoral must be detailed and nuanced; but our "no" to nuclear war, must, in the end, be definitive and decisive.

174. In Pope John Paul II's assessment we perceive two dimensions of the contemporary dilemma of deterrence. One dimension is the danger of nuclear war, with its human and moral costs. The possession of nuclear weapons, the continuing quantitative growth of the arms race, and the danger of nuclear proliferation all point to the grave danger of basing "peace of a sort" on deterrence. The other dimension is the independence and freedom of nations and entire peoples, including the need to protect smaller nations from threats to their independence and integrity. Deterrence reflects the radical distrust which marks international politics, a condition identified as a major problem by Pope John XIII in *Peace on Earth* and reaffirmed by Pope Paul VI and Pope John Paul II. Thus a balance of forces, preventing either side from achieving superiority, can be seen as a means of safeguarding both dimensions.

186. These considerations of concrete elements of nuclear deterrence policy, made in light of John Paul II's evaluation, but applying it through our own prudential judgments, lead us to a strictly conditioned moral acceptance of nuclear deterrence. We cannot consider it adequate as a long-term basis for peace.

187. This strictly conditioned judgment yields *criteria* for morally assessing the elements of deterrence strategy. Clearly, these criteria demonstrate that we cannot approve of every weapons system, strategic doctrine, or policy initiative advanced in the name of strengthening deterrence. On the contrary, these criteria require continual public scrutiny of what our government proposes to do with the deterrent.

188. On the basis of these criteria we wish now to make some specific evaluations:

1. If nuclear deterrence exists only to prevent the *use* of nuclear weapons by others, then proposals to go beyond this to planning for prolonged periods of repeated nuclear strikes and counterstrikes, or "prevailing" in nuclear war, are not acceptable. They encourage notions that nuclear war can be engaged in with tolerable human and moral consequences. Rather, we must continually say "no" to the idea of nuclear war.

2. If nuclear deterrence is our goal, "sufficiency" to deter is an adequate strategy; the quest for nuclear superiority must be rejected.

3. Nuclear deterrence should be used as a step on the way toward progressive disarmament. Each proposed addition to our strategic system or change in strategic doctrine must be assessed precisely in light of whether it will render steps toward "progressive disarmament" more or less likely.

150. We do not perceive any situation in which the deliberate initiation of nuclear warfare, on however restricted a scale, can be morally justified. Non-nuclear attacks by another state must be resisted by other than nuclear means. Therefore, a serious moral obligation exists to develop non-nuclear defensive strategies as rapidly as possible.

153. This judgment affirms that the willingness to initiate nuclear war entails a distinct, weighty moral responsibility; it involves transgressing a fragile barrier—political, psychological, and moral—which has been constructed since 1945. We express repeatedly in this letter our extreme skepticism about the prospects for controlling a nuclear exchange, however limited the first use might be. Precisely because of this skepticism, we judge resort to nuclear weapons to counter a conventional attack to be morally unjustifiable. Consequently we seek to reinforce the barrier against any use of nuclear weapons. Our support of a "no first use" policy must be seen in this light.

169. In the post-conciliar assessment of war and peace, and specifically of deterrence, different parties to the political-moral debate within the Church and in civil society have focused on one aspect or another of the problem. For some, the fact that nuclear weapons have not been used since 1945 means that deterrence has worked, and this fact satisfies the demands of both the political and the moral order. Others contest this assessment by highlighting the risk of failure involved in continued reliance on deterrence and pointing out how politically and morally catastrophic even a single failure would be. Still others note that the absence of nuclear war is not necessarily proof that the policy of deterrence has prevented it. Indeed, some would find in the policy of deterrence the driving force in the superpower arms race. Still other observers, many of them Catholic moralists, have stressed that deterrence may not morally include the intention of deliberately attacking civilian populations or non-combatants.

173. Having offered this analysis of the general concept of deterrence, the Holy Father introduces his considerations on disarmament, especially, but not only, nuclear disarmament. Pope John Paul II makes this statement about the morality of deterrence:

> In current conditions "deterrence" based on balance, certainly not as an end in itself but as a step on the way toward a progressive disarmament, may still be judged morally acceptable. Nonetheless in order to ensure peace, it is indispensable not to be satisfied with this minimum which is always susceptible to the real danger of explosion.

Chapter Nine
Sexuality

Most ethical questions, as observed earlier on, ultimately reduce to person-to-person relationships, whether they are in the form of a simple act of kindness or an intricate financial fraud. Thus every person-to-person relationship forms the context for its own set of ethical considerations. In this chapter, we are to consider a context entirely different from any other we've undertaken thus far, different precisely in that it is *sexuality* that makes a *male*-person to a *female*-person relationship possible.

On the grounds that no person is more or less human than any other and that the male–female relationship is recognized universally as a fundamental ingredient of human life, it would seem to be a reasonable expectation that a similarity of sexual conduct would prevail in all cultures. Though this may be true in many respects, it certainly is not true over all. Sexual conduct has been subject to wide variations in actual practice, some of which exist presently in different cultures throughout the world, and others of which have been discovered from the past by social archeologists. Examples abound: the practice of polyandry; the community focus of male/female behavior rather than private; considering children as belonging primarily to the community instead of the biological parents; the choice of mates where the preference of the marrying couple is unheard of; the prescribing of gender roles; family assimilation as dictated, in favor of the father in patriarchal societies, or in favor of the mother in matriarchal societies; the protocols or rites governing the social legitimacy of marriage, the acceptability of divorce and the procedures for remarriage; and social acknowledgment of the partnership of homosexuals. Without going into the question as to which society or culture is superior or inferior to any other, it is clear that the western Hellenic-Hebraic-Christian tradition has cradled the experience of several thousand years and has had to come to grips with countless facets of the male–female relationship, while still striving to understand others today. This chapter, as well as the text as a whole, speaks from within that tradition as the one we live in and not to other traditions except in passing (R #1).

It's into one of these cultures that individuals are born and form the context in which their moral lives are developed, but individuals are still meant to develop a moral compass of their own, which they do by amalgamating their personal experience of moral fittingness with the mores of that culture.

ACKNOWLEDGING THE BODY

No discussion of sexuality is going to go very far without first saying a word about the most obvious factor in our makeup as human beings, namely, the *body*. We are literally immersed in the world through our bodies. It's through our bodies, our embodied selves, that we come to know ourselves, becoming aware that this small fragment of reality is identified as "me," made individual by the very body that I am. My intellect cannot begin to function unless it first receives the deliverances of the body, or, as the main epistemological tradition puts it, there is nothing in the intellect unless it's first in the senses. By means of my body-self, I come into contact with other body-selves, by my seeing, hearing, or touching them. I locate myself in the world by locating my body. I am born bodily, I live bodily, and I die bodily. I communicate with others using my body as a vehicle to convey my message to them. Do I want to express an idea to another?—it must be by words on my lips, or a bodily sign of some kind. Do I want to show my love for another?—this too must be through words or some other bodily response. No feeling or emotion has any meaning for me, nor anyone else, if it is not a response in and of my body. A young man tells the girl of his dreams "I love you with all my heart" and she warmly responds to the overture; but what kind of response would she give him if he told her "I love you with all my SAT scores!" Everyone understands that when we say, "I have a body," we do not mean to say that the body is external to me, distinctly separate from me; rather, we mean "I am a body." However, there have been philosophers for whom "having" a body is literally true. The early, pre-Aristotelian Greeks supported the idea that the real "me" is not a bodily entity at all. Pythagoras, for example, relying on his favorite doctrine of the transmigration of souls, held that "I" pass from one body to another until I have been sufficiently purified to return from whence I came. The body is not where "I" belong; it's a burden, a yoke, a prison—it's not me. Later on Plato, holding fast to the notion of body and soul as separate entities, had to develop a system for our getting to know things by downplaying the epistemological need for a material world. Knowledge had to begin with ideas already in our minds because they could not be generated by a body. Though the lower world is meant by Plato to reflect a higher reality, its attractiveness is so intense that it may even hinder our intellect from rising to a grasp of that reality. That's why he has Socrates announce his conviction that " . . . if we are ever to have pure knowledge of anything, we must get rid of the body," and finally that death is a blessing because it frees the soul " . . . from the shackles of the body" (*Phaedo*, p. 66). For Plato the intellect is what defines us and distinguishes us from the animal, so much so that "body" cannot enter into the definition of man, as opposed to Aristotle's definition of man as "rational animal." Body and soul, for Plato, are united, but only *functionally*; not, as for Aristotle, *essentially*.

A position similar to the Platonic was developed in the seventeenth century, at the beginning of the modern period, by René Descartes, a position referred to as Cartesian dualism. Descartes was a mathematician-philosopher who, in looking for some way to ground certitude, ingeniously turned his mathematical laser beam inward to locate the irreducible truth "I think, therefore I am" (*cogito ergo sum*). From this, he directly deduced (better, intuited) that "I" *am* a "thinking being," period! The nature of man is spirit, mind, thought; man *possesses* a body to serve him as an instrument. Body, exactly as for Plato, does not enter into the definition of man. This cleavage between body and mind was the controlling problem in continental epistemology for the next 200 years.

Neither Plato nor Descartes, however, in working out the problems of a "higher" and "lower" form of knowledge, belittled the goodness of the body but simply cautioned us not to be "led astray" by the body in our efforts to comprehend reality. The history of mankind also offers many instances in which the body was looked upon, not only as "lower" existentially, but also as an absolute hindrance to the soul in its *spiritual* growth. In the west, for example, there was the Manicheism of the fourth and fifth centuries which held to a two-god system of reality. To explain the existence of both good and evil in the world, since the ultimate could never be the source of good and evil at the same time, Manicheism postulated two gods: one the lord of good, and the other the lord of evil. The realm of good is the realm of the spirit, and the realm of evil is the realm of the body. "Higher" and "lower" now have a new meaning, for whatever is "higher" is good, spiritual, god-like, and holy, while whatever is "lower" is evil, material, ungodly, and sinful. Any interaction with matter, with the body, counts against the spirit and draws a person down. This supposed opposition of body to spirit helps to comprehend the long tradition of Christian asceticism in which extreme practices were frequently engaged in, like severe fasts or lashings of the body to keep it in subjection. During the early, Puritan days of America, pleasures associated with the body were under strict surveillance, like music, dancing, card playing, or uncontrolled mirth. What these historical episodes teach us is that a failure to understand the true reality of the body leads to a misunderstanding of the body and soul wholeness, and of male-and-female sexual embodiment as an inherent goodness of the natural world.

DIFFERENCE AND SAMENESS IN PERSONAL RELATIONSHIPS

As to terminology, the words *sexuality* and *sex* circle around each other, but normally *sexuality* is used to distinguish between the two kinds of human embodiment, male and female; to be sexual is the existential state of being human—it is our *way of being* and *acting* in the world. *Sex* can refer to the designation of a person biologically as male or female, or it can refer to any activity associated with the organs of reproduction. Sometimes they are used interchangeably, so their meaning has to be garnered from the context in which they are used.

Because sexuality is founded in nature, its existence doesn't have to be proven or established—just recognized. And what you recognize is a difference that is a deep, thorough-going *constituent* of the human being, so much so that an asexual human being is a natural impossibility. Further, the difference is also registered in what is popularly called "personality," the complex of distinctive behavior patterns that attend each sex, manifested in countless ways, for example, in nurturing activities, in modes of communication, in emotional response, in showing affection, and in certain kinds of intuition or epistemological sensitivity.

Yet, as radically different as male and female are, sexual difference is not a difference in human *personhood*; as persons they are radically the same. Both are defined in the same terms of humanity; both are beings of intellect and have the same range of intelligence; both are possessed of freewill which they can exercise toward good, or evil; both are of divine creation and are the image of God, the *imago* Dei, a definition of "man" that transcends Aristotle's "rational animal" in that it addresses the reverential, immanence-of-God character of the human being. It is this *difference-in-sameness* that forms the context of ethical relations between the two sexes, a respect for the *difference in sexuality* and a respect for the *sameness in humanity*.

Sexuality adds a different tone to a relationship between male and female, call it completion, complementarity, wholeness, which is expressed in a *special kind of friendship*. Friendship of any kind is a good thing, for it possesses the potential for enrichment in the mutual sharing of ideas, hopes, joys, sorrows, art, humor, and remembrance of things past. But in a male and female relationship, the tone is heard in the very difference in sexual personality. Though it is sometimes overwritten, the term "platonic" is often used of such a relationship and suggests, along the lines of platonic dualism, that there are higher ends of friendship that can be achieved without physical involvement, and to which physical involvement may even be a hindrance. But there are *extremes* in male–female relationships just as there are in any other kind of relationship. One extreme is the distancing of one person from another out of inordinate respect that results in hampering normal interaction, such as Cyrano de Bergerac's inability to tell Roxanne directly that he loves her. Or the distancing from another out of fear that one's own individual freedom may be compromised, as in Camus' portrayal of Meursault whose cold indifference prevented him from asking his girlfriend to marry him. Another extreme is disrespect for the opposite sex in which one uses the other as a means to an end, as a throw-away object when usefulness is over, tantamount to an act of depersonalization.

LOVE AND SEX

By now we've learned to accept the fact that any profound reality lends itself to manifold understandings, giving rise to verbal confusion because a single word can be used to express those different meanings. This should not surprise us, for language simply does not have the calibration we need for expressing the wide range of our sensitivities and perceptions, all of which vary according to time, place, and culture. This is true of the word *love*, with myriad nuances attached to it, like romantic love, courtly love, filial love, Platonic love, spousal love, puppy love, erotic love, and divine love. Greek literature did develop a vocabulary for several of the differences in the meaning of love in that it made a distinction among *philia, eros,* and *agape. Philia* is the love of friendship, respect or regard for another; *eros* pertains to any kind of yearning or desire; and *agape* is a free, self-giving love, of the kind found in intimate friendship. These different types of love are not found separately as though absolutely independent of one another, but are found together in a kind of amalgam in which one predominates. The distinction between eros and agape has become a favorite with theologians of recent years who are inclined to speak of divine agape as the unique self-giving of God in His love for man, a self-giving that endures even when unrequited.

Given the role of the body in the male–female relationship, it is far from naive to raise questions like, what is sex for? What is its function? Why do we have it in the first place? Because sexuality can have multiple meanings, it is rich in its signification, as the philosopher Paul Ricoeur writes, "It is not rigid or inflexible but mobile . . . it is inexhaustible" (*The Symbolism of Evil*, p. 15). It can be a sign of love, of tenderness, of forgiveness, of generosity, of understanding, of compassion. Or, as is the sad possibility attached to any good thing, it can be used perversely to humiliate another, to depersonalize, or to destroy, as in the case of rape, especially the violent rape of subjugation in the fierce waves of ethnic cleansing of recent times. But before it is a sign, it is an objective reality, and the way to understand it is to recognize it as a fact of nature, so it is to nature we must turn to determine its role, not merely as a physical fact considered in its pure physicality, but in conjunction with all the other capacities, responses, and urgings that are expressed by the term *human nature*. In its *biological* end, sex is ordered to the procreation of children, but it has, at the same time, a *personal* end as the expression of love between man and woman. This does not mean that the two ends cannot be joined together so that one and the same act is both an act of procreation and an act of love. Neither does it mean that every sex act is, or has to be, procreative, but that the power in itself has procreation, or the continuation of human kind, as its natural biological end. But, lest we get so taken up in the natural routineness of "propagating the species," Plato reminds us of the singular beauty of procreation, for it is a power of mythic depth, which Socrates, in the *Symposium*, touchingly describes: "procreation is the union of man and woman, and is a divine thing; for conception and procreation are an immortal principle in the mortal creature" (*Symposium*, 206c).

Plato also set the course for a remarkable tradition as to the role of love. He recognized that the power of love comes first of all from love's lacking possession of what it yearns for and now tries to move toward. But because the yearning is so profound, love always attempts to satisfy itself by climbing higher on the *ladder of love*, moving away from want to possession, from ignorance to knowledge, and from material to spiritual until it rests in the transcendent company of Beauty/Good itself. As these notions migrated into Christian times, with a generous injection of the matter-is-evil philosophy as spoken of above, the plea for detachment from the body became more pronounced, as though *bodily things in themselves* were inimical to piety and the spiritual life. That being so, sex and sexual activity, in this view, were assigned to the darker side of humanity and somehow had to be held in submission, or at least subject to rigorous rational control.

This downside picture of sex is repeatedly borne out in the writings of many of the outstanding names in the medieval period, names like Saints Jerome, Ambrose, Augustine, and Thomas Aquinas who, right alongside the utmost regard they had for God's good creation, had some severe reservations about sexual relationships, even in marriage. St. Augustine, for example, decided, some while before his conversion, not to marry. Why? Because, among other reasons, "I know nothing which brings the manly mind down from the heights more than a woman's caresses and that joining of bodies without which one cannot have a wife" (*Soliloquies*, I, p. 10). He maintained that opinion years later in his *City of God* where, in writing of the "evil of lust," he insists on the power it has to destabilize a person's mind: "So intense is the pleasure that when it reaches its climax there is an almost total extinction of mental alertness; the intellectual sentries, as it were, are overwhelmed," as though there were something spiritually suspicious about "intense pleasure" (*City of God*, XIV, p. 16). So, it followed for him, that the genital organs had become "the private property of lust" and that anyone seeking wisdom would prefer, if possible, to beget children some other way. Augustine simply did not see the compatibility of sex and love in nurturing the humanity of husband and wife.

St. Thomas Aquinas too had strong suspicions with regard to the enjoyment of sensual pleasure in the conjugal act apart from the intention of begetting children: "Consequently, whenever one engages in the conjugal act, he is not wholly excused from sin, except insofar as the act is intended to produce offspring" (*Summa Theol.*, III,

Sup, 49,5, ad 1). And following the not unusual evaluation made by commentators on a particular passage in Sacred Scripture, he let it be known that the meritorious reward of virginity is a hundred-fold, of widowhood sixty-fold, and of the married state only thirty-fold (II-II, 152, 8 ad 2).

But alongside these influential ecclesiastical figures in the Middle Ages which, after all, are referred to as the Age of Faith, was the general acknowledgment of a healthy attitude toward sexuality and the human body among the populace. Folk customs, and the works of art and literature, convey a matter-of-factness regarding the needs of the body: "Sex was simply an integral part of the whole man, no more and no less . . . not a breath of impurity was attached to it, not the slightest hint of its being a thing that should preferably not exist" (A, Adam, *The Primacy of Love*, p. 43) (R #2). In the ensuing centuries, however, when faith lost its place as the organizing principle of social life, moral attitudes began to develop along radically different lines and the earlier matter-of-factness gave way to a stricter view on sexual relationships and practice. This was particularly true in the Anglo-Saxon sphere of influence where a curtain of reticence and correctness was drawn over sexual conversation and behavior, so that it would have been in bad taste or a breach of good manners to discuss sexual matters in an open, public fashion, despite what one might do privately, and the term "immorality" meant, in the main, "sexual wrongdoing."

It's characteristic of changing cultures that it takes time to retrieve a waning tradition or to begin another, and so it has been for the notion of sexual love in making its way to becoming re-valued as an integral part of human wholeness. For the Greeks, as we saw earlier, the universe of things was dominated by *eros*, the term that refers to any kind of desire or yearning, or tendency, whence even inanimate things were referred to as having a "desire"; for example, a stone's desire to fall. In reference to the human being the term reaches down to the very source of *being human*, in the thrust to reach beyond oneself to fulfill oneself, to establish an emotional contact between lover and beloved—the basic mystery of persons in love. Fulfillment is a feature of the self-love proper to eros, for love and self-love go hand in hand; that is, the lover knows that in loving the beloved, the lover loves himself as well. So, taking the human being in its totality, it is true that the *natural end* of the sex act includes not only the *biological end*, but also the *personal end* of expressing love between man and woman: the same act is a unity of two natural ends, biological and personal. This means then that every sexual act, in all its biological integrity, excitement, and sensuality, should be an expression of personal love as well. The sexual act, denied love, is stripped of its personal meaning and damages the wholeness of the man–woman relationship (R #3).

Though love for another is founded on the *person* of the other, this does not lessen the role of *physical appeal*, which may indeed be the first attraction one has for the other. Physical attractiveness can, and does, meld with the personal attractiveness of the other and so it has the power to lead to a transcendent, spiritual level of love, felt perhaps in every experience of falling in love. For a literary example, we can turn again to the classical poet, Dante Alighieri, who, as he dramatically recounts in his *Vita Nuova* (My New Life), was smitten early in his pre-adolescent life by the subtle and mysterious beauty of the just as young Beatrice: "At that moment, I say most truly that the spirit of life, which hath its dwelling in the secretest chamber of the heart, began to tremble so violently that the least pulses of my body shook therewith . . . from that time forward, Love quite governed my soul." It was this experience that, in later years, Dante shaped into the unforgettable symbol of love in the *Divine Comedy*, presenting the now lady Beatrice as the personification of his search for love (R #4).

ROMANTIC LOVE AND MARRIAGE

The sex act, fitted to its dual purpose, reaches a level of male and female relationship beyond the platonic to that of *romantic love*, which has its culmination the union of man and woman as husband and wife, expressed by the time-honored term of *marriage*. There is no way of defining this kind of love, or any kind of love for that matter, for it is an original datum; that is, it is a basic, fundamental fact that is self-evident to the persons in love and to no other. It is known only by being in love. It is discoverable only in possessing it. It is a profound reality and inexhaustible in its tokens of expression—the touch, the look, the caring, the sacrifice, the anxiety, the trust, the flower, the ring, the box of sweets: "How do I love thee?" asks the poet, "let me count the ways." What we see here are so many attempts, some perfectly natural and some of one's own invention, to nurture the togetherness of husband and wife, and to signify the reciprocity of love and the need for unity (R #5 and #6). The reaching out is an indication of the continuous pursuit to bring about the finishing in each of what is unfinished, to fulfill what is wanting in each. This is not to say that the call to full humanity resides only in marriage, for many a single person has shown how he or she satisfies the need for fulfillment in their own way, but there is a natural fittingness in marriage for sexual completion. In a humorous vein, to show how much a man and a woman need each other, Plato has the comic poet Aristophanes recount the legend that, of old, man and woman were combined in one sex but that Zeus, for political reasons, separated them, which explains why ever since they've been frantically trying to get back together again!

Marriage then, as the relationship of man and woman seeking fulfillment, rejects time limitations. It hardly makes any sense for a bridegroom to inform his bride that he will love her for two years and two months, or for the bride to tell the bridegroom that she will love him until his money runs out. As a unique person-to-person relationship, the *person*, rich or poor, sick or healthy, beautiful or faded, handsome or disfigured, is always there, and always to be loved. Not indeed with the same frenzied excitement as in the beginning but with a permanent and steady acceptance of the same person. Love, if given with a stated time for ending it, is not love at all, and certainly not the kind of love sought for as a marriage ideal. That's why, in Jesus' view, the bond of marriage is also the divine call to an unbroken commitment, "What God has joined together let no man put asunder" (Mt 19, 6). Permanence in marriage is naturally looked forward to in the bringing up of a family, whose stability is a daily unspoken expectation for children, given the need across the years for the seemingly never-ending care of their bodies and minds—burdensome, of course, but suffused with a sense of loving duty to children who were presented as living gifts of nature to their parents and to each other.

The union of man and woman as husband and wife is wrought by the man and woman themselves; they endow each other with the married state even though an official may be present to certify its public status. They enter, even if only implicitly, into an agreement regarding their new life together. This agreement is often referred to as the *marriage contract* because it guarantees the mutual rights and obligations husband and wife have toward each other. It also guarantees the public and social entailments of their agreement, such as ownership of property and education of children, and all those other benefits and duties that come under the heading of social justice. These are highlighted in calling marriage a contract; perhaps a complaint can reasonably be made against the word *contract* because it comes out sounding too "business-like" for a person-to-person relationship. This incongruity can be avoided by using the word *covenant*, a biblical term that emphasizes the personal aspect of the promises to be kept and obligations honored. It asserts the sacred character of love and marriage.

Thus, marriage entails a basic commitment of man and woman to each other without which you may well ask if there is any marriage at all. The commitment can be made formally, by using an agreed-upon formula, or informally, by living together for a length of time that would signify commitment. It is not intrinsic to marriage to make the commitment public, except to secure a place in society with all its social and political consequences. The "yes," given as a sign of commitment, even though given as a single event, is actually spelled out in the course of time and in the unforeseen happenings of life. A marriage commitment does not mean a rigorously defined pattern of life, but a certain flexibility, a freedom that in no way negates commitment nor yields to a suffocatingly narrow interpretation of it. Experience is always the key to further discoveries, and the experience of married couples shows that a measure of independence in the workplace, in developing friendships or separate interests, need not tell against commitment but can even advance it.

As regards living together, or cohabitation, it should be noted that it has surged upward as a social phenomenon throughout the world in the last fifty or sixty years, and would lead one to think that it is entirely new. In fact, cohabitation harkens back centuries when there was a more experiential view taken toward it. For many it was considered to be a *process*, so that marriage would reasonably be looked upon as beginning a relationship with an expectation, or promise (betrothal), of marriage, thus, a consent formally or informally given that ratified the relationship as it worked its way to a consummation, not essentially sexual intercourse, but a de facto permanence of love.

It would be helpful to recall that the term *agape*, spoken of above, refers to the intimate relationship of love characterized by a free giving of oneself to another, here husband to wife, and wife to husband. In their day-in-day-out nearness to each other, they become closer in every respect, personally, spiritually, and bodily—they share home, food, drink, daily chores, cooking, washing, exercising, reading, traveling, recreating, spending leisure time, sleeping, all of which require mutual self-giving. Such closeness demands respect and love for the very body of each and for the acceptance of the fleshly intimacy of sexual activity between them, such that no act rising from that natural intimacy can be called "unnatural" or morally objectionable. The repertoire of activity springing from the love relationship between husband and wife would be tyrannized if sexuality were reduced to the genital act, for then it would be a deceitful repudiation of the romantic love between two who "belong together" (R #7).

If marriage is the union between male and female, what can be said of a union between two members of the same sex? No case is being made here for or against *homosexuality*, which can only be settled by social recognition and further scientific study into the deep-seated biological and psychological structure of those who call themselves homosexual. But taking facts as they are "on the ground," there is no reason to contest the identity homosexuals proclaim, nor to contest their personal yearning for a committed relationship for persons of the same sex. The notion of commitment today exhibits a far wider berth than it did as recently as a generation ago, and experience has shown that a binding union between homosexuals is as much a desideratum as it is between heterosexuals. The campaign for marital status is best understood as an anxiety on the part of committed gay persons to be accepted as co-equals in a society that prides itself as a democracy which secures civil and social rights for all. It's in that light that public agitation for the term *marriage* should be understood.

DIVORCE

Very seldom, if ever, does a person enter marriage with the intention of breaking it up. That would be the equivalent of *intending* to fail. Nor has any poet ever written about how many ways do I "unlove" you! When you realize that all relationships have a fragility open to a thousand enemies, the ancient troubadour had it right when he sang of selfish pride as the arch-enemy of love: it is a barrier to reciprocity. Earlier on we saw that permanence in marriage, or indissolubility, is built into the very nature of love commitment. What then is to be said of *divorce* as a rupture in that commitment? Certainly in this country the easy acceptance of divorce has grown apace in the last hundred years and has given us an unenviable rate of divorce among the countries of the world. Does the fact of widespread divorce require us to revisit the whole notion of permanence as sketched out above? This is not a question of whether the divorcing persons think, in conscience, that they are doing the right thing; of course they think so; that's the *subjective* side of it. But it's a question of whether there is *objective* validity to divorce as a moral option, an entirely different kind of question. Let's see. There are physical, health, and financial worries in every marriage which, of themselves, are not reasons for terminating it. On the contrary, they become the very reasons for not doing so. But what about brutality, continual infidelity, injury to children, incest, abandonment, and personal despoliation, are they not so many radical negations of the original reasons that brought husband and wife together in the first place? Are not these real changes in the very person who married? That is, it is not the same person I knew, or thought I knew, when I made the promise of forever. That a spouse becomes sick, financially strapped, or mentally unstable does not militate against personal commitment, for they are not willed states of affairs. The same cannot be said about brutality or abandonment. So, if love is a primary constituent of the marriage covenant, can it not be argued that the annihilation of love is a reason for dissolving the marriage? This is not saying that there may not be good and generous reasons for staying together, such as the welfare and education of young children, but it may also be that this praiseworthy objective, in some instances, is more satisfactorily accomplished by separation, as in the case of unbridled and open friction which can devastate the children as well as the parents.

As to the lifestyle of "living together" mentioned above, it can be argued that the notion of commitment, never to be dispensed with, has to respond to the actual state of affairs. The experience of many couples living together is proof that such an arrangement does not necessarily violate personal commitment, and of itself does not make divorce more likely. That being so, a formal declaration of commitment, as in a marriage rite, gives way to the de facto nonformal commitment attested to by the quality of life a couple has experienced in their life together. Commitment has not lost its place, nor permanence its desirability, but have been re-created in an informal and nontraditional way.

CONTRACEPTION

Many textbooks end their treatment of sexuality without taking up the question of *contraception* because it is considered ethically nonproblematic. It's a non-question. But inasmuch as the morality of contraception has entered the political arena by withholding public funding to combat HIV in third-world countries, something more needs to be said about it. The view that contraception is wrong, often referred to as the *traditional* view, is that any artificial means taken against conception frustrates the biological end of sex, is against nature and consequently immoral. If the control of birth is consonant with the natural rhythm of the fertile and infertile periods of the female generative cycle, it's in accordance with nature, and moral.

No beliefs or ideas ever enter history like a bolt out of the blue but meld their way into human affairs in the course of time. The pessimistic strain regarding sex prevalent in the early Christian centuries spoken of above was in large part inherited from Stoic philosophy which prized rational control in all things including sexuality. A detached view of sex is one of the possible consequences of such rational control, but so is antipathy to sex, which is the aspect that worked its way into the moral discourse of the early Christian writers exemplified, as we've seen, in the fourth and fifth century in St. Augustine. His elaboration of the procreation and education of offspring as the primary end of marriage—the first of the "blessings" of marriage—has held through centuries and, though modified in various ways, was spelled out to mean that intercourse was morally permissible only for the begetting of offspring. It's only in recent times that mutual love between spouses has achieved its rightful attention as one of the primary ends of marriage and an unapologetic reason for sexual intercourse.

Changes in long-standing views take time and require the coalescence of many causes, like the time it takes to assimilate one's own life experiences, or to readjust to new understandings of the role of civic authority, or to recognize the impact of ongoing social, economic, and health problems, or to evaluate new medical knowledge, and so on. From a philosophical point of view we can locate a significant engine of change in the *rise of personalism* beginning with the humanist turn in the mid-nineteenth century. It is not because the human being was ignored in previous centuries, but because practices, especially those that become institutionalized, have a way of taking on a life of their own at the expense of the very people exercising them. So at any given time in history a wake-up call may be necessary to reshape a forgotten truth or to nurture an emerging one. In the matter at hand, if sex is seen *only* as a biological activity, then marriage is nothing more than the union of two biological entities, not two human beings, not two *persons*. The recognition of love in its rightful place as a primary end of the sexual act asserts the moral legitimacy of using the sexual act as an expression of love while controlling it as an act of reproduction.

READINGS

READING 1
Sexuality and Its Meanings
Margaret A. Foley
(from *Just Love*)

If our historical and cross-cultural considerations of sexual ethics in previous chapters and our explorations of embodiment and gender in this chapter have served us well, we do not start from zero in our thinking about the meanings of sexuality. The term itself is relatively new (appearing in English dictionaries only since the early nineteenth century). Its meaning in the abstract remains difficult to identify, despite the dictionaries. I take it here to include everything that pertains to the sexual—in the sense of sexual desires and loves, feelings, emotions, activities, relationships. As such, sexuality can have physical, psychological, emotional, intellectual, spiritual, personal, and social dimensions. When we ask about its meanings, we can include individual, relational, species, and cosmic meanings, private and public meanings, biological and cultural meanings. Sex can refer to genital and non-genital sex, sex with or without desire, sex with or without pleasure. The aims and goals of sex and sexuality include, but do not necessarily reduce to, the aims and goals commonly thought to be intrinsic to sexual desire or sexual activity.

Just about everyone today thinks that sex has something to do with love—somewhere, somehow, for some persons; or at least that this is possible. Sex and sexual desire, of course, cannot be reduced to or equated with sexual love. Moreover, it is always a risk to focus on love in relation to sexuality since it tends to escalate the rhetoric about love in ways that imply that sex, no matter what, is always about love—and about certain forms of love.

Despite these caveats, it is important to focus at some point on the meanings of sexuality in relation to love. At least in a Christian context, this is reasonable, since commandments and calls to love are arguably at the heart of any Christian ethic. From this perspective, it is important to offer a reminder of the significance of love. I do this, initially, not by examining psychological, theological, philosophical, biblical analyses of love. I begin only with some reminders of experiences of human interpersonal love—sexual and nonsexual. We need here to remember an array of such experiences: tender love as when a longtime friend touches one's arm to express sympathetic understanding; sweetly memorable love as when parents taking a drive with their children begin to sing the love songs of their youth; endearing love as when a child offers a wild flower to her grandmother; love as shared excitement and relief when colleagues working intensely together on a treasured project collapse united in satisfaction and fatigue. We need also to remember experiences (vicarious or our own) of fierce love, when separation between lovers is like an arm being torn off; or "first love," when the whole world becomes patterned with the color of love. We must remember troubled loves, when feelings are disparate, or love becomes war, or insecurity threatens to destroy the future of love. Insofar as we can, we must remember, too, the love that dawns between persons from vastly different cultures as they grow in mutual knowledge and respect. We remember courageous love, when parents struggle against those who would be unjust to their child, or when co-believers challenge what they consider distorted practices of faith. We remember love's experience of peace and of turmoil, of gentleness and of passion, of wisdom and confusion, bitterness and respect, companionship and death, endurance and transcendent hope.

READING 2
Love Is Personal
Rollo May
(from *Love and Will*)

The fact that love is personal is shown in the love act itself. Man is the only creature who makes love *face to face,* who copulates *looking* at his partner. Yes, we can turn our heads or assume other positions for variety's sake, but these are variations on a theme—the theme of making love vis-à-vis each other. This opens the whole front of the person—the breasts, the chest, the stomach, all the parts which are most tender and most vulnerable—to the kindness or the cruelty of the partner. The man can thus see in the eyes of the woman the nuances of delight or awe, the tremulousness or the angst; it is the posture of the ultimate baring of one's self.

This marks the emergence of man as a psychological creature: it is the shift from animal to man. Even monkeys mount from the rear. The consequences of this change are great indeed. It not only stamps the love act as irrevocably *personal*, with all the implications of that fact, one of which being that the lovers can speak if they wish. Another consequence is the accentuation of the experience of intimacy in giving the side of the person closest to "ourselves" in the sexual experience. The two chords of love-making—one's experience of himself and his experience of the partner—are temporarily merged here. We feel our delight and passion and we look into the eyes of the partner also reading there the meaning of the act—and I cannot distinguish between her passion and mine. But the looking *is* fraught with intensity; it brings a heightened consciousness of relationship.

. . .

If love were merely a *need*, it would not become personal, and will would not be involved: choices and other aspects of self-conscious freedom would not enter the picture. One would just fulfill the needs. But when sexual love becomes *desire*, will is involved; one chooses the woman, is aware of the act of love, and how it gets its fulfillment is a matter of increasing importance. Love and will are united as a task and an achievement. For human beings, the more powerful need is not for sex per *se* but for relationship, intimacy, acceptance, and affirmation.

This is where the fact that there are men and women—the polarity of loving—becomes ontologically necessary. The increased personal experience goes along with the increased consciousness; and consciousness is a polarity, an either/or, a saying "yes" to this and "no" to that. This is why, in an earlier chapter, we referred to the negative–positive polarity held in the theories of both Whitehead and Tillich. The paradox of love is that it is the highest degree of awareness of the self as a person and the highest degree of absorption in the other. Pierre Teilhard de Chardin asks, in *The Phenomenon of Man*, "At what moment do lovers come into the most complete possession of *themselves*, if not when they are *lost* in each other?"

The polarity which is shown ontologically in the processes of nature is also shown in the human being. Day fades into night and out of darkness day is born again; yin and yang are inseparable and always present in oscillation; my breath expires and I then inspire again. The systole and diastole of my heartbeat echo this polarity in the universe; it is not mere poetry to say that the beat of the universe, which constitutes its life, is reflected in the beating of the human heart. The continuous rhythm of each moment of existence in the natural universe is reflected in the pulsating blood stream of each human being.

READING 3
The New Life
Dante Alighieri

IN that part of the book of my memory before which little can be read is found a rubric which says: *Incipit Vita Nova* [The New Life begins]. Under which rubric I find the words written which it is my intention to copy into this little book—and if not all of them at least their meaning.

Nine times now, since my birth, the heaven of light had turned almost to the same point in its own gyration, when the glorious Lady of my mind, who was called Beatrice by many who knew not what to call her, first appeared before my eyes. She had already been in this life so long that in its course the starry heaven had moved toward the region of the East one of the twelve parts of a degree; so that at about the beginning of her ninth year she appeared to me, and I near the end of my ninth year saw her. She appeared to me clothed in a most noble color, a modest and becoming crimson, and she was girt and adorned in such wise as befitted her very youthful age. At that instant, I say truly that the spirit of life, which dwells in the most secret chamber of the heart, began to tremble with such violence that it appeared fearfully in the least pulses, and, trembling, said these words: *Ecce deus fortior me, qui veniens dominabitur mihi* [Behold a god stronger than I, who coming shall rule over me].

At that instant the spirit of the soul, which dwells in the high chamber to which all the spirits of the senses carry their perceptions, began to marvel greatly, and, speaking especially to the spirit of the sight, said these words: *Apparuit jam beatitudo vestra* [Now has appeared your bliss].

At that instant the natural spirit, which dwells in that part where our nourishment is supplied, began to weep, and, weeping, said these words: *Heu miser! quia frequenter impeditus*

ero deinceps [Woe is me, wretched! because often from this time forth shall I be hindered].

I say that from that time forward Love lorded it over my soul, which had been so speedily wedded to him: and he began to exercise over me such control and such lordship, through the power which my imagination gave to him, that it behoved me to do completely all his pleasure. He commanded me of times that I should seek to see this youthful angel; so that I in my boyhood often went seeking her, and saw her of such noble and praiseworthy deportment, that truly of her might be said that word of the poet Homer, "She seems not the daughter of mortal man, but of God." And though her image, which stayed constantly with me, gave assurance to Love to hold lordship over me, yet it was of such noble virtue that it never suffered Love to rule me without the faithful counsel of the reason in those matters in which it were useful to hear such counsel. And since to dwell upon the passions and actions of such early youth seems like telling an idle tale, I will leave them, and, passing over many things which might be drawn from the original where these lie hidden, I will come to those words which are written in my memory under larger paragraphs.

READING 4
Lover to His Love
Song of Songs

What a wound thou hast made, my bride, my true love, what a wound thou hast made in this heart of mine! And all with one glance of an eye, all with one ringlet straying on thy neck! Sweet, sweet are thy caresses, my bride, my true love; wine cannot ravish the senses like that embrace, nor any spices match the perfume that breathes from thee. Sweet are thy lips, my bride, as honey dripping from its comb; honey-sweet thy tongue, and soft as milk; the perfume of thy garments is very incense. My bride, my true love, a close garden; hedged all about, a spring shut in and sealed! What wealth of grace is here! Well-ordered rows of pomegranates, tree of cypress

and tuft of nard; no lack there whether of spikenard or saffron, of calamus, cinnamon, or incense-tree, of myrrh, aloes or any rarest perfume. A stream bordered with garden; water so fresh never came tumbling down from Lebanon.

North wind, awake; wind of the south, take and come; blow through this garden mine, and set its fragrance all astir.

. . .

How graceful thou art, dear maiden, how fair, how dainty! Thy stature challenges the palm tree, thy breasts the clustering vine. What thought should I have but to reach the tree's top, and gather its fruit? Breasts generous as the grape, breath sweet as apples, mouth soft to my love's caress as good wine is soft to the palate, as food to lips and teeth.

My true love, I am all his; and who but I the longing of his heart? Come with me, my true love; for us the country ways, the cottage roof for shelter. Dawn shall find us in the vineyard, looking to see what flowers the vine has, and whether they are growing into fruit; whether pomegranates are in blossom. And there thou shalt be master of my love. The mandrakes, what scent they give! Over the door at home there are fruits of every sort a-drying; I put them by, new and old, for my true love to eat.

READING 5
Trying to Say "I love you"
Virginia Woolf
(from *Mrs. Dalloway*)

All of which seemed to Richard Dalloway awfully odd. For he never gave Clarissa presents, except a bracelet two or three years ago, which had not been a success. She never wore it. It pained him to remember that she never wore it. And as a single spider's thread after wavering here and there attaches itself to the point of a leaf, so Richard's mind, recovering from its lethargy, set now on his wife, Clarissa, whom Peter Walsh had loved so passionately; and Richard had had a sudden vision of her there at luncheon; of himself and Clarissa; of their life together; and he drew the tray of old jewels towards him, and taking up first this brooch then that ring, "How much is that?" he asked, but doubted his own taste. He wanted to open the drawing-room door and come in holding out something; a present for Clarissa. Only what?

. . . And, flicking his bowler hat by way of farewell.

Richard turned at the corner of Conduit Street eager, yes, very eager, to travel that spider's thread of attachment between himself and Clarissa; he would go straight to her, in Westminster.

But he wanted to come in holding something. Flowers? Yes, flowers, since he did not trust his taste in gold; any number of flowers, roses, orchids, to celebrate what was, reckoning things as you will, an event; this feeling about her when they spoke of Peter Walsh at luncheon; and they never spoke of it; not for years had they spoken of it; which, he thought, grasping his red and white roses together (a vast bunch in tissue paper), is the greatest mistake in the world. The time comes when it can't be said; one's too shy to say it, he thought, pocketing his sixpence or two of change, setting off with his great bunch held against his body to Westminster to say straight out in so many words (whatever she might think of him), holding out his flowers, "I love you."

. . . But he would tell Clarissa that he loved her, in so many words. He had, once upon a time, been jealous of Peter Walsh; jealous of him and Clarissa. But she had often said to him that she had been right not to marry Peter Walsh; which, knowing Clarissa, was obviously true; she wanted support. Not that she was weak; but she wanted support.

As for Buckingham Palace (like an old prima donna facing the audience all in white) you can't deny it a certain dignity, he considered, nor despise what does, after all, stand to millions of people (a little crowd was waiting at the gate to see the King drive out) for a symbol, absurd though it is; a child with a box of bricks could have done better, he thought; looking at the memorial to Queen Victoria (whom he could remember in her horn spectacles driving through Kensington), its white mound, its billowing motherliness;

but he liked being ruled by the descendant of Horsa; he liked continuity; and the sense of handing on the traditions of the past. It was a great age in which to have lived. Indeed, his own life was a miracle; let him make no mistake about it; here he was, in the prime of life, walking to his house in Westminster to tell Clarissa that he loved her. Happiness is this, he thought.

It is this, he said, as he entered Dean's Yard. Big Ben was beginning to strike, first the warning, musical; then the hour, irrevocable. Lunch parties waste the entire afternoon, he thought, approaching his door.

The sound of Big Ben flooded Clarissa's drawing-room, where she sat, ever so annoyed, at her writing-table; worried; annoyed. . . .

And the sound of the bell flooded the room with its melancholy wave; which receded, and gathered itself together to fall

once more, when she heard, distractingly, something fumbling, something scratching at the door. Who at this hour? Three, good Heavens! Three already! For with overpowering directness and dignity the clock struck three; and she heard nothing else; but the door handle slipped round and in came Richard! What a surprise! In came Richard, holding out flowers. She had failed him, once at Constantinople; and Lady Bruton, whose lunch parties were said to be extraordinarily amusing, had not asked her. He was holding out flowers—roses, red and white roses. (But he could not bring himself to say he loved her; not in so many words.)

But how lovely, she said, taking his flowers. She understood; she understood without his speaking; his Clarissa. She put them in vases on the mantelpiece. How lovely they looked! she said.

READING 6
Love Shared Is Love Gained
Thomas Merton

(from *No Man is an Island*)

There is a false and momentary happiness in self-satisfaction, but it always leads to sorrow because it narrows and deadens our spirit. True happiness is found in unselfish love, a love which increases in proportion as it is shared. There is no end to the sharing of love, and, therefore, the potential happiness of such love is without limit. Infinite sharing is the law of God's inner life. He has made the sharing of ourselves the law of our own being, so that it is in loving others that we best love ourselves. In disinterested activity we best fulfill our own capacities to act and to be.

Yet there can never be happiness in compulsion. It is not enough for love to be shared: it must be shared freely. That is to say it must be given, not merely taken. Unselfish love that is poured out upon a selfish object does not bring perfect happiness: not because love requires a return or a reward for loving,

but because it rests in the happiness of the beloved. And if the one loved receives love selfishly, the lover is not satisfied. He sees that his love has failed to make the beloved happy. It has not awakened his capacity for unselfish love.

Hence the paradox that unselfish love cannot rest perfectly except in a love that is perfectly reciprocated: because it knows that the only true peace is found in selfless love. Selfless love consents to be loved selflessly for the sake of the beloved. In so doing, it perfects itself.

The gift of love is the gift of the power and the capacity to love, and, therefore, to give love with full effect is also to receive it. So, love can only be kept by being given away, and it can only be given perfectly when it is also received.

Chapter Ten
Virtue and Vice

DISCOVERING VIRTUES

Right along we have been considering the question of morality as it pertains to the performance of an act here and now, which is why we spent several chapters on the norm of morality and how to make moral judgments of specific acts. There is, however, another feature of our experience we have to consider that will shed further light on the nature of moral activity. It is the feature of a certain kind of *consistency* in a person's moral behavior. A neighbor is not always taking the elderly lady next door shopping but is always *ready* to do so, and does, when the occasion arises; a nurse is not always comforting a sick child but is always *ready* to do so, and does, when the occasion arises; a professor is not always giving extra time to an inquiring student but is always *ready* to do so, and does, when the occasion arises. We begin to realize that in cases like these we are not dealing with a merely accidental series of good actions, atomized and unconnected with each other, but with an *interior disposition* the neighbor, the nurse, and the professor possess from which the actions readily proceed, a *habit* to perform the actions without having to think them over every time. Such habits moralists refer to as *virtues*. They are permanent signs of a person's character; they allow us to say "a person is what a person does."

A virtue displays itself to be an inner readiness to respond to a situation wanting the human thing to be done; a deep-seated potentiality, poised to be activated. The response is unhesitating and even spontaneous, like water in a spout, ready to run when the tap is turned on. Virtues give an insight as to the kind of person a person is; they define one; they shape one's character. When we say that John is generous or Jane is gentle, we are saying that generosity is part of his character and gentleness part of hers; we would not understand either person without an awareness of these virtues. The Bible depicts Job as a figure who endured every kind of suffering, loss of wealth, of children, of reputation and yet, however much he complained, he would never abjure the God of his faith, holding that, in a way unknown to him, God too would prove His faithfulness in return, whence the virtue bringing him through these trials has become legendary in the phrase, "the patience of Job."

Virtue is a broad concept and is specified in any number of ways. If you were to make a list of some specific kinds of virtue, you might include sympathy, temperance, faithfulness, generosity, tolerance, concern, courage, helpfulness, mercy, forbearance, gratitude, agreeableness, humility, respectfulness, tolerance, modesty, thoughtfulness, politeness, justice, gentleness, joy, and love. Every one of these involves a good act and suggests that *any* good act you can think of can be the subject matter of virtue. Virtue lies in making the good real in practice, something, we'll recall, that Socrates had in mind when he taught that "knowledge is virtue," meaning that to know what's to be done without doing it is not really knowledge at all; knowledge demands enactment—it's the mark of a person's wisdom to do what he knows should be done; it is the wise person who is virtuous (R #1). This chapter, therefore, is to be seen as the completion of the overall project of the book, to affirm the centrality of the good.

THE HISTORICAL FACE OF VIRTUE

Virtue is produced by a person's internalizing a goal he judges to be good and worth striving for, and in the course of repeated actions he creates an inner resource ready to respond when the occasion demands. The notion of good and the notion of virtue are essentially united: what is held to be virtuous is also held to be good, and the doing of good is held to be virtuous. In following Alastair MacIntyre's magisterial work on virtues, we learn that historically what is prized as good in one society may not be so in another, and likewise with virtue. In primitive western culture, for example, it was the warrior who could always be depended on for his bravery and strength of character; he was expected to display the virtue of manliness, to win victory for his cause and glory for himself. The word *virtue* itself expresses this notion, for *vir* in Latin means man, strength, and power. In Hebrew literature, those leaders were honored who would fight to sustain the Israelites in their belief in the divinely given promise of the holy land, whence Saul was proclaimed for killing thousands, but David even more for killing tens of thousands. In the epic poems of Homer, whoever excels in one or another remarkable feat is a man of heroic virtue, but always with the recognition of "the central place that strength will have in such a conception of human excellence." Think of Achilles, the Greek hero, who, after he was prodded out of his sulkiness, rallied the Greek forces to victory over the Trojans. A similar example of heroic virtue is seen in the early Anglo-Saxon epic *Beowulf,* of the eighth or ninth century, in which the Danes celebrated their deliverance from tyranny by the mighty Beowulf, an example of an heroic code of honor in which "the attainment of a name for warrior-prowess among the living overwhelms any concern about the soul's destiny in the afterlife" (*Beowulf,* Heaney, p. xi).

After Homer, the rich culture of Athens during the fifth and fourth centuries was expressed in poetry, drama, religion, music, science, polity, and even sport, but the philosophical presentation of virtue was found in the writings of Plato and Aristotle. The central role of physical strength as the defining virtue of the Homeric age, though never completely lost, gave way to the *polis,* society in the form of the city-state, within which the citizen would discover the meaning of virtue, in Plato's words, "writ large." Plato, having thoroughly imbibed Socrates' reverence for the ethical life, placed his mentor in the center of his early dialogues, all of which, in one way or another, touched on the meaning of virtue. Several were conversations on individual virtues, like courage in the *Laches,* or piety in the *Euthyphro.* Later he devoted the entire *Republic,* his best known work, to an elaboration of justice and its role in the ideal state. Though Plato never offered an analysis or definition of virtue as such, as his pupil later would, on several occasions he presented a list of virtues subsequently called 'cardinal' virtues: wisdom, temperance, courage, and justice, to which he added holiness.

Aristotle's ideas on ethics and virtue were spread throughout his writings but formally put forth in several books on ethics, principally the *Nicomachean Ethics,* referred to simply as the *Ethics*. What Aristotle's view is on the meaning of virtue cannot be separated from his view on what the meaning of man is, a question we discussed in earlier chapters. Every action is directed toward some good, some goal (*telos*) and, in the often quoted opening words of the *Ethics*, "the good has rightly been declared to be that at which all things aim." But each thing, naturally, has to aim at the good according to the kind of thing it is: the human being does not seek the good as the rock crystal does, nor the maple tree, nor the lion, but as befits the existential status of being human. What do we intend to say when we say a person is good? Not that he has public stature or wealth or physical prowess, or raw intelligence, but only when he has those qualities we truly call "human," namely virtues. Aristotle writes, "in speaking of a man's moral character we do not say that he is bright or intelligent, but gentle or temperate; and a man praised as wise is actually being praised for his disposition, and praiseworthy dispositions we term virtues" (I,13,1103e).

There is another aspect of the good for Aristotle—the *fulfillment* that comes from the possession of virtue, call it by whatever name, "well-being," or "blessedness," or "happiness." If all action is for something, then the acquisition or possession of that something is the final goal of action and is to be understood as its final good: "Happiness is something final and self-sufficient, and is the end of action"; it is the reason for all activity. Virtue is not to be looked upon as a *means* to happiness, for its possession *is* happiness itself: "Virtuous actions must be in themselves pleasant. But they are also *good* and *noble*, and have each of these attributes in the highest degree. . . . Happiness then is the best, noblest, and most pleasant thing in the world." Simply put, Aristotle, together with Socrates and Plato, held that the life of virtue is the fulfillment of what-it-means-to-be-human.

Today, the popular use of the word *stoic*, conveying the idea of steely steadiness a person has in facing the rough times ahead, is an inheritance of the long period of Stoic philosophy, running from pre-Aristotelian times well into the Christian. It was less a philosophy than it was a way of managing life in all its pain and sorrow, thus a person's main project was to create an equilibrium, a balance, and an even-temperedness in bringing anxiety and the swings of emotion under control. Such constant effort would develop a habit, a virtue therefore, of balance and equanimity in one's daily life. Marcus Aurelius, second-century emperor and author of the perennially attractive *Meditations*, sought this balance in the harmony of nature: if nature can produce harmony in the manifold activity of the universe, then to live in accordance with nature can produce harmony in the manifold activities of one's life, whence "tranquility is nothing else than the good ordering of the mind."

The early Christian writers were much impressed with the ethical teachings of the Stoics because they foreshadowed their own doctrine of morality, but the sense of morality took on a totally new orientation based on the love of God as the center of Christian life. Certainly the ancient Greeks could refer to an action as "wrong" or "unjust," but in the Christian economy what is morally wrong or unjust was expressed by the word *sin* because it had the profoundly personal consequence of breaching the bond of love between God and man. If the core meaning of redemption meant a turning away from sin, what, then could be more opposed to a life of sin but a life of virtue? Much of this was formalized by theologians in the thirteenth century, the high point of intellectual activity in the Middle Ages, the age of faith, with St. Thomas Aquinas as its best known representative. As a theologian he exemplified the goal of theology, succinctly stated in the logo of the period, *faith seeking understanding (fides quaerens intellectum)*. Theology's purpose is to transpose the language of belief into a workable human vocabulary, to make faith as understandable as possible in human terms, in terms that shed some light on the mysteries of faith. Otherwise, reason and revelation would be incompatible, inhabiting as it were two totally different skewed planes circling one above the other without ever touching. Aristotle's philosophy became one of Thomas's favorite vehicles for conveying the truths of faith, manifested, for example, in his acceptance of the Athenian's treatment of virtues and its broad classification into what, by then, were known as the *four cardinal virtues*: temperance, courage, justice, and prudence. But something more was called for in the case of a believer, some role for virtues of a different, higher texture, the basis for which was found in a text of St Paul: "faith, hope and love abide, but the greatest of these is love"; theologians refer to faith, hope, and charity as the *three theological virtues*.

When reference is made to the *classical* view on virtues, it is usually the Aristotelian-Thomistic scheme that is meant. Such a reference does not mean, of course, that it was universally held, or that it was always or exclusively favored, or that others did not produce substantial insights into the understanding of virtues. It rather acknowledges that it has been a perennially substantial effort to bring together the role of reason and faith as they fit into the plain person's explanation of man's innate tendency toward the good life. But during the later Renaissance period the relationship between reason and faith began to wane, and for two centuries, beginning in the seventeenth, Aristotle's philosophy, mediated by Thomas Aquinas, gave way to new forces: the declining role of authority, namely that of Aristotle and the Bible; the expansion of scientific knowledge, for which Galileo's confirmation of a revolutionary world-system became a permanent icon; the rationalist philosophies of Descartes and Spinoza; and the diminishing influence of the Church. In the Aristotelian tradition, reason always had an honored place and was the human being's faculty of prudent judgment in the sphere of morality. No less did St. Thomas respect the integrity of reason even when it engaged the domain of revelation. As the modern age of philosophy began, however, the meaning of virtue at first lost its mooring in religion, and then, as the increased reliance on reason drove it to the extreme of rationalism, the meaning of virtue also lost its mooring in reason, with the overall result that virtues, as with all values, had to find a reinterpretation *outside* both reason and religion. Let's see how this works out with two prime examples, Hume and Nietzsche.

The objective of the eighteenth-century Scottish philosopher, David Hume, whose general view of morality we considered in an earlier chapter, was to develop a position on virtues that relied neither on religion nor reason. The existence of God had no significant place in the thinking man's repertoire, so that religion, and even reference to God, could never be construed as the foundation for virtuous activity. Neither could reason have a function in recognizing or shaping virtues; it is not the source of moral discernment. For Hume, then, the approval or disapproval of human actions rises from the *sentiment* you feel within "your own breast"; "reason" therefore "is the slave of passions and must obey them." On such an account of virtues it is difficult to rise above the idea that virtues are in the interest only of the individual, rendering virtues, like justice, involving *the other*, impossible. Though Hume undermined reason and religion as the foundations for virtue, he never denied them as human values to be cherished and cultivated in a new setting. The separation of virtues from both reason and religion never ran its full course in Hume as it did in Friedrich Nietzsche in the century following.

Nietzsche, along with Soren Kierkegaard and Karl Marx, was one of three influential philosophical humanists of the second-half nineteenth century who made their mark by insisting that human beings, over the course of time, had alienated themselves from a genuine understanding of what being human really meant, and with them the phrase "alienation of man" entered into the mainstream of philosophical thought. Though a brilliant young scholar trained in the classics, Nietzsche never wrote in academic style but rather in the style of personal reflection and admonition touching upon his favorite theme of how western philosophy and religion destroyed the very thing they cared about most—man. Man, trying to invest an imagined deity "out there" with fitting attributes, purloined them from himself, so that by an inverted calculus, the more enriched God became the more impoverished man became; thus man *alienated* himself from himself. But, as Nietzsche discovered, values are truly irrepressible—that is, if you push them down here, they'll emerge over there; and if you push them down over there, they'll show up again elsewhere. It wasn't that Nietzsche, though sometimes referred to as an absolute nihilist, was out to destroy values as such, but only those "false" values which proved to dehumanize man in the course of western history. It was these values that had to go. That's why Nietzsche called for a *revaluation of values*; that is, we can restore man's true meaning to himself only by rediscovering genuine human values. This we can do, not by reason or religion, but by seeing them at work in a person who is the perfect human, the perfect one, the ideal man, the Superman, the Overman, the Ubermensch—someone, perhaps, who is an amalgam of Christ and Caesar. From him, the rest of us will learn what human values are and the human virtues they entail. Though Nietzsche's philosophy is an extreme departure from the core of western moral thought, it is a strong wake-up call for the centrality of virtue in the life of human beings.

The guarded let-down of the moral tradition by Hume and the doomsday prophecy of Nietzsche serve to underscore the observation made above that virtues are so much part of the human moral infrastructure that they cannot be obliterated. The meaning of the moral life is inseparable from the meaning of humanity and will permanently command the attention of philosophers as it commands the attention of everyman in the pursuit of a rewarding life.

THE CARDINAL VIRTUES

In general, we've seen that virtue is a habitual disposition toward doing the right thing and that there is an endless spectrum of different kinds of virtue. As a convenient way of speaking of them, tradition has developed a scheme for classifying virtues under four categories—*temperance, courage, justice*, and *prudence*—which is a guide to all virtues (wisdom, practical wisdom, or Aristotle's term *phronesis*). Obviously these are broad categories but they express lines of distinction helpful for understanding them, whence they are called *cardinal virtues* (from the Latin cardines, hinges) around which they all turn, even though specific virtues may be addressed under more than one category.

Temperance

In everyday usage, "temper" refers to the notion of balance or moderate proportion, as a temperate zone is neither too hot nor too cold, an even-tempered person is neither too aggressive nor too casual, and Bach's well-tempered clavier is a piano in which the strings are pitched so that they are neither too flat nor too sharp. Because almost everything we do is subject to extremes, either too much or too little, we refer to a person who follows a middle path as temperate, avoiding the extremes of *excess*, let's say, in taking too much to drink, whence "intemperate"; or of *defect*, in not taking enough to satisfy his needs. To act along the middle path between these two extremes is the heart of Aristotle's system of morality in locating the course of virtuous action, sometimes referred to as the *golden mean*. Thus, the virtue of courage is the mean that lies between foolhardiness and cowardice, modesty the mean between shamelessness and bashfulness, hope the mean between false optimism and despair, and humility the mean between arrogance and self-hate. In an often quoted passage from the *Ethics*, Aristotle writes, "It is possible to go too far, or not to go far enough, in respect of fear, courage, desire, anger, pity, and pleasure and pain generally, excess and deficiency are alike wrong; but to experience these emotions at the right times and on the right occasions and towards the right persons and for the right reasons and in the right manner is the mean, that is, the good which characterizes virtue."

What is it that calls for temperance? What is it that has to be tempered? One of the most striking features about being human is our yearning for things, the whole domain of desire, including those of spirit and body. But what yields to temperance in the first instance are the yearnings of the body, under the general caption of *sensual desire* (appetite, concupiscence). These desires are the wants of the human body for satisfaction and whose fulfillment is the source of pleasure and enjoyment which, as seemingly opposed to desires of a loftier type, are perfectly natural and not to be demeaned or suppressed. If there are those who want to be strict on themselves with regard to sensual desires for some higher goal, it is for them to work out their priorities without becoming apathetic or insensible; apathy, or insensibility, for St. Thomas is a defect, a vice against temperance: "Nature has attached enjoyment to the activities necessary for human life" and anyone who would repudiate their necessity for human wholeness "would be committing a sin" (*Summa theol.* II-II, 142, c). In a poem of philosophical whimsy, *No, Plato, No*, W.H. Auden gently rebukes Plato for his suspicions against bodily things:

> I can't imagine anything less
> that I would like to be
> than a disincarnate Spirit,
> unable to chew or sip
> or make contact with surfaces
> or breathe the scents of summer
> or comprehend speech and music
> or gaze at what lies beyond.
> No, God has placed me exactly
> where I'd have chosen to be:
> the sub-lunar world is such fun.
> where Man is male or female
> and gives Proper Names to all things.

Humans want more, then more, then more; you never hear of anyone who wants less. It was Karl Marx's view that an unchecked profit motive was the main fault of capitalism, and the desire for power has often proved to be unquenchable, as Thomas Hobbes observed, there is "a general inclination of all mankind, a perpetual and restless desire of power after power that ceases only in death" (I, ch 11). Desire is limitless, and the failure to recognize that what is limitless can never be achieved is the root cause of most unhappiness. Though we have seen that desires are naturally good, they can get out of control, thus the precise role of temperance is to master our pleasures lest they master us. We can learn to be satisfied with less.

Courage

What temperance is in the domain of desire, *courage* is in the domain of fear. Everyone recognizes that, in the face of some impending evil, there is not only a natural tendency to avoid it, but also a physical and psychological change, called fear, an intense worry that one's personal self is about to crumble, or one's personal world. Fear, as Aristotle puts it, is our personal response to the "expectation of evil" (1115a12). Though it is, perhaps, possible to ignore the evil and impassively let it take its destructive course, one's first impulse is to counteract it, deploying a built-in capacity to allay the fear within us or overcome it, whence the *capacity to overcome fear* is the traditional definition of *courage.* As can be expected, the first notion of courage, or fortitude, comes from the battlefield and how the warrior reacts to its dangers. The warrior who is adamant, who is fearless in his attack, and who is able to rally his weaker comrades to put the enemy to rout is the one whose valor is praised, like Homer's Achilles, or the First World War's Sergeant York, a once popular hero for his exploits in the Ardennes Forest in 1918. There are many other examples of one's use of physical strength which are deemed courageous because of the bodily harm they entail, such as defending a woman in a rape assault, straining to rescue a swimmer battered by a storm, or braving the winds to save a hiker lost on Mt. Everest. In situations beyond the physical, there are also risks beyond the physical: personal, intellectual, economic, political, or professional risks—the senator who refuses to make a deal in a matter that is politically correct but ethically wrong; the whistleblower on corporate misbehavior; the scientist who refuses to fudge the data even though his job depends on it; the soldier who becomes a conscientious objector; the woman who suddenly becomes a widow and must face the future as the mother of four children. In everyday life, one has to have the courage bravely to face the hardships one encounters to achieve a worthwhile goal in education, supporting a family, or working toward a professional career.

An interesting question: can a person be called courageous who is fearless in doing what is wrong? Is the thief courageous who, bent on stealing a piece of jewelry, proceeds without fear, even knowing that the police might well catch him or kill him? How about the terrorists in the infamous 9/11 attacks on the Twin Towers when they appeared not only to be fearless, but even joyful? Surely the answer to the question has to be that courage, as a virtue, is courage only when the act it is attached to is good. To say there is such a thing as "courageous wickedness" is tantamount to saying there is such a thing as virtuous evil; as one philosopher aptly puts it, "courageous wickedness is still wickedness" (Comte-Sponville, p. 49). In a similar vein, fearlessness should not be confused with recklessness. A youngster who would show his friends how brave or fearless he is by holding a lighted firecracker in his fingers is not fearless but foolhardy. Just as in the case of temperance, a judgment has to be made as to the golden mean for an act to be called courageous: the balance between the excess of foolhardiness and the defect of cowardice.

Justice

To get to the meaning of justice we should first realize how broad the range is in our use of the word. We speak of a just law, or call a person who observes the law a just person. A society is just when it distributes the benefits and burdens of its undertakings like access to the vote, taxation, education, safety, health care, to all its members equitably, whence we refer to such a system as "fair." In our private dealings with others, it's the just, or fair, thing for the buyer to give the seller equal value for the object of transaction; or to keep a promise made to another. It would be unjust for a witness to withhold the truth, or a teacher to give a student a higher or lower grade because of his or her ethnic background. Children are quick to recognize unfairness in those who don't play according to the rules, or cheat in the classroom. On the international scale, it would be just if the inhabitants of an undeveloped country shared the wealth of its natural resources even if foreign capital had exclusive access to them; it would be unjust to wage an offensive war. Almost every action you can think of has an aspect that can be referred to as just or unjust, fair or unfair, which is why, for Aristotle the philosopher, justice is the "greatest of virtues," and for Aristotle the astronomer, it is more wonderful than "the evening or morning star." In short, justice is a "complete virtue" because "every virtue is contained in it" (1129b31ff).

The word *justice* comes from the Latin *jus*, which means both "law" and "right." In the *public* domain, the rights of individuals pertain to *civil* law, and in the *private* domain they pertain to the *moral* law, a matter of *justice* in either case because what is rendered to the individual is what is due. That's why Thomas Aquinas defines "justice," as it resides in the individual, as a virtue: "justice is the habit whereby a person renders to each his due" (II, II, 59, 1).

Regarding *civil law*, society has to have the authority to enact laws for its well-being, for the good of the community at large, and for every member of the community; they are meant to achieve goals which would be impossible for individuals acting on their own. We look to a long line of political philosophers who have developed theories of government in which law must be made to apply to all equitably, philosophers like Plato, Aristotle, Augustine, Thomas Aquinas, Hobbes, Locke, Spinoza, Kant, Rawls. We must turn to historians and political scientists, however, for a realistic evaluation of governments to see how well they have done, whether or not they were successful in employing public law for common justice, or whether they were dictatorial regimes bending the law to serve their own political power. The vexing questions of what the laws should be in a given society, who has the rightful authority to make them, and what price is to be paid for breaking them make us wonder, given the mischief human beings are capable of, how law has enjoyed the measure of success it has had in advancing the cause of justice in the world. The struggle during the past several hundred years has been how to achieve a system in which the people themselves, as the governed, have an essential role in deciding how they are to be governed. That this is a goal worth striving for is pithily expressed in the words of Reinhold Niebuhr, one of the last generation's best-known theologians: "Man's capacity for justice makes democracy possible, but man's capacity for injustice makes democracy necessary" (*Children of light and Children of Darkness*, Foreword).

Regarding *moral law*, which we fully discussed in Chapter 3, we are talking of law in a much wider sense than civil law because we are talking of those principles that guide *all* our actions toward the achievement of ends befitting what-it-means-to-be-human, including therefore the ends of civil society but going beyond them. What this highlights for us is the *private context* in which "right" has a profound meaning that civil law does not touch. It, too, is a guide as to what is to be done toward another, such as showing respect, marital fidelity, keeping one's word, loving one's children. One who does these things is observing the moral law and can be called "just." In our everyday conversation we don't use the word *just* in this way, preferring the word *right*, thus the person who shows respect is faithful in marriage, keeps his word, loves his children, and is doing the "right" thing. As we've seen, it is this disposition, or habit, permanently abiding in the person to do the right thing toward another, that is referred to as the *virtue of justice* (R #2 and #3).

In a public context, there is a reciprocity in civil law between the citizen and society: a citizen does the "right" thing by observing the law because he is rendering society what is its due; at the same time the law guarantees the rights of each individual citizen, so that society can be spoken of as rendering what is due him by law. But it is quite possible for the law to come up short of its purpose when it does not take into account the actual state of public affairs. Thomas Hobbes had this in mind when he observed that inasmuch as it is authority that makes the law, not truth, it's possible for a law to have defects and even injustices if it does not reflect the real state of affairs which, for him, is the truth. It's possible, then, for a given law to contravene the truth and, to that extent, be unjust, such as a law forbidding marriage between black and white persons. Truth, in this case moral truth, sits in judgment on civil law.

Prudence

We call a person *prudent* who is careful in making his decisions; who is circumspect in his actions; who manages a balanced judgment in sensitive situations; who exercises caution in taking risks. Prudence is exhibited in the architect's choice of design, a mother's nutritional plan for her family, a hiker's selection of the safest trail up the mountain, an investor's weighing of the stock market. Think of any course of action, and there you'll find prudence at work, telling you to do it, avoid it, or simply to try it provisionally. It is the precondition of all the virtues in that if the conditions discerned by prudence are not met, then the action is not a virtuous one. Prudence differs from the other cardinal virtues and, in a sense, is more of an intellectual virtue than a moral one, but it is so closely allied with the moral virtues as we've been discussing them that, for the most part, it has been considered as the traditional fourth moral virtue. The difference lies in the fact that the other cardinal virtues pertain to different *classes* of moral activity, whereas prudence pertains to them all: temperance is the doing of a temperate act, but prudence discloses why it's temperate; courage is the doing of a courageous act, but prudence discloses why it's courageous; justice is the doing of a just act, but prudence discloses why it's just. Prudence is the golden key to virtue, for without it no other virtue stands. It is the breathing system that gives life to virtue.

Looking back to our treatment on the need for *judgment* as to the morality of an act, we'll recall how it entails the need for an understanding of the goal and texture of the act, and why such understanding is referred to as wisdom. Prudence is wisdom, but a wisdom in practice, a *practical wisdom* in that, amid complications and hidden entanglements of every sort, it recognizes the uniqueness of a situation, the people involved, feelings displayed, emotions stirred up, consequences likely to ensue, personal cost, and takes them into account to arrive at a balanced judgment. Aristotle put it in words we've seen before, "to feel them at the right times, with reference to the right objects, towards the right people, with the right motive, and in the right way" (R #4 and #5).

Interestingly, there must be something on the feminine side of human nature to explain why it is that in literature, wisdom is always referred to as a woman. In *Proverbs* "Wisdom raises her voice, she cries aloud on the walls of the city, and at the city gates." For Parmenides, it was the "goddess of light" who ushered the wayfarer into the realm of Truth. For Socrates, it was the mysterious Lady of Mantineia who disclosed the meaning of true wisdom. For Boethius, Lady Wisdom is the true philosopher. And for Dante, it is Beatrice who is his guide to paradise.

To these four cardinal virtues, knowable of themselves, medieval theologians added three more, traditionally referred to as the three cardinal *theological* virtues: *faith, hope,* and *charity.* Though "theological," it serves a purpose to mention them here because they show how the notion of virtue can be extended to shed light on its deeper meaning. *Faith* is the enduring readiness to believe whatever has been revealed; *hope,* the abiding confidence that one will receive whatever is needful to lead a good life and to achieve ultimate happiness; *charity,* or *love,* the abiding personal union with another, culminating in the person-to-Person union with the divine. That love is the virtue on which the meaning of the universe depends, it would be worthwhile to reread Chapter 4.

VICE

Up to now we have been making a distinction between an *act* that is good and a *virtue* (*habit*) that disposes us to it, between, let's say, an individual act of charity and the virtue of charity. But virtue has an opposite, namely *vice*: just as virtue is a habit disposing us to acts that are good, so vice is a habit disposing us to acts that are bad— evil, immoral, wrong, or traditionally *sinful.* Here, as in other instances, we've seen of popular usage of moral terms, the distinction between "sin" and "vice," between the act and the habit, is not often acknowledged, so it's not unusual to hear phrases like "pride is a sin" instead of "pride is a vice"; though the distinction is not generally clear, the moral world remains quite undisturbed! Vices, like virtues, are numberless, but just as tradition has sensed that there are four main categories of virtue, the "cardinal" virtues, so it has sensed that there are seven main vices, variously called *capital vices, capital sins,* or even *deadly sins*: pride, avarice, lust, envy, gluttony, anger, and sloth (if you like mnemonics, try "pale gas"). Let's say a word about each (R #6).

Pride

We can be brought up sharp in being told that pride is a vice, especially when we expect a person to take "pride" in his work; or when we rebuke a person for not standing up for himself with the words "have you no pride?" And we are not all surprised that an engineer working in the bush would take pride in the water system he has just built for a barren village, or that parents would be proud of their daughter's achievement in school. So there is a "proper pride" we can and ought to have in those values that make life more livable, a pride Aristotle points to as lying midway between "empty vanity" and "undue humility." But there are times when a show of qualities or possessions is an effort on the part of a person who, consciously or not, is trying to entice recognition of superiority from another, or to "lord it over" him; if those qualities or possessions are really had, then the possessor is demeaning the other for not having them; if they are not really had, then the would-be possessor is laying out a false claim, hoping to advance himself by belittling the other. In cases like these, in which honor, or praise, is sought for itself, a more appropriate word might be "vainglory" rather than "pride," for "vainglory" signifies self-seeking for empty grandeur. Thus it is the vainglorious meaning of pride, the self-centered glorification, that is condemned in the traditional catalog of vices and is the reason why theologians like Augustine and Aquinas, reflecting on the biblical fall of Lucifer after straining to be like God, would agree that pride is "the head and origin of all evil" and is "the beginning of every sin" (*City of God,* xiv, 3, *Summa theol.* II-II, 34, 2, c).

Avarice

Avarice, also called greed or covetousness, though it can refer to any good whatsoever, usually refers to the immoderate desire for money, riches, or temporal goods. "Immoderate desire" is an elastic concept because it's hard to show what immoderate limits are. But we do know that something is amiss when one seeks wealth to the detriment of values he is bound to observe, such as duties to spouse or family, or care of his health, or personal obligations to others. Greed, by definition, knows no limits and elicits a fixation that is its own drive toward endless acquisition. Though this can be found in anyone of any economic class, it is particularly visible in those striving for wealth, as seen in many public cases of the past score of years in which every manipulation and secret device were used to enlarge their holdings as though wealth were life's only goal, a contemporary example of Aristotle's fear that "wealth becomes the standard of value for everything else" (1391a1).

Lust

The word *lust*, in earlier English, was used in the sense of unqualified pleasure or desire, with the later qualification of "passionate"; in its current use, for the most part, it means "passionate sexual desire." The last chapter presented an extended treatment of sexual love, of love as a virtue; the vice opposite love is referred to as "lust," whence an apt definition of *lust* is: *the disordered desire for sexual pleasure.* Its meaning bears not on its being overmuch, but on its being contrary to moral integrity. Desire is a natural movement toward a good, so sexual desire, in itself, is naturally good, but it becomes disordered, and therefore lust, if that desire can only be fulfilled contrary to the other's will, capacity, or personal commitments.

Lust, like vices in general, is a disordering of a natural faculty, making its first appearance on the individual scale of one person's desire for another. But in our day, it goes far beyond the individual scale to a larger scale of ugliness found in the national and international tracking of women to satisfy the sexual desire of men, which can only be described as sexual enslavement. The unspeakable barbarity of kidnapping young girls to groom them into prostitution is not only a crime, but a sin against the humanity of the youth of our society on the part of inhuman predators.

Envy

Envy, or jealousy, in Shakespeare's words, is a monster: "O! beware my lord, of jealousy;/It is the green-eyed monster which doth mock/The meat it feeds on." (*Othello*, III, 3 1)—envy is self-destructive of the very person who is envious. Without question, each of us has felt a slight sting or a bit of distress—Aristotle calls it pain— at the success or good fortune of another, a promotion, a public word of praise, admission to an elite college, prowess in a sport, usually on the part of someone we know, even a friend, perhaps seeking the same things we are. Envy arises, not so much because we want what others have for ourselves but merely because they have it; what they have, and we don't, is interpreted as lessening us. If allowed to run its course, it veers toward hatred, as it did with Joseph's brothers as they sold him into Egypt.

Gluttony

Just as lust is a disorder regarding the natural good of sex for the preservation of life for the species, so gluttony is a disorder regarding the natural good of food and drink for the preservation of the life of the individual. It's a paradox that, in a culture constantly reminding us of the danger of over-eating or eating certain foods, and the danger of drinking certain drinks, especially alcoholic, that we must still talk about vice in consuming them: that natural needs are open to abuse is an irony we've learned to live with. But the measure of need is precisely the role of temperance, that is, the reasonable control of the quantity and quality consumed. It's unreasonable to think that food or drink known to be injurious to one's health should be taken in any sizable amount. The abuse of alcoholic drink, for example, quickly impairs one's faculty of self-control, a fact grimly confirmed in the daily papers.

Anger

When it comes to speaking of anger, we first recognize it as an emotion or passion, an unsought and immediate bodily response to a situation we perceive as causing irritation or pain. At this level, anger is perfectly normal and morally indifferent. If the cause of anger is really of minor moment your appointment is late, or your friend failed to return a notebook helpful for an exam—a little patience restores equanimity; if the cause is really grave—a person swindled out of his or her life's savings, or a spouse killed by a drunken driver—anger is not only understandable but is what Aristotle calls "righteous." Anger as a vice enters the picture when the response is out of all proportion, as beating another to a pulp who accidentally stepped on your toe; or when the cause of the pain is used as an excuse for "getting even," or for vengeance, as when a jilted fiancé kills his fiancée exclaiming "if I can't have her no one else can either." On a personal level, perhaps the worst kind of anger is the anger one feels at some good thing happening to another, like an increase of salary or praise for a job well done, in which case it would be the eruption of jealousy into hatred.

There are some who would argue that anger is one of the greatest causes of sorrow and turmoil in the world, for the consequences of anger in the form of rage or wrath on the part of an individual, or of many at the same time, can be enormous. As early as the first Greek epic, Homer's opening line is the theme of the *Iliad*, "Sing, 0 Muse, of the rage of Achilles," and so . . . on to the Trojan War. History has shown, right down to the present day, how anger can generate frenzy beyond any semblance of rational control, to pit ethnic or religious groups against each other, and to drive parliaments to adopt measures in which sanity has little part. In the first century, the Roman Stoic, Seneca, devotes a lengthy moral essay *On Anger* to the horrors of unrestrained anger, likening it to temporary insanity and then paints a grim picture of the violence that anger can stir up: "If you want to see the results, the damage, that anger has wrought you will find no plague more harmful to mankind than anger. You will see bloodshed and poisoning . . . the destruction of whole cities and nations, whole areas set aflame . . . anger stabbed one in his own room, struck down another during a sacred ritual, speared another within the law as a spectacle in the forum, commanded a son to spill his own father's blood . . . and look at, if you care to, entire groups cut down by the sword, and people whacked to pieces by soldiers or brought to ruin by wholesale condemnation."

Sloth

In a wide sense, all of us have felt a certain lassitude in getting around to do the things we expect to do, a kind of slowness or foot-dragging because they require some effort we're not ready to give. It's a burden, a labor we don't want to face just yet, so we put it off. We recognize it when we postpone replacing that broken window, or for frivolous reasons never getting around to studying for that tough exam, or putting off writing that get-well card to a sick friend. But there is a far deeper level at which sloth has a more significant moral or spiritual meaning, and that is as a lethargy in, or an apathy against, doing the right thing; it's an unarticulated sense of weariness with life, a nagging feeling that life is not worth living. Giving up is easier than living up. The French polymath of the seventeenth century, Blaise Pascal, put it this way: "Nothing is as unbearable for man as to be completely without interests, without passion, without activity, without diversion, without study. That's when he feels his nothingness, his loneliness, his insufficiency, his dependence, his weakness" (*Pensees*, #131). So, inasmuch as sloth designates unconcern with the overall goodness of life, its antidote is the virtue that stands as its opposite, namely, love, which, together with its essential constituents of goodness and happiness, is the key to the meaning of man (R #7).

THE DEFINITION OF A GOOD PERSON

Granting that moral philosophy aims at discovering what there is about our acts that persuade us to call them good, it's arguable that to make a person good is not its immediate goal: to know good, and to do it, are distinctly different activities. But, even if the immediate goal of moral philosophy is not to make a person good, it is intimately bound up with it. Abstractly, a person may be a good moralist without being a good person, just as one may be a good mathematician or a military strategist without being a good person. But in practical terms it's impossible to understand how a good moralist could fail to see in his philosophizing the imperative for leading a good life. In this sense, Socrates was absolutely right in insisting that knowledge of the good is barren unless it puts forth a good life. At first it would seem that the most natural way to bring this about is to adopt the blueprint approach, that is, we can take the image, or package of qualities, of the good person already present in our minds and use it to measure our acts. Isn't this what Plato recommended to us, to contemplate the "idea of man," whose perfect essence is discernible in the World of Ideas, and then use it to shape our lives to fit the world we live in? It seems to be a simple approach, and the one who adopts it can be confident that it offers a consistent guide to a good life. But Plato himself knew that such a blueprint was not given to us directly, that we had to rise to it as in Diotima's invitation to rise to the higher world through the lower one around us. What Plato, top-down thinker par excellence, was trying to do in advising us to contemplate the "idea-l" world was to emphasize the priority of the transcendent in our lives, for it is the transcendent that gives meaning to the here-and-now.

Aristotle agrees with his mentor, that we act out of an idea, or blueprint, of the good person; but the idea of a good person, which is transcendental or metaphysical in meaning, has to be arrived at through experience, and as our experience expands and reacts to changes in the course of time, so does our idea of the good person. Acting out of an idea of man is just as important for Aristotle as it is for Plato but, for his part, Aristotle wants to emphasize the temporal priority of the experiential to guarantee the metaphysical priority of the transcendental: no experience, no idea.

Because of the relationship between the transcendental and the experiential, the higher and the lower, the lasting and the here-and-now, the blueprint approach can begin to make some sense. We would never call a person a "good person" because of the rare instances of good they've done: the doctor who is curt and short with his patients even though once in a great while he treats them as human beings, the manager who sends shock waves throughout the office when he finally gives a word of praise to his secretary, or the plain man who seldom has a kind word to say of another. On the contrary, what we expect is a consistency of action consonant with the human context in which the actions are done and adapted to the particularities of the individuals we are destined to be with. We realize that, in speaking of a "good person," we are not speaking of a person as a mere collection of the good acts he or she has performed, as though the acts are unrelated to each other, but as they are coherent expressions of an inner core in which they are held together, a permanent character serving as their source and center of unity.

From a philosophical point of view, what we are actually trying to do is to apply the epistemological principle that we come to know what things *are* by what they *do*: if a thing *does* such and such, then it must *be* such and such. If the unknown specimen lives and moves, it must, we say, be an animal; if the sample of crystal behaves this way and not that, it must be sugar, and not salt. If a person does things that are thoughtful, respectful, sympathetic, charitable, gentle, polite, generous, just, compassionate, tolerant, full of good faith and humor, then of course we rightly conclude that he or she is precisely what he or she *does*. Without forcing ourselves, we naturally tend to conclude that one's actions, over time, are a recognizable extension of one's *person* that they reveal an internal portrait of the individual which we can reasonably accept as the wellspring of the actions we admire. As we saw above, it's a narrow vision of morality to say that a good person is but the sum total of all their good actions, for that casts a shadow of the quantitative on the meaning of morality. Rather does it make sense to say that the good person displays a *total disposition* to do the right thing whatever it is, to feel it, once again in Aristotle's words, "at the right times, with reference to the right objects, towards the right people, with the right motive, and in the right way."

To show respect for the humanity of others comes as close as we can to a definition of the good person. It involves the sensitivities in all those private and public relationships that arise in the course of everyone's life, so the good person is careful of not hurting another, not imputing motives, and not insinuating evil or malevolence. Conversation is recognized for what it should be, a friendly exchange, open to pleasantries and matters of importance equally but always avoiding the pitfalls of irritation; debate is the laying out of one's opinions without denying the good faith dissent of the other. The deliberate attempt to stir up opinions you can clash with, to damage feelings, to nurse suspicions, or to feed embarrassment are outside the pale of the good person. To provide for the comfort of others, to be generous without being mean-spirited, to be ready to extend favors without expecting recompense, to be firm without being overbearing, to be gentle without agitation, to be decisive without being dogmatic, to be gentle without being coy, to be just without being pharisaical, to be compassionate without being maudlin, to be sincere without the taint of arrogance, and to be loving without counting the cost—all these are signs of the good person for whom the life of virtue is truly identified with "understanding morality" (R #8).

READINGS

READING 1
A Preface to Virtue
Andre Comte-Sponville
(from *A Small Treatise on the Great Virtues*)

What is a virtue? It is a force that has or can have an effect. Hence the virtue of a plant or a medication, which is to cure, or of a knife, which is to cut, or of a human being, which is to will and to act in a human way. These examples, which come from the Greeks, say more or less what is essential: virtue is a capacity or power, and always a specific one. The virtue of hellebore is not that of hemlock; a knife's virtue is not that of the hoe; man's virtue is not that of the tiger or the snake. The virtue of a thing or being is what constitutes its value, in other words, its distinctive excellence: the good knife is the one that excels at cutting, the good medicine at curing, the good poison at killing . . .

If every being or thing has its specific capacity in which it excels or can excel (the excellent knife, the excellent medicine), we might well ask what man's distinctive excellence resides in.

. . .

It is a man's virtue that makes him human, or rather it is this specific capacity he has to affirm his own excellence, which is to say, his humanity, in the normative sense. Human, never too human. Virtue is a way of being, Aristotle explained, but an acquired and lasting way of being: it is what we are (and therefore what we can do), and what we are is what we have become. And how could we have become what we are without other human beings? Virtue thus represents an encounter between biological evolution and cultural development; it is our way of being and acting humanly, in other words (since humanity, in this sense, is a value), our power to act *well.* "Nothing is so fine and so justifiable," wrote Montaigne, "as to play the man well and duly." To do so is virtue itself.

· · ·

In the general sense, virtue is capacity; in the particular sense, it is human capacity, the power to be human.

· · ·

Every virtue is a summit between two vices, a crest between two chasms: hence courage stands between cowardice and temerity, dignity between servility and selfishness, gentleness between anger and apathy, and so on. But who can dwell on the high summits all the time? To think about the virtues is to take measure of the distance separating us from them. To think about their excellence is to think about our own inadequacies or wretchedness. It's a first step— possibly all we can ask of a book. The rest we must live, and how can a book do that for us? I do not mean to say that thinking about the virtues is useless or of no moral consequence. Thinking about the virtues will not make us virtuous, or, in any case, is not enough in itself to make us so. But there is one virtue it does develop, and that virtue is humility—intellectual humility in the face of the richness of the material and the tradition, and a properly moral humility as well, before the obvious fact that we are almost always deficient in nearly all the virtue and yet cannot resign ourselves to their absence or exonerate ourselves for their weakness, which is our own.

READING 2
Virtue and the Highest Good
Plato
(from *Laws*)

ATHENIAN. "Friends," we say to them—"God, as the old tradition declares, holding in His hand the beginning, middle, and end of all that is, travels according to His nature in a straight line towards the accomplishment of His end. Justice always accompanies Him, and is the punisher of those who fall short of the divine law. To justice, he who would be happy holds fast, and follows in her company with all humility and order; but he who is lifted up with pride, or elated by wealth or rank, or beauty, who is young and foolish, and has a soul hot with insolence, and thinks that he has no need of any guide or ruler, but is able himself to be the guide of others, he, I say, is left deserted of God; and being thus deserted, he takes to him others who are like himself, and dances about, throwing all things into confusion, and many think that he is a great man, but in a short time he pays a penalty which justice cannot but approve, and is utterly destroyed, and his family and city with him. Wherefore, seeing that human things are thus ordered, what should a wise man do or think, or not do or think?"

CLEINIAS. Every man ought to make up his mind that he will be one of the followers of God; there can be no doubt of that.

ATH. Then what life is agreeable to God, and becoming in His followers? One only, expressed once for all in the old saying that "like agrees with like, with measure measure," but things which have no measure agree neither with themselves nor with the things which have. Now God ought to be to us the measure of all things, and not man, as men commonly say (Protagoras) the words are far more true of Him. And he who would be dear to God must, as far as is possible, be like Him and such as He is. Wherefore the temperate man is the friend of God, for he is like Him; and the intemperate man is unlike Him, and different from Him, and unjust. And the same applies to other things; and this is the conclusion, which is also the noblest and truest of all sayings,—that for the good man to offer sacrifice to the Gods, and hold converse with them by means of prayers and offerings and every kind of service, is the noblest and best of all things, and also the most conducive to a happy life, and very fit and meet. But with the bad man, the opposite of this is true: for the bad man has an impure soul, whereas the good is pure; and from one who is polluted, neither a good man nor God can without impropriety receive gifts. Wherefore the unholy do only waste their much service upon the Gods, but when offered by any holy man, such service is most acceptable to them. This is the mark at which we ought to aim. But what weapons shall we use, and how shall we direct them? In the first place, we affirm that next after the Olympian Gods and the Gods of the State, honour should be given to the Gods below; they should receive everything in even numbers, and of the second choice, and ill omen, while the odd numbers, and the first choice, and the things of lucky omen, are given to the Gods above, by him who would rightly hit the mark of piety. Next to these Gods, a wise man will do service to the demons or spirits, and then to the heroes, and after them will follow the private and ancestral Gods, who are worshipped as the law prescribes in the places which are sacred to them. Next comes the honour of living parents, to whom, as is meet, we have to pay the first and greatest and oldest of all debts, considering that all which a man has belongs to those who gave him birth and brought him up, and that he must do all that he can to minister to them, first, in his property,

secondly, in his person, and thirdly, in his soul, in return for the endless care and travail which they bestowed upon him of old, in the days of his infancy, and which he is now to pay back to them when they are old and in the extremity of their need. And all his life long he ought never to utter, or to have uttered, an unbecoming word to them; for of light and fleeting words the penalty is most severe; Nemesis, the messenger of justice, is appointed to watch over all such matters. When they are angry and want to satisfy their feelings in word or deed, he should give way to them; for a father who thinks that he has been wronged by his son may be reasonably expected to be very angry. At their death, the most moderate funeral is best, neither exceeding the customary expense, nor yet falling short of the honour which has been usually shown by the former generation to their parents. And let a man not forget to pay the yearly tribute of respect to the dead, honouring them chiefly by omitting nothing that conduces to a perpetual remembrance of them, and giving a reasonable portion of his fortune to the dead. Doing this, and living after this manner, we shall receive our reward from the Gods and those who are above us [i.e. the demons]; and we shall spend our days for the most part in good hope. And how a man ought to order what relates to his descendants and his kindred and friends and fellow-citizens, and the rites of hospitality taught by Heaven, and the intercourse which arises out of all these duties, with a view to the embellishment and orderly regulation of his own life— these things, I say, the laws, as we proceed with them, will accomplish, partly persuading, and partly when natures do not yield to the persuasion of custom, chastising them by might and right, and will thus render our state, if the Gods co-operate with us, prosperous and happy.

READING 3
Small Inhumanities?
Nicolay Gogol
(from *The Overcoat*)

When and at what time Akaky Akakievich entered the department and who appointed him, this no one could recall. However often directors and all sorts of superiors were changed, he was always seen at one and the

same place, in the same position, in the same post, the same copying clerk, so that later they were convinced that he, evidently, was born into this world already entirely finished, in a uniform and with a bald spot on his head.

In the department he was shown no respect whatsoever. The porters not only did not get up from their places when he passed by, but didn't even glance at him, as if a simple fly had flown through the reception hall. Superiors treated him some-how coldly and despotically. Some department head's assistant would thrust papers right under his nose, not saying even: "Copy it," or, "Here's a nice little interesting case," or something pleasant, as is done in well-bred offices. And he would take it, looking only at the paper, not noticing who presented it to him and whether he had the right to. He would take it and right away get set to copy it. The young clerks laughed at him and made jokes about him to the degree that clerk wit permitted; right in front of him they told various stories that had been made up about him; about his landlady, a seventy-year-old lady, they said she beat him, asked when their wedding would be, scattered bits of paper on his head, calling it snow.

But not one word would Akaky Akakievich answer to this, just as if nobody were in front of him; it didn't even affect his work: among all these annoyances he would not make a single mistake in writing. Only when the joke was too unbearable, when they jogged his elbow, keeping him from doing his work, he would say: "Leave me alone, why do you insult me?" And something strange was contained in the words and in the voice in which they were pronounced. In it resounded something so evoking of pity that one recently appointed young man who, by the example of the others, was on the verge of permitting himself to laugh at Akaky, suddenly stopped as if transfixed, and from that time on it was as if everything had changed for him and appeared in another form. Some preternatural force alienated him from the comrades he had become acquainted with, having taken them for decent, well-bred people. And long after, at the gaiest moments, the short little clerk with the bald spot on top would appear to him with his penetrating words: "Leave me alone, why do you insult me?" And in these penetrating words rang other words: "I am your brother." And the poor young man would cover his face with his hands, and many times later in his life he would shudder, seeing how much inhumanity there is in man, how much fierce coarseness is hidden in refined educated breeding, and God! even in the very man whom the world deems noble and honorable.

READING 4
Practical Wisdom
Aristotle
(from *Ethics*)

We may ascertain the nature of prudence, or practical wisdom, by considering who are the people whom we call prudent.

It seems to be characteristic of the prudent man to be capable of deliberating well upon what is good or expedient for himself, and that not in a particular sense, e.g. upon the means of health or strength, but generally upon the means of living well. This view derives support from the fact that we go so far as to speak of people who deliberate well in some particular line as "prudent," when their calculations are successfully directed to some good end, if it is such as does not fall within the scope of art. It may be said generally then that a person who is successful in deliberation is prudent.

But nobody deliberates upon such matters as are incapable of alteration, or upon such as lie beyond his own power of action.

Now science implies demonstration, and demonstration is impossible in matters where the first principles are variable *and not necessary*; for all the results of such principles are variable. On the other hand such things as are necessary do not admit of deliberation. It follows then that prudence cannot be a science or an art—not a science, because the sphere of action is variable and not an art, because *all art is productive and* action is generally different from production. It remains therefore that prudence should be a true rational and practical state of mind in the field of human good and evil; for while the end of production is different from the production itself, it is not so with action, as right action is itself an end. It is in this view that we consider Pericles and people like him to be prudent, as having the capacity of observing what is good for themselves and for mankind; and this is our conception of such persons as are successful in administering a household or a State. This too is the reason why we call temperance by its name *(sophrosyne)*, as being preservative of prudence. It is prudential opinion that temperance preserves, for pleasure and pain do not destroy or distort every opinion; they do not e.g. destroy or distort the opinion that the angles of a triangle are, or are not, equal to two right angles, but only such opinions as relate to practice. For

the first principles of actions are the ends for which actions are done; but no sooner is a person corrupted by pleasure or pain than he loses sight of the principle, he forgets that this ought to be the object or motive of all his choice and action, as vice is destructive of principle. We conclude then that prudence must be a true rational state of mind which is active in the field of human goods.

It must be added that, while art admits of excellence, prudence does not, and that, while in art voluntary error is preferable to involuntary, in the case of prudence, as of the virtues generally, it is worse. It is clear then that prudence is a virtue or excellence and not an art.

As there are two parts of the soul in rational beings, prudence will be the virtue of one of them, viz. of the part which opines; for the sphere of prudence as of opinion is that which is variable. At the same time it is something more than a rational state of mind, as may be inferred from the fact that, while such a state may be lost by forgetfulness, prudence can not be so lost.

READING 5
Moral Virtue and the Mean
Aristotle

(from *Ethics*)

6. The nature of virtue has been now generically described. But it is not enough to state merely that virtue is a moral state, we must also describe the character of that moral state.

It must be laid down then that every virtue or excellence has the effect of producing a good condition of that of which it is a virtue or excellence, and of enabling it to perform its function well. Thus the excellence of the eye makes the eye good and its function good, as it is by the excellence of the eye that we see well. Similarly, the excellence of the horse makes a horse excellent and good at racing, at carrying its rider and at facing the enemy. If then this is universally true, the virtue or excellence of man will be such a moral state as makes a man good and able to perform his

proper function well. We have already explained how this will be the case, but another way of making it clear will be to study the nature or character of this virtue.

Now in everything, whether it be continuous or discrete, it is possible to take a greater, a smaller, or an equal amount, and this either absolutely or in relation to ourselves, the equal being a mean between excess and deficiency. By the mean in respect of the thing itself, or the absolute mean, I understand that which is equally distinct from both extremes: and this is one and the same thing for everybody. By the mean considered relatively to ourselves I understand that which is neither too much nor too little; but this is not one thing, nor is it the same for everybody. Thus if 10 be too much and 2 too little we take 6 as a mean in respect of the thing itself; for 6 is as much greater than 2 as it is less than 10, and this is a mean in arithmetical proportion. But the mean considered relatively to ourselves must not be ascertained in this way. It does not follow that if 10 pounds *of meat* be too much add 2 be too little for a man to eat, a trainer will order him 6 pounds, as this may itself be too much or too little for the person who is to take it; it will be too little e.g. for Milo, but too much for a beginner in gymnastics. It will be the same with running and wrestling; *the right amount will vary with the individual*. This being so, everybody who understands his business avoids alike excess and deficiency; he seeks and chooses the mean, not the absolute mean, but the mean considered relatively to ourselves.

Every science then performs its function well, if it regards the mean and refers the works which it produces to the mean. This is the reason why it is usually said of successful works that it is impossible to take anything from them or to add anything to them, which implies that excess or deficiency is fatal to excellence but that the mean state ensures it. Good artists too, as we say, have an eye to the mean in their works. But virtue, like Nature herself, is more accurate and better than any art; virtue therefore will aim at the mean—I speak of moral virtue, as it is moral virtue which is concerned with emotions and actions, and it is these which admit of excess and deficiency and the mean. Thus it is possible to go too far, or not to go far enough, in respect of fear, courage, desire, anger, pity, and, pleasure and pain generally, and the excess and the deficiency are alike wrong; but to experience these emotions at the right times and on the right occasions and towards the right persons and for the right causes and in the right manner is the mean or the supreme good, which is characteristic of virtue. Similarly there may be excess, deficiency, or the, mean, in regard to actions. But virtue is concerned with emotions and actions, and here excess is an error and deficiency a fault, whereas the mean is successful and, laudable, and success and merit are both characteristics of virtue.

It appears then that virtue is a mean state, so far at least as it aims at the mean.

Again, there are many different ways of going wrong; for evil is in its nature infinite, to use the Pythagorean figure, but good is finite. But there is only one possible way of going right. Accordingly the former is easy and the latter difficult; it is easy to miss the mark but difficult to hit it. This again is a reason why excess and deficiency are characteristics of vice and the mean state a characteristic of virtue.

"For good is simple, evil manifold."

Virtue then is a state of deliberate moral purpose consisting in a mean that is relative to ourselves, the mean being determined by reason, or as a prudent man would determine it.

It is a mean state *firstly as lying* between two vices, the vice of excess on the one hand, and the vice of deficiency on the other, and secondly because, whereas the vices either fall short of or go beyond what is proper in the emotions and actions, virtue not only discovers but embraces the mean.

Accordingly, virtue, if regarded in its essence or theoretical conception, is a mean state, but, if regarded from the point of view of the highest good, or of excellence, it is an extreme.

But it is not every action or every emotion that admits of a mean state. There are some whose very name implies wickedness, as e.g. malice, shamelessness, and envy, among emotions, or adultery, theft, and murder, among actions. All these, and others like them, are censured as being intrinsically wicked, not merely the excesses or deficiencies of them. It is never possible then to be right in respect of them; they are always sinful. Right or wrong in such actions as adultery does not depend on our committing them with the right person, at the right time or in the right manner; on the contrary it is sinful to do anything of the kind at all. It would be equally wrong then to suppose that there can be a mean state or an excess or deficiency in unjust, cowardly or licentious conduct; for, if it were so, there would be a mean state of an excess or of a deficiency, an excess of an excess and a deficiency of a deficiency. But as in temperance and courage there can be no excess or deficiency because the mean is, in a sense, an extreme, so too in these cases there cannot be a mean or an excess or deficiency, but, however the acts may be done, they are wrong. For it is a general rule that an excess or deficiency does not admit of a mean state, nor a mean state of an excess or deficiency.

7. But it is not enough to lay down this as a general rule; it is necessary to apply it to particular cases, as in reasonings upon actions general statements, although they are broader, are less exact than particular statements. For all action refers to particulars, and it is essential that our theories should harmonize with the particular cases to which they apply.

We must take particular virtues then from the catalogue *of virtues*.

In regard to feelings of fear and confidence, courage is a mean state. On the side of excess, he whose fearlessness is excessive has no name, as often happens, but he whose confidence is excessive is foolhardy, while he whose timidity is excessive and whose confidence is deficient is a coward.

In respect of pleasures and pains, although not indeed of all pleasures and pains, and to a less extent in respect of pains than of pleasures, the mean state is temperance, the excess is licentiousness. We never find people who are deficient in regard to pleasures; accordingly such people again have not received a name, but we may call them insensible.

As regards the giving and taking of money, the mean state is liberality, the excess and deficiency are prodigality and illiberality. Here the excess and deficiency take opposite forms; for while the prodigal man is excessive in spending and deficient in taking, the illiberal man is excessive in taking and deficient in spending.

(For the present we are giving only a rough and summary account *of the virtues*, and that is sufficient for our purpose; we will hereafter determine their character more exactly.)

In respect of money there are other dispositions as well. There is the mean state which is magnificence; for the magnificent man, as having to do with large sums of money, differs from the liberal man who has to do only with small sums; and the excess *corresponding to it* is bad taste or vulgarity, the deficiency is meanness. These are different from the excess and deficiency of liberality; what the difference is will be explained hereafter.

In respect of honour and dishonour the mean state is highmindedness, the excess is what is called vanity, the deficiency littlemindedness. Corresponding to liberality, which, as we said, differs from magnificence as having to do *not with great but* with small sums of money, there is a moral state which has to do with petty honour and is related to highmindedness which has to do with great honour; for it is possible to aspire to honour in the right way, or in a way which is excessive, or insufficient, and if a person's aspirations are excessive, he is called ambitious, if they are deficient, he is called unambitious, while if they are between the two, he has no name. The dispositions too are nameless, except that the disposition of the ambitious person is called ambition. The consequence is that the extremes lay claim to the mean or intermediate place. We ourselves speak of one who observes the mean sometimes as ambitious, and at other times as unambitious; we sometimes praise an ambitious, and at other times an unambitious person. The reason for our doing so will be stated in due course, but let us now discuss the other virtues in accordance with the method which we have followed hitherto.

Anger, like other emotions, has its excess, its deficiency, and its mean state. It may be said that they have no names, but as we call one who observes the mean gentle, we will call the mean state gentleness. Among the extremes, if a person errs on the side of excess, he may be called passionate and his vice passionateness, if on that of deficiency, he may be called impassive and his deficiency impassivity.

There are also three other mean states with a certain resemblance to each other, and yet with a difference. For while they are all concerned with intercourse in speech and action, they are different in that one of them is concerned with truth in such intercourse, and the others with pleasantness, one with pleasantness in amusement and the other with pleasantness in the various circumstances of life. We must therefore discuss these states in order to make it clear that in all cases it is the mean state which is an object of praise, and the extremes are neither right nor laudable but censurable. It is true that these mean and extreme states are generally nameless, but we must do our best here as elsewhere to give them a name, so that our argument may be clear and easy to follow.

In the matter of truth then, he who observes the mean may be called truthful, and the mean state truthfulness. Pretence, if it takes the form of exaggeration, is boastfulness, and one who is guilty of pretence is a boaster; but if it takes the form of depreciation it is irony, and he who is guilty of it is ironical.

As regards pleasantness in amusement, he who observes the mean is witty, and his disposition wittiness; the excess is buffoonery, and he who is guilty of it a buffoon, whereas he who is deficient in wit may be called a boor and his moral state boorishness.

As to the other kind of pleasantness, viz. pleasantness in life, he who is pleasant in a proper way is friendly, and his mean state friendliness; but he who goes too far, if he has no ulterior object in view, is obsequious, while if his object is self interest, he is a flatterer, and he who does not go far enough and always makes himself unpleasant is a quarrelsome and morose sort of person.

There are also mean states in the emotions and in the expression of the emotions. For although modesty is not a virtue, yet a modest person is praised as if he were virtuous; for here too one person is said to observe the mean and another to exceed it, as e.g. the bashful man who is never anything but modest, whereas a person who has insufficient modesty or no modesty at all is called shameless, and one who observes the mean modest.

Righteous indignation, again, is a mean state between envy and malice. They are all concerned with the pain and pleasure which we feel at the fortunes of our neighbours. A person who is righteously indignant is pained at the prosperity of the undeserving; but the envious person goes further and is pained at anybody's prosperity, and the malicious person is so far from being pained that he actually rejoices *at misfortunes*.

We shall have another opportunity however of discussing these matters. But in regard to justice, as the word is used in various senses, we will afterwards define those senses and explain how each of them is a mean state. And we will follow the same course with the intellectual virtues.

READING 6
On Different Kinds of Vice

Thomas Aquinas

(from *Summa theologiae*, I-II, 84)

Under this head there are four points of inquiry: (1) Whether covetousness is the root of all sins? (2) Whether pride is the beginning of every sin? (3) Whether other special sins should be called capital vices, besides pride and covetousness? (4) How many capital vices there are, and which are they?

FIRST ARTICLE

Whether Covetousness Is the Root of All Sins?

According to some, covetousness may be understood in different ways.—First, as denoting inordinate desire for riches: and thus it is a special sin.—Secondly, as denoting inordinate desire for any temporal good: and thus it is a genus comprising all sins, because every sin includes an inordinate turning to a mutable good, as stated above (Q. 72, A. 2).—Thirdly, as denoting an inclination of a corrupt nature to desire corruptible goods inordinately: and they say that in this sense covetousness is the root of all sins, comparing it to the root of a tree, which draws its sustenance from earth, just as every sin grows out of the love of temporal things.

Now, though all this is true, it does not seem to explain the mind of the Apostle when he states that covetousness is the root of all sins. For in that passage he clearly speaks against those who, because they *will become rich, fall into temptation, and into the snare of the devil . . . for covetousness is the root of all evils.* Hence it is evident that he is speaking of covetousness as denoting the inordinate desire for riches. Accordingly, we must say that covetousness, as denoting a special sin, is called the root of all sins, in likeness to the root of a tree, in furnishing sustenance to the whole tree. For we see that by riches man acquires the means of committing any sin whatever, and of sating his desire for any sin whatever, since money helps man to obtain all manner of temporal goods, according to Eccles. x. 19: *All things obey money*: so that in this sense desire for riches is the root of all sins.

SECOND ARTICLE

Whether Pride Is the Beginning of Every Sin?

Some say pride is to be taken in three ways. First, as denoting inordinate desire to excel; and thus it is a special sin.—Secondly, as denoting actual contempt of God, to the effect of not being subject to His commandment; and thus, they say, it is a generic sin.—Thirdly, as denoting an inclination to this contempt, owing to the corruption of nature; and in this sense they say that it is the beginning of every sin, and that it differs from covetousness, because covetousness regards sin as turning towards the mutable good by which sin is, as it were, nourished and fostered, for which reason covetousness is called the *root*; whereas pride regards sin as turning away from God, to Whose commandment man refuses to be subject, for which reason it is called the *beginning*, because the beginning of evil consists in turning away from God.

Now though all this is true, nevertheless it does not explain the mind of the wise man who said (*loc. cit.*): *Pride is the beginning of all sin*. For it is evident that he is speaking of pride as denoting inordinate desire to excel, as is clear from what follows (*verse* 17): *God hath overturned the thrones of proud princes*; indeed this is the point of nearly the whole chapter. We must therefore say that

pride, even as denoting a special sin, is the beginning of every sin. For we must take note that, in voluntary actions, such as sins, there is a twofold order, of intention, and of execution. In the former order, the principle is the end, as we have stated many times before (Q. 1, A. 1 *ad* 1; Q. 18, A. 7 *ad* 2; Q. 15, A.1 *ad* 2; Q. 25, A. 2). Now man's end in acquiring all temporal goods is that, through their means, he may have some perfection and excellence. Therefore, from this point of view, pride, which is the desire to excel, is said to be the *beginning* of every sin.—On the other hand, in the order of execution, the first place belongs to that which by furnishing the opportunity of fulfilling all desires of sin, has the character of a root, and such are riches; so that, from this point of view, covetousness is said to be the *root* of all evils, as stated above (A. 1).

THIRD ARTICLE

Whether Any Other Special Sins, Besides Pride and Avarice, Should Be Called Capital?

The word capital is derived from *caput (a head)*. Now the head, properly speaking, is that part of an animal's body, which is the principle and director of the whole animal. Hence, metaphorically speaking, every principle is called a head, and even men who direct and govern others are called heads. Accordingly a capital vice is so called, in the first place, from *head* taken in the proper sense, and thus the name *capital* is given to a sin for which capital punishment is inflicted. It is not in this sense that we are now speaking of capital sins, but in another sense, in which the term *capital* is derived from head, taken metaphorically for a principle or director of others. In this way a capital vice is one from which other vices arise, chiefly by being their final cause, which origin is formal, as stated above (Q. 72, A. 6). Wherefore a capital vice is not only the principle of others, but is also their director and, in a way, their leader: Because the art or habit, to which the end belongs, is always the principle and the commander in matters concerning the means. Hence Gregory (*Moral.* xxxi. 17) compares these capital vices to the *leaders of an army*.

FOURTH ARTICLE

Whether the Seven Capital Vices Are Suitably Reckoned?

As stated above (A. 3), the capital vices are those which give rise to others, especially by way of final cause. Now this kind of origin may take place in two ways. First, on account of the condition of the sinner, who is disposed so as to have a strong inclination for one particular end, the result being that he frequently goes forward to other sins. But this kind of origin does not come under the consideration of art, because man's particular dispositions are infinite in number.—Secondly, on account of a natural relationship of the ends to one another; and it is in this way that most frequently one vice arises from another, so that this kind of origin can come under the consideration of art.

Accordingly therefore, those vices are called capital, whose ends have certain fundamental reasons for moving the appetite; and it is in respect of these fundamental reasons that the capital vices are differentiated. Now a thing moves the appetite in two ways. First, directly and of its very nature: thus good moves the appetite to seek it, while evil, for the same reason, moves the appetite to avoid it. Secondly, indirectly and on account of something else, as it were: thus one seeks an evil on account of some attendant good, or avoids a good on account of some attendant evil.

Again, man's good is threefold. For, in the first place, there is a certain good of the soul, which derives its aspect of appetibility, merely through being apprehended, viz. the excellence of honor and praise, and this good is sought inordinately by *vainglory.*—Secondly, there is the good of the body, and this regards either the preservation of the individual, e.g. meat and drink, which good is pursued inordinately by *gluttony*—or the preservation of the species, e.g. sexual intercourse, which good is sought inordinately by *lust.*—Thirdly, there is external good, viz. riches, to which *covetousness* is referred. These same four vices avoid inordinately the contrary evils.

Or again,—good moves the appetite chiefly through possessing some property of happiness, which all men seek naturally. Now in the first place happiness implies perfection, since happiness is a perfect good, to which belongs excellence or renown, which is desired by *pride* or *vainglory*. Secondly, it implies satiety, which *covetousness* seeks in riches that give promise thereof. Thirdly, it implies pleasure, without which happiness is impossible, as stated in *Ethic.* i. 7, x. 6, 7, 8, and this *gluttony* and *lust* pursue.

On the other hand, avoidance of good on account of an attendant evil occurs in two ways. For this happens either in respect of one's own good, and thus we have *sloth*, which is sadness about one's spiritual good, on account of the attendant bodily labor:—or else it happens in respect of another's good, and this, if it be without recrimination, belongs to *envy*, which is sadness about another's good as being a hindrance to one's own excellence, while if it be with recrimination with a view to vengeance, it is *anger*. Again, these same vices seek the contrary evils.

READING 7
Virtue and Happiness
Aristotle
(from *Ethics*)

6. . . . We must define happiness as an activity of some kind, as has been said before, and if activities are either necessary and desirable as a means to something else or desirable in themselves, it is clear that we must define happiness as belonging to the class of activities which are desirable in themselves, and not desirable as means to something else; for happiness has no want, it is self-sufficient.

Again, activities are desirable in themselves, if nothing is expected from them beyond the activity. This seems to be the case with virtuous actions, as the practice of what is noble and virtuous is a thing desirable in itself. It seems to be the case also with such amusements as are pleasant, we do not desire them as means to other things; but they often do us harm rather than good by making us careless about our persons and our property. Such pastimes are generally the resources of those whom the world calls happy. Accordingly people who are clever at such pastimes are generally popular in the courts of despots, as they make themselves pleasant to the despot in the matters which are the objects of his desire, and what he wants is to pass the time pleasantly.

. . .

As has been frequently said, therefore, it is the things which are honourable and pleasant to the virtuous man that are really honourable and pleasant. But everybody feels the activity which accords with his own moral state to be most desirable, and accordingly the virtuous man regards the activity in accordance with virtue as most desirable.

Happiness then does not consist in amusement. It would be paradoxical to hold that the end of human life is amusement, and that we should toil and suffer all our life for the sake of amusing ourselves. For we may be said to desire all things as means to something else except indeed happiness, as happiness is the end *or perfect state.*

7. If happiness consists in virtuous activity, it is only reasonable to suppose that it is the activity of the highest virtue, or in other words, of the best part of our nature. Whether it is the reason or something else which seems to exercise rule and authority by a natural right, and to have a conception of things noble and divine, either as being itself divine or as relatively the most divine part of our being, it is the activity of this part in accordance with its proper virtue, which will be the perfect happiness. . . . to be realized in this activity. This then will be the perfect happiness of Man, if a perfect length of life is given

it, for there is no imperfection in happiness. But such a life will be too good for Man. He will enjoy such a life not in virtue of his humanity but in virtue of some divine element within him, and the superiority of this activity to the activity of any other virtue will be proportionate to the superiority of this divine element in man to his composite *or material* nature.

9. Man, as being human, will require external prosperity. His nature is not of itself sufficient for speculation, it needs bodily health, food, and care of every kind. It must not however be supposed that, because it is impossible to be fortunate without external goods, a great variety of such goods will be necessary to happiness. For neither self-sufficiency nor moral action consists in excess; it is possible to do noble deeds without being lord of land and sea, as moderate means will enable a person to act in accordance with virtue. We may clearly see that it is so; for it seems that private persons practise virtue not less but actually more than persons in high place. It is enough that such a person should possess as much as is requisite for virtue; his life will be happy if he lives in the active exercise of virtue. Solon was right perhaps in his description of the happy man as one "who is moderately supplied with external goods, and yet has performed the noblest actions,"—such was his opinion—"and had lived a temperate life," for it is possible to do one's duty with only moderate means. It seems too that Anaxagoras did not conceive of the happy man as possessing wealth or power when he said that he should not be surprised if the happy man proved a puzzle in the eyes of the world; for the world judges by externals alone, it has no perception of anything that is not external. . . .

Again, he whose activity is directed by reason and who cultivates reason, and is in the best, *i.e. the most rational,* state of mind is also, as it seems, the most beloved of the Gods. For if the Gods care at all for human things, as is believed, it will be only reasonable to hold that they delight in what is best and most related to themselves, i.e. in reason, and that they requite with kindness those who love and honour it above all else, as caring for what is dear to themselves and performing right and noble actions.

It is easy to see that these conditions are found preeminently in the wise man. He will therefore be most beloved of the Gods. We may fairly suppose too that he is most happy; and if so, this is another reason for thinking that the wise man is preeminently happy.

READING 8

On the Definition of a Gentleman

John Henry Cardinal Newman

(from *Apologia*)

It is almost a definition of a gentleman to say he is one who never inflicts pain. This description is both refined and, as far as it goes, accurate. He is mainly occupied in merely removing the obstacles which hinder the free and unembarrassed action of those about him; and he concurs with their movements rather than takes the initiative himself. His benefits may be considered as parallel to what are called comforts or conveniences in arrangements of a personal nature: like an easy chair or a good fire, which do their part in dispelling cold and fatigue, though nature provides both means of rest and animal heat without them. The true gentleman in like manner carefully avoids whatever may cause a jar or a jolt in the minds of those with whom he is cast;—all clashing of opinion, or collision of feeling, all restraint, or suspicion, or gloom, or resentment; his great concern being to make every one at their ease and at home. He has his eyes on all his company; he is tender towards the bashful, gentle towards the distant, and merciful towards the absurd; he can recollect to whom he is speaking; he guards against unseasonable allusions, or topics which may irritate; he is seldom prominent in conversation, and never wearisome. He makes light of favours while he does them, and seems to be receiving when he is conferring. He never speaks of himself except when compelled, never defends himself by a mere retort, he has no ears for slander or gossip, is scrupulous in imputing motives to those who interfere with him, and interprets every thing for the best. He is never mean or little in his disputes, never takes unfair advantage, never mistakes personalities or sharp sayings for arguments, or insinuates evil which he dare not say out. From a long-sighted prudence, he observes the maxim of the ancient sage, that we should ever conduct ourselves towards our enemy as if he were one day to be our friend. He has too much good sense to be affronted at insults, he is too well employed to remember injuries, and too indolent to bear malice. He is patient, forbearing, and resigned, on philosophical principles; he submits to pain, because it is inevitable, to bereavement, because it is irreparable, and to death, because it is his destiny. If he engages in controversy of any kind, his disciplined intellect preserves him from the blundering discourtesy of better, perhaps, but less educated minds; who, like blunt weapons, tear and hack instead of cutting clean, who mistake the point in argument, waste their strength on trifles, misconceive their adversary, and leave the question more involved than they find it. He may be right or wrong in his opinion, but he is too clear-headed to be unjust; he is as simple as he is forcible, and as brief as he is decisive. Nowhere shall we find greater candour, consideration, indulgence: he throws himself into the minds of his opponents, he accounts for their mistakes. He knows the weakness of human reason as well as its strength, its province and its limits. If he be an unbeliever, he will be too profound and large-minded to ridicule religion or to act against it; he is too wise to be a dogmatist or fanatic in his infidelity. He respects piety and devotion; he even supports institutions as venerable, beautiful, or useful, to which he does not assent; he honours the ministers of religion, and it contents him to decline its mysteries without assailing or denouncing them. He is a friend of religious toleration, and that, not only because his philosophy has taught him to look on all forms of faith with an impartial eye, but also from the gentleness and effeminacy of feeling, which is the attendant on civilization.

Not that he may not hold a religion too, in his own way, even when he is not a Christian. In that case his religion is one of imagination and sentiment; it is the embodiment of those ideas of the sublime, majestic, and beautiful, without which there can be no large philosophy. Sometimes he acknowledges the being of God, sometimes he invests an unknown principle or quality with the attributes of perfection. And this deduction of his reason, or creation of his fancy, he makes the occasion of such excellent thoughts, and the starting-point of so varied and systematic a teaching, that he even seems like a disciple of Christianity itself. From the very accuracy and steadiness of his logical powers, he is able to see what sentiments are consistent, in those who hold any religious doctrine at all, and he appears to others to feel and to hold a whole circle of theological truths, which exist in his mind no otherwise than as a number of deductions . . . such are some of the lineaments of the ethical character, which the cultivated intellect will form, apart from religious principle . . .

Suggestions for Further Reading

Over and above the authors and books already presented in the text and cited in the index, the following list of readily accessible titles offers suggestions for further reading.

Bacevitch, Andrew, *The New American Militarism: How Americans Are Seduced by War*, New York: Oxford University Press, 2005. (A strong indictment of recent American war policy.)

Cherlin, Andrew J., *The Marriage-Go-Round: The State of Marriage and Family in America Today*, New York: Knopf, 2008.

Cottingham, John, *On the Meaning of Life*, New York: Routledge, 2008.

Ciulla, Joanne B., Martin, Clancy W., and Solomon, Robert C., eds., *A Business Ethics Reader*, New York: Oxford University Press, 2007.

Dasgupta, Partha, *Economics: A Very Short Introduction*, New York: Oxford University Press, 2007.

Kleinberg, Aviad, *7 Deadly Sins: A Very Short List*, Cambridge, MA: Harvard University Press, 2008.

Moore, Gareth, *A Question of Truth: Christianity and Homosexuality*, London: Continuum, 2003.

Ramsey, Paul, *The Just War*, new edition with foreword by Stanley M. Hauerwas, New York: Continuum, 2002. (A 1968 classic by an influential moral philosopher.)

Salzman, Todd A., and Lawler, Michael G., *The Sexual Person*, Washington, D.C.: Georgetown University Press, 2008.

Sandler, Michael J., *Justice: What's the Right Thing to Do?* New York: Farrar, Straus and Giroux, 2009.

Scanlon, T. M. *What We Owe to Each Other*, Cambridge, MA: Harvard University Press, 1999.

Stiglitz, Joseph E., *Globalization and Its Discontents*, New York: Norton, 2002.

Wiesel, Elie, *Night*, new translation and preface, New York: Hill and Wang, 2006.

Wilson, E. O., *An Appeal to Save Life on Earth*, New York: Norton, 2006.

Credits

Index